General Directions for a Comfortable Walking with God

General Directions
for a Comfortable Walking with God

Robert Bolton

Introduced by John MacArthur

 Soli Deo Gloria Publications
. . . for instruction in righteousness . . .

Soli Deo Gloria Publications
An imprint of Reformation Heritage Books
2965 Leonard St. NE
Grand Rapids, MI 49525
616-977-0889
orders@heritagebooks.org
www.heritagebooks.org

Paperback reprint 2019

ISBN 978-1-60178-669-2

General Directions for a Comfortable Walking with God was originally published in 1626. This volume is a facsimile of the edition published by the Religious Tract Society in 1837.

For additional Reformed literature, request a free book list from Reformation Heritage Books at the above regular or e-mail address.

An Introduction to the 20th Century Edition
of Robert Bolton's
*General Directions for a
Comfortable Walking with God*

Robert Bolton has given us a comprehensive guidebook for the Christian's spiritual walk. Modern readers will find Reverend Bolton's words as fitting and helpful as they were for Bolton's original 17th century audience - perhaps more so, because Bolton clearly and carefully unfolds rich modern truth modern preachers often ignore or avoid as out of step with the times.

These are words straight from the heart of a man of God who candidly and fearlessly spoke the truth - but with great tenderness and compassion. There's a refreshing, simply honesty to be found in most of the Puritan literature, and it is surely evident in abundance here.

Bolton sees walking with God as the crown of the Christian's character. He defines it as:

> *a sincere endeavour, punctually and precisely, to manage, conduct, and dispose all our affairs, thoughts, words, and deeds, all our behaviour and conversation, in reverence and fear, with humility and singleness of heart, as in the sight of an invisible*

INTRODUCTION

God, under the perpetual presence of his all-seeing, glorious, pure eye; and, by a comfortable consequence, to enjoy, by the assistance and exercise of faith, an unutterable sweet communion and humble familiarity with his holy Majesty; in a word, to live in heaven upon earth.

"To live in heaven upon earth!" That's what the Christian life is supposed to be. It is the abundant life our Lord promised (John 10:10).

As Robert Bolton understood so well, to live thus in God's presence is perfect bliss. The Christian seeking satisfaction and contentment needs only to apply himself to a deeper spiritual walk. Fulfillment for the deepest desires of his heart may be found only in a close walk with God. That's why Bolton speaks of a "comfortable walking with God."

Unfortunately, the spirit of our age substitutes good feelings and self-satisfaction for spiritual contentment. Modern believers seem obsessed with personal relationships, emotional needs, temporal possessions, and earthly pleasures. Little wonder that most Christians feel their walk with God is seriously deficient.

When, for example, was the last time you read a book or heard a sermon that spoke of the

INTRODUCTION

spiritual harm caused by excessive sleep? That's one of the issues Bolton addresses in this intensely practical handbook. Others include living by faith, guarding against worldliness, meditating on the assurance of heaven, avoiding profane company, dealing with anger and fear, governing the tongue, choosing suitable recreations, and much more. Reverend Bolton maintains a sensible, biblical perspective throughout. His uncomplicated wisdom stands in stark contrast to much modern teaching on these issues.

You'll find Robert Bolton warm, engaging, insightful, and thoroughly biblical. More important, he will challenge you to a deeper, richer walk with God than you ever thought possible.

John MacArthur
November 1990

TO

THE RIGHT HON. AND TRULY NOBLE,

EDWARD, LORD MONTAGUE,

OF BOUGHTON:

A fruitful increase of all heavenly graces; and all watchful preparation for the glory that shall be revealed.

MUCH HONOURED AND NOBLE LORD,

Although the eminence of your other personal worth, great wisdom, and noble parts, a sufficient attractive to every honest heart, by reason of the particular interest it hath in the common state of goodness; or your special bounty to myself, which ought to stir up an ingenuous mind to apprehend any opportunity of due and deserved acknowledgment; or your public deportment in the face of our country, so worthy and honourable, and managed with such true honesty, grave moderation, and nobleness of spirit, which cannot but draw from every heart truly sound to our great Lord in heaven, and his royal deputy our highest sovereign upon earth, a great deal of reverence and love; I say, though any of these severally might draw from me a more exact and able demonstration of the thankful devotions of my heart, yet, my lord, (and you may believe me,) there is another thing besides all these, which was the strongest and most predominant motive to quicken me to this duty and dedication, even your sincere and invincible affection to the gospel of Jesus Christ, his faithful ministers, and most precious ways. And this, to tell you the truth, is far the fairest and most orient flower in the garland of all your goodness, and incomparably above all your greatness, were you advanced even to desert, nay, to the highest top of all earthly felicities and mortal honour. For, however the world, ever beside itself in point of salvation, and stark blind in the right apprehension of heavenly things, doth dote upon gilded miseries, stinging vanities, golden fetters; and wickedly deems pursuit of purity the height of folly; yet I can assure you, in the word of life and truth, the richest and rarest confluence of all human happiness, the most exquisite excellency and variety of the greatest worldly pomp and splendour that ever the sun saw since the first moment of its creation, or shall look upon while it shines in heaven, is but dust in the balance to one grain of grace; it is but dross to an humble mind, savingly enlightened with a foretaste but of the least glimpse of that incomprehensible endless glory which shall shortly be revealed. It is all, in the true valuation, but as a vain smoke, which doth not only vanish as it riseth, and utterly loseth itself at the highest, but also draws tears from a man's eyes; nay, at last wrings the very heart-strings of every impenitent soul with that extreme everlasting horror which would burst ten thousand hearts, seriously and sensibly to think upon before-hand.

It is not only " vanity," but also " vexation of spirit." Let worldly wisdom say what it will, and hold them melancholy and mad, who, by the help of the Holy Ghost, hold a constant counter-motion to the course of the world, and corruptions of the time,—that they may keep a good conscience, (the richest treasure and dearest jewel that ever the heart of man was acquainted with;) who infinitely desire rather to be religious, than rich; to be good, than great; to enjoy the favour of God, than the sovereignty and pleasures of all the kingdoms of the earth;—yet assuredly, when all is said, and truly summed up, it is only the true fear of God's blessed name, a zealous forwardness for his glory, (at this day, unhappily, and to the ruin of immortal souls, called by the world pragmaticalness, and too much preciseness,) which can truly beautify and adorn both all other personal sufficiencies, and indeed sanctify and bless all public employments and services of state.

For the *first*. A professor, even something popish, doth yet truly teach, that "Heroical nobility is an illustrious eminency shining in a man by the heavenly infusions of supernatural grace, whereby he is made by adoption the son of God, the spouse of Christ, the temple of the Holy Ghost; without which all other nobilities are nothing."* Suppose a fair and goodly horse to the eye, as exquisitely featured, coloured, paced, as that feigned by Bartas to be managed by Cain, yet if he wanted mettle, he were worth nothing to a man of spirit. The most magnificent glorious worldling that ever trod upon earthly mould, richly crowned with all the ornaments and excellences of nature, art, policy, preferment, or what heart can wish besides, yet without the life of grace to animate and ennoble them, he were to the eye of heavenly wisdom but as a rotten carcass stuck over with flowers, magnified dross, gilded rottenness, golden damnation! And that which is more dreadful, when the sun of his short summer's day is set, the hot gleam of transitory prosperity past, and the bitter tempestuous winter's night of death approaches, from which all the gold and pearl of east and west can no more deliver him than can a handful of dust; I say, then shall be poured upon his head a terrible shower of snares, fire and brimstone,

* Gers. Tractat. de Nobilitate.

and a horrible tempest, Psa. xi. 6. His soul sinks in a moment into the depth of remediless misery, and is desperately plunged for ever into the bottom of the burning lake. His body descends into the grave as into a dungeon of rottenness and horror, arrested, as it were, by the second death, in the devil's name; and, at length, hailed and dragged unto the terror of that great and last day, where no creature can rescue him, no mountain cover him, from that unquenchable wrath, and never-dying worm, which shall everlastingly, day and night, feed upon his soul and flesh. Whereas now, on the other side, that poor neglected one, who hath in truth given his name unto Christ and his profitable service, perhaps by the world most disdainfully and contemptuously trampled upon, even into the dust, with the feet of cruelty and pride; at least, most certainly ever made extremely vile and contemptible by the villainy of tongues, and cruel mockings, yet is such a one as the world is not worthy of, Heb. xi. 36—38. In the mean time, in the meaning of the Holy Ghost, a crown of glory in the hand of Jehovah, Isa. vi.

1—3, as beautiful and amiable as the blood of Christ and his righteous robe can make him, crowned full gloriously with God's own comeliness which he hath put upon him, Ezek. xvi. 14, designed from all eternity in due time, for so his sanctification now assures him, to wear an everlasting crown of bliss. And when his pilgrimage is past, death is to him the daybreak of eternal brightness. Upon his last bed, his blessed soul shall find that fresh-bleeding fountain for sin and for uncleanness set wide open unto it, by the hand of faith, ready now at its departure to raze out the last sinful stain. It may confidently, in the name of Christ, cast itself into the open arms, enlarged bosom, and dearest embracements of the Father of all mercies; it may feel the glorious presence of the sweetest Comforter, presenting unto it a foretaste of heavenly joys; it shall have the last sweetness, and triumphant truth of all the promises of life, able to confront and confound the utmost rage of all the powers of darkness, made good unto it: a mighty guard of blessed angels shall attend upon it, waiting with longing and joy to bear it triumphantly into the bosom of Abraham. His body shall go into the grave as into a chamber of rest, and bed of down, sweetly perfumed unto it by the sacred body of the Son of God lying in the grave; locked there full fast with the bars of the earth, and fenced with the omnipotent arm of God, as a rich jewel in a casket of gold, until the resurrection of the just. And then, after their joyfullest meeting and glorious re-union, they shall both be for ever filled with all those unmixed pleasures, blessed immortalities, and crowned joys, which the dwelling-place of God, the glory of heaven, and the inexhausted fountain of all bliss, Jehovah himself blessed for ever, can afford.

Now let the scornfullest opponent to the power of godliness tell me, in cold blood, whether that honourable wretch, or this honest man, be more truly noble and happy.

For the *second*. "So natural," saith Hooker, " is the union of religion with justice, that we may boldly deem there is neither where both are not. For how should they be unfeignedly just, whom religion doth not cause to be such; or they religious, which are not found such by the proof of their just actions? If they which employ their labour and travail about the public administration of justice follow it only as a trade, with unquenchable and unconscionable thirst of gain, being not in heart persuaded that justice is God's own work, and themselves his agents in the business, the sentence of right God's own verdict, and themselves his priests to deliver it; formalities of justice do but serve to smother right, and that which was necessarily ordained for the common good, is, through shameful abuse, made the cause of common misery." Full well did this learned man perceive, and rightly apprehend, that the purity and power of religion alone, doth truly honour all honours, dignify all dignities, actuate with acceptation and life all moral virtues and endowments of art, sweeten all government, strengthen all states, settle fast all imperial crowns upon princes' heads. It is no humorous conceit, but a matter of sound consequence, that all, either personal duties, or employments of state, are by so much the better performed, by how much the men are more religious from whose abilities the same proceed. When heaven is made too much to yield to earth, piety to policy, public good to private ends, there authority is embittered, inferiors plagued, and, too often, law and justice turned into wormwood and rapine. He truly intimates what a deal of hurt is done, what a world of mischief is many times wrought, insensibly and unobservedly, when a wicked wit and wide conscience wield the sword of authority. For it is easy and ordinary for a man so mounted by legal flights, putting foul businesses into fair language, and by a dissembled pretence of deeper reach, to compass his own ends, either for promotion of iniquity, or oppression of innocency; especially, since he knows himself backed with that principle in policy—It is not safe to question or reverse transactions of state, though tainted perhaps with some impressions of miscarriage and error; and that it is holden a solecism in state wisdom, and unseemly for private innocency, to contest too busily with passages of public tribunals.

These things I thus discourse and declare unto your lordship, to represent unto you the vanity of that honour which is not directly and sincerely subordinate to the honour of God: at the best, it is but a breath, and yet not able to blow so much as one cold blast upon ungodly great ones, when, being suddenly carried from their stately and sumptuous dwellings, they shall be cast into unquenchable flames. To let you see the excellency and worth of those happy ways to which it hath pleased the Lord of heaven, out of his special mercy, to bend the eye of your noble mind; and that you may know what it is alone hath had power, and the prerogative (and shall for ever, in whomsoever takes God's part) to make you both more truly honourable in yourself, and more faithfully serviceable to our king and state; both to cast a diviner lustre upon your personal virtues, and to make your managing of public businesses (many times most unworthily swayed awry, by that foul fiend, faction, partiality, and private ends) worthy, conscionable, and just. For which, every honest eye in our country that looks upon you blesseth you;

and shall mourn most bitterly for your absence from amongst us, when you shall be gloriously gathered to your fathers. So let all that truly love the Lord Jesus, his blessed gospel, and servants, " be as the sun, when he goeth forth in his might," and at last full sweetly set in the boundless ocean of immortal bliss.

In these ways of life, my noble lord, which in the opinion of truth itself are ways of pleasure, and paths of sweetest peace, Prov. iii. 17 ; it is the infinite desire of my heart, and drift of this treatise I now offer into your honour's hands, that you would still advance forward, and do more nobly still. That you would improve to the utmost the height of your excellent understanding to a further and more full comprehension of the mystery of Christ; which, though it be a sealed book to the sharpest sight of the most piercing human wisdom, yet reveals to every truly humble, spiritual eye, the rich and royal treasures of all true sweetness, contentment, and peace. That you would hold it your greatest honour and happiness, as it is indeed, to grow still in fruitfulness, in every good work,

Col. i. 10; in fervency of spirit, Rom. xii. 11; in purity, 1 John iii. 3; in heavenly mindedness, Phil. iii. 20; Col. iii. 2; in precise walking, &c. Eph. v. 15; with singular watchfulness, and the more punctual and frequent search and perusal of your spiritual state; both because the depths and delusions of Satan are most intricate and infinite, and because " not many noble are called," 1 Cor. i. 26. That you would hold on in that valiantness for the truth, and all good causes, which ordinarily gather vigour and strength proportionably to the swelling fury of all adversaries, either mortal or infernal powers. Ever patiently passing by, with generous magnanimity and brave contempt, all the vile railings and contradictions of Satan's revellers, and popish insolency; for vainly to affect the acclamations and applause of worthless men, or to be dejected unmanlily with their unjust accusations and anger, are both equally ignoble, and most unworthy a man of honour and virtuous resolution. Yours shall be the crown and comfort, when all popery and profaneness shall lie buried in the dust and dungeon of hell. In a word, the thirsty longing of my heart, and heartiest prayer shall ever be, that you may shine every day, more and more gloriously in all personal sanctity, a plantation of godliness in your own family, and where you have any thing to do; and in a holy zeal for setting forward the affairs of God, when and wheresoever you have any power or calling. That when the last period of your mortal abode in this vale of tears, which draws on apace, shall present itself, you may look death in the face without dread; into the grave without fear; upon the Lord Jesus with comfort; and upon Jehovah blessed for ever, with everlasting joy. Thus let all the saving blessings of our most bountiful heavenly Father, through Jesus Christ, by the Holy Ghost, be plentifully and for ever upon your honourable self, and all your sweet and noble children.

Your honour's most truly in all services for

the salvation of your soul,

ROBERT BOLTON.

CONTENTS.

	Page
Introductory remarks	1
The servants of God are singular from others in holiness	2
God's free grace the fountain of all our goodness	10
The wonderful mercies of God	12
Our horrible ingratitude	13
Personal goodness brings comfort and blessings upon posterity	17
True saving grace can never be lost	21
Some cautions	25
Means of perseverance	27
Christians ought to live apart from the corruptions of the times	28
Walking with God the crown of the christian's character	30

GENERAL PREPARATIVES.

I. Abandon thy beloved sin	34
How to discover our bosom sin	37
We may deceive ourselves by exchanging one sin for another	40
II. Hate hypocrisy	46
Various classes of hypocrites described	46
Our particular calling not to be given up	52
III. Build thy resolutions on self-denial	55
IV. Live the life of faith	57
Benefits arising from living a life of faith	58
V. Settle in thy heart a right conception of the substance and power, nature and materials of christianity	62

CONTENTS.

	Page
VI. Guard against worldliness	66
VII. Let thy heart be thoroughly warmed with the love of God	67
The motives and obligations	67
VIII. Prize the fruition of God's reconciled face	68
IX. Watch over thy heart, and keep it in a spiritual temper.	69
X. Meditate on thy future bliss	71

PARTICULAR DIRECTIONS.

	Page
I. On family duties	73
Observe, 1. A right disposition before family duties	74
2. A spiritual behaviour in the performance of them	75
3. A holy carriage afterwards	75
II. On idleness	77
III. On solitary seasons of meditation	78
IV. On company	80
Danger of profane company	80
How to converse with unconverted persons	94
V. On the government of the heart	97
Captivation and conformity of the heart to the rules of grace	98
Watchful guard over the heart	101
Elevation of the heart towards heaven	104
VI. On repressing raging passions	105
Anger, moral remedies against	106
Religious remedies	111
Fear, the vanity and tyranny of	116
Antidotes and cordials against	121
VII. On the government of the tongue	127
The duty of christian reproof	127
Characters of those called "dogs," and those called "swine."	130
Beware of a sinful silence and a furious zeal	135, 136
Reasons enforcing the duty of christian reproof	137

The duty of observing a sanctified silence	143
From rash censuring	143
From slandering, backbiting, false accusing	157
From unsavoury communication	168
Heavenly discourse	169
VIII. ON MANAGING CONSCIENTIOUSLY EVERY ACTION OF OUR LIVES	171
Circumstances requisite in a comfortable action.	172
On Recreations	178
They should not be costly.	178
Nor cruel	179
Nor engrossers of time	179
Nor encroach upon heavenly comforts.	193
Differences between spiritual and carnal joy.	195
Visits to unsanctified great men	207
Some reasons to show that they prove snares	209
Some cautions to prevent ensnarement	214
Natural actions	225
Against gluttony	225
Against drunkenness	229
Against excessive sleep	229
Civil affairs	232
Do as thou wouldst be done by	232
Abhor unjust dealing	235
Be moderate in your attachment to earthly things	241
Directions as to *marriage*	262
Convenient entrance into that state	262
Duties peculiar to both husband and wife.	265
Duties peculiar to the husband	270
Duties peculiar to the wife	277
Works of mercy	282
Spiritual works of mercy.	283
Corporeal works of mercy	283
Motives to alms-deeds	287
Believers often falsely accused of covetousness	301

CONTENTS.

	Page
Occasions of this imputation	305
Some occasions ministered by *profane men*.	305
Some occasions from the *parties slandered*.	313
Worldly-mindedness infinitely unbecoming an heir of heaven	322
Our spiritual state.	327
Two extremes to be avoided	327
1. Self-admiration, and a proud overprizing of our own graces	327
The mystery of self-deceit opened	333
Work of grace in the true convert	344
A sanctified man may be assured of his spiritual safety, and how	355
Sound persuasion distinguished from delusion	369
Preservatives against spiritual pride.	383
2. A dejected, distrustful undervaluing of God's mercies, the promises of life, and our graces.	399
Some saints expostulated with for their heavy, pensive walking	399
Real causes and motives of the joy of believers	405—432
Some conceits and occasions of discomfort removed.	431

SOME

GENERAL DIRECTIONS

FOR A

COMFORTABLE WALKING WITH GOD.

***

GEN. VI. 8, 9.
BUT NOAH FOUND GRACE IN THE EYES OF THE LORD.
THESE ARE THE GENERATIONS OF NOAH: NOAH WAS A JUST MAN AND
PERFECT IN HIS GENERATIONS, AND NOAH WALKED WITH GOD.

***

In this dreadful and dismal story of the old world's degeneracy and destruction, falling away, and final ruin, here stands in my text a right orient and illustrious star, shining full fair with singularity of heavenly light, spiritual goodness, and God's sincere service, in the darkest midnight of Satan's universal reign, and amidst the strangest confusions, idolatrous corruptions, cruelties, oppressions, and lust, that ever the earth bore. Noah, a very precious man, and preacher of righteousness, and his family, were alone excepted. The true worship of God was confined to them, when all the world besides lay drowned in idolatry and paganism, ready to be swallowed up in a universal grave of waters, which was already fashioned in the clouds by the angry, irresistible hand of the all-powerful God, who was now so implacably, but most justly, provoked by those rebellious and cruel generations, that he would not suffer his Spirit to strive any more with them; but inexorably resolved to open the windows or floodgates of heaven, giving extraordinary strength of influence above, and abundance to the fountains of the great deep, commanding them to cast out the whole treasure and heap of their waters; and taking away the retentive power from the clouds, that they might pour down immeasurably, for the burying of all living creatures which breathed in the air. From whence, by the way, before I break into my text, take this note.

Doctrine. The servants of God are men of singularity. I mean it not in respect of any fantasticalness of opinion, furiousness of zeal, or turbulency of faction, truly so called; but in respect of abstinence from sin, purity of heart, and holiness of life.

Reasons. 1. God's holy word exacts and expects from all that are new born, and heirs of heaven, an excellency above ordinary, Prov. xii. 26; Matt. v. 20, 47. Being taken forth as the precious from the vile, Jer. xv. 19, by the power of the ministry, they must not only go beyond the highest civil perfections of the exactest moral purity amongst the most honest heathens, Heb. xii. 14, but also exceed the righteousness and all the outward religious conformities of the devoutest pharisees, whose sufficiences, Luke xviii. 11, 12, many thousands in these times come short of, and yet hope to be saved: or they can in no case enter into the kingdom of heaven. But, lest any be proudly puffed up with a sense of this singularity and excellency above his neighbour, let him know that humility is ever one of the fairest flowers in the whole garland of supernatural and divine worth; and that self conceit would poison even angelical perfection.

2. They must upon necessity differ from a world

of wicked men, by a sincere singularity of abstinence from the course of this world, the lusts of men, the corruptions of the times, familiarity with graceless companions, the worldling's language, profane sports, all wicked ways of thriving, rising, and growing great in the world, and so forth.

3. They make conscience of those duties and Divine commands, which the greatest part of men, even in the noontide of the gospel, are so far from taking to heart, that their hearts rise against them. As, to be warm in religion, Rev. iii. 16; to be zealous of good works, Tit. ii. 14; to walk precisely, Eph. v. 15; to be fervent in spirit, Rom. xii. 11; to strive to enter in at the strait gate, Luke xiii. 24; to pluck out their right eyes; that is, to abandon their bosom delights, Matt. v. 29; to make the sabbath a delight, Isa. lviii. 13; to love the brotherhood, 1 Pet. ii. 17; with a holy violence to lay hold upon the kingdom of heaven, Matt. xi. 12.

4. Experience, and examples of all ages, from the creation downward, clearly prove the point. At this time, as you see, the saints of God were all harboured under one roof, and yet not all sound there. Survey the ages afterward: the time of Abraham, who was as a brand taken out of the fire of the Chaldeans; the time of Elijah, when none appeared to that blessed man of God; the time of Isaiah, who cried, "Who hath believed our report?" chap. liii. 1; the time of Manasseh, who built altars for all the host of heaven, in the two courts of the house of the Lord; the time of Antiochus, when he commanded the sanctuary and holy people to be polluted with swine's flesh, and unclean beasts to be sacrificed, the abomination of desolation to

be set up upon the altar; that darksome time when the glorious Day-star, Christ Jesus himself, came down from heaven to enlighten the earth; the time of Antichrist, when all the world wondered after the beast; our times, wherein, of six parts of the earth, probably scarce one of the least is christian. And how much of christendom is still overgrown with popery, and other exorbitant distempers in point of religion; and where the truth of Christ is purely and powerfully taught, how few give their names unto it! and of those who profess, how many are false-hearted, or merely formal

5. Methinks worldly wisdom should rather wonder that any one is won unto God, than cry out and complain, Is it possible there should be so few? since all the powers of darkness, and every devil in hell, oppose, might and main, the implanting of grace in any soul; since there are more snares upon earth to keep us still in the invisible chains of darkness and sin, than there are stars in heaven; since every inch, every little artery of our bodies, if it could, would swell with hellish venom to the bigness of the greatest Goliath, the mightiest giant, that it might make resistance to the sanctifying work of the Holy Ghost; since our souls, naturally, would rather die and put off their immortality and everlasting being, than put on the Lord Jesus: in a word, since the new creation of a man is held to be a greater work of wonder than the creation of the world.

6. First, let us set aside in any country, city, town, family, all atheists, papists, and distempered exorbitants from the blessed truth of doctrine taught in our church: secondly, all whoremongers, drunkards, swearers, liars, revellers, worldlings, usurers, and fellows of such infamous rank : thirdly,

all merely civil men, who come short of Cato, Fabricius, and other honest heathens, and, wanting holiness, shall never see the Lord, Heb. xii. 14: fourthly, all gross hypocrites, whose outsides are painted with superficial flourishes of holiness and honesty, but their inward parts filled with rottenness and lust, who have their hands in godly exercises, when their hearts are in hell: fifthly, all formal hypocrites, who are deluded in point of salvation, as were the foolish virgins, and that proud pharisee, Luke xviii. 11: sixthly, all final backsliders, of which some turn sensual epicures, and plunge themselves into worldly pleasures with far more rage and greediness, by reason of former restraint by a temporary profession; others become scurrilous deriders of the holy way; some, bloody goads in the sides of those with whom they have formerly walked into the house of God as friends: seventhly, all unsound professors for the present, of which you would little think what a number there is:—I say, let these and all other strangers to the purity and power of godliness be set apart, and tell me how many true-hearted Nathaniels we are likely to find.

Uses: 1. Try then the truth of thy spiritual state by this mark of a sober and sincere singularity. If thou still holdest correspondence with the world, and conform to the fashions thereof, if still thou swimmest down the current of the times, and shiftest thy sails to the turn of every wind; if thine heart still hankers after the tasteless fooleries of good fellowship, and follow the multitude to do evil; if thou be carried with the swing and sway of the place where thou livest, to uphold, by a boisterous combination, lewdness and vanity, to profane the Lord's day, to scorn profession, oppose the ministry, and walk in the broad way; in a word, if thou doest as the most do, thou art utterly undone for ever. But if with a merciful violence thou art pulled out of the world by the power of the word, and happily weaned from the sensual, insensible poison of all bitter-sweet pleasures, and fellowship with unfruitful works of darkness; if, by standing on God's side, and hatred of all false ways, thou art become the drunkard's song, as David was, and a by-word amongst the sons of Belial, as was Job; if the world lower and look sour upon thee for thy looking towards heaven, and thy good-fellow companions abandon thee as too precise; if thy life be not like other men's, and thy ways of another fashion, as the epicures of those times charged the righteous man when the Book of Wisdom was written; in a word, if thou walkest in the narrow way, and be one of that little flock which lives amongst wolves, and therefore must needs be little; so that by all the leopards, lions, and bears about thee, I mean all sorts of unregenerate men, thou art hunted for thy holiness as a partridge on the mountains, at least by the poison and persecution of the tongue;—I say then thou art certainly in the high way to heaven.

2. If the saints of God be men of singularity in the sense I have said, then away with those base and brainless cavils against those who are wise unto salvation. What! are you wiser than your forefathers? than all the town? than such and such learned men? than your own parents? are you wiser than your head? may the husband say, &c. Nay further, to Noah it might have been said by the wretches of those times, Art thou wiser than all the world? He, out of the height of his heroical resolution, easily endured and digested the affronts and indignities of

this kind from millions of men. But take thou these spiteful taunts, and bind them in the mean time as a crown unto thee, and advance forward in thine holy singularity with all sweet content and undauntedness of spirit, towards that glorious immortal crown above; and let those miserable men, whose eyes are hood winked by Satan, and so blinded with earthly dust that they cannot possibly discern the invisible excellences and true nobleness of the neglected saints, follow the folly of their worldly wisdom, and sway of the greater part, to endless woe, and then give losers leave to talk.

3. Let every one, who in sincerity of heart seeks to be saved, ever hold it a special happiness and his highest honour to be singled out from the universal pestilent contagion of common profaneness, and the sinful courses of the greatest part, and to be censured as singular in that respect. Neither is this a singular thing that I now suggest, but it hath been the portion of the saints in all ages to be trod upon with the feet of imperious contempt, as a number of odd despised underlings; whereas indeed they are God's jewels, and the only excellent upon earth. "Behold," saith Isaiah, chap. viii. 18, "I and the children whom the Lord hath given me are for signs and wonders in Israel." "I am as a wonder unto many," saith David, Psalm lxxi. 7. "I am in derision daily, every one mocketh me," saith Jeremiah, chap. xx. 7. "We are made," saith Paul, "a spectacle unto the world, and to angels, and to men," 1 Cor. iv. 9. "We are made as the filth of the earth, the off-scouring of all things," v. 13. In Augustine's time, those that made conscience of their ways, durst not plunge into the corruptions of the times, and play the good fellows,

were scornfully pointed at, not only by pagans, but even by unreformed professors, professors at large as we call them, as fellows that affected a preciseness and purity above ordinary and other men: they would thus insult and scoffingly fly in the face of such a holy one, "You are a great man, sure you are a just man, you are an Elias, you are a Peter, you come from heaven!" In after times, if a man were but merely civil, ingenuous, chaste, temperate, he was made a by-word and laughing-stock to those about him. They presently said, He was proud, singular, beside himself, hypocrite, &c. Thus it was, is at this time, and will be to the world's end, that every vile whoremonger, beastly drunkard, ignorant scoundrel, scoffing Ishmael, and self-guilty wretch, will have a bitter sneer or reproach to throw, like the madman's firebrand, into the face of God's people, as though they were a company of odd-humoured fellows, and a contemptible generation. This, I say, ever was and ever will be the world's opinion of the ways of God's people. The children of darkness ever harbour such conceits, and peremptorily pass such censures upon the children of light.

It is strange, men are content to be singular in anything save in the service of God, and the salvation of their souls! They desire, and labour too, to be singularly rich, and the wealthiest in a town; to be singularly proud, and in fashion by themselves; to be the strongest in the company to pour in strong drink. They would, with all their hearts, be in honour alone, and adored above others. They would dwell alone, and not suffer a poor man's house to be within sight. They affect singularity in wit, learning, wisdom, valour, worldly reputation, and in all other earthly precedences; but they can by no means endure a loneness and singularity in zeal and the Lord's service. In matters of religion they are resolved to do as the most do, though in so doing they certainly damn their own souls, Matt. vii. 13. Basest cowardliness and fearfulness fit for such a doom! Rev. xxi. 8. They are afraid of taking God's part too much, of fighting too valiantly under the colours of Christ, of being too busy about the salvation of their souls, lest they should be accounted too precise, fellows of an odd humour, and engrossers of more grace than ordinary. It is one of Satan's dreadful depths, as wide as hell, and brim-full with the blood of immortal souls, to make men ambitious and covetous of singularity in all other things but in godliness and God's services; not to suffer it in themselves, and to persecute it in others.

Now, in this story of Noah, so highly honoured with singularity of freedom from the sinful contagion of those desperate times, and happily exempted from that most general and greatest judgment upon earth that ever the sun saw,—a universal drowning,—gloriously mounting up upon the wings of salvation, and safety both of soul and body, when a world of giant-like rebels sunk to the bottom of that new sea as a stone or lead, I consider,

1. The cause of such a singular blessed preservation, which was the free grace and favour of God; "But Noah found grace in the eyes of the Lord," v. 8.

2. The renown and honour of Noah's name; in that he stands here as the father of the new world, the holy seed and progenitors of Jesus Christ; "These are the generations of Noah," ver. 9.

3. The description of Noah's personal goodness, preservation, and posterity. These latter two follow.

His personal description stands in the end of ver. 9; "Noah was a just man and perfect in his generations; and Noah walked with God:" where we find him honoured with three noble attributes, which make up the character of a complete christian—honesty, uprightness, and piety. And they receive much excellency and lustre from a circumstance of time; "In his generations," which were many and mainly corrupt.

Without any further unfolding my text's coherence and dependence upon either precedent or following parts, (for historical passages are plainer, and do not ever exact the length and labour of such an exact resolution as other Scriptures do,) I collect from the first point, wherein I find God's free grace to be the prime and principal cause of Noah's preservation, this

Doct. The free grace and favour of God are the first mover and fountain of all our good. Consider for this purpose such places as these: Jer. xxxi. 3; Hos. xiv. 4; Deut. vii. 7, 8; Rom. ix. 11, 12, 13; John iii. 16; Josh. xxiv. 2, 3; Ephes. i. 5.

And it must needs be so. For it is utterly impossible that any finite cause, created power, or anything out of God himself, should primarily move and incline the eternal, immutable, uncreated, omnipotent will of God. The true original and prime motive of all gracious, bountiful expressions and effusions of love upon his elect, is the good pleasure of his will. And therefore to hold that election to life is made upon foresight of faith, good works the right use of free will, or any created motive, is not only false and wicked, but also an ignorant and absurd tenet. To say no more at this time, it robs God of his all-sufficiency, making him go out of himself, looking to this or that in the creature, upon which his will may be determined to elect. The school-men, though otherwise a rotten generation of divines, yet are right in this.

That distinction which I learn from my master* in his heavenly sermons, published since his death, doth lead unto aright, and truly enlighten this head-spring of all our good. " 1. Some actions of God's love unto us," saith he, " are so in Christ, that they are wholly suspended on him, and his merits are the only procuring cause of them: for example, forgiveness of sins is an action of God's love unto us, and yet this wholly depends upon Christ and his merits; so that his precious blood must either procure this mercy for us from God, else they will never be forgiven; and this and the like love of God is both in Christ and for Christ. 2. There are some other actions of God's love which arise merely and only out of the absolute will of God, without any concurrence of Christ's merits; as the eternal purpose of God, whereby he hath determined to choose some men to salvation: this is an action of God's love, merely rising out of his absolute will, without Christ's merits. For Christ is a Mediator, and all his merits are the effects of his love, not the cause of it. And yet this love, though it be not for Christ, yet is it in Christ. ' According to the eternal purpose which he wrought in Christ Jesus our Lord,' Eph. iii. 11, that is, in regard to the execution of it; for even this eternal purpose, and all the actions of God's love, which arise from his absolute will, are effected and brought to pass in and through Christ." We

* That most worthy, wise, holy, and learned minister of God, John Randall, sermon 2, upon Romans viii. p. 44.

may take an estimate of the absolute and infinite freeness of this inconceivable love of God to his, which reacheth from everlasting to everlasting, by looking upon the description of Jerusalem in Ezekiel xvi. In the beginning of the chapter she lies most filthy and foul in her own blood, pitied by no eye, abhorred of all; which loathsomeness should rather have begot loathing than love; aversion and hatred, than affection and liking; yet God himself doth there profess, out of a melting pang and overflowing abundance of his free grace, that that time was unto him the time of love: he spread his skirt over her and covered her nakedness: in a word, after she was dressed and adorned with God's most skilful, merciful hand, she became a most lovely thing; first, washed with water, cleansed from blood, anointed with oil; then clothed with embroidered work, shod with badgers' skin, girded about with fine linen, covered with silk, decked with ornaments of silver and gold; with bracelets upon her hands, a chain on her neck, a jewel on her forehead, ear rings in her ears, and a beautiful crown upon her head; fed with fine flour, honey, and oil; so that she became exceedingly beautiful, and renowned through the whole world for her perfect comeliness, "even mine own comeliness which I put upon her, saith the Lord God."

Uses. 1. All praise then is due unto Jehovah, the Author of all our good, the Fountain of all our bliss, the Well-spring of immortality and life, "in whom we live and move, and have our being;" our natural being, the being of our outward state; our gracious being; the everlastingness of our glorious state. Were the holiest heart upon earth enlarged to the vast comprehension of this great world's wideness;

nay, made capable of all the glorious and magnificent hallelujahs and hearty praises offered to Jehovah, both by all the militant and triumphant church, yet would it come infinitely short of sufficiently magnifying, admiring, and adoring the inexplicable mystery and bottomless depth of this free, independent mercy, and love of God, the Fountain and First Mover of all our good. We may, and are bound to bless God for all the means, instruments, and second causes, whereby it pleaseth him to confer and convey good things unto us; but we must rest principally, with lowliest thoughts of most humble and hearty praisefulness, at the well head of all our welfare, Jehovah, blessed for ever. We receive a great deal of comfort and light from the moon and stars, but we are chiefly indebted to the sun; from the greater rivers also, but the main sea is the fountain. Angels, ministers, and men may please us, but Jehovah is the principal. Let us then imitate those lights of heaven and rivers of the earth; do all the good we can with those good things God hath given us by his instruments; and then reflect back towards, and return all the glory and praise unto, the Sun of righteousness and Sea of our salvation. The beams of the moon and stars return as far back to glorify the face of the sun, which gave them their beauty, as they can possibly; so let us ever send back to God's own glorious self the honour of all his gifts, by a fruitful improvement of them, in setting forth his glory, and by continual fervent ejaculations of praise to the utmost possibility of our renewed hearts.

And here I cannot forbear, but must needs most justly complain of the hateful, intolerable unthankfulness of us in this kingdom, the happiest people under the arch of heaven, had we hearts enlarged to conceive aright of God's extraordinary love, and such miraculous mercies as never nation enjoyed. Walk over the world, peruse the whole face of the earth from east to west, from north to south, and from one side of heaven to another, thou shalt not find such another enlightened Goshen as this island wherein we dwell. Of six parts of the earth, five are not christian; and in christendom, what other part is so free from the reign of popery, the rage of schism, or the destroying sword? Or where besides doth the gospel shine with such glory, truth, and peace? Or in what nook of the world are there so many faithful souls who cry unto God day and night against the abominations of the times, for the preservation of the gospel, that God's name may be gloriously hallowed, his kingdom come, his will be done in every place, and who themselves serve him with truth of heart? And yet we are too ready, if we have not the height of our desires, and our wills to the full, instead of patience, tears, and prayers, which best become the saints, to embitter all other blessings, and to discover most horrible unthankfulness for them, by repining, grumbling, and discontent; by not rejoicing, as we ought, in every good thing which the Lord our God hath given unto us, and by not improving the extraordinariness of his mercies to our more glorious service of him, and more humbly and precisely walking before him. Away then with all sour, melancholy, causeless, sinful discontent; and "praise ye the Lord; sing unto the Lord a new song, and his praise in the congregation of the saints. Let Israel rejoice in him that made him: let the children of Zion be joyful in their King. For the Lord taketh pleasure in his people: he will beautify the meek with salvation. Let the saints be joyful in glory: let them sing aloud upon their beds," Psa. cxlix. 1, 2, 4, 5. In a word, let us of this island, as we have just cause above all the nations of the earth, and above all ages of the church, from the very first creation of it, praise Jehovah most heartily, infinitely, and for ever.

2. Never reproach any for deformity of body, dulness of conceit, weakness of wit, poorness in outward state, baseness of birth, &c. "For who makes thee to differ from another?" 1 Cor. iv. 7; either in natural gifts, as comeliness of body, beauty, feature, stature, wit, strength, &c.; see Job x. 10, 11; Psa. cxxxix. 13—15; in civil endowments, or any artificial skill, until it come even unto matters of husbandry; see Isa. xxviii. 24—28; in outward things; see Psa. cxxvii.; more particularly in preferment and promotion, see Psa. lxxv. 6, 7; in children, 1 Sam. i. 27; Psa. cxxvii. 3; in a good wife; see Prov. xix. 14; in spiritual things; see Ezek. xvi.; in any thing thou canst name. We are all framed of the same mould, hewed out of the same rock, made as it were of the same cloth, the shears as they say only going between; it is therefore only the free love and grace of God which make all the difference. Whereupon it was an excellent speech of a French king, as his chronicler reports: "When I was born, there were a thousand other souls more born; what have I done unto God more than they? It is his mere grace and mercy which doth often bind me more unto his justice; for the faults of great men are never small."

Let none then, I say, overlook, disdain, or browbeat their brethren, by reason of any extraordinary gifts, eminence of parts, singularity of God's special favour, or indulgence towards him in any good thing, which he denies to others. Especially, thyself being vouchsafed the mercy of conversion, never insolently and imperiously insult over those poor souls who are beside themselves in matters of salvation, who, like miserable drudges, damn themselves in the devil's slavery, and suffer their corrupt nature to carry them to any villany, lust, or lewd course. Alas! our hearts should bleed within us at beholding so many about us imbruing their cruel hands in the blood of their own souls, by their ignorance, worldliness, drunkenness, lust, lying, scoffing at profession, hating to be reformed, &c. What heart, except it be hewed out of the hardest rock, or hath sucked the breasts of merciless tigers, but would yearn and weep to see a man made of the same mould with himself wilfully, as it were, against the ministry of the word, a thousand warnings, and God's many compassionate invitations, cast himself, body and soul, into the endless, easeless, and remediless miseries of hell? And the rather should we pity and pray for such a one who follows the swing of his own heart to his own everlasting perdition, because the matter whereof we were all made is so nearly alike; only the free mercy, goodness, and grace of God make the difference. If God should give us over to the unbridled current of our corrupt nature we might be as bad, and run riot into a world of wickedness as well as he: if the same God visit him in mercy, he may become every way as good, or better than we.

3. If the free love of God be the fountain of all our good, away then with that feigned foresight of

faith, right use of free will, and good works, which should move God to elect before all eternity; and that luciferian self-conceit of present merit, a fit monstrous brood of that beast of Rome, "who opposeth and exalteth himself above all that is called God," 2 Thess. ii. 4. For works meritorious foreseen are equally opposite to grace as works meritorious really existing. Here you must call to mind those eight considerations which I opposed against that wicked tenet of merit, which doth justly deserve never to taste of God's free mercy.*

From the second point, in these words, "These are the generations of Noah." Whereas the fame and memorial of all the families upon earth besides lay buried and rotting in the gulf of everlasting oblivion, as their bodies in the universal grave of waters, the family of Noah, a righteous and holy man, is not only preserved in safety from the general deluge, but his generations registered and renowned in the book of God, and conveyed along towards the Lord Jesus, as his progenitors and precedent royal line: I observe this point—

Doct. Personal goodness is a good means to bring safety, honour, and many comfortable blessings upon posterity; see Deut. v. 29; Exod. xx. 6; Psa. xxxvii. 25, cxii. 1—3; Prov. xx. 7; xi. 21; Acts ii. 39.

Reason 1. Parents professing religion in truth make conscience of praying for their children before they have them, as did Isaac and Hannah; when they are quick in the womb, as did Rebecca; when they are born, as did Zacharias; in the whole course of their lives, as did Job; at their own death, as did Isaac: Gen. xxv. 21; 1 Sam. i. 10; Gen. xxv. 22; Luke i. 64; Job i. 5; Gen. xxvii. 4. And prayers, we

* Referring to a former course of Sermons.—ED.

know, are, for the procuring of all favour at the hands of God, either for ourselves or others, the most undoubted sovereign means we can possibly use.

2. Godly parents do infinitely more desire to see the true fear of God planted in their children's hearts, than, if it were possible, the imperial diadem of the whole earth set upon their heads. And therefore their principal care is, and the crown of their greatest joy would be, by good example, religious education, daily instruction, loving admonitions, seasonable reproofs, restraint from wicked company, the corruptions of the times, &c., by all dearest means and utmost endeavours, to leave them gracious when they go out of this world. And "godliness," saith Paul, "hath the promise of the life that now is, and of that which is to come," 1 Tim. iv. 8. It gives right and full interest to all the true honour, blessings, and comforts, which are to be had in heaven or in earth.

3. Children are ordinarily apt, out of a kindly instinct of natural lovingness, from many and strongest motives, to imitate and follow their parents either in baseness or better carriage, to heaven or hell.

4. A father that truly fears God dare not for his heart heap up riches or purchase high stations for his children by wrong doing, or any wicked ways of getting; whereupon both he and his fare far the better, and happily avoid the flaming edge of those many fearful curses denounced in God's book against all unconscionable dealers. Such as that, Eccles. v. 13, 14, "There is a sore evil which I have seen under the sun, namely, riches kept for the owners thereof to their hurt. But those riches perish by evil travail: and he begetteth a son, and there is

nothing in his hand." And Hab. ii. 9, 10, "Woe to him that coveteth an evil covetousness to his house, that he may set his nest on high, that he may be delivered from the power of evil! Thou hast consulted shame to thy house by cutting off many people, and hast sinned against thy soul."

Use. 1. Wouldest thou, then, have thy little babes thou lovest so dearly, blessed upon earth, truly noble, God's favourites, and meet thee in heaven? be holy thyself. Men are very careful and curious to have their seed-corn and breed of cattle choice and generous; and will they not endeavour to nurture, manage, and conduct the immortal souls of their children with grace, by godly education, to the highest advancement of which those noble natures are capable, to everlasting bliss, fruition of all heavenly joys, and world without end?

2. This may also serve to reprove and correct those covetous madmen that labour more to have their children great than good, rich than religious. It is a madness of that kind which wanteth terms to express it: that a man should go to hell himself, and fit his children to follow him, in seeking to establish his house and raise his posterity by sacrilege, simony, bribery, usury, oppression, depopulation, or any other course of cruelty and wrong. For so they lay their foundation in fire-works, which is able to blow up themselves and their posterity, body and soul, root and branch.

3. Let this fill the heart of the dying christian with sweetest peace. For, whereas the bloody knife of profane men's unconscionable and cruel negligence in training up their children religiously doth stick full deep in their souls, and, leaving this life, they bequeath unto them the curse of God,

together with their ill-gotten goods, the christian happily finds his conscience, by reason of his former thirsty desire and sincere endeavour to do his children good spiritually, freed from the horror of such blood-guiltiness, and leaves them to that comfortable outward estate which no injury or usury hath impoisoned, and to that never-failing providence of our heavenly Father, which then is wont to work most graciously and bountifully for us, when we, renouncing the arm of flesh, the favour of man, riches of iniquity, and all such broken staves, depend most upon it. If we will needs be our own carvers for things of this life, either by right or wrong, fraud or fair dealing — all is one, so that we may thrive and grow great in the world—then we are justly cast off from all merciful care over us, and exposed to ruin and curse. But, if we rest sincerely for ourselves and ours upon the all-powerful Providence, it will never fail nor forsake us, but ever exercise and improve its sweetness and wisdom for our true and everlasting good.

In the third point, we have a description of Noah's spiritual state, which is the complete character of a true christian, consisting of three attributes: 1. Justness. 2. Sincerity. 3. Piety. I collect from the first this note:—

Doct. Every truly religious man is also a righteous and true-dealing man. From the second, this:—

Doct. Sincerity is the sinew and touchstone of true christianity.

But these two I have so often pressed in the course of my ministry, that I will pass by them at this time.

Look what kind of honesty to men that is which is not accompanied with religion towards God; the same is that religion towards God which is not attended with honesty to men. Dishonest religion, irreligious honesty, insincere religion and honesty, are all in one predicament, as they say, and all out of the right path. If thou hast respect only to the commandments of the first table, and outward performance of religious services, but neglect duties of the second, and conscientious carriage to thy brethren, thou art but a pharisee and formal professor. If thou dealest justly with thy neighbour, and yet be a stranger to the mystery of godliness, canst not pray, nor sanctify the Lord's day, nor submit to a sincere and searching ministry, which the first table enjoins, thou art but a mere moral man. If thou put on a flourish and outward face only of obedience and conformity to both, and yet be true-hearted in neither, as did the pharisees, Matt. xxiii. 14—23, thou art but a gross hypocrite. Bear thyself holy towards God, honestly towards man, and true-heartedly towards both, or thou art nothing in Christ's kingdom, but still in the gall of bitterness and bond of iniquity. Put on righteousness and true holiness in this life, Eph. iv. 24, or thou shalt never put on a crown of glory in the life to come.

"In his generations," which were many, and mainly corrupt, Noah stood out, and stuck unto God through so many ages, and against so wicked a world; from which we may learn—

Doct. That constancy is ever an inseparable attendant upon true christianity. But because a double constancy is here implied,—1. One in respect of continuance of time; 2. Another in respect of opposition to the corruptions of the times,—I may observe two points.

1. Grace once truly rooted in the heart can

never be removed. See for this purpose, Matt. xxiv. 24; 1 John ii. 19, 27; John x. 28; Rom. viii. 35, 38, 39; Luke xxii. 32; 2 Cor. i. 21, 22; Eph. iv. 30, &c

Reasons may be taken from, 1. The dearness, strength, constancy, inviolableness of God the Father's love unto his children. It is dearer than a mother's to her sweetest babe, Isa. xlix. 15; it is stronger than the mountains, Isa. liv. 10; it is as constant as the courses of the sun and moon and stars; of the day and of the night, Jer. xxxi. 35, 36, and xxxiii. 20, 21 ; it is as sure as God himself, Psa. lxxxix. 33—35. 2. Christ's triumphant sitting down and intercession at his Father's right hand; which may for ever, with sweetest peace, and freedom from slavish trembling, assure us of our rootedness in Christ, constancy in grace, and everlasting abode with him in the other world. Being once implanted into Christ by a lively fruitful faith, and blessedly knit unto him by his Spirit, as fast as the sinews of his precious body are knit unto his bones, his flesh to his sinews, and his skin to his flesh, he that will rend us from Christ's mystical body, must pull him out of heaven, and remove him from the right hand of his Father. What furious or infernal power can or dare lay a finger on us in this kind ? Christ hath taken the poisoning power out of every thing that would hurt us, or drag us back to hell. He hath conquered, led captive, carried in triumph, and chained up for ever, all the enemies of our souls, and enviers of our salvation. They may, in the mean time, exercise us for our good, but they shall never be able to execute their malicious wills, or mortally hurt us, either here, or in the next life. 3. The irrevocable sealing of the blessed

Spirit, Eph. i. 13, 14, and iv. 30. And who or what can or dare reverse the deed, or break up the seal of the Holy Ghost? Here then, as you see, the blessed Trinity is the immovable ground of our going on in grace. 4. The lasting and immortal power of the word when once rooted in a good and honest heart, Luke viii. 15; 1 Pet. i. 23. 5. The certainty and sweetness of promises to this purpose, Jer. xxxii. 39, 40; Zech. x. 12; John viii. 12; 2 Sam. vii. 14, 15; Psa. lxxxix. 33—37. 6. The force and might of faith, 1 Pet. i. 2—9. 7. The efficacy of Christ's prayer, Luke xxii. 32; John xvii. 15—20; Rom. viii. 34. 8. The durable vigour of saving graces, John iv. 14; Rom. xi. 29. 9. The inability, nay, impossibility, of all causes or creatures to pluck out of God's hand, John x. 29, or to draw any of his to a total or final falling away. It is not the devil himself can do it, 1 John v. 18. It is not the world, 1 John v. 4; John xvi. 33. It is not the concurrent fury and united forces of all the powers of darkness, Matt. xvi. 18. It is not sin, 2 Sam. vii. 14, 15; Psa. lxxxix. 31, 32. It is not weakness of faith, or other graces, Matt. xii. 20. It is not the imposture of false prophets, Matt. xxiv. 24. It is no creature, or created power, Rom. viii. 38, 39.

Use 1. This point, thus confirmed, doth confound that forlorn tenet of the popish doctors, which tells us that a justified and sanctified man may fall finally and totally from grace. In which I have heretofore upon another occasion, in your hearing, punctually refuted those which I conceived Bellarmine's best arguments. I will not now trouble you with his sophistry again.

2. This sweet and precious truth may crown the hearts of all those that are truly Christ's with joy unspeakable and glorious. Let new converts and babes in Christ, who are wont to be very fearful and much troubled lest they should not hold out, because upon their first entrance into the ways of christianity they are cunningly and concurrently encountered with so many oppositions:—from the devil, who then rageth extraordinarily; from the world, which then tendereth more and more alluring baits; from the flesh, which naturally is very impatient of any spiritual restraint; from carnal friends, who cannot endure their change; from their old companions, who cry out, They are turning puritans; from the times, which lower and look sour upon their zeal: sometimes from the father who begat them; from the mother who gave them suck; from the wife who lies in their bosom; from a world of enemies to grace:—I say, in such a case, let them grasp in the arms of their faith the proofs and promises in the present point, and ride on, because of the word of truth. Let them sweetly, with full assurance and unconquerable resolution, repose upon that everlasting encouragement, for the finishing of their spiritual building, which Zerubbabel received from the mouth of God himself, for success of the material building, a type of this: "Not by might nor by power, but by my Spirit, saith the Lord of Hosts. Who art thou, O great mountain? before Zerubbabel thou shalt become a plain; and he shall bring forth the head stone thereof with shoutings, crying, Grace, grace unto it," Zech. iv. 6, 7.

And that they may more comfortably and constantly go on, let them cast their eyes betimes upon these and the like cautions, at their very first giving their names unto Christ.

(1.) Propose such interrogatories as these to thine own heart: Art thou content to abandon thy bosom sin, and the sensual froth of former pleasures, hereafter to delight in God, as thy chief joy? Canst thou take up thy cross, and follow Christ, his truth and holy track, amidst the many by-paths that lead to hell, and different opinions of multitudes of men? Art thou willing to suffer adversity, disgrace, and discountenance with the righteous, and contemned godly ones? Canst thou endure to have things laid unto thy charge thou never didst, thoughtest, or dreamedst on; to become the drunkard's song; a by-word to those that are viler than the earth; to be music at the feasts of those that sit in the gate? Lam. iii. 63. In a word, canst thou, for Christ's sake, deny thyself, thy worldly wisdom, natural wit, carnal friends, old companions, pleasures, profits, preferments, ease, excellency of learning, acceptation with the world, outward state, liberty, life, or whatever else thou canst name dearest unto flesh and blood? If thine heart answer not affirmatively, (I mean, out of the resolution of a well-advised regenerate judgment; for I know the flesh will grumble and reclaim,) thou wilt certainly fall away, or end in formality.

(2.) Look to thy repentance that it be sincere, universal, constant, from the heart, for all known sins, to thy dying day. 1. If some worldly cross be the continued principal motive: 2. or the humour of melancholy: 3. if it be confusedly only for sin, and in general: 4. or for some one special notorious sin only: 5. or for some lesser sins, with neglect of greater, as for tithing mint, &c.: 6. if it be only legal : 7. but for some sins, of what kind soever; leaving but so much as one known sin not taken to heart : 8. or but for a time;—all will come to naught. A foundation of godly sorrow, deliberately, advisedly, and sincerely laid at first, will be for ever after a comfortable encouragement to faith, spiritual joy, well-doing, and walking with God.

(3.) Take the touchstone of fruitful, powerful, and special marks, to discern and distinguish justifying saving faith from all false and insufficient faiths; for a temporary faith may go far.

(4.) Let knowledge and affection grow up together in thee, and mutually transfuse spiritual vigour into each other. Presume not upon any knowledge, without a humble inflamed affection; neither build too much upon the heat of zeal, without the light of knowledge : either of these may be single and superior in some, who afterwards may shamefully fall away.

(5.) Above all things, look unto thy heart. If thy change were angelical, in words, actions, and all outward carriage, and yet thy thoughts still the same and reserved, thou art but a gilded tomb, and canst not be saved. Let a man take a wolf, beat it black and blue, break its bones, knock out its teeth, cut away its claws, put upon it a sheep's skin, yet still it retains its wolfish nature : let a man become ever so harmless outwardly, yet without a new heart all is in vain.

(6.) Incorporate thyself into the company of God's people, by all engagements and obligations of a profitable, intimate, and comfortable fellowship in the gospel. There is a secret tie unto constancy in the communion of saints. He is not likely to walk long that walketh alone, especially if he might enjoy good company. Shunning society with the godly is a plain sign of a temporary faith.

(7.) Consider well (for the contrary is a notable discovery of counterfeits) that thy calling to grace must settle thee more surely in thine honest particular calling; and make thee therein more faithful, conscientious, and laborious.

Let christians also of longer standing, and more strength in their assaults about perseverance, have recourse unto this tower of truth, and labour to prevent that which they fear:—

1. By constancy, in a careful use of all the means; the word, prayer, conference, meditation, sacraments, &c. To which, let them preserve their love, and practise what they hear, without omission or delay. He that gives way to a heartless neglect, or customary hardness of heart, in the use of the ordinances, may justly suspect his nearness to some fearful sin, or fierce temptation, to some heavy judgment, or dangerous apostacy.

2. As soon as they discover any spiritual weakness or decay, assault or temptation, let them complain betimes unto the throne of grace, and mightily oppose with the most fervent prayers of extraordinary private humiliation.

3. Let them keep perfection still in their eye and aim; and, towards the attainment thereof, acquire and acquaint themselves with rules of holy life, daily directions, courses of most mortified men, &c.

4. Let them watchfully decline all occasions of falling back: spiritual pride, known hypocrisy, desire to be rich, undervaluing and declining the most searching means, form and negligence in religious duties, discontinuance of intimateness with the

godly, neglect of distractions upon the Lord's day, &c.

5. Let them consider that all which is past is lost, if they fall off, 2 John 8.

This former point of constancy in grace did arise from a consideration of blessed Noah's continuance in goodness through so many ages. Now, in that he did not conform to the iniquities of the times, but did stand unstained, amidst the most wicked generations that ever dwelt upon earth, I collect the necessity of another constancy, and that is in respect of opposition to the corruptions of times.

Doct. The servant of God must not serve the times. Or thus: The true christian ought to stand at a distance from the corruptions of the times.

Reason. He is bound unto it by his baptism. Of such as profaned themselves, being christians, with irreligious delight in the ensigns of idolatry, as heathenish spectacles, shows and stage-plays, Tertullian, to strike them the more deep, claimeth the promise which they made in baptism. He is not of the world, John xv. 19; his life is hid with Christ in God, Col. iii. 3. There is a secret, heavenly vigour infused into every gracious soul by the sanctifying Spirit, which deadens it to the world, and makes it delight in God. He ought to shine in the world, as a light "in the midst of a crooked and perverse nation," Phil. ii. 15. Light and darkness cannot endure one another; neither the power of grace those works of darkness in which the world lies drowned. He is by no means to be conformed to this world, Rom. xii. 2, nor to run with the wicked to the same excess of riot, 1 Pet. iv. 4. He is now new-born, and become a child of eternity; whereby his heart is fallen in love with new and everlasting delights, and the eye of his soul turned from the dung of this world towards the glory of the second life. As the worldling cannot relish the sweet joys of gracious exercises, so neither can the christian the frothy pleasures of carnal fellowship. You can as hardly draw the sound professor to an assembly of swaggering companions, as a lover of pleasure to a day of humiliation.

Use 1. Howsoever, then, thou mayest seem to stand on God's side, by an artificial acting of some affected forms in religion, by countenancing the ministry, if thou art a great man, and outwardly conforming to the ordinances; yet, if in thy practice thou art plunged into the corruptions of the present, and thine heart still hanker and hunt in secret after youthful delights, the lusts of men, the most applauded fashions of the greater part, thou art not a christian in truth, but a counterfeit. Assure thyself, if thou swim down the current, and sail with the tide of the times, thou mayest justly look every moment to fall upon the sudden, perhaps, in the height of thy temporal happiness, and hottest gleam of thy worldly glory, into the irrecoverable and everlasting lake of brimstone and fire.

2. Let every one who hath given his name unto Christ, ever hold it his crown and comfort to hold a strong and unconquerable countermotion to the courses of the world. Let him still discover the true nobleness of his christian spirit, and of a mind spiritually generous, by gathering vigour, and growing invincible, from the very oppositions of the wicked, and villanies of the age. See Psa. cxix. 126, 127; 1 Kings xix. 14; 1 Thess. ii. 2.

It was the saying of a moral heathen, "that to do well where was no danger was a common thing;

but to do well where was both peril and opposition was the peculiar office of a man of virtue:" much more, say I, of a man of God.

"And Noah walked with God." Walking with God was the top and flower of all Noah's excellences and spiritual felicities upon earth. Whence note,—

Doct. That walking with God is the crown of the christian's character.

It is the duty and property of every true christian to walk with his God. By walking with God, I mean, a sincere endeavour, punctually and precisely, to manage, conduct, and dispose all our affairs, thoughts, words, and deeds, all our behaviour and conversation, in reverence and fear, with humility and singleness of heart, as in the sight of an invisible God, under the perpetual presence of his all-seeing, glorious, pure eye; and, by a comfortable consequence, to enjoy, by the assistance and exercise of faith, an unutterable sweet communion and humble familiarity with his holy Majesty: in a word, to live in heaven upon earth.

God's covenant and commandment to Abraham, and in him to all the faithful unto the world's end, require it, Gen. xvii. 1. The practice and protestations of the saints and servants of God seal unto it. Enoch's walking with God, chap. v. 22, 24, was a happy preparative to his extraordinary translation to glory. "The Lord, before whom I walk," saith Abraham, chap. xxiv. 40, will do thus and thus. "I will walk before the Lord in the land of the living," saith David, Psa. cxvi. 9. "O Lord God of Israel," saith Solomon, "there is no God like thee in the heaven, nor in the earth; which keepest covenant, and showest mercy unto thy servants that walk before thee with all their hearts," 2 Chron. vi. 14. "I have walked before thee in truth and with a perfect heart," saith Hezekiah. 2 Kings xx. 3 "And herein do I exercise myself, to have always a conscience void of offence toward God, and toward men," saith Paul, Acts xxiv. 16; which sounds the same way. "Let their money perish with them who esteem all the gold in the world worth one day's society with Jesus Christ and his Holy Spirit,"* said that noble Marquess of Vico, well skilled and experienced in a heavenly conversing with his God.

Reason 1. And it must needs be so: for howsoever natural men and worldlings, out of their obnoxiousness and secret terrors, slavishly retire, they do not willingly, neither dare they, draw near to that God, who to them is "a consuming fire," Heb. xii. 19; yet all those who have truly tasted how gracious and glorious he is, will find their hearts, out of a secret sense of God's love unto them first, kindly inflamed with infinite desire to live under the comfortable influence of his pleased countenance, to enjoy his holy Majesty with constant peace, and a humble spiritual access and acquaintance continually. The spirit of prayer, infinite love, exercise of repentance, temptations, and troubles from Satan; pressures and oppressions from the world, loss of inward peace, faintness of faith, want of spiritual strength, assault of some special sin, sweetness of meditation, daily favours showered down upon him without number and above measure; forethought of the great and last account, motions of the blessed Spirit, spiritual desertion, &c., but above all, the inexplicable blessedness, goodness,

* The Life of Galearius, chap. 28.

and excellency of the highest Majesty himself, drive him to his God many times a-day.

2. All God's love unto us, his loving kindnesses, protections, preservations, bounty, patience, divine illuminations, spiritual blessings; in a word, every link of that golden chain of mercy, grace, and glory, far thicker set with sweetest blessings in all kinds than the heaven with stars, which our happy souls have, do, or shall enjoy, from the first springing of it up (if everlasting could have any beginning) out of the adored fountain of his free grace, to the last moment of eternity in highest heavenly bliss, (if eternity could possibly ever determine,) should be so many keen spurs, deepest obligations, strongest chains, to draw our hearts most eagerly to this infinite delight in him, and thus with a humble familiarity to converse with his holy Majesty.

3. Consciousness of our former walking comfortably with God, sanctified by the life of faith, will mightily and incredibly support our spirits and courage in the times of confusions and fear. The hearts of sensual worldlings, for w nt of reconcilement and acquaintance with God in calm and comfortable times, sink and tremble in the day of distress and God's dreadful visitations, as the heart of a woman in her pangs, and fall asunder in their breasts like drops of water. But that happy one, who in his prosperity hath made God his portion, and walked humbly in his presence, will in the time of trouble stand like a strong immovable mountain, impregnable against the rage of wind and weather, against the cruel incursions of all adverse power: when the wicked, with useless cries, shall call upon the mountains to cover them, he will be able to say with David, " The Lord is my refuge

and my strength, therefore will I not fear, though the earth be removed, and the mountains be carried into the midst of the sea," Psa. xlvi. 2. He shall, by the mercies of God, and humble dependance upon his omnipotent arm, encounter and entertain the terrors even of the evil day, of the hour of temptation, of the king of terror, and last judgment, with confidence and peace.

4. Thy walking with God will make thee extraordinarily powerful, and mightily to prevail in prayer; one of the greatest blessings, and sweetest comforts, which can be named or enjoyed in this life. As the king's favourite, who still stands in his presence, and under the immediate and gracious influence of his royal eye, doth far sooner and much more easily obtain both his own and friends' suits, than those who are more estranged from the court, so it is in this case.

5. But, above all, that which should most quicken and urge us to this duty, is that particular interest we have, by Jesus Christ, in Jehovah himself, blessed for ever;—a mystery which, if I should offer to open and enlarge, I should be endless, and yet come infinitely short.

Oh, then, let us infinitely love, and learn exactly the most sweet and heavenly art of walking with God! For a more comfortable enlightening and guiding us wherein, before I come to give some general instructions, give me leave to premise these quickening preparatives.

GENERAL PREPARATIVES.

1. Look that thou livest not in any one known sin against thy conscience, hating to be reformed. Do not cherish, allow, or go on in any lust, corruption, or lewd way in thine heart, life, or calling. Suffer not any work of darkness, or service of Satan, to reign and domineer in thee ; for, if so, thou art so far from ability, or possibility of walking with God, or delighting in him, that thou wearest the devil's brand, and art yet most certainly one of his. See and search the true meaning of such places as these : 1 John iii. 3, 6, 8, 9; James ii. 10; Ezek. xviii. 21, 30; Psa. lxvi. 18, and cxix. 6, 101; Matt. xviii. 8, 9; 2 Cor. vii. 1.

Suitable hereunto is the concurrent judgment and doctrine of our best divines and worthiest writers, graciously instructed unto the kingdom of heaven. These are their several assertions to the same sense, in their own words :

1. "A man can have no peace in his conscience that favoureth and retaineth any one sin in himself against his conscience."

2. "A man is in a damnable state, whatsoever good deeds seem to be in him, if he yield not to the work of the Holy Ghost, for the leaving but of any one known sin, which fighteth against peace of conscience."

3. "So long as the power of mortification destroyeth thy sinful affections, and so long as thou art unfeignedly displeased with all sin, and dost mortify

the deeds of the body by the Spirit, thy case is the case of salvation."

4. "A good conscience stands not with a purpose of sinning; no, not with an irresolution against sin."

5. "The rich and precious box of a good conscience is polluted and made impure, if but one dead fly be suffered in it." (He means, any one known sin, allowed and delighted in impenitently.)

6. "Where there is but any one sin nourished and fostered, all our other graces are not only blemished, but abolished; they are no graces."

7. Most true is that saying of Aquinas, that "all sins are coupled together, though not as to seeking the same temporal good; for some look to the good of gain, some of glory, some of pleasure, &c., yet, in regard of aversion from eternal good, that is God; so that he that looks but toward one sin, is as much averted and turned back from God as if he looked to all. In which respect St. James says, 'He that offendeth in one point, is guilty of all.'"

8. "Every christian should carry in his heart a constant and resolute purpose not to sin in anything; for faith and the purpose of sinning can never stand together."

Thou seest, then, if Satan keep possession but by one reigning sin, it will be thy everlasting ruin. Thou shalt, then, be so far from ever enjoying any humble, holy, acquaintance with our God, that thou art gone, body and soul, for ever. One breach in the walls of a city exposeth it to the surprise of the enemy: one leak in a ship neglected will sink it at length into the bottom of the sea: the stab of a penknife to the heart will as well destroy a man as all the daggers that killed Cesar in the senate-house: if thou hedge thy close as high as the middle region of the air in all other places, and leave but one gap, all thy grass will be gone: if the fowler catch the bird, either by the head, or the foot, or the wing, she is surely his own. It is so in the present case: if thou live and lie with allowance and delight, in any one known sin, without particular remorse or resolution to part with it, thou as yet carriest the devil's brand; he hath thereby marked thee out for his own. As obedience is universal and catholic, if sincere, so repentance, if true, is also general. "It strips us stark naked," as a worthy divine says well, "of all the garments of the old Adam, and leaves not so much as the shirt behind: in this rotten building it leaves not a stone upon a stone. As the flood drowned Noah's own friends and servants, so must the flood of repentant tears drown our sweetest and most profitable sins."

The premonition, therefore, I tender in the first place is this: thou canst never possibly be fitly qualified, either for the right understanding or saving practice of this sacred and sweetest art of walking with God, except thou resolve to stand for ever sincerely at the sword's point against all sin. Even thy bosom-sin must be abandoned, if thou look for any blessing in this kind.

And because this darling pleasure, this minion delight, is Satan's strong-hold, his tower of greatest confidence and security, when he is driven out elsewhere, and so consequently is most powerful and peremptory in keeping a man's heart estranged, with largest distance and incompatible aversion from all holy acquaintance with God; I will, in short, labour to enlighten and disentangle any one who unfeignedly desires an utter divorce from this bosom-devil, by telling him, 1. What it is: 2. The marks to discover it: 3. How he may be deceived about it.

1. As in every man there is one element, one humour, and ordinarily one passion predominant; so also one work of darkness, and way of death. And it is that which his corrupt and original crookedness, upon the first elective survey and prospect over the fool's paradise of worldly pleasures, fleshly lusts, and vanities of this life, by a secret, sensual inclination, and bewitching infusion of Satan, singles out, and makes special choice of, to follow and feed upon with the greatest delight and predominant sweetness: afterward, by custom and continuance, grows so powerful and attractive, that it extraordinarily endears and draws unto it the heat of all his desires, and strongest workings of his heart, with much affectionate impatience and headlongness: and at the height, by an irresistible tyranny, it makes all occasions and occurrences, friends and followers, the deepest reach of policy, and utmost projects of wit, religion, conscience, credit with the world, the universal possibility of body, soul, outward state, serviceable and contributary unto it, as the captain and commanding sin; as to the devil's viceroy, domineering in the wasted conscience. In some it is worldliness, wantonness, ambition, opposition to godliness, usury, pride, revenge, or the like: in others, it may be drunkenness, the swaggering vanity of good fellowship, gluttony, pleasures of play-house haunting, gaming, scurrilous jesting, obstinate insatiableness in allowed recreations, idleness, or such like.

2. Thou mayest discover it by such marks as these:—

(1.) It is that which thy truest friends, thine

own conscience and the anger of God in the ministry, many times find out, meet with, and chiefly check thee for.

(2.) It is that which if it break out into act, and be visible to the eye of the world, thine enemies most eagerly observe and object, as matter of their chief insult, and thy greatest disgrace.

(3.) That which thou art loth to leave, art oftenest tempted unto, hast least power to resist, and which most hinders the resignation and submission of soul and body, of all thy courses and carriage, heartily and unreservedly to the word and will of God.

(4.) It is that which God oftenest corrects in thee, even in the interpretation and guilty acknowledgment of thy self-accusing heart. It may be, at several times thou hast been afflicted with some heavy cross in thine outward state, loss of a child, some fits and pangs of bodily pain, terrors and troubles of mind, or some such proportionable visitations: now in all these and like afflictions, upon the first smarting apprehension, thy conscience, if any whit awaked, on its own accord seized upon that sin we now seek for, as the principal Achan and author of all thy misery.

(5.) If ever thou wast so sick, as out of extremity to receive sentence of death against thyself, and despair of recovery; if thy conscience was stirring, this sin affrighted thee most, and gave the deadliest blow to drive thee to final despair. And, if thou shouldest die in it without repentance, (which God forbid,) it would infuse most hellish vigour and venom into the never-dying worm, which would thereby more mightily gnaw upon thy conscience through all eternity. If ever the sword of the Spirit shall cleave it from thy bosom, (which is infinitely to be desired,) and strike through thy sensual heart with true repentance, it will cost thee the bitterest tears, most sighs, and deepest groans.

(6.) It is that which thou art most loth to have known. If it were possible, thou couldest be well content that no John Baptist should ever hear of thy Herodias. And therefore thou beatest thy brains, and improvest thy wit, to devise (if it be capable of daubing) distinctions, evasions, excuses, extenuations, whole cart-loads of fig-leaves, to colour and cloak this foul fiend, though favourite to thy bewitched soul.

(7.) That which thou art in a bodily fear the minister will meddle and meet with when thou art going to a faithful and searching sermon. For thou thinkest with thyself, If this day he disclose my bosom, I shall both be disgraced amongst my neighbours that know it, and cast also into melancholy by his denouncing of terror against it.

(8.) Thoughts, plots, and projects about it, a thousand to one, ordinarily seize upon thine heart, with first and most acceptable entertainment at thy very first waking; if they have not broken off thy sleep, and troubled thee in thy dreams.

(9.) The cares, pleasures, and appurtenances of it are wont to thrust and throng upon thee on the Lord's day with extraordinary eagerness, importunity, and irresistibleness. For the devil, that desires to have thy mind most distracted upon that day, makes choice of the fittest and most pleasing baits to draw away and detain thy heart, and the most alluring objects for diversion.

(10.) In the darkness and discomforts of the night, if thou art suddenly awakened with some dreadful thunder, lightning, or terrible tempest, the guilt and accusations of thy beloved sin are wont to come into thy mind in the first place, and with greatest terror.

3. A man may be deceived, in conceiving that he is utterly divorced and quite delivered from his bosom sin, and yet it may be but a mere exchange, or some other mistake. This gross, affected self-imposture may be seen in such cases as these:—

(1.) He may change only the outward and visible form of it. For instance: whereas the same sin of covetousness doth utter and express itself by usury, simony, sacrilege, bribery, grinding poor men's faces, crushing, and unmercifully keeping under the poorer of the same trade, stealing, overreaching by tricks of wit, all manner of wrong-doing, all kinds of oppression, detaining ill-gotten goods without restitution, &c., he may insensibly glide out of one gulf of griping cruelty into another; he may fall from one of these, being a more notorious and cursed trade of hoarding, to some other of them less observed and odious in the world, and yet still abide in the chambers of death, and under the tyranny of a reigning sin. The foul sin of uncleanness doth actuate itself by fornication, adultery, and other impurities. Now, he may pass from one of these pollutions, more crying and abominable, to some other of them, not affrighting the conscience with such grisliness and horror, and yet still lie in the impenitent and damnable snares of lust.

(2.) He may cease and refrain from the outward gross acts of such hateful villanies, and yet his inward parts be still defiled with insatiable sensual hankerings after them, delightfully revolving them in his mind, and contemplative commission of them.

For instance, he may hold his hand both from the crying violence of oppressions and wrong, and the closer conveniences of cunning and fraud, and yet covetousness may still reign in him by the earthly exercise of the heart. He may forbear the external acts of uncleanness, and yet lie and languish abominably in speculative wantonness and adulteries of the thought; the visible executions of revenge, and yet nourish in his distempered affections the hellish vipers of heart-burning hatred and spite; all indirect ambitious climbing into high rooms, and yet be passingly proud and over greedy of precedence.

(3.) Nay, he may every way change the kind of his bosom sin in respect of matter, form, object, and yet, upon the matter, it is but the exchange of one foul fiend for another. For instance, wantonness may be his sweet sin in youth, and worldliness in old age; revelling in his younger years, downright drunkenness in his declining time; prodigality may sway in some part of his life, pinching in some other; hypocrisy may reign at one time, apostacy at another; furious zeal for one while, profane irreligion for another.

(4.) When the blasting frosts and feebleness of old age have, with a sottish deadness and listlessness, wasted the ambitious vigour of his mind, and the boisterous heat of his affections have dried and drunk up the milk in his breasts, and marrow in his bones, his darling sin may then at length bid him adieu, without any penitent discharge, and he may say unto it, I have no more pleasure in thee. Whereupon he may falsely conclude a mortification and final conquest over it; a secure deliverance from the guilt and curse of it.

(5.) He may unsoundly please himself with an

involuntary and enforced cessation from it, when there is no want of good will, as they say, but only of matter, means, opportunity, enticement, company, provocation, or something for the full and free acting and enjoyment of it. So, want of money may restrain a man, but full sore against his will, from strange apparel, gaming, ale-house haunting, buying of benefices, offices, high places, &c.

(6.) He may for a time pull his neck out of the strongest yoke of Satan, only out of a melancholic pang of slavish terror, serious forethought of death, and lying everlastingly in hell, and true apprehension of the impossibility of being saved without abandoning it; upon some desperate horror of bringing again his beloved sin in his bosom to the communion, after so many causeful provocations of Divine justice; observation of some remarkable vengeance seized upon his fellow delinquents; or sensible smart of some terrible blow from God's visiting hand in one kind or other: I say, upon some such occasion, he may for a time forbear his vile oaths, usury, drunkenness, gaming, play-house haunting, impurity, or what other sin soever doth reign in him, and retain him strongest in the devil's slavery. But, because it is not the work of the word, humbling him soundly under God's mighty hand, planting faith, and infusing mortifying power, he is not able to hold out long; but the unclean spirit returns, and rules in him again far more imperiously and sensually, out of indignation of its discontinuance, and proportionably to the party's new collected strength and eagerness to recommit it, after his extraordinary and impatient forbearance. I know it is not impossible but that a man, after his conversion, by the sudden surprisal of some violent temptation and cunning train of Satan, may be dragged back to commit his sweet sin again; especially if it be of some nature, (though it be a very heavy case, and to be lamented, if it were possible, with tears of blood;) yet he never doth nor can return to wallow in it again, or allow it. After such a dreadful relapse, his heart bleeds afresh with extraordinary bitterness of penitent remorse, he abhors himself in dust and ashes, as exceedingly vile, cries more mightily unto God in a day of humiliation for the return of his reconciled countenance, repairs and fortifies the breach with stronger resolution, and more invincible watchfulness against future assaults and all attempts to re-enter. But the temporary professor I talk of, after his formal enforced forbearance, ingulfs himself again with more greediness into the pleasures and sensuality of his bosom sin, lies and delights in it again as the very life of his life, and hardens himself more obstinately in it, as a thing impossible to leave, and live with any comfort. Upon his return, the unclean spirit rages more than before, Matt. xii. 45.

Thus, to lend thee some light for a more full discovery, and thorough disentanglement out of its pleasing snares, I have intimated briefly what a beloved sin is, what thine may be, and how thou mayest be deceived about it. For if thou wouldest truly taste how gracious and glorious the Lord is in a sweet communion with his blessed Majesty,—if thou wouldest be intimately acquainted with the mystery of Christ, wherein are hid infinite heavenly treasures, and such pleasures as "eye hath not seen, nor ear heard, neither have entered into the heart of man," 1 Cor. ii. 9,—if thou wouldest ever be fitly qualified to walk humbly with thy God in the way which is called holy,—as thou must fall out for ever with all sin, so must thou principally and impartially improve all thy spiritual forces and aid from heaven, utterly to demolish and beat to the ground the devil's castle; to dethrone and depose from its hellish tyranny over thee, that grand impoisoner of thy soul, and the strongest bar to keep out grace, and all acquaintance and sweetest intercourse with God, —thy bosom sin.

Take notice, by the way, that since we concurrently and constantly teach that justifying faith doth purify the heart from the reign and allowance of any lustful or evil course, and plants, by the power of the Holy Ghost, a sincere universal new obedience, and regular respect to all God's commandments, to all good works of justice, mercy, and truth; and that we neither do nor dare give any comfort to any man of his being justified and assured of God's love, who goes on impenitently in any one known sin against his conscience, hating to be reformed; I say, since it is thus, take notice how unworthily and wrongfully the antichristian doctors, having received foreheads from the whore of Babylon, deal with us in this point. Hear them speak: "So that their justification," (meaning ours,) saith Fitzherbert, "may, according to their opinion, stand with all wickedness." "These words," saith Arnoux, (meaning of the French confession,) "are set down to assure the most wicked man that is, of the righteousness of the Son of God." " By the application of Christ's satisfaction by faith," saith Lessius, "he (meaning the protestant) is reputed just before God, though he find no change of will at all within." The scarlet fathers in the Trentish conventicle say, that Luther, from justification by faith alone, collected not only that good works are not necessary, but also that a dissolute liberty in observing the law of God and of the church will serve the turn. Bellarmine also says, "They seem altogether to think that a man may be saved, although he do no good works, nor observe God's commandments:" which he there only seems and assays to prove, but indeed plays the calumniating sophister. "The justifying faith of the adversaries," saith he in another place, "takes clearly away prayer, sacraments, good works, and whatsoever God hath instituted for our salvation." "The protestants," saith Stapleton, "will have certainty of grace to be in a man, not only without any respect, necessity, consequence, presence, or convenience of good works, but also whatsoever sins being present." The Rhemists also most slanderously affirm, that we "condemn good works as unclean, sinful, hypocritical." Arnoldus also swells with malicious popish poison and the rancour of a slanderous spirit when he fathers upon us such falsehoods as these; as though we should teach that all men are bound to believe that they are elected to eternal life; that we bid all wicked men be secure as those who can fall from salvation by no wickedness.

Now the Lord rebuke thee, Satan, who sittest with such extreme malice and falsehood in the foul mouths of the popish proctors and Rabshakehs of Rome, that they should with such prodigious lies and villanous slanders revile the Lord's champions, and traduce the glorious heavenly truth of our most holy and righteous religion.

But to my purpose, and to conclude the point; thou must either, with a resolute and everlasting divorce, abandon and abominate thy bosom sin, thy darling delight, to the pit of hell, whence it hath formerly received much enraged sensual poison, to the woful wasting of thy conscience, and the stronger and longer barring thee from grace; or else thou must continue an everlasting stranger from all communion and conversing with God: thou shalt never be able to meet him in his ordinances with true reverence and delight, or look him in the face with comfort at the last day.

II. Scorn with an infinite and triumphant disdain to serve the mighty Lord of heaven and earth servilely, slavishly, or formally, for selfish and private ends, or any thing save his own sweet, gracious, glorious self. Hate hypocrisy from the very heart-root; which foul fiend, painting himself more unobservedly in the warm sun and shining prosperity of the gospel's flourishing estate with an outward gilt and superficial tincture, doth with greater variety and stronger imposture deceive both men's own souls and others in the glorious noontide thereof: nay, this great agent for the prince of darkness is so politic, that he prevails too much many times in causing the decline and damp of profession and christian zeal. For though at this day professors of the gracious way be in greatest disgrace with the most; and a drunkard, a swaggering good fellow, a usurer, a son or daughter of Belial, shall find more favour, applause, and approbation with the world, than a man who makes conscience of his ways; so that it may seem the greatest madness to make profession of religion hypocritically,—yet, even in these times, there are some causes in which the devil takes occasion to cause some to play the hypocrite notoriously.

Some there may be, who, being weak and worthless, yet vain-glorious and over greedy of reputation, finding that they obtain no acceptation and applause with worldlings, by reason of their worthlessness, and that natural men entertain them not with that estimation and account proportionable to their proud expectation; and conceiving also that, by their association and siding with the saints, (who in preciousness of regard and dearness of love ever infinitely prefer the poorest christian before the proudest Nimrod,) they shall be prized above vulgar esteem and ordinary valuation, purposely put on a mask of outward conformity to the courses of christianity, that thereby they may procure and purchase some special credit and remarkable respect, and with some, at least, be accounted somebody in the world.

Others there are, who, seeing they cannot so easily and excessively satisfy and glut their greedy humours by their commerce, dealings, and mutual negotiations with natural men; for such are well able with equal cunning to countermine against their crafty and cozening underminings; their consciences will serve them to encounter and retaliate their unconscionableness, with like overreaching retributions of circumvention and wrong; they can well enough sound and fathom with the crooked line of their own deceitful hearts the invincible depths of their Machiavelian projects, and plots, and knavery;—I say, others there are, who upon such occasion, that they may thrive in the world, and grow in wealth more easily and unobservedly, put on a cloak of outward profession, and in policy only and hypocrisy draw towards the better side, mix and join themselves with God's children, hang upon and adhere unto true christians; because they pitch upon them, make special choice of, and single out such upon purpose, as those from whom, by reason of the singleness and simplicity of their hearts, the unsuspiciousness of their charity, the equity and conscionableness of their dealings in these cozening, supplanting, and undermining days, they may most fairly and easily suck out the greatest advantage, and prey upon most plentifully with the devouring teeth of covetousness and craft, gilded over only with a veil of seeming, and varnish of hypocrisy.

Some there may be, whom only the very terrors and sting of slavish fear, and forethought of the wrath and torment to come, may drive and restrain from the execution of grosser villanies, excite and enchain to the outward exercises of holy duties, and many actual religious conformities. For instance, some may repair to the house of God on the Lord's day, not for any such great love to God's truth or a searching ministry, but for fear that, being then alone, or walking idly abroad, their guilty consciences should work more fearfully and fiercely upon them; and that thoughts of their sins, death, hell, damnation, and other such terrible considerations would come into their minds with affrighting forms and apparitions of horror. Some, it may be, for fear they should be justly censured and marked out by men acquainted and experienced in the mystery of grace and ways of God, with the odious deserved brand of prayerless and atheistical sinners; or lest they should be seized upon with some remarkable judgment in their own persons, families, or goods, by fire, robbery, tempest, ill success, death, horror, despair, or other fearful accident, dare not for their lives but continue a course and formal task of prayer, evening and morning, in their houses.

Some also, in times of trouble and terror especially, as of extraordinary thunders, impetuous tempests, dreadful appearances in the air, &c., fly into the company and communion of christians, driven thither by the fearfulness of their spirits, and hope to receive protection of their guiltiness and preservation from wrath, by the prayers, presence, and acceptation of such holy ones. We see in men's conduct, as to human laws, that even fear of them restrains many from many lawless outrages, and constrains to many civil conformities, against which their sensual hearts and humours do rise up against with much distaste and aversion. Do you not think that many drunkards would as well live in murder and upon the spoil, as in their present abominable swinishness, did they not hold it a more horrible thing to be hanged than to pay five shillings, or sit in the stocks? Would not many at sermon-time rather be in the ale-house than in the house of God, were not the constitutions of men a curb unto their corruptions? Would not some desperate wretches as well strike through at once, and quite despatch those they hate, as kill them all the year long with their cruel thoughts and dreadful malice, were not thought free, and actual murder death by the laws of men? It may be so proportionably in men's behaviour towards divine laws, the holy statutes of heaven, and that highest tribunal. But as in the former we ought to be subject "not only for wrath, but also for conscience' sake," Rom. xiii. 5, so in the latter much more, not only for terror of God's judgments, but also for love of his truth.

A worthy divine sums up all I would say in this point thus: "Sometimes the fear of God's judgments, as of the rack of an accusing conscience, of the torments of hell-fire, &c., holdeth men in a slavish obedience."

I fear there are too many abroad in the world, especially great ones, who by forbearance of other gross sins, to which their sensual affections are not so endeared, by outward performance of some holy duties, formal presence at religious exercises, or by countenancing and patronage of godly ministers and good men, hope to make amends, as it were, and to purchase protection and dispensation for the vengeance due unto the sinful pleasures of some bosom and beloved lust wherein they secretly lie. And, therefore, their outside conformity in other things is caused by fear of being horribly and remarkably plagued for that close darling delight.

Others there are, who, by reason of respect to, correspondence with, dependance upon, or gainful expectation from, some gracious great one, christian friend, reverend pastor, patron, landlord or governor, religious rich kindred, &c., or other such by-respects, conform to the outward forms of religion, and live reservedly under the canopy of a counterfeit profession. The false and hollow hearts of men many times harbour many private ends in their outward services of God; and howsoever they openly pretend religion, yet they secretly intend, and plot the satisfaction of their humour and serving of their own turns, by an artificial, enforced, temporary taking part with the better part. Such servile professors as these, ordinarily in the mean time stand at a stay in an external conformity to christian courses; for no spiritual life warms their affections, no root of grace grows in their hearts. Formality of this kind is ever void of all vital vigour, vegetation, and activity; such men are constant only in a heartless, plodding course and coldness; and many times, at length, when the motive of their religious representations and shows is removed, and the end compassed for which they counterfeited, they put off their visors, and appear again plain carnal men and lewd fellows, as they were before.

Some there may be, who, out of a greedy pursuit of a general applause from all sorts of men, and ambitious hunting after a promiscuous reputation, and equal acceptance both with professors of religion and men of this world, put on a show of religious deportment, at least, in the company of such as are ready and forward to commend their conformity, and forwardness that way, and by relation abroad, to enrol their names amongst the number of those who are noted to be on the best side. In a word, such fellows as these, out of a base and unblessed ambition to be well spoken of by all, though a woe waits upon such, Luke vi. 26, furnish themselves both with a form of profession to content christians, and flourishes of good fellowship to please the profane.

Others there are, who may gloriously pretend and protest, with great bravery and confidence, their assent and assistance to the best and holiest courses; put on a temporary counterfeit profession, and fashionable conformity to the communion of saints; that thereby they may pass more fairly and plausibly out of one calling into another: from a baser, lower, more neglected, and toilsome trade, into some other of more liberty, acceptation, and ease; or else break out of all callings, and so by the unhallowed mystery of a sacred cozening, if I may so call it, live upon their profession; and by amusing the tender consciences of weak christians, with the controlling and countermanding tyranny, as it were, of an affected furious zeal, suck out of them no small advantage, and prey too plentifully upon the people of God. Such as these are ready to pretend and intimate that such base, earthly, and worldly employment and spending of their time is disgraceful and derogatory to the providence of God and their christian liberty; that unworthy detainments and avocations interrupt them in the pursuit of their general calling, disable and hinder them in the discharge of holy duties. But let them know, that christianity, if sound and true, doth not nullify, but sanctify our particular callings. Thou oughtest to continue with conscionableness and constancy in that personal calling wherein thy calling to grace did find thee, if it be warrantable and lawful: see 1 Cor. vii. 20. No comfortable change of a calling, but in case of private necessity, or common good; and that truly so, not hypocritically, pretended, or for by-respects.

If any man, then, upon giving his name to religion, shall grow into neglect, distaste, or dereliction of his honest particular calling, we may ever strongly suspect him of hollowness and hypocrisy. It is the confident conclusion of a very learned and holy divine, "Though a man be endued with excellent gifts, and be able to speak well, conceive prayer, and with some reverence to hear the word and receive the sacraments, yet, if he practise not the duties of godliness within his own calling, all is but hypocrisy."*

(1.) What son or daughter of Adam can challenge and plead exemption from that common charge laid upon them by the Lord of heaven, "In

* Perkins, of Callings, p. 734.

the sweat of thy face shalt thou eat bread till thou return unto the ground," Gen. iii. 19; either by travail of body or toil of mind, or both?

(2.) Diligence in a civil calling is necessary for a comfortable provision of earthly necessaries.

(3.) He is a cursed drone, a child of idleness and sloth, the very tennis-ball of temptation, most unworthy the blessings and benefits of human society, who doeth not, one way or other, co-operate, as it were, and contribute to the common good, with his best endeavours, in some honest particular calling.

(4.) A seasonable employment in a civil calling is a sovereign preservative and curb for prevention of infinite swarms of idle, melancholy, and exorbitant thoughts; and for restraint from many wicked and unwarrantable meddlings and miscarriages.

(5.) An honest calling is a school of christianity, in which a man, performing duties for the Lord's sake, may daily profit in the practice and increase of many heavenly graces, faith, obedience, patience, meekness, constancy, truth, fidelity, invocation, thanksgiving, experience of God's providence, &c.

A true convert, therefore, is so far from casting off his personal calling, that, after his calling to christianity, he is wont to discharge the duties thereof with far more care and conscience, though with a better mind, more moderate affections, and for a more blessed end.

Some there may be, who, seeing the iniquity of these last and worst times, lying in wait for the surprise and suppression of forwardness and zeal, and that they may gain, or grow into credit with the world by some special service against the forwarder sort, serve themselves in the mean time (plausibleness of profession taking away the sense of their intrusion) into the company and communion of the most noted religious people, that at length they may do them the more mischief, and drive to the head the bitterness of their lurking malice with a more desperate and deadly sting. These are men of great imposture and cunning in their carriage. They inform themselves thoroughly and exactly in the ways and zealous behaviour of profession, and so, with great satisfaction and contentment, apply and accommodate themselves for a time to their desires and devotions. But if once they pry into a point of seeming advantage, which by their wresting and outfacing may create matter of molestation, and spy their supposed season to win by betraying, they turn Turks and traitors to those which are true of heart, to serve their own turns.

Many there are, who, out of a fond and groundless conceit that only an outward conformity to the word, sacraments, and other religious exercises, will serve their turn for salvation, give their names to profession, and so walk on plodding in the comfortless, unzealous forms of a frozen, outside christianity, even unto their dying day. These men mar and unsanctify themselves by making moderation in religion a saint; and undo their souls by adoring discretion as an idol. Moderation and discretion, truly so called, and rightly defined by the rules of God, are blessed and beautifying ornaments to the best and most zealous christians; but being tempered with their coldness, and edged with their eagerness against forwardness and fervency in spirit, which the apostle enjoins, Rom. xii. 11, become the very desperate cut-throats to the power of godliness, and pestilent consumption of the spirits, heart, and life of true zeal. These fellows are most insolent and confident in their pharisaical brags, spiritual security, and hopes for heaven. They admire and applaud, with much self-estimation of their singular skill and rare felicity, in pitching just upon the golden mean, as they conceive, between profaneness and preciseness, infamous notoriousness and persecuted strictness. But that proverb, in the mean time, falls pat upon their pates, "There is a generation that are pure in their own eyes, and yet is not washed from their filthiness," Prov. xxx. 12. And at length, most certainly, the just execution of that terrible threatening, Rev. iii. 16, will crush their hearts with everlasting horror, confusion, and woe.

But I should be endless in the discovery of this hidden and hellish gulf of hypocrisy, wherein thousands are swallowed up, even in this glorious midday of the gospel. For a man may as soon find out the way of an eagle in the air, the way of a serpent upon a rock, and the way of a ship in the midst of the sea, as to track the cunning and crooked footsteps of this foul fiend in the false hearts of Satan's followers. Only take notice, that thou canst never possibly delight in God, nor ever comfortably come near him, if thou give any entertainment unto it, in what form soever it represents itself, or whatsoever visor it offers unto thee, though ever so fairly varnished, and gilded over with the devil's angelical glory.

III. Build and erect all thy resolutions and conclusions for heaven and God's service upon that strong and purest pillar, that main and most precious principle of christianity,—self-denial, Luke xiv. 26, 27. No walking with God, no sweet communion and sound peace at his mercy-seat, except for his sake, and, keeping a good conscience, thou be content to deny thyself, thy worldly wisdom, natural wit, carnal reason, acceptation with the world, excellence of learning, favour of great ones, credit and applause with the most; thy passions, profit, pleasures, preferment, nearest friends, ease, liberty, life, every thing, any thing. And fear no loss; for all things else are nothing to the least comfortable glimpse of God's pleased face.

From this principle sprung all those noble resolutions and replies of God's worthiest saints and soldiers. That of Esther for the preservation of the people of God; Well, saith she, "I will go in unto the king, which is not according to the law; and if I perish, I perish," Esth. iv. 16. That of Micaiah, when solicited strongly by the messenger to temporize in managing his ministry with suitableness and conformity to the king's pleasure, and plausibleness of the false prophets; "As the Lord liveth, what the Lord saith unto me that will I speak," 1 Kings xxii. 14. That of Nehemiah; "Should such a man as I flee?" Neh. vi. 11; as if he should have said, Tell not me of fleeing, my resolution was fixed long ago, if need require, to lay down my life and lose my blood in the Lord's battles. That of Paul, when his friends were weeping and wailing about him; "What mean ye to weep and to break mine heart? for I am ready not to be bound only, but also to die at Jerusalem for the name of the Lord Jesus," Acts xxi. 13. That of Jerome; "If my father stood weeping on his knees before me, and my mother hanging on my neck behind me, and all my brethren, sisters, children, kinsfolk, howling on every side to retain me in sinful life with them, I would fling my mother to the ground, despise all my kindred, run over my father and tread him under my feet, thereby to run to Christ when he calleth me." That of Luther, when dealt with earnestly and eagerly, not to venture himself amongst a number of perfidious and blood-thirsty papists; "As touching me," saith he, "since I am sent for, I am resolved and certainly determined to enter Worms in the name of our Lord Jesus Christ; yea, although I knew there were as many devils to resist me as there are tiles to cover the houses in Worms." That of a most renowned Italian marquis, Galeacius Carracciolus, when tempted by a jesuit with a great sum of money to return from God's blessing at Geneva to the warm sun in Italy; "Let their money perish with them who esteem all the gold in the world worth one day's society with Jesus Christ and his Holy Spirit." That of George Carpenter, martyr; "My wife and my children are so dearly beloved unto me that they cannot be bought from me for all the riches and possessions of the duke of Bavaria; but for the love of my Lord God I will willingly forsake them." That of Kilian, a Dutch school-master, to such as asked him if he loved not his wife and children; "Yes," said he; "if the world were gold, and were mine to dispose of it, I would give it to live with them, though it were but in a prison; yet my soul and Christ are dearer to me than all."

IV. Exercise thyself continually, and be excellent in that only heaven upon earth, and sweetest sanctuary to a tried soul,—the life of faith; which to live, in some good measure, is the duty and property of every living member of Christ Jesus. Love therefore, and labour to live by, the power of faith, which is the life of salvation, sanctification, preservation.

1. Of salvation—thus: let thy truly humbled soul, grieved and groaning under the burden of sin, throw itself into the meritorious and merciful arms of Jesus Christ, wounded, broken, and bleeding upon the cross, and there let it hold and hide itself for ever, in full assurance of eternal life by virtue of that promise, "He that believeth on the Son hath everlasting life," John iii. 36. For, having thus laid hold upon him, he, by his Spirit, doth communicate first himself unto thee; then both the merit of his death, for remission of thy sins, and of his active obedience, for thy right to salvation and happiness: and withal, the power of his Spirit to quicken thee to the life of grace in this world, and to raise up thy body to the life of glory at the last day.

2. Of sanctification: if thou keep thy faith, the fountain, root, and heart, as it were, from which all thine other graces spring, in life and vigour, thou shalt pray more comfortably, be more courageously patient, hear the word more fruitfully, receive the sacraments more joyfully, pass the sabbaths more delightfully, confer more cheerfully, meditate more heavenly, walk in all the ways of new obedience with more strength, and conquest over corruptions. For, ordinarily, every christian shall find the exercise of other graces to be comfortable or cold, according to the liveliness or languishing of his faith.

3. Of preservation, both temporal and spiritual.

In crosses, afflictions, and all God's outward, angry visitations, by the power of such promises as those, Psa. lxxxix. 33, and l. 15; Heb. xii. 7, 8, 11; 1 Thess. iii. 3; Acts xiv. 22; Luke ix. 23; Isa. lxiii. 9.

In the course and carriage of thy particular calling, the duties and works whereof if thou discharge with conscience, diligence, and prayer, thou mayest go on with comfort, contentment, and freedom from that torturing and racking thoughtfulness; from those restless and cursed carkings of carnal worldlings, wherein they basely languish and lose their souls; and leave the success, issue, and event of all thy labours and undertakings unto the Lord, whatsoever it may be, resting sweetly and ever relying upon that gracious promise, "I will never leave thee nor forsake thee," Heb. xiii. 5.

In ordering and guiding the affairs of thy family, depend by faith upon God's blessing, the strength and sinew of all sound comfort and true contentment that way: see Psa. cxxvii.

In the loss of outward things for thy love and service unto God, by believing that man of God, "The Lord is able to give thee much more than this," 2 Chron. xxv. 9. Nay, in the loss of all earthly things in every kind, see Hab. iii. 17, 18; "Although the fig-tree shall not blossom, neither shall fruit be in the vines; the labour of the olive shall fail, and the fields shall yield no meat; the flock shall be cut off from the fold, and there shall be no herd in the stalls: yet I will rejoice in the Lord, I will joy in the God of my salvation." Consider also for this purpose Job's patient blessing of God upon the surprise and concurrence of a universal misery, Job i. 21.

In pangs of the new birth, spiritual infancy, weaknesses of faith, prayer, godly sorrow, and other graces; by those cordial refreshing promises, Rev. xxi. 6; Matt. v. 6; Isa. xl. 11, and xlii. 3, and lvii. 15.

In oppositions against the raising or restoration of spiritual buildings by the ministry of the word; or in temptations against a man's personal progress, and holding out against God's ways unto the end; by renouncing our own strength, disclaiming the arm of flesh, and crying in every encounter, "Not by might, nor by power, but by my Spirit, saith the Lord of Hosts. Who art thou, O great mountain?" &c., Zech. iv. 6, 7.

In languishings and tremblings after relapse into some old, or fall into some new sin; by such precious places as these, Luke xvii. 4; 1 Sam. xii. 20; 1 John i. 9, ii. 1. From this last place a reverend divine collects this comfort: "If we see our unworthiness, and with broken hearts acknowledge it, God is faithful and just to forgive it, be it ever so great." But this is a jewel fit only for the ear of a sincere christian, when, out of the fearfulness of his distrustful spirit, he puts off all comfort, though truly humbled, after insnarement in some more special affrighting sin. Let no swine trample upon it.

In all kinds of temptations, by the power of that promise, 1 Cor. x. 13. Nay, even amidst a variety of them by obeying that precept, "My brethren, count it all joy when ye fall into divers temptations," James i. 2.

In spiritual desertion, by refreshing, and resting thy sinking soul, in the mean time until the Lord return, upon that sure rock, "Blessed are all they that wait for him," Isa. xxx. 18. Most blessed, dear, and sweetest sanctuary! If the christian die in that waiting state, he shall be certainly saved; for the Holy Ghost pronounceth him blessed.

In the deep and almost despairing apprehensions

of thine extreme vileness, and, as it were, nothingness in grace, by apprehending that most merciful promise from God's own mouth, Isa. xliii. 25.

In thy perplexed and troubled thoughts about return after backsliding; by those comfortable encouragements, Jer. iii. 1, 12—14, 22; Hos. xiv. 1, 2, 4.

In doubts of losing the love of God, and life of grace; by consideration of those passages in God's book, where it appears that the love of God unto his child, in respect of tenderness and constancy, is infinitely dearer than that of a most loving mother to her little one, Isa. xlix. 15; stronger than the stony mountains and rocks of flint, Isa. liv. 10; as constant as the courses of the sun, and of the moon, and of the stars, and of the day, and of the night, Jer. xxxi. 35, 36, and xxxiii. 20, 21; as sure as God himself, Psa. lxxxix. 33—35.

In the hail-storms of slanderous arrows, and impoisoned darts of disgrace, by cleaving to most glorious promises, 1 Pet. iv. 14; Matt. v. 11.

In the valley of the shadow of death, by an assurance of God's merciful omnipotent presence, Psa. xxiii. 4.

In the extremity and depth of such desperate distresses and perplexities, wherein in thy present feeling thou canst see, and find no possibility of help from heaven or earth, God or man, but art both helpless and hopeless, as the church complains, Lam. iii. 18, by such like places as those, Isa. xxxiii. 9, 10; 2 Chron. xx. 12; Gen. xxii. 14; Exod. xiv. 13; Psa. lxxviii. 63—65.

In every thing, or any thing that shall or can possibly befall thee; prosperity or poverty; cross or comfort; calmness of conscience or tempests of terror; life or death, &c.; by extracting abundance of unconquerable patience and peace of soul, from those three heavenly golden conduits of sweetest comfort, Rom. viii. 18, 28, 32.

Thus, in any trouble of soul, body, good name, outward state, present or to come, thou mayest, by the sovereign power of faith working upon the word, not only draw out the sting, and expel the poison of it, but also create a great deal of comfort to thy truly-humbled soul, and maintain it, in despite of all mortal or infernal opposition, in a constant spiritual gladness. For all those promises, whereupon thy heavy heart in such cases may repose and refresh itself, have their being from the blessed name Jehovah, (see Exod. vi. 3,) and therefore are as sure as God himself; they are sealed with the bloody sufferings of his only Son, and therefore as true as truth itself; and, if thou be in Christ, are all as certainly thine, as the heart in thy body, or blood that runs in thy veins. Nay, and a little more for thy comfort, the glory of God's truth is mightily advanced, and himself extraordinarily pleased, by thy more resolute, stedfast, and triumphant cleaving unto them. What a blessed, sweet, and heavenly life, then, is the life of faith!

V. Apprehend in thy mind, and settle in thine heart, a true estimate and right conception of the substance and power, inward nature and materials, of christianity.

This doth not consist, as too many suppose, in outward shows, profession, talking; in holding strict points, defending precise opinions, contending against the corruptions of the times; in the work wrought, and external forms of religious exercises, set tasks of hearing, reading, conference, and the like;

in some solemn, outward, extraordinary abstinences and forbearances, censuring others, &c.; but in righteousness, peace, joy in the Holy Ghost; in meekness, tender-heartedness, love; in patience, humility, contentedness; in mortification of sin, moderation of passion, holy guidance of the tongue; in works of mercy, justice, and truth; in fidelity, painfulness in our callings, conscientious conversing with men; in reverence unto superiors, love of our enemies, an open-hearted, real, fruitful, affectionateness, and bounty to God's people; in heavenly-mindedness, self-denial, the life of faith; in disesteem of earthly things, contempt of the world, resolute hatred of sin; in approving our hearts in God's presence, a sweet communion with him, comfortable longing for the coming of the Lord Jesus, &c.

Yet mistake me not; thou must make a show, profess, and talk, if thou wouldst have Christ Jesus to own thee at that last and dreadful day, Mark viii. 38.

It is therefore an idle and brainless cavil of some lewd ignorant men to say, "We can by no means endure these shows; cannot a man be religious to himself, except he hang out his flag, and let all the world know it?" For where the power of religion is, there will be the show also. Painted fire shines not, ascends not, heats not; but true fire is ever inseparably attended with these properties. We cannot put a candle in a lantern but the light will show itself through; if true grace be planted in the heart, it will shine forth in our words, gestures, actions, and our whole conversation. He that will take show from the substance of religion, let him take brightness from the sun, glittering from gold, breathing from a live body. Show and profession of Christ before men is commanded, as well as the substance and soundness of heart, Rom. x. 9, 10.

Thou must be a patron, and in some good measure a practiser, of precise points, if ever thou wilt have true peace and assurance of walking in the narrow path that leads unto life; as, of walking circumspectly, Eph. v. 15; being fervent in spirit, Rom. xii. 11; striving to enter in at the strait gate, Luke xiii. 24; self-denial, Luke xiv. 26; surpassing the righteousness of the scribes and pharisees, Matt. v. 20; laying violent hands and hold upon the kingdom of heaven, Matt. xi. 12: in a word, of the way which is called holy, and yet so spoken against everywhere, Acts xxviii. 22. For I mean only that preciseness which is commended unto us, and commanded by the blessed Spirit in God's pure and holy word. I know that all passages of sanctification are too precise in the interpretation of worldly wisdom, and paradoxes intolerable and burdensome to flesh and blood, which, notwithstanding, are easy and sweet to mortified men.

Thou must stand opposed against the sins of the times, and, like the eagle, prune up thyself against a storm, or else thou art a temporizer.

Outward exercises of religion are, as it were, the body, without which the soul of christianity hath no existence.

Thou must be content to abridge and confine thy christian liberty at any time, according to opportunities and exigences, for the enlargement of God's glory, the building up of thy brother, and curbing thine own rebellious nature.

Thou mayest, and must judge by the fruits. It is Christ's rule, Matt. vii. 16. If, therefore, thou seest the abominable and unsavoury fruits of lying, swearing, drunkenness, sabbath-breaking, usury, scoffing at religion, &c., hanging out in the sight of the sun, thou mayest justly censure the tree to be rotten, and, for the present, fuel for the fire of hell. Thou mayest judge no man rashly, nor of his final estate. If we see a malefactor cast and condemned for some grievous crime, yet reprieved unto the next assize, no man can say that he shall be certainly hanged, because a pardon may be procured, and come from the king in the mean time; it is so in the present case. But thou mayest call a spade, a spade; a drunkard, a drunkard; a usurer, a usurer. Otherwise, if thou daub and dissemble, how shalt thou ever be able to escape liableness to that abomination, "He that justifieth the wicked, and he that condemneth the just, even they both are abomination to the Lord," Prov. xvii. 15. And to the sting of that woe, "Woe unto them that call evil good, and good evil; that put darkness for light, and light for darkness; that put bitter for sweet, and sweet for bitter," Isa. v. 20. Yet know, that speaking the evil thou certainly knowest of another, must be seasonable, charitable, and discreet; not out of humour, spleen, imperiousness, at thy pleasure; but for God's honour, the good of the party, thine own discharge, upon a warrantable calling, &c., according to the rules I shall hereafter deliver for guiding the tongue.

My meaning, then, in this point is, that those greater matters be most dearly prized, and principally plied proportionably to their worth and weight; and yet these lesser things not neglected. It is too true, that those who are more fierce and forward about the ceremonials and circumstantials, than truly hot and zealous in the essentials and substantials of christianity, prove, too often, vain-gloriously and proudly mounted upon that foul, hellish fiend, hypocrisy, and posting apace towards some fearful apostacy or frenzy.

VI. Let thy spirit, mindful of its own heavenly birth, immortal nature, and everlasting home, ever generously fortify itself with victorious resolution against worldliness, (the canker and cut-throat of all heavenly-mindedness,) and hearty conversation above. Of all the foul fiends that haunt the hearts of carnal men, there is none that holds a stronger opposition and countermotion to walking with God than covetousness. Ambition, sensuality, and other ways of death, cut off their slaves with an accursed disacquaintance and estrangement far enough from all comfortable access unto the throne of grace; but affections nailed and glued to the earth have this pestilential precedence, that they hold the remotest point of declination from the warmth and influence of any sweet communion with the Sun of righteousness and God's glorious face. All earthly-minded men ordinarily, howsoever they may be outwardly restrained and reserved, are secret deriders of the power of godliness, holy strictness of the saints, and mysteries of grace. "And the pharisees also, who were covetous, heard all these things: and they derided him," Luke xvi. 14; even mocked, and made themselves merry with the searching and heart-piercing sermons of the Son of God. Their hearts and hopes are wholly anchored upon the earth, and locked up in their chests; and therefore they dream of no other heaven than their golden hoards, heaps of wealth, and present temporal happiness. Whereas, notwithstanding, one refreshing glimpse shining and shed into our hearts from God's reconciled face, and well-grounded assurance of being his, is infinitely more worth than all the gold in the world.

VII. Let thy holy affections be ever thoroughly warmed and extraordinarily enraptured with the love of God; to which there are infinite inflaming motives and obligations.

1. God, being absolutely considered, is immeasurably lovely. The most attractive objects of insatiable love, and all-amiable excellences, are eminently and transcendently triumphant in him, eternally; beauty, glory, worth, wisdom, greatness, goodness, holiness, purity, any thing, every thing, that is in any ways admirable and loveworthy.

2. Or consider him in relation to thyself; and shouldest thou every moment, through an interminable time, lay down ten thousand lives for his sake, thou couldest never come near the requital of the least part of his infinite love towards thee, which reacheth from everlasting to everlasting. (1.) He bore thee in the bosom of this his free love from all eternity; and that so dearly, that from the same eternity he decreed that his own dear Son should die for thee. (2.) He brought thee out of the abhorred state of being nothing, into the rank of his reasonable and noblest creatures. (3.) He bought thee, when thou hadst wilfully lost thyself, with the heart's blood of his only Son. (4.) He preserves thee every day from a thousand dangers, a thousand deaths, which might seize upon thee, both from within and from without. (5.) He will shortly crown thee with everlasting life, fulness of joy, and pleasures at his right hand for evermore.

3. Consider the unquenchable nature of Christ's

inflamed love unto thee, if now washed with his blood, and beautified with his grace. "Thou hast ravished my heart," saith he to the church, and by consequence to every true christian, "my sister, my spouse; thou hast ravished my heart with one of thine eyes, with one chain of thy neck," Cant. iv. 9. Now, love is of that alluring nature, that many times it will draw love from a man when there is no lovely part in the party loving. How much love, then, doth the sovereign Lord of all goodness, the wellspring of all beauty, excellence, and sweetness, require of us! especially since we are his mere creatures, in respect both of our natural being, outward state, gracious state, and state of glory. See how his spiritual amiableness is shadowed by outward beauties, Cant. v. 10.

VIII. Prize the fruition of God's reconciled face, a nearer communion and acquaintance with his blessed Majesty, the love and light of his countenance, and thereupon a free and frequent access, with humble boldness, unto the throne of grace, at a far higher and more invaluable rate than heaven and earth, as a very real, fruitful foretaste of eternal joys. For, to say no more at this time, if thou hold a holy familiarity with thy God, and he look pleasedly upon thee, thou shalt grasp Jesus Christ more sweetly and feelingly in the arms of thy faith; partake more plentifully of the joyful freedom, presence, and communication of his comforting Spirit; be guarded more strongly and narrowly by his glorious angels; gain more sweetness and heavenly manna out of the ministry, and his other blessed ordinances; walk in safety amongst the creatures like an unconquerable lion. "Thou shalt be in league with the stones of the field; and the beasts of the field shall be at peace with thee: when thou goest, thy steps shall not be straitened; and when thou runnest thou shalt not stumble: when thou liest down, thy sleep shall be sweet; thou shalt dwell safely, and shall be quiet from fear of evil. Thou shalt never more be afraid of any evil tidings, or of destruction that wasteth: when thou passest through the waters, thy God shall be with thee; and through the rivers, they shall not overflow thee: when thou walkest through the fire, thou shalt not be burned; neither shall the flame kindle upon thee," Job v. 23; Prov. iv. 12; iii. 24; i. 33; Psa. cxii. 7; xci. 6; Isa. xlii. 2. And if, at any time, thou art seized upon with any cross or calamity from any of the creatures, any trouble or temptation from man or devil, any lowering or cruelty from the iniquity of the times, or persecutors of the truth; yet the refreshing beams of God's reconciled face shining upon thy heart, through the darkness of such discomforts, will sweetly mitigate, revive, and infinitely make amends for all. The poison and curse of them shall never come near thy soul. The Lord, in the mean time, like an eagle fluttering about her nest, will most tenderly defend and protect thee, Deut. xxxii. 11; Isa. xxxi. 5; and at length most certainly come, like a young lion roaring on his prey, for thy rescue and glorious enlargement, Isa. xxxi. 4.

IX. Labour, by a constant watch, to keep thy heart in a spiritual temper still, and still sweetly content and fruitfully conversant in the mystery of Christ, and the secrets of his kingdom, which thou shalt more easily do, if thou first rejoice in God, his word, and graces, as thy chief joy and greatest advantage. Secondly; by all earthly things, be drawn to the love of heavenly. For though God hath appointed but one sabbath in seven days for his more solemn public worship, yet, to a christian, every day is sanctified to be a rest from all the deeds of the flesh, wherein he is to walk with his God, and show forth the religious keeping of his heart and good conscience in every action of his whole life; so making every passage of his particular calling a part of christian obedience and duty unto God. Thirdly; let the nobleness of thine enlarged spirit as infinitely disdain to be any ways, upon any terms, in bondage to the corruptions of the times; so find a far sweeter relish, and take incomparably more contentment, in the services of thy Lord and his holy ordinances, than in all the outward benefits and favours of this life. For as the best of these abused, will most certainly, at the bar of God, turn scourges and scorpions to the worldling's conscience; so the other will prove unto the christian, having been conscientiously exercised in them, as a rich stock, to bring in comfort, patience, and inward peace in his greatest need. Fourthly; as soon as thou discoverest any spiritual weakness or decay, any extraordinary assault, temptation, deadness, &c., complain betime, cry mightily unto God, give him no rest, neither give over seeking until he return unto thy soul with power and life again. If ordinary means will not prevail, press upon him with extraordinary; if then he do not revive thee with wonted quickening vigour, wait with a patient wakeful longing of all the powers of thy soul, and then all this while thy soul will be still in its true spiritual temper, and a most blessed state, see Isa. xxx. 18. Fifthly; watchfully decline all occasions of falling from thy first love, fervency, and heavenly-mindedness; as spiritual pride, known hypocrisy, desire to be rich, discontinuance of thine intimateness with the godly, neglect of thy particular calling, or daily watch over thy heart, ungodly company, form in religious duties, coldness and customariness in the use of the means, &c. Sixthly; suffer not thine affections to be chained down and set too much upon those things which the common sort and greatest part of men seek after insatiably, and slavishly sink under; praise, profit, credit, acceptation with the world, favour of the great ones, mirth, pleasure, ease, fear, sorrow, earthly contentment, preferment, wealth, long life, or any worldly thing; but debase and disesteem all other delights, in respect of doing God's will, which should ever be unto thee thy meat and drink, thy chief and choicest recreation, and thy only paradise upon earth.

X. Let thy soul full often soar aloft, upon the wings of faith, unto the glory of the empyrean heaven, where God dwelleth, and bathe itself beforehand with many a sweet meditation in that everlasting bliss above. Oh, think with thyself, (though it far pass the reach of any mortal thought,) what an infinite, inexplicable sweetness it will be to look for ever upon the glorious body of Jesus Christ, shining with incomprehensible beauty; and to consider that even every vein of that blessed body bled to bring thee to heaven; and that it, being with such excess of glory hypostatically united into the second Person in the Trinity, hath honoured and advanced thy nature in that respect far above the brightest cherub. To say nothing of the beauty and brightness of that ever-blessed place, that unapproachable light which besets God's dreadful throne, the walking in closest fellowship with the angels of God, that everlasting joyful communion and conversing with the dearest christian friends and all the crowned saints, and innumerable felicities more, which infinitely surpass in excellence and sweetness the comprehension of the largest heart, and expression of an angel's tongue. Contemplate principally the fountain of all thy bliss, how the mighty Jehovah, God blessed for ever, will pour out of himself, by the influence of beatifical vision, perpetual rivers of unutterable joys and pleasures upon thy glorified body and soul through all eternity; even as the sun pours out his beams and shines every day afresh upon the world, without emptiness or end; and with such variety, (for He is infinite,) that they shall be unto thee as fresh, as new, as sweet, as enrapturing, millions of years after thou hast dwelt in those mansions of rest, as they were the very first moment thou enteredst that blissful place. Such fixed considerations as these of things above will serve as notable helps to draw and keep thy heart heavenward, and may mightily move thee to delight in God, and to hold it the sweetest life upon earth to walk with him in the ways of purity and peace. Methinks, if a man do but once a day seriously and solemnly thus cast up the eye of his faith upon that never-fading crown of life, which, after an inch of time, shall eternally rest upon his head, the goodly splendour thereof, and beams of that incomparable joy, should be able to dispel those mists of fading vanities and hurtful fumes of honours, riches, and earthly pleasures, which this great dunghill of the world, heated by the fire of inordinate lust, doth evaporate and interpose between the sight of the soul and celestial bliss; so that he might, with more affectionate freedom and contempt of earth, have his conversation above, and turn the current of all his delights, love, and longings, with more resolution and constancy, towards his heavenly home.

PARTICULAR DIRECTIONS.

These preparatives thus premised, I proceed to some general directions for a more comfortable walking in the way that is called holy.

I. ON FAMILY DUTIES.

First, and before all other things, have a special eye and attendance to a sincere, constant, and fruitful performance of holy duties, of God's services. I say nothing particularly at this time of private reading the Scriptures, public hearing the word, personal prayer, and with thy yoke-fellow, if thou live in that state, singing of psalms, meditation, conference, days of humiliation, &c., of which thou must proportionably make conscience in their due place, observing also in them the ensuing cautions; for a known gross customary neglect of any holy duty, religious exercise, divine ordinance, in its season, may bring a damp upon the rest, and a consumption upon the whole body of christianity. To leave these and the like, in their courses and turns also, to be performed with all good conscience and following cautions, I only at this time purposely advise, for the better sanctifying thyself and all about thee to a more comfortable and successful managing of all affairs, businesses, and undertakings, either spiritual or civil, that thou, being master of a family, (for I single out such a one for instance,) be ever sure to glorify God amidst thy family, by morning and evening sacrifices of prayers and praises to his heavenly Highness.

In the discharge of which important duty of

christianity, utterly neglected by the most, and impoisoned to many, by their resting only in the work wrought, take heed of growing into form, customariness, carelessness, which will most certainly draw the very life-blood and breathing out of those holy businesses; being ever the canker and cut-throat of all true godliness, and gracious acceptation with God. Labour, therefore, by a reverend collecting all the powers of thy soul, and fresh renewing and strengthening thy watch at every several time, to preserve heart and spirit in those daily devotions and family duties: which thou shalt the better do if thou look to, 1. A right disposition before; 2. A spiritual behaviour in the doing; 3. A holy carriage afterward.

1. For the first: 1. Come not before God with any sin lying upon thy conscience unrepented of, or delighted in; see Psa. lxvi. 18. 2. Neither with passion, wrath, or heart-burning against any. 3. Stir up and quicken the activeness and particular apprehensions of thy faith about the things desired and deprecated; in a word, in the apostle's language, for that is my meaning, " Lift up holy hands without wrath and doubting." Bring resolution against all sin, in respect of God; peace and appeased passions, in respect of men; assurance to be heard, in respect of thyself. Or thus, before thou fall upon thy knees, shake off three impoisoning and heavy hinderances, which will clog and clip the wings of thy prayers, that they will never be able to ascend up into heaven,— sin, anger, distrust; and possess thy heart of three excellent helps and inflaming furtherances: a right apprehension of God's dreadfulness, purity, power, &c.; a true sense of thy own vileness, abominableness, nothingness, &c.; a hearty survey of the infiniteness

and inexpressibleness of God's bounty, blessings, and many compassionate forbearances towards thee.

2. For the second, 1. Repel, with an undaunted spirit and resolute contempt, Satan's blasphemous infections, if he be busy that way, (and he is ordinarily most spiteful against the best businesses,) and the rather because, if they be heartily abominated and abandoned with heart-rising and loathing, they are put upon the devil's score, and are only thy crosses, not thy sins. 2. Watch over the world with all care and timely opposition, that, if it be possible, not an earthly thought may creep into thy heart all the while. 3. Strive to hold thy heart in a lively frame, as well in confession as deprecation; in deprecation as petition; in intercession as for personal blessings; as well for purity of heart, as pardon of sin, throughout; though there may be difference of fervour, and crying unto God, according to the necessity and nearness of the passage in the prayer to our particular, or the more universal good desired. Prayer is the creature of the Holy Ghost, every part whereof we should heartily wish, and earnestly wrestle for, that He would proportionably animate, as it were, and thoroughly enliven, even as the soul doth the body.

3. For the third, with all intention and watchfulness pursue and press after the things prayed for, by a timely apprehension, fruitful exercise, and utmost improvement of all occasions, ordinances, helps, and heavenly offers, which may any ways concur to the compassing of them. For instance: thou prayest for knowledge; walk then, when thou hast prayed, with a constant endeavour, in the strength of thy prayer, through all the means, reading, hearing, conferring, practising, (for even that also is a means

to increase knowledge, John vii. 17, especially experimental,) catechising, &c., for the storing of thy understanding, with all sacred illuminations and holy senses of God's saving word. Let no opportunity pass, be earnest in catching all occasions for the enriching of thy mind with such heavenly knowledge, and hoarding up in thine heart such hidden treasures. "If thou criest after knowledge," saith Solomon, "and liftest up thy voice for understanding;" there is the prayer: "if thou seekest her as silver, and searchest for her as for hidden treasures;" there is the endeavour: "then shalt thou understand the fear of the Lord, and find the knowledge of God;" there is the blessing, Prov. ii. 3—5: see Psa. xxvii. 4. Again, thou prayest to be preserved out of ill company; thou doest well: but, when thou hast done, dost thou make conscience of the counsel of Solomon, Prov. iv. 14, 15, and, by the power and impression thereof, confront and oppose the cunning enticements and cursed importunities of thine old companions and brethren in iniquity? "Enter not," saith Solomon, "into the path of the wicked, and go not in the way of evil men. Avoid it, pass not by it, turn from it, and pass away." He that makes prayer the end of prayer, prays only to pray, and rests in his prayer, thinking, when that holy duty is done, that there is no more to be done, prays to no purpose. There must be good doings as well as good duties. He that doth not earnestly, and in good spirit, afterwards set himself against sins deprecated, and pursue with zeal and conscience the graces and good things petitioned, his prayer is worth nothing.

II. ON IDLENESS.

Decline idleness, the very rust and canker of the soul, the devil's cushion, pillow, chief reposal; his very tide-time of temptation, as it were, wherein he carries with much ease, and without all contradiction, the current of our corrupt affections to any cursed sin. Be diligent, with conscience and faithfulness, in some lawful, honest, particular calling, (a good testimony, if other saving marks concur of truth, and true-heartedness, in thy general calling of christianity,) not so much to gather gold and engross wealth, as for necessary and moderate provision for family and posterity; and in conscience and obedience to that common charge, laid upon all the sons and daughters of Adam to the world's end, "In the sweat of thy face shalt thou eat bread, till thou return unto the ground," Genesis iii. 19. 1. But ever go about the affairs of thy calling with a heavenly mind, seasoned and sanctified with habitual prayer, ejaculatory elevations, and willingness, if God so please, to be dissolved, and to be with Christ; filled with heavenly matter and meditation, picked out of the passages of thy present business. For instance, let the husbandman, in seedtime, collect this sacred soliloquy and heavenly thought: —If I now take not the season, I shall have no harvest, but starve in winter; so, proportionably, if I gather not grace in this sunshine of the gospel, and day of my visitation, I shall find nothing but horror upon my bed of death, and burn in hell for ever hereafter, &c. 2. In all the civil businesses of thy personal calling, let thy eye and aim be upon God's glory, as the prime and principal end of all thy actions. 1 Cor. x. 31, and in them seek and serve the glorious end of God's honour, not so much in procuring thine own, as the good of the church, commonwealth, neighbours, and family. 3. By earthly employments do not become an earthworm. In using the world, grow not a worldling, and such a one as finds more sweetness and pleasure in worldly dealings, and the coming-in of thy profits, than in thy heavenly traffic and treasures through the practice and business of christianity.

III. ON SOLITARY SEASONS OF MEDITATION.

In thy solitary seasons, 1. Single out some special, profitable choice matter to meditate on all the while; thereby both to prevent the ordinary intrusion of many vain, foolish, noisome thoughts, impertinent wanderings, and woful trifling cut thy precious time; and also to keep thy spirits and the powers of thy soul at work, lest, as millstones wanting grist grate and grind one another, they waste themselves in a fruitless, barren melancholy. When canst thou be alone, and not have just cause either to busy thy mind about some lawful affairs of thy calling; or wrestle with some corruption, which troubles the peace of thy conscience; or break out into the praises of God, or some other holy passage of heavenly meditation, whereof there is great variety and store? 2. Watch and withstand, with all godly jealousy and care, two dangerous evils: (1.) Thoughts of pleasures from thy youthful sins and unregenerate time, which at such seasons are ready to make re-entry, and very eagerly, being aided by the devil's cunning and the heart's corruption, to re infect and pollute thy soul again with sensual lusts, and renewed guiltiness. And in this point take heed lest the devil delude thee in the glory of an angel, or, by the flashes of his counterfeit light, cast into thy heart his secret wildfire and sparks of lust. For in thy solitary musing thou mayest resume into thy memory the abominations of thy former life, especially of that sin which was thy minion delight and darling pleasure, upon purpose to bewail and detest them; and yet, without a very vigilant eye, the devil will insinuate some secret temptations of wonted sinful sweetness, and that which was intended for an exercise and increase of repentance, may end in the iteration and re-enjoyment of old sensual pleasures. (2.) Take heed, also, at such times, of acting any new sins, from sensual suppositions and imaginary plots; as of worldliness, lust, speculative wantonness, ambition, revenge, dishonouring God's providence, by an unnecessary distrustful forecasting of fearful accidents upon thyself, family, goods, posterity, the state, &c. Some sons of Belial there are who encourage all manner of uncleanness (horrible impurity in the inward parts!) by the mere work of imagination. When they cannot compass and attain the real accomplishment of their furious and sinful projects in outward acts, and upon objects abroad, their abominable desires rebounding, as it were, with an impetuous and unsatisfied rage upon their heated and envenomed passions, act and execute any kind of villany upon the invisible forge of a cursed contemplation. It is strange to consider how many, who carry a counterfeit heaven in their outward behaviour, should harbour such execrable hells in their hearts. 3. Let not pass such a golden opportunity for thy spiritual good, without some sweet comfortable conference with thy God in secret. Call and cry out towards heaven for some special graces, by which thou mayest be most enabled to glorify God, and to keep in thy breast a cheerful and heavenly spirit, as for precious and incomparable jewels to be purchased with the loss of ten thousand worlds, but not to be parted with for as many worlds as thou hast hairs upon thy head. Beg with greatest earnestness, and extraordinary intention of spirit, for mortifying grace, and spiritual strength for the crushing and conquering of those special lusts and unruly passions that most haunt thee, and hurt the peace of thy conscience. Let a sorrowful survey of all thy sins draw from thee some hearty groan and fervent ejaculations for mercy and pardon ; or a summary view of God's blessings and favours towards thee, fill thy heart with many joyful, lowly, and most thankful thoughts, &c. Thus, or in the like manner, let some part of thy solitary time be sure to be seasoned with holy musings and talk with God.

IV. ON COMPANY.

Concerning company, I advise,—

1. That thou never cast thyself into wicked company, or press amongst the profane, especially from choice, voluntarily and delightfully ; and abide no longer with them at any time, upon any occasion, than thou hast found warrant and a calling thereunto. It is uncomely, and incompatible with good conscience, and is not for the honour or comfort of God's children, to keep company, or familiarly converse, with graceless men.

In which point, to prevent misconceptions and

mistakings, consider there is a double fellowship: 1. Common, cold, and more general: in trading, bargaining, buying, selling, saluting, eating and drinking together, and in other passages of humanity and intercourse of civil society, to which charity, nature, necessity, or the exigencies of our general or particular calling, do warrantably lead us. 2. Special, dear, intimate: in consultations and counsels about matters of special secrecy, greatest weight, and highest consequence; in spiritual refreshments, religious conferences, prayer, marriage, all manner of nearest engagements; in a free, unreserved communication of their souls, mutual exchange of the thoughts of their hearts, faithful revelations of the spiritual state of their consciences one to another, and in such like blissful pangs and passages of christian love and ardent sanctified affection.

The former of these the christian must of necessity entertain and exercise sometimes with the men of this world, except he will go out of the world, 1 Cor. v. 10. But the second fellowship is peculiar to the saints. The christian is bound by the book of God, by the law of heaven, by his allegiance to his Lord and Sovereign, and by the common charter of God's children, from conversing with delightful intimacy, and from the exchange and exercise of those special passages of dearest acquaintance, with profane men, children of darkness, and enemies of God. For these, and the like reasons, he thereby incurs a double hazard: the one, of infection with sin; the other, of infliction of punishment.

"He that toucheth pitch," saith the wise man, " shall be defiled therewith; and he that hath fellowship with a proud man, shall be like unto him." " Can a man take fire in his bosom, and his clothes not be burned ? Can one go upon hot coals, and his feet not be burned?" Prov. vi. 27, 28. Neither can any familiarly and intimately converse with a profane man but he shall be corrupted.

There is a strange attractive and imperious power in ill company to impoison and pervert even the best dispositions. 1. By holding familiar correspondence with lewd companions, there first steals upon a man a secret and insensible dislike of his former sober courses. He begins within himself to censure and renounce his former ways of innocence and harmless conversation, as too restraining and distasteful to the ordinary liberty of youth, and common frailty of flesh and blood; and as too much dissweetened and straitened with unnecessary strictness and abridgment. 2. There slily insinuates into his heart a pleasing approbation and delightful assent to the sensual courses and sinful pleasures of his lewd companions. 3. There follows a resolved and habitual change of affections and conversation, a transformation into the manners and conditions of those with whom he doth so familiarly converse. 4. He grows ill-affected and opposed to good men and godly exercises, because in the profane, boisterous, and furious conventicles of good fellowship, he hears them daily railed upon, jested at, belied, and slandered, and there is not a man to take their parts, and to stand on God's side; and therefore, by little and little, he himself is also transformed into a scoffing Ishmael, an accuser of the brethren, and so becomes at last as much the child of hell as any of that graceless company. Thus, and by such steps and degrees as these, many, many times, especially in the universities and inns of court, men of good nature, honest disposition, and perhaps religious education, are by little and little caught and fearfully corrupted, and at length brought to horrible and utter confusion, both of reputation and outward state, both of soul and body, by the infectious villanies of lewd and wicked companions.

But, ordinarily, God's children are not in such danger from notorious sinners, and from men of such desperate and reprobate conversation. For who in his right senses will run upon a man whom he clearly sees has the plague-sore running upon him? What christian, in his right mind spiritually, having any fear of God in his heart, life in his soul, or tenderness in his conscience, will delightfully thrust himself into the company of swearers, drunkards, scorners, filthy talkers, profane jesters, or any fellows of such infamous rank; especially since the soul is a thousand times more capable of the contagion of sin, than the body of any infectious disease?

The hurt which the christian doth take in this regard is most from merely moral men, as such as only profess in form, who being more tolerable and plausible companions, and yet unacquainted with the great mystery of godliness, unseasoned with the power of inward sanctification, and unpractised in the ways of sincerity, do secretly and insensibly infuse, if not a notorious infection with some scandalous sin, yet many times a fearful defection from zeal, forwardness, and fervency in the ways and services of God. Throw a blazing firebrand into the snow or rain, and its brightness and heat will be quickly put out and quenched: let a christian but for awhile abandon his holy conference and comfortable communion with God's children, and plunge himself into the company of those who are but cold and careless, lazy and lukewarm professors, and he shall, in very short time, find his zeal to be very much cooled, his forwardness abated, the tenderness of his conscience too much qualified with worldly wisdom, much dulness of heart, deadness of spirit, drowsiness and heartlessness in his affections to holy things, and a universal decay of his graces insensibly to grow upon him.

In this respect many christians do themselves much wrong, and afflict their souls with many unnecessary spiritual miseries. For they do sometimes unadvisedly, by reason of kindred, for old acquaintance, advantage, and carnal contentment, because of the worldly wisdom, immunity from gross sins, and other good parts of the parties, hold a too near, intimate, and delightful correspondence with such as are only moral men, or pharisees at the best. With whom spending most of their time, and they wanting both heart and skill to uphold any holy conferences, or to afford any reciprocal or mutual help in the feeling passages of sanctification, are occasions to put God's children out of use with the language of Canaan, from the embracing of many joyful considerations, and the exercise of those comfortable meditations and holy conversation above, which christian company would occasionally and seasonably put into them, and keep fresh and working in their minds. Consequently they bereave themselves thereby of much zeal, comfort, feelings of God's favour, joyful springings of heart, boldness in their ways, cheerfulness in the exercises of religion, and that comfortable fruition of other prerogatives of christianity, which many other of their brethren possess; and which they, by the benefit of religious companions, and delightful conversing with the saints, might plentifully enjoy.

Apprehend this passage aright; I say, a christian may be much weakened in his graces by companying too much and conversing delightfully with mere moral men, or whited tombs; for he may spend with such men whole weeks, nay, months and years, and have not one word of sanctified discourse and holy talk ministered unto him; scarce a word to be had from them of the word of God and way to heaven; no conference of the secrets of sanctification, of perplexities of conscience, of their everlasting abode together in the mansions of heaven. Motions that way would be very irksome and tedious unto them; such talk would quickly beget silence, melancholy, sadness, and a desire to break off company. Now the christian, by this means, neither having his tongue exercised, nor his ears much acquainted with edifying christian discourse, grows negligent of storing his memory with holy things, unzealous and cold in the apprehensions of heaven, dull and heartless to godly duties.

As the christian incurs by the company of profane men evident hazard, either of infection with their sins, if they be notorious, or defection from zeal and forwardness, if they be something more tolerable and formal; so every hour that he is in their company, without a warrantable calling and just dispensation out of the word, and from a good conscience, he is in great danger of being involved within the flames of the just confusions, and inwrapt within the compass of those outward curses and plagues, which God's indignation enkindles and inflicts upon wicked men. All profane men being unreconciled to God, are every moment liable to all those miseries and fearful judgments which either man or devil, any of God's creatures, or his own immediate hand, can bring upon them: they are only respited and reserved by God's mercy, and deferred only unto those opportunities and seasons which seem best and fittest to his holy wisdom. Now if, when they light upon them, (as they may justly at any time,) any of God's children be found amongst them unwarrantably and delightfully, it is righteous with God that they receive their portion amongst them at that time, and be fearfully infolded within the fury of the greatest temporal visitation. It is righteous with God, that if his own child will needs be unwarrantably familiar with his enemy, that he also be partaker of any temporal plague, especially with his enemy, even to the loss sometimes of his natural life. Take then, I beseech you, the holy counsel of the blessed apostle, "Be not ye therefore partakers with them," Eph. v. 7; and let his reason fright you out of their company: "Let no man deceive you," saith he, "with vain words, for because of these things cometh the wrath of God upon the children of disobedience," ver. 6. For such things, to wit, "fornication, uncleanness, covetousness, filthiness, foolish talking, jesting," and such like. Take heed, therefore, of conversing with the practisers of these uncomely things.

Again: there must very shortly be an everlasting separation between christians and profane men; at the furthest they must part upon their death-beds, and never see one another again until the day of judgment, and then they must part for world without end. For there is set between them, by God's immutable and irrevocable decree, a vast and immeasurable gulf, which stands as fast and immovable as God Almighty in his throne of majesty; so that they can never possibly meet. "Between us and you," saith Abraham to the rich man in hell, "there is a great gulf fixed; so that they which would pass from hence to you cannot; neither can they pass to us, that would come from thence," Luke xvi. 26. If it be so, then, that after an inch of time there must be between them an endless divorce, and an impassable distance through all eternity, it is best for a christian to begin this separation and disacquaintance in time, and not to repose his special love, the sweetest and noblest of all his affections, upon an object where it must not eternally rest; nor intimately converse with him, whose company he shall not have hereafter in heaven everlastingly. Let him ever only afford the dearest pangs of his kindest affection unto God's children, and convey the sweetest meltings of his heart, and the most passionate embracements of his soul, into their bosoms alone; for he shall be sure to meet them in heaven, and there the lesser streams of their former christian love shall grow into a mighty torrent, and, falling into the great and universal confluence of the united zeal and seraphical fervour of all the saints and angels, run with a sweet and everlasting current into the bottomless and boundless sea of all love and lovely excellences, God himself, blessed for ever.

Again: a good man conversing with those who are graceless, doth very foully distain and obscure, if not quite lose, his christian reputation and credit with good men; for a man is still reputed to be of their humour and conditions with whom he doth ordinarily and intimately converse. "All flesh," saith the wise man, "comforteth according to kind, and a man will cleave to his like. What fellowship hath the wolf with the lamb? so the sinner with the godly." Now, it is a most disgraceful and uncomfortable thing to be justly cast out of the favour and good opinions of judicious and understanding christians. I would have a christian never much trouble himself, or labour with too much curiosity and intrusion, too anxiously, vexingly, and solicitously, to give the world satisfaction for the unjust censures and misconceptions of senseless and worthless profaneness; only he may thence take occasion to examine his heart more narrowly, to walk more warily, to live more holily, and to pray more heartily. Let profane men rage, and swell, and burst; in despite of all, I would have the christian sweetly and calmly to enjoy those blessed comforts which God's compassionate hand hath put into his heart. But, methinks, he should much take to heart and be very sorry for the just dislike and disesteem of true christians, or for any scandal taken upon good ground, from unadvisedness and aberration in his carriage and conversation. As the christian, then, desires to be dearly esteemed of the godly, and tenders the preservation of his good name with good men, "which is rather to be chosen than great riches," Prov. xxii. 1, "than precious ointment," Eccles. vii. 1, "and maketh the bones fat," Prov. xv. 30, which indeed is the most inestimable jewel he possesseth in this life, next unto his own crown of christianity; I say, as he would maintain and uphold a good opinion and esteem in the hearts and consciences of christians, let him fly the company of profane men; for there is no reason he should be reputed God's friend who converses familiarly with his professed enemies.

No profane man can heartily and directly love a christian for his zeal and spiritual graces; nay, naturally and ordinarily he hates all holy impressions wrought upon him by God's sanctifying Spirit. 1. Partly, by reason of that everlasting, irreconcilable, and implacable enmity and antipathy between the Seed of the woman and the seed of the serpent, between light and darkness, Christ and Belial, grace and profaneness. 2. Partly, also, because every unregenerate man, though furnished with the best perfections and excellences attainable in that state, thinks that his lukewarmness and formality are censured and condemned by the zeal and forwardness of the true christian; and that, if these gracious endowments and holy strictness be real, and necessarily required, they plainly proclaim the awful danger of his state, which he securely reposes upon as sufficient for salvation. David, a man after God's own heart, and of a sweet and loving disposition, yet was most heavily pressed and pursued with much causeless spite, and this hatred was even for his goodness. "They that hate me without a cause," saith he, "are more than the hairs of mine head: they that would destroy me, being mine enemies wrongfully, are mighty: then I restored that which I took not away," Psa. lxix. 4. And in another place he saith, "They that hate me wrongfully are multiplied. They also that render evil for good are mine adversaries; because I follow the thing that good is," Psa. xxxviii. 19, 20.

But yet, understand this further in the point. The expression and exercise of this hatred of the forwardness and zeal in the christian, which naturally and ordinarily lurks in the heart of every profane man, may be sometimes restrained for advantage and in policy, by accident, and for by-respects. The sting and fury of it may be weakened and lessened by the ingenuousness of the unregenerate man, or by other good, natural, and moral parts in the christian. Nay, I do not see but that sometimes it may be, as it were, quite dashed and confounded, by the extraordinary innocence and heroical height of spiritual excellences in a good man: as moralists say of virtue, that though it be ordinarily attended by envy, as the body with a shadow, yet it may grow so incomparable and glorious, that envy is glad to hide its head, and fly away like a weak mist from the sun shining in his strength. As soon as virtue, say they, is grown out of ignorance, she entereth by-and-by into envy, till mounting aloft, like as the sun being vertical abateth all shadows, so she, in the top and height of perfection, abateth all envy. Why may it not be so in zeal and piety; that, though it be ordinarily persecuted with extreme hatred, yet sometimes it may attain that extraordinariness, incomparableness, and excellence, that hatred may even hate itself for opposing such unreprovable sanctity? But to my purpose: if it be so, that a profane man cannot possibly love a christian heartily for his christianity and grace, but rather maliciously and mortally hate him, what heart can a christian have to converse intimately and delightfully with a profane man? Who would ever vouchsafe his company, and afford the best of his time, and dearest of his affections, to a person who disdains and despises the most precious jewel he bears about him, I mean, his religious zeal; and labours powerfully, though insensibly, to dim the brightness, and stain the glory of it; either by the contagion of his notoriousness, or at least by his formality, coldness, and unzealousness?

Once more; no christian ought to enter league or entertain fellowship with the enemies of God. It is absurd that a member of Christ should exercise familiarity and intimate passages of love with a child of Satan. What earthly prince could endure with patience to have one of his nearest servants, and of chief trust, to be conversant continually amongst professed rebels and open traitors to his crown and dignity; or to converse intimately with his deadliest enemy? Would any great man in the state retain any as a special favourite who should be intimate with his greatest counter-factionist? What ingenuous child would delightfully digest that company wherein he should hear his father in a foul and shameful manner disgraced and railed upon? How then should Almighty God hold him as his friend who is familiar with strangers to the life of God, and enemies to his grace? How can that man look for the prerogatives and protections of a child of God, who haunts such company with delight; where he hears daily his Almighty Father foully and shamefully dishonoured, perhaps, with oaths and blasphemies, with obscenities and railings, at least with many idle and profane speeches?

Again, conversing with profane men doth cross and overthrow a common christian duty, which is this,—in all companies either do good or take good, or both. For, in this case, the christian both takes hurt and doth hurt. 1. He hurts himself; because he throws himself upon temptation and hazard of being infected with notoriousness, if his companions be very lewd and profane; or, at least, with formality and coldness, if they be but only morally honest, or formal professors. 2. He hurts also others. (1.) He hardens his companions in their unregenerate courses, because, they think, he would not so familiary converse with them, except he had a good opinion of their spiritual state; and so they rest with security and confidence in their unregeneration. (2.) He is a stumbling-block to the weak christian, who, by looking upon his example, may be led awry from the straight path of his profession, and, by taking thereupon liberty of imitation, may have his young beginnings of grace choked and smothered by the delightful vanities of good fellowship in the press of profane company. (3.) He grieves also strong and understanding christians to see him so far forget himself and disgrace his profession as to converse with the enemies of God; and by his practice to persuade the world, that the base fooleries of good fellowship are more sweet and tasteful than the glorious pleasures of the communion of saints.

There is another reason, which, though it be not very obvious to men's apprehensions, or much taken notice of, yet, in my understanding, it should be very powerful and of very great weight to drive christians out of the company of unregenerate men, and to restrain them from a familiar and delightful correspondence and conversing with them; except they have a warrantable calling, and the testimony of their consciences to converse with them for their conversion and spiritual good. It is this: when an unregenerate man observes that a christian presseth into his company, desires to spend time with him, and is well enough content to exchange mutually many offices of intimate kindness, he presently conceives and concludes that sure he sees in him matter worthy of christian company, and endowments sufficient to rank him amongst the saints, else he could not take such contentment in his conditions and conversation. Whereupon he is fearfully hardened in his present courses, and settles with resolution, confidence, and security, upon the plausible deceitfulness of his unregenerate state; and thinks himself well that he may both enjoy the pleasures of the present, and also a good testimony and hope of his rightness in the way to heaven, because it is well known and acknowledged, that his companion both knows and walks in the right path. And, since he hath one to take part with, he takes it not much to heart that other christians are more unfamiliar and strange unto him, for he imputes it only to their sourness and unsociableness. Assuredly, there are many christians very faulty this way, who have very much to answer for in this kind. They familiarly converse with unregenerate men, and because they would not displease and be distasteful, they say nothing unto them of the cursedness of their condition towards God, and of the fearfulness of their case in respect of salvation. Hereupon they grow into a conceit that they are well satisfied with their spiritual state, and so walk far more resolutely and confidently towards hell, by reason of the society and silence of their christian companions. I think, verily, that profane men do not only sometimes desire the company of christians, to win reputation from the better sort, and to gild over the rottenness of their conversation with some little tincture and lesser spendour, reflected from the glory of their christianity, but also to purchase some counterfeit comfort to their consciences, and false hope unto their hearts, that their case is the better towards God, because God's children vouchsafe to keep company and converse familiarly with them.

But, above all, for this purpose peruse often, and ponder well, 1. the effectual prohibitions in God's word; 2. the protestations and practice of the saints; 3. the punishments inflicted for familiarity with the ungodly. For the last, see 2 Chron. xix. 2, and xx. 37. For the second, see Psa. xxvi. 4, 5; Jer. xv. 17; 2 Kings iii. 14. For the first, see 1 Cor. v. 11; Eph. v. 11; Prov. xiv. 7; 2 Thess. iii. 6; where he solemnly commands them, in the name of our Lord Jesus Christ, that they withdraw themselves from every brother that walks disorderly. He specially aims in that place at idle persons; by consequence then, and good proportion, at more notorious fellows. If we must withdraw ourselves from those who have leisure to be for all companies, at all times, upon all occasions, and are therefore accounted the only companions, how fast must we run from liars, swearers, whoremongers, drunkards, scorners, revellers, and fellows of such infamous rank! In Prov. iv. 14, 15, the repetition of the same sense, in variety of phrase, argues the necessity of the duty and earnestness of the holy penman to persuade; "Enter not," saith he, "into the path of the wicked, and go not in the way of evil men. Avoid it, pass not by it, turn from it, and pass away." Deep apprehensiveness of the excellency and worth of the matter, or extraordinary fervency to impress and persuade the point, doth many times in Scripture clothe the same thing with divers forms of speech and variety of phrase.

2. Now, in a second place, if thou desirest to converse with some of thine unconverted kindred, friends, neighbours, old acquaintance, &c., for their spiritual good, observe these three rules: 1. Let

there be a good probability, proportionably, of more power of grace, knowledge, sanctification, spiritual wisdom, christian resolution, &c., in thee to convert them, than poison of unregenerate stubbornness, sensual malice, sinful wit, worldly wisdom, Satanical sophistry in them to pervert thee. 2. See that thy heart be sincere, and that in the singleness thereof thou seek truly their conversion, and not thine own secret contentment; for in this point thine own heart will be ready to deceive thee. Thou mayest put thyself into such company with pretence and purpose to solicit them for salvation, and prevail with them about the best things, and yet, before thou be aware, be plunged and ensnared in the wonted unwarrantable delights of good fellowship, pleasant passages of wit, idle and impertinent follies and familiarities, which thou wast accustomed to exchange and enjoy with them in thy unregenerate time. So that, instead of the discharge of a christian duty, thou mayest both hurt thyself and harden them. 3. As physicians of the body arm and animate themselves with strong preservatives and counter-poisons when they visit contagious and pestilential patients, so, in such cases, be thou sure to furnish and fortify thyself beforehand with prayer, meditation, the sword of the Spirit, store of persuasive matter, strength of reasons, and unshaken resolution, to repel and beat back all noisome insinuations of spiritual infection.

Into christian company, which thou shouldest prize as thine only paradise and heaven upon earth, the very flower and festival of all thy refreshing time in this vale of tears, ever bring, 1. a cheerful and lightsome heart. Methinks, though thou shouldest come amongst the saints with a sad heart, and something overcast with mists and clouds of heaviness and discomfort, yet the presence and faces of those whom hereafter thou shalt meet in heaven, and there, with incomparable joy, behold for ever clothed and shining with eminency and eternity of glory, should disperse and dispel them all, and infuse comfortable beams of heavenly lightsomeness and spiritual joy. I know them, who, being cast sometimes full sore against their wills amongst profane company, are quite out of their element all the while, struck dead in the place, as they say, as solitary as in the most silent desert. But let them come amongst christians, and they are quite other men; as full of lightsomeness and life, as full of heart and heaven, as if they had the one foot in the porch of paradise already. Sadness is not seasonable where such precepts as these have place; "Be glad in the Lord and rejoice, ye righteous; and shout for joy all ye that are upright in heart," Psa. xxxii. 11. 2. A fruitful heart, full of gracious matter, to uphold edifying conference and sanctified talk; being forward and free to communicate, without any hurtful bashfulness or vain-glorious aim, to others the hidden treasures of heavenly knowledge, which thou hast happily digged out of the precious quarry, as it were, of the great mystery of grace; and also by moving of questions, and ministering occasion mutually to draw from them with a holy greediness the waters of life, for a reciprocal refreshing and quickening of the deadness and unheavenliness of thine own heart. And here it will be a profitable wisdom to take notice of and observe each other's singularity of gifts and several endowments, and thereafter, with wise insinuations, to provoke and press them to pour out themselves in those things wherein they have best experience and most excellency. Some are more dexterous and skilful in discussing controverted points, others in resolving cases of conscience; some in discovering the devil's depths and treading the maze of his manifold temptations, others in comforting afflicted spirits, and speaking to the heart of mourners in Zion, &c. I am persuaded many times many worthy discourses lie buried in the breasts of understanding men, by reason of the sinful silence, I think I may say so, and barrenness of those about them; and therefore christians ought to be more forth-putting, active, and fruitful this way. 3. An humble heart, ready and rejoicing to exchange and enjoy common comforts, soul-secrets, heavenly consultations, with the poorest and most neglected christian. If thou be haunted with the white devil of spiritual pride, it is likely thou wilt be either too prodigal and profuse, and so ingross all the talk, which is sometimes incident to new converts or counterfeits; or else too reserved and curious, and so say no more than may serve to breed an applause and admiration of thy worth, which is a very fearful fault. There is no depth of knowledge, no height of zeal, no measure of grace, but may be further enlarged, more inflamed, blessedly increased, by conference with the poorest faithful christian; see Rom. i. 12, and xv. 24, how Paul, that great, learned, and divinely inspired doctor of the gentiles, stood affected in this point.

V. ON THE GOVERNMENT OF THE HEART.

V. But, above all, be most busy with thy heart, for it is the root that either poisons or sweetens all the rest; that is the fountain which causes all the streams of thy desires, purposes, affections, speeches, and the whole current of thy conversation, to run either muddy or clear. Ply, therefore, amongst others, these three points of special and precious consequence for the present purpose, with all seriousness and zeal.

1. Captivation and conformity of the thoughts and imaginations of thy heart to the sovereignty and rules of grace. If thy change in words, actions, and all outward carriage were angelical, yet if thy thoughts were the same, and unsanctified still, thou wert still a limb of Satan. Purity in the inward parts is the most sound and undeceiving evidence of our portion and interest in the power and purity of Christ's saving passion and sanctifying blood-shedding; see Jer. iv. 14; Isa. lv. 7. Now, that thou mayest the better conquer and keep the thoughts of thy heart in subjection and obedience unto Christ, be persuaded and acknowledge, 1. The pestilency of that wicked proverb, "Thoughts are free." It is true, the immediate invisible productions and projects of the heart lie not within the walk of human justice, neither are liable to the censure of earthly courts and consistories; but there is an all-seeing and omniscient eye in heaven, to which the blackest midnight is as the brightest noontide, Psa. cxxxix. 12; which sees our most secret thoughts afar off, ver. 2, and sets them in the light of his countenance, Psa. xc. 8. Hence it is that many humble souls, sensible of their secret provoking the glory of God's pure eye, are more grieved (setting aside the ill of example and scandal, ordinary attendants upon open and visible miscarriages) for the rebelliousness of their thoughts than the exorbitance of their actions. For the sting of these is something eased and

lessened, as they think, by the absence of hypocrisy, and because the world sees the worst. But, concerning the other, it cuts them to the very heart that they are not as well able to preserve their inward parts in purity towards the all-searching eye of that God who stretched forth the heavens, and laid the foundations of the earth, as their words and actions in plausibleness towards man, who shall die, and the son of man, which shall be made as grass. Whereas, then, the natural man is wont to let his heart run riot and at random into a world of idle imaginations, without remorse or restraint, do thou make thy sanctification sure unto thyself by this infallible sign,—that thou sufferest the consideration of God's all-seeing eye, the curb of the last commandment, and check of a tender conscience, to range thy thoughts into order, to confine and keep them within a holy compass from their vain and impertinent vagaries. 2. That thou must be accountable and answerable for every wandering thought, as well as for idle words and wicked actions. Now consider what numberless swarms of imaginations pass the forge of thy fancy every day; and therefore, if thou be not extraordinarily and exactly vigilant and eyeful over thy heart, thou mayest justly fear that, upon the opening and enlightening of the book of thy conscience at those two dreadful days of death and the last judgment, innumerable armies of exorbitant thoughts, which have lain in ambush, as it were, in the secret corners of thy deceitful heart, will charge upon thee with a far heavier account than perhaps thou art aware of, or hast seriously thought upon heretofore. 3. That God's glory must as well shine in thy thoughts, in the invisible workings, intentions, desires, and elevations of the heart, as in thine outward conversation. As God exacts and expects honour and service from his children in words and works, so there is also a thought service, a thought worship, that I may so call it, which is very pleasing and precious in his eyes, as springing more immediately from the heart, wherein he principally delights; and because the secrecy of it is attended with more sincerity. Remember therefore to render with all reverence and zeal unto the Father of Spirits and Lord of thy soul the daily tribute of thy thought service, as well as the tongue service and hand service. And the rather and more plentifully, because opportunities, abilities, and means may fail for outward performance, but the heart is ever at leisure and liberty to think nobly. No times, no tyrants, no wants or restraint, can hinder it from an invisible fruition of God's own self, with thoughts of sweetest rapture and reverence, of love and lowliest adoration, from bathing itself in the meritorious blood of the immaculate Lamb, with thoughts of inexplicable peace, joy, and triumph; from cleaving to the promises of life, and diving into the mystery of grace with extraordinary dearness, purest delight, and victorious faith; from being as a mountain of myrrh and incense, sending up a spiritual sacrifice of praiseful thoughts, infinitely admiring and magnifying the glory and goodness of that merciful hand which wrote thy name with the golden characters of his endless love in the book of life from all beginnings,—suffered the dearest and warmest blood in his Son's heart to be spilled as water upon the ground for the washing of thy body and soul from sin; and after a span of time will set a crown of eternity upon thy head, composed of all comfort, rest, and peace, joys, pleasures, and felicities. And also because, besides God's more special acceptation and more certain sincerity of this inward invisible service, it is ordinarily full of more spiritualness, intention, and life, by reason that it is nearest and most immediate to the object of adoration. The best man, though he may labour to do his best every way, yet he shall find a difference and degrees in his ability to discharge, and the execution of his duties, devotions, and services towards God. His works do not ever answer with that exactness to his words : his words cannot express so to the life the thoughts of his heart : the thoughts of his heart come infinitely short of the excellency of God. Those streams which are next to the well-head are strongest and purest: the thoughts of a sanctified heart laying hold upon, with immediate apprehension and nearest embracements, that most amiable, holy, and glorious object, God himself, blessed for ever, and his sweetest attributes, give him his due and reverend attributions with more heartiness, life, and heavenliness, than his words or actions are wont; though all a man's best and utmost, in thought, word, and deed, fall fearfully short of that which we owe and ought to do.

2. A continual, narrow, watchful guard over thy heart. It is like a city liable every moment both to inward commotion and outward assault. The fountain of original impurity, though its main stream and bloody issue be stayed, and in some good measure stopped, by the sanctifying power of Christ's saving blood, yet it doth still, more or less, bubble up rebelliously. The world doth labour continually with her three great battering engines of pleasures, riches, and honours, to lay it waste,

and rob it of all heavenly treasures. The devil watches every opportunity to hurl in his fiery darts, to cast all into combustion, and thereby further to envenom and enrage the already too much impoisoned viciousness and impetuousness of our corrupt nature. Precious therefore, and worthy all practice, is that precept of Solomon, "Keep thy heart with all diligence," Prov. iv. 23; which thou mayest do with more success and comfort, if first thou watch over the windows of thy soul, the fences, as the worthies of old were wont, with extraordinary care, see Job xxxi. 1; Psa. cxix. 37. It is incredible what a deal of pollution and ill the devil conveys insensibly through these flood-gates of sin into their bosoms who are careless and watchless this way. To instance in the ear and eye: what balls of wild-fire, as it were, doth many an obscene and filthy tongue, set on fire of hell, throw through their ears into men's hearts with rotten and ribald talk, which afterwards begets within worlds of speculative wantonness and flames of lust! Many false reports drop from the slanderer's mouth into the ear, which afterwards in the heart become the cursed seed of heartburning, spite, and mental murder at the least. And such wicked weeds cannot but fructify very rankly in such a naturally sinful soil. A tale-bearer tells thee, that such an one said of thee so and so, when in truth it was not so. Thou presently thereupon conceivest thoughts of unkindness, displeasure, and, it may be, of rage, against that man that never thought thee ill. Here thou spillest innocent blood, for thy heart may kill as well as thy tongue and hand. It is fit, therefore, for every honest face to furnish and fill itself with frowns of distaste and indignation at the approach of any tale-teller. As "the north wind driveth away rain, so doth an angry countenance a backbiting tongue," Prov. xxv. 23. Concerning the eye, David's woful example may warn the holiest men to the world's end to be very watchful, with a most restless and eyeful jealousy, over that wandering sense. An idle glance upon Bathsheba was like a thievish boy thrust in at a rich man's window, who lets in a number of villanous, desperate cutthroats to ransack and rob the house; it being not resisted at the first, drew after it such a black and bloody train, that robbed his royal heart of much heavenly wealth, and wounded his soul as deeply and dangerously as perhaps any of God's servants ever since. 2. Resist and crush every exorbitant thought, which draws to sin at the very first rising. Encounter it with this dreadful dilemma: say unto thyself, If I commit this sin, it will cost me unspeakably more heart-breaking and spiritual smart, before I can obtain assurance of pardon and peace of conscience, than the sensual pleasure is worth: if I never repent, it will be the death and damnation of my soul. See what a world of misery man brings upon himself by giving way to the first wicked thought. 3. Entertain ever with all holy eagerness, and make exceedingly much of, all good motions put into thy heart by the blessed Spirit, howsoever occasioned, whether by the ministry of the word, mindfulness of death, christian admonition, reading some good book, some special cross, extraordinary mercy, any way, at any time. Feed, enlarge, and improve them to the utmost, with meditation, prayer, and practice. So thou shalt preserve thine heart in a soft, holy, comfortable temper, and heavenward, which is a singular happiness.

3. Elevation, and often lifting up of the heart towards heaven. What christian heart can endure to discontinue its sweet familiarity and humble intercourse with God for one day? Let thy broken heart, therefore, every day, besides solemn and ordinary ejaculations, evening and morning, and upon other special occasions, be sure, 1. To bathe itself deliciously in the blissful depths of God's boundless mercies in Christ, that it may be happily kept, spiritually joyful, thankful, and in love with all holy duties. 2. To kiss sweetly the glorified body of our crucified Lord, with the lips of infinitely dearest, and inexpressibly affectionate love,—though the distance be great, yet the hand of faith will bring them easily together,—that it may be preserved in peace, purity, and revengeful opposition unto sin. For, as the application of his meritorious blood is a sovereign remedy to heal the wounded conscience, to turn crimson and scarlet into snow and wool, so, methinks, a serious and compassionate commemoration of the dear effusion thereof should be both a precious corrosive to eat out the heart of corruption, and a special preservative to keep from sin, since sin was the principal in slaughtering the Lord of life. 3. To cast the eye of hope upon the glory, everlastingness, and unutterable excellences of that immortal, shining crown above, which, after this life, (and this life is but a bubble, a smoke, a shadow, a thought,) shall be set upon thy head by the hand of God; a very glimpse of the goodly splendour and enrapturing beauty whereof, is able both to sweeten the bitterest villanies and basest wrongs from the world and wicked men, and to dispel those mists of fading vanities and hurtful fumes of honours, riches, and earthly pleasures, which this great dung-

hill of the world, heated by the fire of inordinate lusts, is wont to evaporate, and interpose between the sight of men's souls and the bliss of heaven.

VI. ON REPRESSING RAGING PASSIONS.

Be very watchful over thy most predominant and troublesome passion, whether it be fear, sorrow, love, anger, &c. All of them are unruly and raging enough, but yet commonly one overrules all the rest, and is the king in the unregenerate man, nay, too often offers to rise in rebellion even against the most sanctified soul.

Whatsoever it be, 1. In thy private morning sacrifice be sure to lay on a load of deepest groans and strongest cries for mortifying grace against it, and comfortable conquest over it. Let that period and passage of thy prayers be enforced and enlarged with an extraordinary pang of fervency, and feelingly sealed, as it were, with the most seraphical selah. 2. Cut off all occasions, whatsoever it cost thee, which may any ways stir, awaken, and kindle it. Withdraw the fuel that ministers unto that passionate flame, though it should be as painful unto thee as the plucking out of thy right eye, or the cutting off of thy right hand. Assuredly, the pleasures of inward quiet, and sweet spiritual calmness of thy so understanding soul, will infinitely recompense any pains in oppositions and resistances in that nature. 3. Consider seriously beforehand, what a deal of disturbance and unsettledness the visible exorbitancy and breaking of it out will breed and bring upon thy inward man. It will be like a dead fly in a box of precious ointment, disgrace all thy graces, and full foully darken the glory of thy profession.

It will be like fire in the thatch, and for the while cast into combustion, as it were, the whole frame of thy spiritual building, and turn the heavenly peace of thy appeased conscience into a bitter tempest. Tell me whether after a lawless transgression of those bonds of moderation, to which thy christian resolution hath confined it, and that it hath prevailed against thee with any notorious excess, I say, whether at night thou find not thy spirit quite down and much deadened to the exercise of prayer, or any other evening duty? And if upon thy waking in the night there should be any terrible wind, dreadful thunder, or any affrighting accident, whether thy heart would not smite thee upon that occasion with much more fear and apprehensions of horror?

I will suppose thy reigning, or rather rebelling, passion (for I speak to the christian) to be choler and anger: and then, first listen to the counsel which the very moral sages minister against this spiritual malady, and to the rules and remedies which the light of reason leads us unto.

Cut off, say they, the causes, and the effect will vanish. Quench the firebrands which enrage this fury, and thou shalt be at quiet; they are such as these:

(1.) Weakness of spirit, unmanliness of mind. Hence it is that old men, infants, and sick folks, are commonly more choleric than others. Impotency and excess of passion ever argue the disgrace and inferiority of the understanding part, the noblest power of the soul. And, therefore, if we would be armed against the sallies and assaults of this domineering raging distemper, we must suffer the highest and heavenliest part of our soul to know and exercise its place and strength. We must not make our understandings underlings, but give reason his right and reigning power.

2. Self-love, a foolish doting upon and adorning ourselves, which springs from the cursed root of self-ignorance, and quite puts out that light of nature's law in our conscience, "Do as thou wouldest be done by." If, before thou loose the reins to that short frenzy, thou wouldest suppose and set thyself in the place of the party with whom thou art angry, and then say and do no more than if thine own person were the patient, it would be a notable means to curb thy choler, and keep the credit of dispassionateness and moderation, and make thee patiently suffer that which perhaps thou hast often confidently offered to others.

3. An over tenderness and delicate niceness in bearing wrongs; an impetuous impatiency for being abused, (whereas insensibility and contempt would better become a great spirit;) an effeminate facility to be moved and touched with every trifle. A spot or wrinkle upon their garments, a dish misplaced upon their table, some error in their dressing, a bird, a dog, a glass, &c., or some lesser toy, will turn some kind of people quite out of tune, and put them out of their humour into a storm of passion. Great minds, and victorious over this furious arch-rebel, are not moved but with great matters. It is a special point of manly wisdom to pass by many petty provocations to wrath without notice or acknowledgement, without wound or passion, and to digest many times the brawlings and indiscretions of hasty men, with the same patience that surgeons do the injuries and blows of madmen when they let them blood.

4. Credulity, lightness in believing whatsoever

comes first to the ear,—that is the highway to hold choler still in combustion. For so the tongues of slanderers, tale-bearers, whisperers, pickthanks, will prove as so many bellows blown by the devil himself to keep this fire in height and fulness of flame.

5. Curiosity, an itching humour, and needless inquisitiveness to know every thing that is done or said. If a man will needs be so meddling, he shall find matter enough to fill his gall. Some men out of this humour are eager to know what is said against them in such and such company, listen to hear what their servants talk concerning them, and if a letter fall into their hands wherein they think themselves to be mentioned, they will not hesitate, against the laws of society, to break it open. Busybodies in this kind never want wrath and woe. Antigonus, as it is said of him, was wise to abandon this vanity. For, when he heard two of his subjects speaking ill of him in the night near his tent, he desired them to go further off, lest the king should hear them.

6. Covetousness, the cutthroat of grace, and canker of the soul, like an eating, insatiable wolf, will either still feed upon gain, or else gnaw upon the heart with fretting; and therefore the very loss of a penny, sometimes the omission of a good bargain, the miscarriage of some domestic trifle, the death of a beast, &c., will presently put a covetous man into choler: for his eyes are so earthly, that they look only upon the secondary, not upon the supreme cause.

7. A dread of being contemned by others in word, deed, or countenance. Many are so weak this way, that, if they spy but any secret smiling, two whispering together in the company, or any talking,

especially with their eyes now and then cast towards them, they presently think that themselves certainly are the aim and object of their scornful observation, and so grow sour, out of tune, and unfit for company all the while after. Such as these are extremely troubled and displeased if they have not the chief place and upper hand at meetings, respect and salutation from those that they salute, exact observance and obeisance from their inferiors, if they are not put first in matters of compliment and services of humanity, &c.

A riddance and restraint of these and the like maladies of the mind will be a notable means to prevent and hinder the assaults and surprisal of this furious and foul fiend.

But if at any time thou feel this viper to receive heat in thy bosom, and that occasions of choler are offered, then, 1. Contain thy body in quiet, and tongue in silence. The stirring and agitation of thy body by stamping or flinging about, inflames the blood and humours, and the talking of thy tongue keeps both the passionate heat in thine own heart, and many times sets on fire those that thou art angry with. The bark of one dog sets all the curs in a town a brawling. Thy breaking forth into raging terms may raise the spirit of raving in others, and therefore silence is a singular cooler to this choleric distemper. If the swelling and boisterous waves rebound from the soft and even sands, there is no great ado, but, if they encounter a rock, they return with great turbulence, and turn into foam. Silence, or a soft answer, stops the overflowing of the gall on both sides; but, if fury be set upon by rage, they grow both almost stark mad for the time. Give reason leave to interpose and resolve. It was good counsel which was given to Augustus, that when the object and occasions of choler were in his eye, he should not be moved before he had pronounced over the letters of the alphabet. It is as absurd for a passion to usurp and domineer over judgment, as for an intemperate scold to justle a reverend judge out of his place, and there to take on in her talkative and scurrilous manner. If thou give the swing and reins unto it at first rising, it will presently quite banish reason and judgment, and be like a man that puts the master out of the house, and sets it on fire, and burns himself alive within; or like a ship that hath neither stern nor pilot, nor sails nor oars, exposed to the mercy of the waves, winds, and tempest, in the midst of a furious sea. 3. Divert to some other business, company, place, pleasant employment, thoughts of content, &c. These are notable coolers, and very convenient to slack this passionate fire, when it first begins to burn in thy bosom.

Habituate thy heart, and keep it exercised and seasoned with considerations: 1. Consider not only the effects of melancholy, a passion which naturally breeds bodily distempers by stirring choler, heating the blood, and the vital spirits, but also consider the brutish deformities and ugly distortions with which this rage disfigures those who are transported with it; as the fieryness of the eyes, inflammation of the face, furiousness of the looks, extraordinary panting of the heart, beating of the pulse, swelling of the veins, stammering of the tongue, gnashing of the teeth, a very harsh and hateful expression of the voice, and many other extremely impotent and unmanly behaviours. Hence it was that angry men were anciently counselled in the heat of their fit to look at themselves in a glass. The monstrous representations of that deformed fury were suited to frighten them out of their choleric humour. 2. Of the sweet loveliness and amiable acceptation of a mild unpassionate spirit. It is the sinew, as it were, and cement of all delightful society, the flower of humanity, the very sweetness of civil conversation. As it is a singular preservative to keep a man's own heart in much calmness and quiet, so it is also an attractive loadstone to draw unto him the hearts and love of others. 3. Of the aim and aspirations of moral wisdom which labours to draw a man's heart to that unshaken, constant, and comfortable temper, that beautiful and noble disposition, which resembles the highest region of the air, where there is no overshadowing cloud nor tempestuous thunder, but perpetual fairness, serenity, and peace.

I have the longer insisted upon these moral instructions purposely to make christians ashamed, who, besides the honest arguments of purer reason, have also rules of religion, and heavenly remedies, and yet are too often overtaken with this mental drunkenness, as some call it. For you must know that all this while I mean hasty, unjust, and exorbitant anger, which misses in measure, object, end, seasonableness, or other circumstances. For there is a sinless and holy anger, and therefore saith Paul, " Be ye angry, and sin not," Eph. iv. 26. Upon the describing and limiting of which, it is not seasonable for me at this time to insist.

Now then, secondly, for religious directions, and more immediately drawn from sacred learning, consider,

1. That all thy wrongs and unworthy usages, thy injuries and indignities, crosses and uncomfortable

accidents, that shall ever any way befall thee, are fore-appointed, ordered, and disposed by God's wise and merciful providence, and that for thy spiritual and everlasting good. This very one thought, that God is ever the principal agent, kept fresh and on foot in thy mind, will be of sovereign power to cool and beat back any intemperate heat which might either rise in thine heart or rage in thy tongue against his instruments, and cause thee many times when thou art chafing ripe and ready to rave, to lay thine hand upon thy mouth, and sweetly say unto God, with David, "I was dumb, I opened not my mouth; because thou didst it," Psa. xxxix. 9. And not like a child to beat the place that hurt him, but rather to walk more heedfully; not like a foolish cur, to snarl and snatch at the stone, never looking after the thrower; or a madman, to bite the sword that sticks in his flesh, but rather to pull it out softly and hasten to the surgeon. There was matter and malice enough in the mouth of Shimei to have made David's royal heart naturally to rise with implacable indignation against that dead dog; unkindness and cruelty enough in the hearts of Joseph's brethren to have made him for ever irreconcilable; wrong and villany enough in the carriage of the Chaldeans to have set Job on fire with rage and revenge against them: but these holy men, by practice of the present point, and from the strength of this consideration which I now commend for the restraint of choler, procured a great deal of sweet peace and patience to their own hearts, pleasedness and acceptation with God, admiration and example to posterity; for they glanced by the means and the men, and fastened their eyes upon their Maker, and the first mover. Joseph looked beyond his brethren's barbarous dealing with him, and said, "The Lord sent me before you;" Job beyond the Chaldeans' lawless outrages, and said, "The Lord hath taken away;" David beyond Shimei's dogged rancour, and said, "The Lord hath bidden him." Jesus Christ himself, blessed for ever, looked beyond the pharisees, priests, jews, Judas, and the soldiers, to his Father's cup, "The cup which my Father hath given me, shall I not drink it?" John xviii. 11, when he commanded Peter to sheath his sword. This christian counsel passeth that which was given to Augustus, when the objects and occasions of choler are in thine eye or ear: when thou art any ways wronged, belied, railed upon, spurned at, or trampled upon by the feet of honoured insolence or dunghill malice; before thou inwardly fret or break out into any impatient behaviour, say first seriously and feelingly in thine own heart, This is from God, for my good; or, with old Eli, " It is the Lord: let him do what seemeth him good," 1 Sam. iii. 18. And let it for ever bridle, nay, sweetly compose, the hastiness and sourness of thy corrupt nature in case of choler.

2. Let the wonderful patience of that mighty Lord of heaven and earth, who is able with one word to cast all the creatures in the world into hell; nay, even with the breath of his mouth to turn hell, and heaven, and earth, and all things into nothing: I say, let his patience against the infinite, intolerable, and endless provocations of his own most obliged creatures, who, like so many desperate traitors, live and lie continually in open rebellion against so great a majesty, be a pattern and precedent unto thee, a silly worm, dust and ashes, earth, or anything that is nought, of pro-

portionable forbearance (if there could be any proportion between infinite and finite) towards thy fellow-creatures. How many black and blasphemous mouths are incessantly open against his blessed majesty! With what dreadful oaths do they tear and re-crucify the precious body of his glorious Son, who sits at his own right hand! With what lies and slanders do they revile his ambassadors and vilify his chosen! How many graceless wretches do wilfully and obstinately profane his sabbaths, pollute his sacraments, and turn their backs upon his word! How many do daily turn themselves into beasts by their swinish drunkenness, to the great reproach of mankind, and dishonour of their reasonable nature! How many inclosing Nimrods and cruel landlords do grind the faces of the poor, nay, pluck off their skins, tear their flesh, break their bones, and chop them in pieces as for the pot, and eat the flesh of God's people! Mic. iii. 2, 3. In a word, how many incarnate devils do march up and down the earth, with hearts and hands as full as hell with all manner of mischief, lewdness, and rebellion! So many, and with such extreme insufferable audaciousness and impudence, that, as a learned divine speaks, if but any tender-hearted man should sit but one hour in the throne of God Almighty, (if it be fit so to suppose,) and look down upon the earth, as God doth continually, and see what abominations are done in that hour, he would undoubtedly in the next set all the world on fire, and not suffer his wrath to be pacified, or the fire to be quenched. And yet, for all this, our gracious God, in the mean time, though he be armed with his own irresistible omnipotence, and a thousand chariots of the whirlwinds,—though he have ever in readiness all the angels in heaven, all the devils in hell, all the creatures in the world, nay, the very hands and consciences of profane wretches, and all that provoke the eyes of his glory with their pollutions, to be the instruments and executioners of his just wrath upon their sin,—yet, I say, our gracious God opposes his infinite patience against all these restless outrageous provocations. He sweetly and fairly tempers and moderates, in the mean time, his most just and causeful indignation, to see if the bountifulness of his forbearance and long-suffering will lead them to repentance. Be thou then for ever ashamed to be angry for every trifle; to break patience upon every trivial provocation; to turn lion in thine own house, and, which is common in carnal worldlings, to rage with extreme folly and baseness against the wife, children, servants, cattle, or any thing that comes in thy way, for every cross accident, worldly loss, domestic miscarriage; nay, many times to torture thine own heart, and trouble others in this kind upon mere mistakings, groundless surmises, and misconstructions, but rather take this gracious lesson from the Lord Jesus' own mouth, "Learn of me, for I am meek and lowly in heart," Matt. xi. 29, and an example of patience from his first martyr, "Lord, lay not this sin to their charge," Acts vii. 60.

3. Let the sweet experience of God's patient and merciful dealing with thee soften thine heart with a compassionate sense of other men's weaknesses, and a melting forwardness to forgive If he, out of the riches of his mercy, hath remitted unto thee ten thousand talents, what a base wretchedness were it to fly in the face of thy fellow-servant, and to take him by the throat for an hundred pence! If he entreated

thee with all love, and with all long-suffering, to come into his stretched-out arms of mercy, when thou layest wallowing abominably in the gore-blood of thy many scarlet and crimson sins, foughtest on the devil's side to the loss of the very life-blood of thy soul, and every time thou camest to the Lord's supper sheddest the precious blood of his blessed Son; what a shame is it unto thee to fall a raging and swell with anger, for the mere oversight, many times unwilling miscarriage, and unpurposed error of those, perhaps, who otherwise treat thee with obsequiousness and love!

4. If a man will not be moved with more fair and ingenuous motives, to master and mortify this bedlam rage, (I speak in this passage to him that hates to be reformed,) let him be amazed, and amend for shame, since the Holy Ghost hath charged every man not to meddle or make any league of friendship with him while he nourisheth and gives the reins to this bosom rebel. "Make no friendship with an angry man; and with a furious man thou shalt not go," Prov. xxii. 24. What a monster is a man of anger, that Solomon should set such a brand upon him, whereby every one is warned to beware of him, and fly from him, as from a nettling, dangerous, unsociable creature!

A word or two of another passion before I pass out of the point, and that is *fear;* which I had not touched at this time, had it been only a rack whereon the hearts of covetous, ambitious, and carnal men are wofully rent, and torn, and tortured all their life long, and not also a cruel engrosser of too much golden time, even from God's children, not without impressions of much fruitless sadness and unnecessary discontent.

The vanity and tyranny of this passion is specially seen and exercised, 1. In putting all real stings into imaginary evils, and drawing true and bitter sorrows from supposed sufferings. 2. In quick apprehension and anticipation of sorrows to come, so that a man, by too much forethoughtfulness and painful apprehension, doth suffer them many times before they seize upon him.

1. For the first: Who feels not the fantasticalness opinion to forge and fasten upon him many dreadful objects, which of themselves have no vigour to vex, because no real being and existence, yet truly torture and afflict by the strength of imagination alone?

Thus one eats his own heart with grief for loss of those riches, and that superfluous wealth, which, if he had ever still possessed, he would never have used. Another lies under the continual slavery of restless fear, lest fire or robbery, some alteration in the state, or desolation of war, should disperse his hoard, or hazard his temporal happiness. One is haunted with much thoughtfulness and carking care, what will become of his children after his death, what men will say of him when he is gone, how it will fare with his wife after his departure. (For naturally our minds are so vain, that, besides the abundance and burden of present cares, they will transport our desires and affections beyond ourselves and being.) Another frettingly fears that he shall be undone in a dear year, or the next rot of sheep, and tires himself with variety of plots for comings-in for many years to come, when he may die in the mean time. Some take up too much precious time from present and more profitable meditations, by troubling their hearts, lest, if the times turn, they should not be able to endure the fiery trial; whereas afterwards, perhaps, they end their life in the peaceful noontide of the glorious gospel. Others, upon the thought or talk of death, are ready to entertain fearful apprehensions lest they should disgrace their christian life with an uncomfortable end, and by some extraordinary temptation, raving, furious carriage, lay open to the world's interpretation, sinister censures, and misconstruction of their former courses; whereas, it may be, they conclude their days calmly, in good memory to the last gasp, without any storm or cloud of feared horror and discomfort, (except former distrustful fears justly bring upon them that which they feared.) For since every one whose life hath been consecrated to God's glory, with truth of heart, doth certainly pass through those dreadful pangs and last pain into pleasures endless and unspeakable, he ought also to submit, with patience and quiet, to glorify him, and to be serviceable to his secret ends, with what kind of death he please; whether it be, 1. Glorious, and untempted: 2. Discomfortable, by reason of bodily distemper: 3. Mingled with temptations and triumphs: 4. Or ordinary, and without any great show or remarkable speeches, after extraordinary singularities of a holy life, which promised an end of special note and observation.

2. For the second: Besides these utterly unnecessary and merely imaginary miseries, many fearful spirits, especially haunted with the humour of melancholy, will not suffer also certain and inevitable evils, which at length must needs befall them, to sleep and keep in their stings until the time appointed, but many times awake them by the cry of fear, like so many sleeping lions, and cowardly provoke them with timorous expectation to rend

their hearts, and sting terribly before the time. Thus our vain minds torment us more with the fear of evils, than with the evils which we fear; spur us on with much unmanly folly to meet in the midway, nay, to overtake, out-run sorrows to come, and make us a thousand times miserable with one individual misery.

For instance; thou hast a child, and perhaps but one, which thou lovest most dearly; for that affection which would be severely strong towards ten, or how many soever, is united in it alone. Thou enjoyest a wife whose death would be unto thee as the loss of half thy heart; and so, proportionably, of any worldly comfort. Now, certain it is, thou must at length part from all these, or what else soever most dear and desirable things in this life; they must be taken from thee, or thou from them. In this case, then, if thou give way and forth unto this faint-hearted tyrant and malicious passion, it will wound thine heart many and many a time with sense of their loss before thou lose them, and mingle amidst thy dearest and most doting apprehensions of their sweetness and worth many bitter thoughts of the day of divorce, and stings of much worldly grief, (for such only I mean,) from a torturing apprehension of painful heartbreak at parting. But the most tormenting rack of this kind, upon which this tyrannical passion doth much terrify and tear the hearts of carnal men, especially, is death; it is called the prince of terror, by reason of its own extreme inevitable pangs; and to them also it is a certain passage to torments without end, and past imagination; and therefore if their consciences be not desperately seared, and sealed up securely with the spirit of slumber against the day of vengeance, they are wont to die almost every day by a slavish fear of death; see Heb. ii. 15. O death, saith the wise man, how bitter is the remembrance of thee to a man that liveth at rest in his possessions, unto the man that hath nothing to vex him, and that hath prosperity in all things! Oh how the heart of such a man doth shrug together for horror, quake like an aspen leaf, and die all the while, when his fear doth represent unto it, in the glass of his imagination, the grisly forms and ugly face of death, with those other dreadful circumstances, as the wailings and outcries of wife, children, and friends about his last bed, parting from all worldly pleasures for ever, rotting in the grave, dragging to the tribunal and terror of the last day! &c.

Besides these imaginary sufferings and untimely sorrows, take notice of three other base pestilential effects and mischiefs which this natural, slavish, distrustful fear (for that I only mean in the whole point) puts upon a man. 1. It may bring upon him the thing which he fears; by fearing to become miserable, he may become that he fears, and so turn his vain fear into certain miseries, according to that saying of Solomon, "The fear of the wicked, it shall come upon him," Prov. x. 24; and that of Isa. lxvi. 4, "I will bring their fears upon them." Thou hast a wife, a child, an outward state, a high place, which thou art immoderately afraid to lose; now this very distrustful fear derogating from the glory of God's merciful providence, which sweetly and wisely disposeth all things, may justly provoke him to deprive thee of them, whereas otherwise thou mightest have enjoyed them still. 2. It robs and bereaves thee of the kindly relish and comfortable enjoyment even of good things. A man can take no delight in the fruition of that good which he feareth to loose. Life itself is loathsome if a man slavishly fear to die. That good breeds the truest present contentment, against the loss whereof we are always prepared. And therefore those who live in continual fear of losing their child, goods, liberty, life, or any other thing that is dear unto them, lose a great deal of that honest joy and allowed pleasure they might have even in these outward things. 3. It dejects and debases his noble nature below the miseries and baseness of beasts in this point, for they are fenced from this folly and vanity by the benefit of their weakness and want of reason; never re-afflicting themselves with evils past, or fearing any to come, but through their whole life enjoying entirely, and with full security, all contentments and pleasures incident to their natures, save only when they are pinched with sense of present pain. What a shame then is it to man, who, being honoured with the excellency of an understanding, reasonable, and provident spirit, whereby he outshines all other creatures like an angel upon earth, should, by the abuse and misemployment thereof, make it a means unto himself to become more miserable in this respect than a brute beast!

Now, many and sweet are the places and promises in God's book, which may serve as precious antidotes and cordials against this carking venom, which too often haunts with insinuations even the most heavenly mind, but eats continually like a canker into the carnal heart. They are such as these; "I will never leave thee, nor forsake thee," Heb. xiii. 5. Shouldest thou fall into the fiery trial, assuredly thy merciful God would either supply thee with a supernatural and extraordinary power and patience over that most exquisite pain, or else abate and lessen the rage of the flames for thy sake. "All things work together for good to them that love God," Rom. viii. 28. Sin, in its own nature, is the deadliest and rankest poison to the soul, and in itself the greatest evil that is or can be; yet God's infinite power and wisdom, which at first drew light out of darkness, as a skilful apothecary deals with poison, so orders and tempers it to his people, that it proves a medicine; much more doth he turn to their good, crosses, disgraces, losses of earthly things, poverty, want, life, death, any thing, every thing. "God is faithful, who will not suffer you to be tempted above that ye are able; but will with the temptation also make a way to escape, that ye may be able to bear it," 1 Cor. x. 13. It is the child of God's peculiar privilege, in the case of afflictions and all future troubles, to expect support in them, benefit by them, deliverance out of them. "He that spared not his own Son, how shall he not with him also freely give us all things," Rom. viii. 32. If Jesus Christ be ours, it is infinitely absurd slavishly to fear either hurt by ill, or want of good. He is incomparably more worth than ten thousand worlds. If thou enjoyest then such a jewel, what a cursed vanity is it to torture and tear thy heart with fear of any earthly loss, or of ever being prevailed against by any created power. Take yet more spiritual armour and heroical resolution against the assaults of this cowardly tyrant, which doth so unworthily afflict the spirits of men, not only with imminent ills, but also with those which are not, and perhaps shall never be, nay sometimes which cannot possibly be, out of those two sweetest psalms for promises of future protection, Psa. xci. and cxxi.; Isa. xliii. 2. But the special preservative which at this time I would commend unto you against this distrustful heart's poison may be extracted from Christ's own words, Matt. vi. 34. After many strong and precious arguments against thoughtfulness and carking, our heavenly Teacher concludes, "Take therefore no thought for the morrow: for the morrow shall take thought for the things of itself. Sufficient unto the day is the evil thereof." Whence I collect and counsel, that the christian ought, in respect of any torturing care or carking forecast, to unite and confine his thoughts, the workings and agitations of his spirit, to the managing of the affairs and mastering the miseries of the present day. The strongest and best composed mind is weak enough to sustain the brunt and encounter of every day's crosses. Temporal troubles, or spiritual temptations, fightings without or fears within, are the certain portion of the saints in this vale of tears. And what day so far comes over the christian's head wherein he escapes free herein? Since, therefore, every day brings forth sorrow sufficient for the exercise of the most retired presence of the most recollected spirit, and the heartiest man shall have his hand full in passing patiently and profitably through present troubles, which many times fall as thick upon him as one wave on the neck of another, what a base and unworthy weakness is it to unfit and disable our already too weak minds for a comfortable dispatch and digesting of daily uncomfortable occurrences, by such needless, senseless, fruitless distractions, vagaries of vanity, and utopian peregrinations?

as either, 1. to lose them in the endless maze of imaginary afflictions; 2. or to waste them by untimely wrestling with certain evils to come; 3. or to wound them with a painful remembrance of sorrows already past. For some there are so bent on grieving themselves, and so transported with the tyrannical vanity of their own minds, that besides their trouble with present, feigned, and future miseries, they collect also matter of mournfulness from time past. For instance: thou has long since, lost thy dearest child, which is one of the extremest earthly crosses, and goes nearest the heart, so that if reasons from reason and religion assuaged not the immoderation and excess of thy sorrow, yet time hath worn out and wiped away thy tears, and made thee weary of weeping; but, notwithstanding, thy vain mind will not suffer that grief, which even length of time hath buried long ago, to lie quietly in the grave, but draws into consideration and remembers its speeches, favour, pretty behaviour, and other lovely circumstances, to make thy heart bleed afresh, and wring from thine eyes new torrents of tears, &c. Sovereign, therefore, against these harpies and devourers of the heart is that counsel of Christ which I have commended unto you from his own mouth, seconded also by the apostle, "Be careful for nothing," Phil. iv. 6; that is, with tearing and torturing the heart, with carking thoughtfulness, anxiety, fretting impatience. Do not waste and weaken thy mind immoderately, unseasonably, imaginarily, untimely, with distrustful anguish, pensiveness, and base prostitution of the flower and sinew of thine immortal spirit, to fruitless and endless impertinences and mis-employments.

For, by the way, we must take notice and acknowledge, notwithstanding what hath been said against carking and other needless distractions and exorbitances of vain minds, that a moderate, christian, provident care and forecast, is both convenient and commanded, both for provision of things necessary, and the prevention of dangers. But this is not distressful, but delightful, because enjoined by God; see 1 Tim. v. 8. For a performance of God's commandment, and the very act of obedience with sincerity, should beget much spiritual sweetness, delight, and joy in the heart. And a fair, easy, unangry providing for things needful and time to come, sweetened with the life of faith and a patient reliance upon God's wise and merciful disposing all our affairs and their success, is one thing; and a restless carking and pursuit after things unnecessary, imaginary, and sometimes impossible, embittered with many slavish fears of feigned or future evils, is another. It is profitable also to gather matter from time past, by contemplation of youthful pollutions, crosses, and corrections for sinful courses, companions in iniquity, or any other aggravating circumstance, for the increase of godly sorrow and hatred of sin. But this is joyful, and easeth the heart; for howsoever carnal joy and sorrow can never consist together at the same time, yet that which is christian sweetly ought, and may, of what sort soever the sorrow be. For first, causes of it from without, as reproaches, persecutions, shame, crown the christian's head with abundance of glory, his heart with joy, his soul with blessedness, 1 Pet. iv. 14; Acts v. 41; Matt. v. 10. Secondly, if it be inward for sin and corruption, there is great matter of much joy, for it sweetly signifies the softening and melting of the heart, and consequently the presence of God's sanctifying Spirit. Such tears as burst out of a heart oppressed with grief for sin, are like an April shower, which, though it wet a little, yet it begets a great deal of sweetness in the herbs, flowers, and fruits of the earth. A great man, guilty of high treason, comes to the block to lose his head; in the very nick of time, when he is ready to lay down his neck, a gracious pardon is shown from the king, whereupon he bursts out abundantly into tears, springing partly from an angry indignation against himself for his traitorous carriage towards so tender-hearted a prince, partly from an inexplicable joyful sense of his own safety. It is proportionably so when we mourn for Him whom we have pierced, and in evangelical repentance. God hath so mercifully ordered all things for his people, that, if they be not wanting to themselves, they may be ever merry, and find a continual matter of rejoicing; for he well knows what great need their poor hearts have of this joyful affection, both to sweeten their outward sufferings and bitterness from the world, and also to season their spiritual sacrifices and services unto himself. and, besides, it is one thing to rake with our remembrance into the grave of buried griefs for sharpening the teeth of worldly sorrow to eat our hearts, another thing to make our memories minister matter from former times of more humiliation under God's mighty hand, deeper detestation of our abominable vileness, and to make our hearts many and many a time melt again and bleed afresh with comfortable softness and godly sorrow for youthful sins.

VII. ON THE GOVERNMENT OF THE TONGUE.

Prize and ply, as a most sweet excellency and comfortable perfection in christianity, a right and religious ordering of thy tongue. It is very material and of special importance for preservation both of outward and inward peace. Original corruption hath naturally put upon every man's tongue an impoisoned fiery edge, whereby, like a sword in a madman's hand, it kills and slays on all sides, wofully wounds his own conscience, infects and envenoms mortally the souls of the present, mangles the good names of the absent with deadly malice, and so bathes itself remorselessly in continual bloodshed, (for there is heart murder and tongue murder, as well as hand murder,) until the attainment of this grace, and the mortifying of such an unruly evil. That it may therefore neither be unseasonably idle nor sinfully exercised, besides many other caveats and constant watchfulness,

1. Take notice of, and apply to heart and practice, that much and generally neglected duty of christian reproof.

By reason of that general and common fellowship, whereof I gave a taste and touch before, (of his arbitary and intimate company every christian makes conscience of better choice,) which thou must sometimes entertain and exercise with the men of this world, except thou wilt go out of the world, thou shalt meet now and then upon unavoidable necessity, and by the exigency of thy calling, with men of intolerable conversation and very scandalous discourse; and unawares and unwillingly fall amongst such companions as will swear, blaspheme God's name, talk filthily, slander the ministry, rail against good men, besides many other scurrilous, base, and profane speeches, much froth and folly in this kind. Now in this case, ordinarily, profane men meddle not. They hold it a point of preciseness to mar the mirth and cast the company into melancholy by calling sin into question. They love not (as they say in their hearts) to be displeasing where they gain nothing, and perhaps do no good to the party. They are commonly quick in railing upon and slandering a good man in his absence; but they are stark-nought and nobody in reproving a notorious wretch unto his face. If they open their mouths this way, it is commonly in jest, in bravery, in form, in derision for some one's sake in the company, who, they know, cannot endure it; or, at best, out of a moral detestation of outrageous villany and furious blasphemies of God's glorious name. But in such cases the christian is truly solicitous and zealous, very much troubled, and careful how to frame and hold a serious, wise, and seasonable contradiction to the language of hell, which consisteth in oaths, lying, slandering, in obscenities, railings, contemptuous insolencies against the ministry and ways of God, defence of popery, and in such rotten and mad talk. He dares not many times in such company let his heart hold his peace, lest thereby he may be guilty, in some degree, of the parties going on in sin, or of betraying God's glory by a cowardly and unchristian silence, or for fear of wounding his own conscience. The omission of the discharge of this duty will sometimes very much vex the conscience, and grieve the heart of the true-hearted professor, when he is departed the place, and considers that by his baseness and frailty he hath failed in so holy a duty, and been faint-hearted in the cause of God.

For this kind of reproving then, and such censuring of the words and works of darkness, the christian is not to be censured as too censorious and precise. Conscience, charity, and God's commandment call and cry upon him for the performance of this needful duty, whensoever unavoidable necessity, or the exigency of a warrantable calling, shall have cast upon him profane wretches, and imprisoned him for the while amongst fellows of lewd discourse and graceless carriage. Except they be dogs or swine: Christ himself hath commanded, that pearls and holy things shall not be cast away upon such: "Give not," saith he, " that which is holy unto the dogs, neither cast ye your pearls before swine," Matt. vii. 6. See also Prov. ix. 8, and xxiii. 9.

The ground of this commandment of Christ I take to be twofold: 1. A dear, compassionate, and tender-hearted care of God, even over the temporal lives of his children; besides the glorious ministry and continual guard of the blessed angels for their preservation, that they hurt not their foot against a stone, his own all-seeing and all-pitying eye doth ever graciously watch over them, to keep them as dearly as the apple of his own eye; and, therefore, he forbids them to cast themselves desperately into the mouth of a barking dog, or upon the paw of a revengeful and blood-thirsty lion; that is, he would not have his child to vouchsafe so much as a reproof to any blasphemous wretch or desperate swaggerer, that would furiously fly in his face for offering him a pearl. 2. A holy jealousy over the glory and majesty of his own blessed word. It is that holy wisdom which issued immediately out of his own infinite understanding. It is far more pure and unspotted than silver tried in a furnace of earth, refined seven-fold. It is a sacred pearl, framed and fashioned by his own almighty hand in the palaces of heaven, which only by an invisible and inspired power can raise those who are dead in trespasses and sins to spiritual life, stop the issue of original corruption, and preserve the souls of men in everlasting health. In a word, it is the word of God, and therefore most unworthy to be trodden under foot, or trampled in the mire by any sensual swine; that is no ways to be vouchsafed to those hateful and swinish men, who, out of a malicious sottishness, entertain so glorious a message from the mighty God of heaven with contempt and scorn.

These two reasons of the commandment lie in the text: " Give not, &c. lest they trample them under their feet, and turn against and rend you." Whence we have also some light to discern who are dogs, who are swine.

By dogs, we see, are meant obstinate enemies, that maliciously revile the ministry of the word, the doctrine of God, and the messengers thereof; who do not only tread the words of instruction and reproof under foot, but also turn again, and all to rend the teachers, and furiously fly in the face of those who fairly tell them of their faults. Consider this, and tremble, all ye that are become scornful and furious opposers to the power and purity of the word, and goads in the sides of the faithfullest ministers. Alas, poor sinners, you cast yourselves desperately into that accursed and horrible condition, that every good man is bound in conscience not to afford you so much as an admonition, or reproof, or a caveat to prevent those curses which are coming upon you. And you wilfully draw upon your own heads that most fearful doom from God's Spirit, and from the church of God, " He which is filthy, let him be filthy still," Rev. xxii. 11. He that is a swine, let him be swinish still. He that rails against the power of grace, let him continue still a mad railer. He that sets himself maliciously against the ministry of the word, let that man receive no comfort or benefit by the word of life. If he will, let him roar still, swagger, be drunk, despair, die, and perish.

By swine are meant those sottish, scurrilous persons, who do scornfully and contemptuously trample under foot all holy instructions, reproofs, admonitions, tendered unto them out of the word of truth.

Some of these are swine, as it were, only in practice : they do not say much, or keep any great grunting against good men ; but they feed insatiably, though silently, upon the dross and filth of sensual pleasures and carnal contentments : and if at any time a pearl be cast in their way, I mean a seasonable reproof ministered unto them, they trample it in the mire, and with a brutish baseness tread it under foot, because indeed they hate to be reformed, and are sottishly and stubbornly resolved not to exchange these worldly pleasures, which they have in present possession and pursuit, for the glory of a hundred heavens, which preachers so much talk of, but they cannot taste of, or tell when to come thither.

Other swine there are, as it were both in practice and profession, who, besides their hating to be reformed, and obstinate resolution not to forego their present pleasures, or forsake their former ways, are also possessed with a spirit of scoffing. These are rather wild boars : for, with a furious and giant-like insolency and outrage, they provoke and challenge the mighty Lord of heaven about the truth of his judgments and promises, making a mock of them.

Let all who are thus sensual and swinish consider this, and tremble ; who with sinful greediness feed upon earthliness, and epicurism, and hate to be reformed ; who wilfully wallow in the mud and filth of vanishing pleasures, and will not be washed ; who many and many times come unto, continue at, and depart from the house of God, with a settled purpose and resolution, not to suffer their hearts to be mastered by the power of the ministry, or to change their old fashions, say the preacher what he will, but to live and end their days in their ordinary former courses of profaneness and good fellowship. They may read their doom and vengeance in Psa. l. 21, 22.

Cursed also is the condition of all you that are scoffers at godliness and good men. You have wearied yourselves so long in walking and standing in wicked ways, that you are not set down at rest in the chair of scorners. And, therefore, all those that stand on the Lord's side are commanded by Christ there to leave you in your condemned case, and to disquiet you no further. And what a horrible depth of spiritual misery is this ; that you run furiously towards the pit of hell, and must have nobody to stay you ; not a man to call and cry unto you, to tell you that the fiery lake is a little before you!

Though we have thus much light from the natural properties of dogs and swine, to descry and delineate those fellows to whom, by Christ's commandment, pearls and holy things, admonitions and reproofs, are not to be vouchsafed; yet christians are sore troubled many times how to behave themselves, when to speak, when to hold their peace, whom to repute dogs and swine, whom not; when upon some unavoidable necessity, or by the exigency of their calling, they are unwillingly and unawares plunged into the company of profane sinners, whose ordinary talk is the language of hell; oaths, scurrilous jests, jesting upon the holy conversation of the saints, slandering good men, disgracing the ways of sincerity, and such other base and mad discourse.

But I do not see how any constant rules or immutable direction can be given for christian carriage in this case; it is so variable, and clothed with such variety of circumstances and constancy of alterations. The advice which I would give in this point to the christian is this: when he is perplexed what to do in this regard amongst profane company, let him consult with these bosom counsellors, look unto his spiritual wisdom, to his heart, and to his conscience. These must be his guides and informers in these cases, and they are counsellors ever at hand; he carries them in his bosom.

His *spiritual wisdom* is to guide him in a right apprehension and discretion of circumstances, and to define the opportunity and seasonableness when he is to interpose, and in what manner to oppose against their furious and rotten speeches. It must tell him secretly, and suggest to him, when the cause of God, or the innocence of a good man, calls specially upon him for an apology, and at what time he hath a calling thereunto. It must inform him how he must reprove; whether directly and downright, or by intimation and indirectly; whether personally, or in the general; whether in a fair and milder manner, or with a more bold and resolute spirit; whether presently upon it, and in hot blood, as it were, or afterward to take occasion to censure the same sin, with aggravation of the odiousness and damnation of it; whether only by discountenance or discourse; by a silent disapprobation, which, I think, may be sufficient for some men, at some times, in some companies, or with solemn protestation, and a professed opposition and dislike.

Let him also look to his *heart;* that his reproof spring not from any imperious humour of censuring and meddling with his brethren; from a proud vein of contradicting and controlling others; out of a stoical sourness and commanding surliness; from any purpose to disgrace and grieve the party; from a formal affectation of pharisaical severity; from a secret ambitious desire of purchasing an opinion and reputation of forwardness, by being forward in finding faults, or from any other by-respect; but from a heart truly humbled with a sight and sense of its own infirmities, zealously thankful unto God for preserving him from the like outrage and excess in sin; graciously resolved into compassion and commiseration of the offender; lifted up in a secret supplication for the pardon of its own sin, success of the reproof, and salvation of the party all at once unto the throne of grace.

His *conscience* must guide and hold him in the right path and golden mean between two extremes, which ordinarily in these cases men are very apt to incur; I mean faint-hearted silence and furious zeal.

Men, many times, by reason of a sinful irresolution and unchristian cowardliness, would gladly make such offenders dogs and swine, that thereby they might challenge the privilege of exemption from the discharge of that christian duty of reproof. Though their ears be filled with the oaths and blasphemies of those that are about them, and grated upon with graceless railings against good men, and foul disgracements of the ways of God, yet they never open their mouth, as though there could be any nobler object, or exercise of their best eloquence and greatest courage, than the just defence of God's glory, and a christian's innocence. Oh, these are vile cowards in good causes, and a kind of traitors to the state of christianity! By such sinful silence they labour to purchase a name of no-meddlers in other men's matters, of merciful men to their brethren's infirmities, of plausible companions, of wiser and more moderate christians. But let them know that such no-meddling is a kind of soul-murdering; such mercifulness is cruelty; such plausibleness is perniciousness; such wisdom is not that of the serpent commended by Christ, but the wiliness of that great red dragon, suggested by hell.

Nay, some men are so strangely lewd and graceless, that they can hear, and digest with patience and silence, the oaths and rotten speeches of their servants, and, perhaps, their sons, without any contradiction or correction. In their own families, some perhaps swear, others talk filthily, some rail against the ministry, others jest upon the sincerity of the saints, &c., and yet the wicked master says never a word. But in this point my purpose is principally to counsel christians; I meddle not at this time with such synagogues of Satan, and dens of atheists.

Some others, it may be, but they are not near so many, may run into the other extreme, and out of a spiritual fool-hardiness, as it were, and furious zeal, with an imperious and unwarrantable boisterousness, fly in the face of some desperate swaggerer, with an undigested and unseasonable reproof; whereby they both incur the guilt of giving a holy thing unto a dog, and unnecessary danger from the graceless fury of the party. Or else, for want of spiritual wisdom, and a holy discretion of circumstances, they may tender an admonition to some such contemptuous swaggerer, who will pass over and put by the precious severity of the word of truth with a scurrilous jest, or, with a dull and scornful sottishness, trample under foot that sacred pearl.

Though it be no constant character of dogs and swine, yet commonly those desperate wretches, to whom by Christ's commandment we must give no holy things, are fellows of dogged, sour, and contracted countenances, especially towards true christians, and have a kind of desperate furiousness impressed upon their foreheads, which is then most visible when they are crossed in their villanies, and hear of any contradiction or condemnation of their graceless courses and contemptuous carriages. And these swinish Gadarenes, before whom we must not cast pearls, are fellows of a gibing and scornful carriage, especially towards good men and godly exercises; they are so drowned in sensuality, and glued to the earth, that they do not only despise, but also deride the precious things of heaven. As

I take it, sensuality and earthly-mindedness, mingled with a great deal of atheism, begetteth in men this sottish swinishness, and brutish contempt of the blessings of grace, and directions to everlasting bliss.

These premonitions and cautions premised and observed, every christian ought to address himself with resolution and conscience to discharge this christian duty of reproving, when a just occasion and a calling thereunto do require and exact it at his hands. For these reasons :—

1. In respect of the party offending.

(1.) A seasonable reproof, mingled and sanctified with the spirit of invocation and compassion, may, by the blessing of God, be an occasion of conversion to the offender. And let him know, that " he which converteth the sinner from the error of his way, shall save a soul from death, and shall hide a multitude of sins," Jam. v. 20. And it is the most glorious work in the world, and the noblest employment under the sun, to have a hand in the holy business of saving a soul. Let hope then of doing spiritual good to thy brother's soul be the special aim, and a principal motive of performing this duty. There is a law, Exod. xxiii. 4, 5, that if a man meet his enemy's ox or ass going astray, he must bring him back again; if he see his enemy's ass lying under his burden, he must help him up again. How much more dear and precious in our eyes should the immortal soul of our brother be than the ass of our enemy! If we must turn back the straying ox of our enemy, and lift up his ass when he is crushed under his burden, with what eagerness and zeal ought we to labour to stop the furious course of a reasonable creature towards the pit of hell; and to put our helping hand to raise up that silly soul, which, by reason of the heavy weight of its sin, is full sorely bruised and bleeding, ready even to breathe out its last, and sink into the misery of endless horror! Speak then boldly in the cause of God when thou hearest thy brother blaspheme his name, jest with his word, talk filthily, rail against holiness, slander good men, and plead for profane pastimes, for they are so many mortal stabs into his own poor soul, besides the natural infectiousness of rotten speeches, which may do much mischief to the by-standers. Though thy reproof prevail not at the present, yet thou knowest not what impression and working it may have afterward upon his hard heart, whereby, perhaps, he may happily think upon a new course, and of conversion to God, and so thou be a blessed instrument of saving a soul.

(2.) But if it have not so happy a success upon his soul, yet it may be thou mayest thereby tame and take down his insolence; so cut his pride by a seasonable contradiction, that he do not carry it away bravely; so cool and confound his swaggering humour, that he do not glory in his villany, that he do not pride himself in his blasphemies and bloody oaths, in his contempt of grace, and other outrageous carriages. "Answer a fool," saith Solomon, "according to his folly, lest he be wise in his own conceit," Prov. xvi. 5,—lest he be too proud. If a desperate and profane wretch will needs swear and swagger, and rail against the servants and services of God, yet let him know that all the while he fights against God, damns his own soul, and pleases none but devils, drunkards, and devilish men. If he will needs labour to be infamous by a furious opposition to the ministry and ways of God, let him know that his name shall rot after him, as vilely as his carcass in the grave, and himself burn in hell everlastingly, if he hold on in that humour without timely repentance and reformation.

(3.) At the least, thou shouldest thereby increase and aggravate his inexcusableness, and so glorify the tribunal of God's justice, when it shall there appear that, besides many other means afforded and offered unto him by God's mercies, thou also didst lend him thine hand to have pulled him out of the fire, and gavest him one call to have stayed him in the furious and wilful pursuit of his own damnation. But because he still hated to be reformed, because variety of means for his amendment made him more malicious and obstinate in his own ways, and that contradiction and counsel to the contrary inflamed and set on fire the lustful viciousness of his corrupt nature, to hunt more greedily after forbidden pleasures,—therefore, I say, he will be more and more fearfully ashamed and confounded at that great and awful day; and the more occasions he hath had of his conversion, the juster cause then will he see of his deserved confusion, and consequently more glory will accrue unto the glorious tribunal of God's justice.

2. In such cases, the christian must speak in respect of himself.

(1.) When the air is impoisoned with any infectious vapour, men fill their sense with some sweet perfume, that so they may guard against the noisomeness of the smell, and repel the contagious insinuation; so, when any profane wretch hath let fall any rotten speech, the christian, with a present counter-poison of a seasonable reproof, should stop his own apprehension, lest any baser infection insinuate, and strain the soul; and to preserve in heat and life a fresh and strong opposition of the heart and affections to all such lewdness and scurrility.

(2.) Silence at such a time will seem to betray either thy cowardliness in the cause of God, or hypocrisy in thy profession. For it will seem strange that thou, who makest a show of standing on the Lord's side, and professest thyself to be a party in the glorious communion of saints, shouldest hear the name of God profaned in a base and blasphemous manner, and sometimes the innocency of a good man carried in triumph by the slanderous tongues of sinners, and trampled upon, as it were, even unto dust, by the feet of pride and malice, and yet never open thy mouth. As thou, therefore, desirest to preserve the glory of thy christian reputation entire and shining, and hold it thy crown and honour to be a champion unto the mighty Lord of heaven, a proctor in his spiritual causes, and the protector of the good names of good men, be ever ready to open thy mouth when a just apology in any of these respects is needful and required at thy hands.

(3.) If thy conscience be enlightened, awake, tender, and rightly informed, it will smite and check thee after the omission of such a duty; when afterwards thou considerest with thyself, that by thy cowardly and unseasonable silence thy soul is entangled in the guiltiness, and hath incurred an accountableness for that sin. As thou then wouldest keep all in quiet at home in thine own bosom, and still possess the paradise of a peaceful heart, suffer not blasphemies, obscenities, railings, and other such ribaldry and rotten talk to pass uncensured and unsorrowed for. Nay, in so doing, besides the invaluable comfort of a peaceful conscience, thou shalt also purchase unto thine heart a sound testimony of that gracious tender-heartedness, which is wont to melt and resolve the hearts of God's children into compassion and commiseration in such cases; and which they used to express and exercise, even towards the lewdest sinners, and such as have no pity upon the spiritual miseries of their own poor and woful souls. See 1 Sam. xv. 35, and xvi. 1; Jer. ix. 1; Phil. iii. 18, 19; 2 Cor. xii. 21; Luke xix. 41, 42. It was the sullen and condemned voice of cruel and cursed Cain to say, " Am I my brother's keeper?" But every true and tender-hearted christian doth grieve to see so many of his brethren stick fast in the clutches of the roaring lion, and between the teeth of the red dragon, and therefore labours, by all means he can, to rescue them: to see so many about him run as fast and furious as they can to drown themselves in the pit of endless perdition; and, therefore, as occasion serves, calls and cries unto them to stay their course, before the gulf of confusion and horror hath shut her mouth upon them.

3. In respect of those who are present.

(1.) By thy speaking in such a case thou mayest lay, as it were, the spirit of profaneness for that time, so that it do not rage and overrule in the rest, as otherwise it would. For we may sometimes observe, that a seasonable reproof, passing from a man of understanding, with resolution and authority, upon a fellow that so behaves himself as though swearing were his profession, and traducing the saints his trade, doth so quell and confound the swaggering humour of the rest of the same crew in the company.

that they are quite put out of their humour, as they say; perhaps, hang down their heads all the while, and think, in their hearts, if once they get out, they will come no more amongst such precise fellows who cannot abide an oath, or where they cannot have their way, and put forth their profane villanies and cursed revelling.

(2.) Thou mayest hereby hold in the weak that they be not scandalized.

(3.) Thou mayest hold up the hearts of stronger christians, that they be not grieved and cast down with the domineering of profaneness, and out-swaggering rage of Satan's revellers.

4. In respect of God himself.

(1.) That though the days wherein we live be strangely profane, and desperately naught,—for this old age of the world is pestered with all the pollutions and abominations which the course and current of all former ages have conveyed and carried into it,—though iniquity mightily abound with much tyranny and triumph, and fearfully prevail in all places, yet, I say, that it may appear that God hath some to speak for him; that though Satan, more is the pity, hath innumerable swarms of knights of the post, as they say, that are ready at a beck to do him any desperate service, yet, notwithstanding, here and there God hath a champion, who dares, fearless of the face of man, with an undaunted and holy resolution, defend his ways, and stand on his side.

(2.) But, above all, let that strict charge from God's own mouth, "Thou shalt not hate thy brother in thy heart: thou shalt in any wise rebuke thy neighbour, and not suffer sin upon him," Lev. xix. 17, frighten and fire every one of us out of our sinful silence and cowardliness this way, and sharpen us with resolution and forwardness to a seasonable discharge of this holy duty.

Take notice of a three-fold duty, which lies upon every christian in his carriage towards men in their presence, and before their faces : 1. Christian admonition; 2. Christian reproof; 3. Christian silence, and forbearance in such cases. 1. If a brother be overtaken with a fault, or some less offence, we are to admonish him in the spirit of meekness, Gal. vi. 1. 2. If he offend more grievously, we are freely to reprove him, and not to suffer sin to rest upon him, Lev. xix. 17. 3. If he be a son of Belial, a scoffing Ishmael, a dog, or a swine, we are commanded by Christ to say nothing, Matt. vii. 6. Neither private admonition nor brotherly reproof is to be vouchsafed to desperate sinners or profane ruffians, who would entertain it with cruelty or scurrility.

II. Observe a sanctified silence.

1. From rash censuring, which is severely censured by Christ himself, and set as a visible brand upon the face of the hypocrite. Let it ever be only the peevish property of those who are themselves naught, and most obnoxious, of pharisees and false hearts, to be the greatest findfaults; uncharitably to entertain causeless disconceits, and to pass rash censures against those who are far better than themselves. Which they will ordinarily do, because,

They were never truly humbled with a sight and sense of their own sinful and accursed state. They never trembled, nor were thoroughly affrighted with the wrathful countenance of God, for their infinite pollutions and provocations of the eyes of his glory. Their consciences were never awakened out of their dead sensual sleep by the trumpet of the law, nor received any special and particular illumination from the sanctifying Spirit. In a word, they have no terror, no trouble, no work or business at home about their own sins, in their own consciences, and therefore they have leisure enough to look about them, and are full enough of sinful curiosity and unnecessary meddling to pry and inquire into other men's courses and carriages; of malice and spitefulness, to mistake and misinterpret; of pride and peremptoriness, to proclaim many times, with great noise and self-applause, their own idle, malignant forgeries and fancies, for faults of those who are much more righteous than they. When they look forward, or any ways about them, they are very sharp-sighted into the fashions and failings of others, most exact in observing their neighbours' ways; eagle-eyed, to pierce beyond the moon, to spy the least mote in the sun, I mean the smallest infirmity in the most glorious saint: nay, they are of such a refined and sublimated eyesight, that they can discern some errors and exorbitances, especially in professors of religion, which never had any existence. But when they should reflect upon themselves, and turn their eyes to contemplate and consider their own corruptions, there lies a great beam of hypocrisy between them and themselves; so that they cannot possibly see so much as those huge mountains of many crying sins, which full heavily press down their own souls towards hell,—those unnumbered swarms of beastly lusts which rage remorselessly within their own bosoms.

Again: it is a point of their hypocritical policy cunningly and confidently to impute those sins unto others which are grossly predominant in themselves; that thereby they might purchase an opinion of a supposed innocence and freedom from the like faults. For, when they cry out with great noise and clamour upon other men, they think they still the cry and stop the mouth of their own sins; and they labour to fasten a persuasion upon their own hearts, that, since they with such confidence and bold faces reprove and censure others, others will not, out of the congruity of a charitable ingenuousness, think them so shameless as to be justly liable to the same imputations, except some few wiser and more judicious christians, who are able by spiritual experience to discover the depths and mysteries of their hypocrisy; and for such they care not much, for, in point of reputation, they rely most upon the common sort and greater part.

Further: it is the natural humour of a hypocrite to be supercilious and censorious. Pride is no where more naturally bred, proudly seated, and highly enthroned, than in his heart. And, therefore, it is his common practice to hunt after estimation by disgracing and disabling others. Since he wants worth in himself, he labours to shine by darkening others,—misconceiving that every detraction from other men's reputation is an addition to his own.

Again: they hold it a point and proof of forwardness to be forward in finding faults. As though the flame of a holy zeal were enkindled in any man's heart only to give him light for the discovery of other men's sins, and not as a sacred fire to burn up the noisome lusts which boil in his own breast.

Thus, and upon such grounds as these, it is the hateful property of hypocrites and self-guilty ones, and a common mark of their cruel security, to wade deeply into the search and censure of other men's ways, and to gore into the consciences of others, whereas they never purged their own. But true zeal ever casts the first stone at a man's self, and plucks the beam out of his own eye, that he may better discern and draw the mote out of another's eye. I mean, a sincere heart is ever most censorious and severe against itself, most searching into and sensible of its own sins; prying with special curiosity and inquisitiveness into the endless maze of its own wicked windings and depths of guile. Though it heartily and unfeignedly detest all sin, in whomsoever it may be, yet its own iniquities and pollutions stick closest, and go nearest, and beget in it a more particular and extraordinary impression of remorse and loathing. The reason is, it hath truly tasted the terrors of a wounded conscience, been scorched with the secret sense of God's angry face, and formerly full sorely crushed under the most grievous burthen of innumerable sins. It knows right well, by woful experience, what bitterness of spirit and anguish of soul spring naturally from the retired survey of scandalous transgressions in cold blood. It feels from time to time deadness of heart, lessening of graces, loss of comfort, to ensue upon every gross relapse or willing fall. It finds too often, to its much grief, that if it foster and hide in itself any sensual corruption or secret lust, the Lord will not hear its prayers. It is full well acquainted with the invaluable preciousness of a peaceful conscience and God's favourable countenance, which it cannot possibly enjoy if it lie delightfully in any one sin against its knowledge. This being the experience, exercise, and constitution of an upright heart, it is the most angry and displeased with, most eagle-eyed and watchful over, most strict and severe against, its own sins. Which home employment happily hinders and moderates a man from too much meddling abroad. This world of work within about his own soul, in discovering, opposing, and mortifying his own unruly lusts and rebellions, ties his tongue from being so busy in censuring other men's faults. As, therefore, thou wouldest have a true testimony of taking thine own sins to heart, and of having been sincerely humbled under God's mighty hand thyself, keep a constant and narrow watch over thy tongue; be very sparing in speaking the evil which thou knowest by others; judge no man rashly, out of spleen, humour, passion, pride, prejudice, pharisaism, &c., or of his final state. For all sound converts and truly mortified men desire and labour to be very charitable, merciful, and seasonable in their censures. Consciousness of their own corruptions makes them compassionate towards others in this kind.

Object. Yea, but will some say, Howsoever you put it upon profane men and hypocrites, yet it is well known your professors are the only shrewd censurers, very quick and severe about other men's faults, and are still ready upon all occasion, by their peremptory judging, to send all others into hell, save themselves and those of their own sect, as they speak, (and so was the way to heaven styled many a year ago.)

Answer. This, I grant, is many times the profane man's censure of the true christian, and therein he discovers himself to be a true hypocrite; for with much bitterness and malice he censures sincere-hearted men to be censorious, when he himself is the only unconscionable critic and censurer. He reproves God's faithful ones for reproving, when he himself full often amongst his companions, out of a pang of imperious choler and implacable hatred to holiness, condemns for counterfeits, without all ground or truth, those whom the Lord himself justifies for true-hearted Nathanaels; and passes sentence of guiltiness and gross hypocrisy, after they be cast by a jury of tipplers, upon those whom the highest tribunal doth mercifully acquit.

To enlighten a little, and rectify thy judgment in this point of private judging, consider with me,

(1.) First, that all judging and censuring is not censurable and condemned, but that, when a man with an evil mind judgeth amiss and uncharitably of others for some evil end, we may judge the tree by its fruit. If we see a fellow constant and incorrigible in his lewd rebellious courses, evidently infamous for rotten fruits hanging out in the open sight of the sun, as drunkenness, swearing, usury, whoredom, persecuting the power of godliness, scoffing religion, or unrighteous dealing, we may, leaving his final doom to the Searcher of all hearts, judge and censure him for the present to be God's enemy, and in a most wretched estate. But, in such cases, besides just cause, be sure of a warrantable calling, conscionable end, and no beam in thine own eye. Matt. vii. 5.

(2.) Again: let us take notice of some differences between the true professor's and the profane man's censuring. It differs in respect

Of the object. The principal aim and object of carnal men's cruel disconceits and bitterest censures is the zealous professor. Dogged they are enough many times amongst themselves about worldly affairs, and maliciously tear one another like wild beasts; mutual brawlings about earthly things, wrongs, encroachments, underminings, cozenings, overreachings, and ambitious contentions, fill their hearts with much gall and greediness of revenge, their mouths with mutual barking at and biting one another. But to the people of God, in their mad fits, they are not only dogs, but even enraged devils, and swell with the very venom of hell, the overflowing thereof doth drown all private discords. Herod and Pilate behaved themselves before like two angry mastiffs one against another; but, when opportunity was offered, they pursued Christ with reconciled malice and united forces. Put up a hare before two greyhounds snarling about a bone, and they will both concur in the pursuit of that harmless beast. It is just so with graceless men against God's child; and ever the more forward he is in the narrow way, the more furiously is he persecuted by the spite of tongues. The most resolute for God's glory and in good causes are ordinarily most railed against and reviled. The foul spirit of good fellowship, as they call it, is still foaming out against God's chiefest favourites the foulest censures; that they are hypocrites, humourists, factionists, traitors, pestilent fellows, and all that naught is. David was so charged by Saul and his courtiers; Jeremiah by the profane nobles; the godly jews by Haman; nay, Christ himself by the scribes and pharisees; Paul by Tertullus; the primitive christians by the heathen; and all that will live godly in Christ Jesus must look for the same portion, the same persecution amongst the men of this world, even to be most vile and contemptible in their opinion and construction. There is no creature that ever God made, not Satan himself excepted, which is more maliciously set against and censured than good men. Neither should any have so bad a name as they, could the hellish mists of virulent tongues obscure and stain the glory of their reputation. If sentence should pass upon the godly at the last and great day, according to the verdict of those who are not friends or parties, we should certainly all be cast and condemned, not a man freed and acquitted. But, blessed be God, the Searcher of all hearts, the almighty Protector of all innocence, who to the shame and confusion of all spiteful opposites will witness for us at that highest tribunal, and then at the furthest before men and angels will bring forth our righteousness as the light, and our judgments as the noon-day. "Oh that one would hear me!" saith Job; "behold my desire is that the Almighty would answer me; and that mine adversary had written a book," xxxi. 35. And in this eager humour of miscensuring the servants of God, the wicked are so wilful and eager, that, rather than they will want matter, they will most basely and unworthily snatch it from the envenomed tongue of a talebearer, from the slanderous folly of some scurrilous jester, the frothy raving of a greasy drunken alehouse haunter; nay, rather than fail, forge it out of a suspicious self-guiltiness in their own profane fancies. But let them know that, when a son of Belial censures a sincere professor, it is as if the darkest nook in hell should find fault with the moon, that great light of heaven, for those little spots in her face, whereas, otherwise, she is fair and goodly: as if the most loathsome dunghill should challenge the fairest garden for unsavouriness, because there is here and there a weed amidst variety of other fragrant flowers: as if a worthless lump of dross should censure a golden coin for want of a grain or two in weight. For, in this case, he who as yet is nothing but an accursed lump of sin and lust, damnation and hell, loads with censorious lies that happy soul, which in the fountain of Christ's meritorious blood is made far whiter than the snow on Salmon, and fairer than the wool of the sheep coming up from washing, though some spots and stains of infirmities and frailties cleave unto it, while it yet dwells in a house of flesh and tabernacle of clay.

But now, on the other side, the ordinary object of the christian's censure is, according to Christ's rule, those trees which discover themselves to be stark naught by the rotten fruits which hang upon them in the sight of the sun; and yet that also must be seasoned with charity, discretion, seasonableness, freedom from spleen, humour, passion, personal hatred, insolence, or any other exorbitant distemper. Those professors prove too often either utterly unsound, or not so thoroughly humbled, who unmercifully insult either over the wretched state of those who are without, or uncharitably blaze abroad the infirmities and failings of the brethren which they ought to conceal, and, as the hand fasteneth a salve upon any sore part of the body, and then covers it, so to apply a plaster of a gentle and mild reproof that it may secretly heal, and the world be never the wiser. Ordinarily, so far as some men are fierce, boisterous, and master-like in searching out, censuring, and secret insulting over the falls, frailties, difference from them in some indifferent things in their fellow-christians, so much many times come they short in mortification, holy wisdom, humility, self-denial, faithfulness in their callings, &c., and that of those perhaps whom they so imperiously disable and undervalue. Commonly busy-bodies this way are either dangerously proud, or sinfully politic: proud, and therefore endeavour to raise their own upon the ruins of other christians' reputations, who are better than themselves: or politic, for, themselves being censurable for some grosser infirmities, or scandalous walking, they labour cunningly to find answerable errors in more noted professors, that they themselves may go more unnoted.

In respect of the order. The true christian ever casts the first stone at himself, and first the beam out of his own eye, Matt. vii. 5; that is, begins with himself, searcheth his own heart, rips up and ransacks his own conscience, censures his own ways, condemns and crucifies his own corruptions, and abandons all his known sins; and then he may with a more comfortable calling, with more sincerity and success, censure others. But hypocrites, and those who hate to be reformed, first begin with others, are most prying into other men's conduct, perusing other men's lives, thirstily hunting after, perhaps by the help of many dogged spies and fawning spaniels, the falls and faults, especially of professors, (for there is the kindly triumph,) ever tampering and meddling with their motes, but have never any leisure or pleasure to look into their own rotten hearts and rebellious courses. The reason of this difference may be this,—every godly man, together with the power of grace, puts on a holy bashfulness, an ingenuous modesty, that he would be foully ashamed, and could not with any face charge others with those crimes which he should allow in himself. But hypocrites wear masks, visors, and whorish foreheads; they will hardly blush or be ashamed at any sinful conduct, especially bringing in pleasure or profit, much less for seeming holy by their strictness and severity against other men's faults, though as full of lewdness and lust themselves as the skin will hold. How often may we hear imperious pharisees mangle and martyr a good man's good name for some lesser infirmity, who never learned to mourn for, or mortify any one of those many gross corruptions and secret villanies which reign in themselves!

In respect of the manner. Self-guilty pharisees are wont peremptorily to pass their rash censures upon the more righteous than themselves with much malice, pride, scornfulness, and profane insult; but the seasonable censures of truly humbled christians ought ever to be mingled with much mercifulness, commiseration, sensibleness of their own infirmities, and love.

In respect of evidence and truth. Profane men's censures of God's servants are many times not only groundless, causeless, and false, but also prodigiously absurd and utterly impossible, without any shadow or show at all of likelihood. The enemies to Christ's ministry confidently censured him of having a devil, John vii. 20; viii. 48—52; x. 20; in whom, notwithstanding, the fulness of the Godhead bodily dwelt, Col. ii. 9. Tertullus judged Paul to be a pestilent fellow, when he was the most precious man upon earth. Elijah was accounted a troubler of Israel, who was in truth the very chariots and horsemen of the same. The princes suggested to the king that Jeremiah was a traitor to the state, Jer. xxxviii. 4., from which he was so far, that he desired his head to be turned into waters, and his eyes into fountains of tears, that he might weep day and night for the desolations of it. Proportionable for monstrousness of falsehood are many and many censures passed upon professors at this day. Opposites to the power of godliness are so impudently perverse, that they commonly cut conditions unto others out of the cursed corruptions of their own rotten hearts.

But now, on the other side, God's people must be very careful and tender what opinions they entertain, and what censures they pass upon others. They are bound by the laws of Divine love to conceive and speak the best of every one, until his words, ordinary carriage, open profaneness, and fruits of the flesh, clearly convince the contrary; to construe and interpret all things in the better part, so far as they may with a good conscience, without prejudice to the truth, or impeachment of God's glory. They ought to be so far from greedy apprehension of imaginary matter, or violent wresting of men's words, actions, and behaviour to the worst sense, that if matters be but probable, poised with equal circumstances, and with even weight of reasons interpretable both ways, they are ever to suffer their opinions and censures to be carried the more charitable way. They ought to be so far from censuring others without ground, truth, and proof, (which is the ordinary practice of most men,) that they should never speak the ill they too certainly know by their brethren, but with fearfulness, as it were, and some kind of enforcement.

In respect of the end. The ends why pharisees and good fellows, as they call themselves, entertain many groundless disconceits, and thereupon exercise such censoriousness against holy men, are such as these:

(1.) To bind up their bleeding souls in the mean

time with a palliating cure, as they call it; to procure some temporary ease to their hearts against the checks and bitings of their guilty conciences. For when consideration in cold blood of their impenitent courses, and of their certain walking in the broad way, by reason of their own sensual liberty and much company, doth sting them with remorse, they have recourse to the ill opinions they have conceived of the best men, and thereupon think within themselves, and take occasion to say unto others, What need we take these things so much to heart, or trouble our thoughts with necessity of more strictness? Are not those who go for the godliest, and are accounted the prime professors, such and such men? Have not they also their infirmities and follies, though they gild them over with goodly shows, and pretence of zeal? Hereupon they somewhat assuage the secret slavish smart of their now-and-then wounded consciences, and walk more merrily towards their eternal perdition: for a settled disconceit of a christian, harboured and applauded, is a strong nail to fasten an unregenerate man to his own ways, and a mighty bar to keep him out of a gracious state. Sensualists are so strangely bewitched by Satan, that he first causeth them to forge in their own brains, or take up from a spiteful tongue, some lying tale of a good man, and then after makes it his means to keep them with security and contentment in the kingdom of darkness, and to stand in everlasting opposition to the ways of sincerity and salvation of their souls.

(2.) To make, by an affected liberty and severity in censuring others, the masks of their own hypocrisy less markable. For by their feigned triumphs and imperious insults in this kind, especially upon fresh news of some professor's scandalous fall, they would have the by-standers to conceive, that howsoever they be not so precise and forward, or make so great a show as others, yet they are fully as honest men as they, and may, perhaps, step into heaven before them.

(3.) To wreak their spite upon the children of light, who are ever eye-sores and heart-sores to all sorts of sinners. " He," meaning the righteous man, (saith the author of the book of Wisdom, though apocryphal, yet ancient,) " is grievous unto us, even to behold: for his life is not like other men's, his ways are of another fashion." And it angers them at the very heart-root to consider, that whereas they hope, and hold themselves sufficiently qualified for heaven, yet the righteous man's forwardness, zeal, and living after another fashion, if ingenuousness dispel the mist of prejudice, clearly demonstrates to their own consciences, and proclaims aloud to all spiritually understanding men, that in truth, and upon trial, they are in the state of wretchedness, and of the family of hell. Hereupon it is that they labour might and main, with many disgraceful censures, to dim the glory of his goodness; and, if it were possible, by publishing their own malicious surmises, other's slanderous tales, or spitefully aggravated frailties, to pull him back, at least in opinion of their favourites and dependants, to the same measure of infirmities and pitch of impiety with themselves.

But now the ends which humble christians propose unto themselves of just dislikes and seasonable censures of unsanctified men, are briefly such as these : 1. To preserve their thoughts innocent from accessariness to sin, by a secret invisible allowance of it in other men; and their tongues from cowardly silence, when they have a calling to disgrace it. 2. Lest a knave go for an honest man, and hypocrites deceive true-hearted Nathanaels. 3. Lest the power of christianity, wherein God's glory is highly interested, suffer and be undervalued. For instance, thou hearest sometimes a fellow notoriously branded with some infamous sin, yet so spoken of by some daubers with untempered mortar, or at least by ignorant worldlings, as though his present condition were tolerable towards God, and hopeful in respect of salvation, by reason of some other good parts, for which they praise him : in this case, if the understanding christian hold his peace, the by-standers may be so far scandalized and mistaken as to conceive and collect, that a man may lie in a sweet sin and yet live in God's favour; that the pleasures of the world and peace of conscience may consist together, which are as incompatible as heaven and hell. And why should not that silence be sinful, which suffers an open, known profane man to carry away the reputation of one in the right way, (if there be time and place for a seasonable, wise, and charitable contradiction,) as well as that which suffers one who is true of heart to be charged with hypocrisy?

2. Be silent from slandering, back-biting, false-accusing. Here I will say nothing of downright forging and fastening a false crime upon the innocent, which is the most pestilent and palpable, and other gross kinds of this very foul sin; for so it is indeed, howsoever to a carnal eye, looking upon it painted with the colours of commonness and self-love, through the false glass of these corrupt times, it appears not so ugly. The very casuists and school-men, none of the precisest divines I am sure, do

deservedly vilify it with a brand of heinousness, far above theft; as they may well, both for a greater breach of love, preciousness of object, unrecompensableness of loss, difficulty of restitution, concurrence of many sins, consequence of much ill, &c. I say, I will be here silent to the grosser sorts of slander, because of them God's children are for the most part more easily sensible, and ordinarily watchful; but let me a little advise and awake thee to further inspection of the present point, lest sometimes, even in telling the truth, thou be entangled in the briers of this base sin, and justly incur the fault of a false accuser, which thou mayest many ways. Detraction, to speak logically, doth not formally consist in the diminution of the truth, but in the blackening of a man's good name. 1. By discovering secret infirmities, which love, that covereth a multitude of sins, would have concealed. It is a base ambition, and most unworthy the noble magnanimity of a christian heart, to hunt after and purchase an opinion of precedence in graces and zeal by the disgrace of another; perhaps every way, save only in the censurer's own overweening conceit, better and more worthy than himself. When thou hearest a man worthily magnified for eminence of parts and spiritual worth, be it far from thee, or any that ever took sin truly to heart, to come in with a *but*, only because out of a pang, or rather predominancy of privy pride, thou wouldest gladly be noted for a nonsuch, and pass for the matchless professor. Let it ever be the property and vein of vain-glorious pharisees to raise their reputations, and sometimes themselves, but with execrable villany, upon the imaginary ruins of good men's innocencies; and to hold every insolent detraction from other men's sufficiencies an addition to their own. 2. By drawing out of other men's words, actions, and behaviours, upon the suspicious rack of a busy wit, aims, insinuations, and intentions, which the author never dreamed of; and by fathering upon them such enforced sinister senses, and wrested crooked constructions, which an ingenuous impartial expositor could never possibly extract. It is the easiest thing of a thousand for a malicious mind to soil the glory of the bravest and most beautiful actions with ill and wrong interpretations, and surmises of by-ends. For the pride of a man's own disdainful nature, and the devil himself, are ready to bring forth such monstrous conceptions. There is some truth in that hyperbolical speech of him who said, Let any man present me with the most excellent and blameless action, and I will oppose it with fifty vicious and bad intentions, all which shall carry a face of likelihood. Upon this very point, tribunals of justice, which hold more upon policy than piety, especially of private spleen, embitter their judiciary power against the party, too often strangely blind the common people's eyes, and do a great deal of wrong. A wicked wit and wide conscience, mounted on horseback amongst a number of princes, walking like servants upon the ground, (the epidemical disease of these worst and most ulcerous times,) upon this advantage many times work a world of revengeful villany. But, howsoever it be easy and too ordinary for black tongues to blast and stain, by wresting and wire-drawing the beauty of the best actions with malicious misconstructions, yet it is villanous and base. To let laws of divine love alone, even the light of reason led wise men to this resolution, as appears by their rules of law, That, in doubtful things, we must ever pitch upon the more favourable construction. We are to be so far from an eager hunting after a spiteful misinterpretation of men's speeches, and violent wresting of their actions and carriage to the worst sense, that if matters be but probable, poised with equal circumstances, and with even weight of reasons interpretable both ways, we are ever to suffer our opinions and censures to be carried the more charitable way. 3. By adding unto the truth, or detracting from it, or intermixing false adulterate glosses, or some impertinent parenthesis of a man's own. Christ's false accusers were deeply and damnably faulty this way. And in this kind many who are their crafts-masters, as they say, in malice, will first of all give good men in their absence their due and deserved commendations, with many magnificent and plausible speeches, but afterward, at the close, premising some formal counterfeit protestation and pharisaical preface, as, I am very sorry to hear it,—I would it were otherwise,—come in with a *but*, steeped in very gall and vinegar, which bites most bitterly, and cuts like the sharpest razor. As thus: a man of very good parts, great worth, extraordinary endowments,—but something proud. He is one that is very well reformed of late, of much knowledge, and grown marvellously forward in religion,—but a little covetous. And thus they speak, not out of any love unto the party, impartiality of censure, or that the imputation is true, but out of a cunning trick to bring their own credit to their own door, a perverse humour of measuring another by their own foot, an envious impatience of being surpassed in any sufficiencies, or, rather than all this, from a base, an irregular, and dunghill desire of having the best men, especially every forward professor, branded with one notorious *but* or another. For hypocrites and enemies to God's grace would rejoice to have the lives of all God's people stained with some gross sin. Rather than fail, they will fasten upon them many a lewd slander that way, hammered only upon the forge of falsehood, and by the efforts of malice in their own crafty pates; or broached upon an ale-bench, or snatched from the distempered tongue of some pedling tell-tale, whence they may supply themselves with imaginary matter both of insolency and triumph against forwardness and zeal, and also nourish a pharisaical persuasion that, howsoever there may be a profession, and shows to the contrary, yet others are as corrupt and censurable as themselves. 4. By relating all the truth, the whole truth, and nothing but the truth, but either with a malicious and spiteful heart towards the party, or in a contemptuous, scornful, and insulting manner, or to a lewd end, and upon purpose to bring into hatred and disestimation, or some way or other, without any warrantable and comfortable calling thereunto.

Here, therefore, it will be seasonable for help and direction against this more plausible, but also pestilent kind of slandering, to tell you, that telling the evil that is true of another, in his absence, doth brand you with the guilt and stain of backbiters, save in such cases as these:—

(1.) First, of profit and good to the party absent. For instance, thou informest thy friend of a third man, telling him that he begins to break out into bad courses, ill company, infamous haunts, and so proceedest to a more particular and punctual discovery of his wicked pranks and exorbitant carriage; but all this purposely for the benefit of the party. And, therefore, thou intreatest thy present friend that he would interpose, engage, and improve the utmost of that power and interest which he hath in his affections, dependence, or some nearer relation, for his reclaiming and amendment.

(2.) Of expediency for him that heareth, when he is any way in danger of injury or infection from the cunning or corruption of the party spoken of. For instance, thou discernest and observest some sly, smooth companion, under a cloak of profession, and formal colour of conformity to the best things, insinuate into liking and acceptation with thy unsuspecting christian friend, whereupon thou foreseest that if he go on without notice and discovery, and get once within him, a thousand to one at length he will either cunningly prey upon him or cursedly betray him. Now, in this case, thou mayest lawfully lay out such a counterfeit in his colours, and, for prevention of the mischief which might ensue upon such a dangerous insinuation, disclose unto thy friend his hollowness and halting, and that lewdness and knavery which he gilds over in the mean time with a veil of seeming and varnish of hypocrisy, but is wont, when once he hath attained his end, or acted his villany, to throw away his visor. For such fellows there are abroad in the world, who purposely mix and join themselves with God's children, hang upon and adhere unto true christians, as men from whom, by reason of the singleness of their hearts, and charitable unsuspiciousness, they may either directly or by accident suck out the greatest advantage.

(3.) Of necessity for him who speaketh. That he may be preserved from guiltiness and accessariness to the sin, which by silence and saying nothing he would incur and bring upon himself. For instance: there comes to thy notice some notorious villanies, which concealment and impunity would mightily animate and easily transport to further excess and outrage, but seasonable advertisement given to authority, as to a magistrate, minister, tutor, father, master, or governor of a family, might be a means to cut the knot and heart of such cursed fellowship, and stay the torrent of that scandalous insolency. In this case thou hast a calling to reveal, inform, and implore superior assistance for suppression of sin. And therefore those of the house of Chloe did well to certify Paul of the disorders and dissensions amongst the Corinthians, 1 Cor. i. 11; and Paul's sister's son, to acquaint the chief captain with that plot of desperate conspirators against Paul, Acts xxiii. 16. Otherwise both thou and they, by cowardly and cruel silence, in such cases, might, in some sort, justly incur the guilt and accountableness even for other men's sins so unhappily concealed.

(4.) When a seasonable, warrantable occasion is given thereby of performing some christian duty, as

[1.] Of instruction and forewarning to others, thus, or in the like manner:—Thou hast a friend, whom thou seest and fearest is entering a licentious course, which at length is like to breed his confusion, whereupon thou tellest him that such or such a man, just as he begins, from contempt of the word, profanation of the sabbath, disobedience to parents, fell fearfully into a desperate knot of lewd companions, then to ale-house haunting, afterwards to gaming, at last to the gallows; and therefore thou advisest him to take heed in time, to let such woful precedents of sin and shame stand still in his eye to stay him from breaking his neck at the bottom of the same stairs; for if he continue the reins but awhile longer upon the neck of his rebellious nature, and still hold on so desperately with such wild colts to the same excess of riot, he shall find no more power in himself to stay, until from the height of sin he falls into the bottom of hell, than a man having begun to run down the steepest hill can stop before he comes at the bottom. He that lays his foundation with fire-works, must look in the end to be blown up; he that premises profaneness and rebellion, shall be sure to conclude in cursedness and confusion.

[2.] Of praising God for the ruin and rooting out of some implacable impenitent persecutor, thus, or in the like manner:—A remarkable vengeance hath seized upon such a scornful sinner, who hath been a perpetual goad in the sides of the saints all his life long; upon which occasion thou discoverest unto thy friend many passages and plots of his cruelty and hate against the kingdom of Christ and his precious people, and that purposely to minister matter also unto others of more heartily magnifying the glories of God's justice, which at length hath happily struck down Antiochus with an incurable and invisible plague, eaten up Herod with vermin, made Pashur a terror to his friends, Zedekiah to run from chamber to chamber to hide himself. For you must know, that the hearts and tongues of all good men and friends to the gospel are wont to be filled with much glorious joy and heartiest songs of praise at the downfal of every cruel persecutor; when the revenging hand of God, not without special terror, hath tumbled from the top of malice and pride any antichristian and enraged enemy. So the Jews feasted after Haman was hanged. But in such cases look into thy heart, with extraordinary watchfulness and search, that he be an enemy indeed, I mean to christianity, that thou do it not out of spleen, humour, faction, personal enmity, for the destruction of the creature, or the like; but simply and sincerely out of zeal to the glory of God's justice, the prosperity of the gospel, and peace of the church. Otherwise, instead of a christian duty, it will prove to thee a cursed cruelty.

[3.] Of prayer. Thus, or in the like manner:— Thou art acquainted with the secret plots of some plausible tyrant against the people of God, whose words, perhaps, may be as soft as butter or oil, and outward deportment promise fair, but his thoughts and invisible intendments against the better side composed all of blood and bitterness, of gall and gunpowder; whereupon, as occasion is offered, thou unmaskest his malice among thy christian friends, to the end that they may communicate and contribute their prayers for the confusion and infatuation of all his devilish depths and devices of hell. Tears, patience, and prayers were ever the defensive weapons of God's people. Let powder plots, Parisian massacres, invincible armadas, slaughtering of kings, and such like horrible and hellish combustions, brand with an everlasting stain of cruelty and blood the popish religion and persecutors of heavenly truth; but let the sons of the gospel be ever content to confront and beat back the implacable rage of all God's enemies and haters of sincerity and grace only with the cutting edge and sharpened point of fervent prayer; which weapon they may discharge three ways; 1. Immediately against all desperate enemies to God, his church, and gospel, without intimation, so much as by thought, of any particular persons. So David, "Let them all be confounded and turned back that hate Zion," Psalm cxxix. 5; Deborah, "So let all thine enemies perish, O Lord; but let them that love him be as the sun when he goeth forth in his might," Judges v. 31. 2. Conditionally, when they perceive some insulting Shebna and insolent Haman to persist and hold on in persecuting the saints and opposing the power of godliness, they may entreat the Lord, if they belong unto him, to humble them in their places, and give them repentance; but, if he purpose to give them over finally to a reprobate mind, and to the impetuous rage of their own cruel dispositions, to cut them off and utterly confound them, that they be no longer a burden to the church, and a vexation to his people. 3. Abstractively, against their extreme oppressions and malicious plots, without any relation at all to their persons. So David, "O Lord, I pray thee, turn the counsel of Ahithophel into foolishness," 2 Sam. xv. 31.

Or thus: Thou observest some one to have continued long a worthy and noted professor, but now, unhappily, begins to fall off from his former forwardness, to grow slack and negligent in family duties, cold and cowardly in good causes, heartless and hanging down the head in godly company; to disregard and underprize the powerful means; to entertain but ordinary affections, if not some kind of strangeness, towards other professors, especially of greater eminence and acceptation for their grace; to suffer immoderate employment and entanglement in the world to waste his heavenly-mindedness; so that, in all likelihood, God will shortly give him over unto some scandalous fall, as a punishment for his backsliding: whereupon thou discoverest unto thy christian friends his declining state, only that they may join with thee in prayer, that the Lord would be pleased to stay him in time, and re-establish him in his first love, lest, by his further falling, the credit of the gospel also receive a bruise and blemish, profession be ill spoken of, and the enemies of sincerity blaspheme.

[4.] Of vindicating the power and truth of religion from the mistakes of ignorants and underprizers. Thus, or in the like manner:—Thou art in company, where thou hearest a mere moral man, or a formal professor at the best, whom the church never discovered or acknowledged to be any of hers; and thyself canst aver, out of thy certain particular knowledge, that he never set himself to seek God with any conscience or constancy, but is utterly unacquainted with the mystery of godliness, family exercises, sanctification of the sabbath, contributions to the saints, exercises of mortification, self-denial: I say, thou hearest such a man commended for his religion, forwardness, and the fear of God; which commendation, if he carry away without contradiction, the rest of the company may be very ready to apprehend such a precedent, and resolve not to pass his pitch of profession, as unaccompanied with such pain and preciseness, and yet approved by wise and understanding men as hopeful and comfortable. Now, in this case, it may concern thee, but with as much wisdom, discretion, and charity as thou canst possibly command, to disrobe such a fellow of his undeserved attributions, and the reputation of that holiness which he never had, lest both the by-standers be hardened to come short of heaven, and the power of christianity be disparaged by an ignorant and hurtful under-valuation.

3. Be silent from all unsavoury communication, as lying, swearing, profane, foolish, filthy jesting, jesting out of Scripture, mocking and making God's people as music at feasts, merry meetings, and cursed conventicles of good-fellowship, and such other rotten, ribald, and mad talk; which, because they are the known and proper language of the sons of Belial, the dung, froth, and vile evaporations of drunken wits, christians, whom alone I labour to direct in this point, are not in such danger of, and therefore I have nothing to do with them at this time.

III. Pray for and practise a holy and discreet dexterity to divert and draw from profane and wicked, or too much worldly and ordinary talk, to more savoury conference and heavenly discourse. Methinks it is a great pity that professors should ever meet without some talk of their meeting in heaven, or of the blessed means and ways that lead thereunto, before they part. Yet many times (such a deadness and damp of zeal and heavenly-mindedness haunts even the holiest hearts in these unhappy days of security and form) worldly matters, talk of others, or some more remarkable accidents and affairs abroad, speculative curiosities, some ceremonial unseasonable controversies, or other such like impertinences in one kind or other, take up and engross, even from God's children, too much of many golden seasons which might preciously serve, by their mutual diving with more christian edifying discourse into the great mystery of godliness and walks of christianity, to nourish and increase amongst them much spiritual warmth, comfort, and resolution against all ungodly oppositions, and to build up one another in their most holy faith, acquaintance with temptations, experimental knowledge, and more comfortable walking with God, To confront this common mischief and mar conference at christian meetings, come unto them prepared, as I advised before, pages 95—97. But if the company be contrary-minded and uninured to the language of Canaan, exercise and interpose all thy wit, courage, authority, and eloquence to draw them from the dunghill of rotten talk; and by a wise diversion, and modestly overruling transition, carry the current of their present discourse all thou canst towards some heavenly good and spiritual end. 1. To which end observe and apprehend all opportunities and occurrences which may minister matter of digression into divine talk, and acquaint thyself with the art of abstracting sacred instructions from the book of the creatures and businesses in hand. It was the practice of our blessed Saviour: upon mention of bread, he pressed upon his disciples a dissuasion from the leaven of the pharisees, Matt. xvi.; when he observed a number of people to throng about him for more miraculous bread, he digressed into a most heavenly discourse of the food of life, John iv. Upon occasion of drink being denied him by the Samaritan woman, he, forgetting his weariness, hunger, and thirst, laboured to allure her to the well-head of everlasting happiness, John iv. 2. Have ever in readiness some common heads of more stirring and quickening motives to mind heavenly things; as the cursed condition of our natural state, the incomparable sweetness of christian ways, the vanity and vexations of all earthly things, the uncertainty and miseries of this short life, the everlastingness of our second state in another world, the sudden executions of God's fierce wrath upon some notorious ones even in this life, especially those which are freshest in memory and recently done, the terrors of death, the dreadfulness of that last and great day drawing on apace, the horrors of a damned soul, &c.; mention of these things many times will strike full cold to the heart of the most swaggering and sensual Belshazzar, the most raging and roaring companions, and drive the most confident and domineering worldling into dejection. Talk, then, of these terrible things may, by God's blessing, prepare and soften sometimes the hardest hearts for some thoughts of remorse and more heavenly impressions.

3. But, above all, get into thine own heart a habit of heavenly-mindedness by much exercise, intercourse, and acquaintance with God, in pouring out of thy soul ever and anon before him, in renewing and recovering thy peace and comfortable access unto him upon every fall and check of conscience, in often contemplation and foretaste of the inexplicable sweetness, glory, and eternity of those mansions above; in diving into the secrets of his kingdom by the help of humbleness and godly fear; upon the most sweet and soul-fattening days of humiliation, mortifying visitations of troubled and afflicted consciences, and often conference with humblest and best experienced christians; by private employment of thy soul in solemn reflections upon itself, fruitfully recounting with what variety of trains it was long detained in the state of darkness; with what delays and tergiversations, lets and assaults, it met in its way to light; what bitterness and terrors it

passed through in its new birth; the temptations incident to its infancy in grace, progress and growth in several graces, and the whole body of christianity; relapses, desertions, their discoveries, recoveries, with all the means and circumstances; in a word, by a punctual observing how God deals with it every day. Be, I say, thus blessedly busied at home in thine own heart, and thou shalt find thyself much more pregnant and plentiful in holy talk when thou comest abroad. We are most apt and readiest to pour out ourselves in public, according to our private provisions, and the most predominant discourses and contemplations of the mind. The conferences of free and unreserved spirits are ordinarily nothing else but the clothing of their ordinary mental conceptions and heart-secrets with familiar forms of speech. Men, for the most part, speak most and most willingly of those things they mind most. I advise thus, in this point, that thou mayest be habituated and encouraged with resolution and delight in the art and exercise of putting forward good talk. Otherwise, thou shalt never be able to hold out with constancy and courage, to cross many times the general mirth of the company, to put worldly-wise men out of their element of all earthly talk, and to draw them to heavenly things.

VIII. ON MANAGING CONSCIENTIOUSLY EVERY ACTION OF OUR LIVES.

Survey thoroughly beforehand with the glorious lamp of the word of life and truth; watch over narrowly with the enlightened eye of a tender conscience, and ever punctually manage, and conduct with the particular light of spiritual prudence, every action thou undertakest, or that shall at any time pass through thy hand, of what kind soever it be, whether natural, recreative, civil, of mercy, or religion.

To which particulars, before I descend, let me commend unto thee and premise this principle concerning actions in general.

Every truly commendable and comfortable action consists of an absolute integrity of all concurrents and requisites. Or thus: that which is good and lawful must be entire; I mean it in that sense, as our divines speak of sanctification, which if saving, say they, must be perfect and entire, though not in respect of degrees, yet in respect of parts. Every part and power of body and soul must have its part of sanctification, though no part its full perfection and all degrees, before the dissolution of our earthly tabernacles. Proportionably in the present point, though some mixture of infirmities and imperfections will cleave unto the face of the fairest action, (an absolute and unstained purity is incompatible with this unglorified state of mortality,) yet notwithstanding, every several ingredient must be attended and tempered with its own particular goodness and honesty, and seasonable conformity to the whole; or else the whole action, howsoever right in other respects, is utterly robbed and disrobed of all true splendour, acceptation, and grace. A little leaven sours the whole lump: one noxious herb brings death into the pot: the goodliest deed or duty is quite perverted and impoisoned by the enormity of any one particular requisite. We say truly in the schools, "The conclusion ever follows the worst part." In like manner in morality, the iniquity, defect, and exorbitancy of any one ingredient, denominates the whole action naught.

In every one of thine actions and undertakings, look ever, if thou look for comfort, that every concurrent be justifiable, that every ingredient be gracious, and approved of God. For instance:—

It must be good in its own nature, and warrantable out of the word; by which all things must be sanctified unto thee, 1 Tim. iv. 5; as a good servant will venture upon nothing but what he knows will please his master. Otherwise, let the person be ever so pleasing unto God, his intention ever so good, his heart ever so zealous, the means, circumstances, and end ever so excellent, yet all is naught. Worshipping Christ in a crucifix is naught in its own nature, abominable, idolatrous, condemned in God's law, Exod. xx. 4, &c. And therefore, be it done with ever so great devotion and good meaning, with ever so much popish daubing or goodly pretence whatsoever, it is still cursed and damnable.

The object whereabout the action is exercised must be qualified according to the rules of religion. Almsdeeds and gifts of charity are sweet and acceptable sacrifices unto God. But, amongst other cautions and considerations to season them, the parties that are to be made partakers thereof are to be singled out with all godly discretion. 1. The true wants of a religious professor should, in the first place, be the principal and most moving object, to draw bounty from a truly charitable heart: according to that, "As we have therefore opportunity, let us do good unto all men, especially unto them who are of the household of faith," Gal. vi. 10. 2. In the next place, the lame, the blind, the sick, the aged, the trembling hand, or any whom God hath made poor. 3. Any whosoever, in a case of true necessity and extremity, whatsoever the party hath been before; for there, not the man as it were, but the common state of humanity, is relieved. But now, if, for such a purpose, thou makest choice of a sturdy beggar, idle rogue, canting companion, (the shame and plague of this noble kingdom,) thou dost not only deprive thyself of the comfort and honour of a truly charitable deed, but thereby incurrest a great deal of guilt, by encouraging and nourishing idleness, filching, many strange unknown villanies, nay, even an execrable irreligious paganism in such lewd, lazy drones, unprofitable burdens of the earth, and intolerable caterpillars of the commonwealth. "For such," saith a worthy divine, "as turn begging into an art and occupation, they are, by order, to be compelled to work for their maintenance, which is the best and greatest alms."

The object of thy special, intimate, and dearest love must be the christian, even the poorest professor of religion, not the complete carnalist, or most magnificent worldling.

Thou must also look unto the matter, else all may be marred. For instance: the matter of thy bounty and beneficence must be thine own goods, got lawfully, not formerly hoarded by usury and wrong; otherwise it will but prove, in respect of Divine allowance, but an abominable sacrifice; for many times "that which is highly esteemed among men is abomination in the sight of God," Luke xvi. 15.

The person must be pleasing, the actor acceptable unto God; otherwise his best and most bountiful deeds are at the best but beautiful abominations: services most sacred in their own nature, as prayer, hearing the word, and receiving the sacrament, are, from him, and the altar of his unsanctified heart, but as the offering of swine's blood. If thou be not justified by faith, and accepted through Christ, all thy actions, natural, moral, recreative, religious, whatsoever is within thee or without thee, the use of the creatures, all thy courses, ways, and passages, are turned into sins and pollutions unto thee, enlarge and aggravate thy woe and damnation: even " the sacrifice" and whole " way of the wicked is an abomination to the Lord," Prov. xv. 8, 9. The pharisee (Luke xviii.) was not the least the better for all his prayers and fastings; nay, by accident more accursed; I mean in respect of any gracious entertainment with God, who was not pleased with him.

The heart must be sincere, else even the noblest duties of religion are nothing. Judas gave his name to Christ, preached, and wrought miracles, and yet all the while was a desperate hypocrite, a very incarnate devil; because his heart was rotten, drenched in the gall of bitterness, and snared in the bond of iniquity. The Israelites' humiliation, seeking God, returning and inquiring early after him, bespeaking him with all terms of dearness and dependance, " our Rock, our high God, our Redeemer," was all but temporary and unsound, because their hearts were not upright. " When he slew them, then they sought him: and they returned and inquired early after God. And they remembered that God was their Rock, and the high God their Redeemer. Nevertheless they did flatter him with their mouth, and they lied unto him with their tongues. For their heart was not right with him," Psa. lxxviii. 34—37.

The means must be good. Otherwise, be the end ever so excellent, let there be ever so exact and absolute concurrence of all other causes, yet the glory and comfort of the action is quite darkened, and desperately impoisoned to the man that willingly, and against the cry of an enlightened conscience, employs and puts his hand to any wicked means for the achievement. Suppose that by a lie thou couldest save a man's life, his soul, the souls of all the men upon earth; nay, win thereby unto God as much glory as accrues unto him by all his creatures; yet, for all this, on thy part all were naught. For it is a sacred principle, sealed by truth itself, We must not do evil that good may come, Rom. iii. 8.

The circumstances must be seasonable. For instance, personal and private prayer is a right precious sacrifice and service; but let it be seasonable for the circumstance of place, or else it may lose its sweet-smelling savour with God, and be tainted with pharisaism. The closet, or some retired place, is fit for this exercise, which the more secret, the more sincere; not the synagogues and corners of the streets, which were the pharisees' vain-glorious places for prayer, who sought more for praise of men than pleasing of God. Meditation upon divine mysteries and quickening spiritual points is an excellent and acceptable exercise, so it keeps its own turn, and be confined to a fit time; but, in the heat of the preacher's pouring out his soul for us in prayer at the throne of grace, it is sinful, because unseasonable. Calling to mind seriously some special passages formerly heard or read, to press them with more life and power upon the conscience, is a right, needful, and religious duty; but so to do at a sermon, in singing a psalm or when we ought to bend all the powers of our souls, and best attention to the present, is but one of Satan's tricks, in the glory of an angel, to make us guilty of the contempt, and rob us of the comfort of the ordinance in hand.

The end also must be answerable in goodness; and, by its excellency and attractiveness, inspire amiableness and allurement into all the means leading thereunto, though they should be in their own nature painful and unpleasing. In all thy enterprises and undertakings thou must principally have in thine eye that universal aim of all our actions, God's glory, 1 Cor. x. 31; otherwise, let the whole affair be carried ever so fairly in the eyes of men, be clothed with ever so goodly a show and glorious outside; yet, in respect of acceptation with God, or true comfort to the party, it is no better than the cutting off a dog's neck. Jehu did right noble and worthy service, by his resolute rooting out, and courageous cutting off, that wicked and idolatrous house of Ahab: and acceptable to God was that great sacrifice of Baal's priests; he marched furiously in this holy business, and was very zealous to execute God's charge in that regard exactly. And yet for all this, all these outward, glorious, visible conformities to God's commandment were to him but as the killing of a man; because his eye was not upon the right end—God's glory. He principally aimed at the secure settling of the crown upon his own head, by an utter extinguishment of the king's family. Had his aim been right, his heart had been as well set against the golden calves in Dan and Bethel, as his hand and sword against the idolatrous house of Baal; but it was not so, 2 Kings x. 29. Now I come to some particulars.

On Recreations.

First, concerning recreations; which, howsoever they ought to be very moderate and sparing, (and in that respect methinks I should rather spare my labour, and not spend many words,) yet, because they are not only insatiably pursued and plunged into by men of this world, but also too much looked after and indulged in, even by some who look towards religion, I shall be somewhat the longer; and advise that they be not,

1. Costly. To curb and confine thine affections to a seasonable and sanctified moderation herein, consider, 1. How the backs and bowels of many poor members of Jesus Christ and distressed saints call, nay, cry even with tears of blood, for relief and compassion from thine abundant and overflowing abilities. 2. That thou must be called upon, and accountable with severity and exactness, at the last and dreadful tribunal for every farthing; how thou didst get it, and with what warrant thou didst keep it, upon what thou didst spend it. 3. The judgment of Austin, that great and renowned father of the church, who, as divines report, would have all things gotten by play taken from the winner, and never restored to the loser, but given to the poor; that both the winner might want what so greedily he gaped for, and the loser not recover what so foolishly he parted with. 4. The resolution of a grave and profound divine of these latter times: " But some say," saith he, " they can take no pleasure in play, except they play for money. But we are to know of them how they would have the money bestowed. Perhaps they will say, upon a common feast. And why not rather upon the poor? But I

say, It is much better, and more safe, that no money be laid to the stake; for, although it may be that thou art not touched with greediness of winning, yet he with whom thou playest may be tainted that way.

2. Cruel. Bathe not thy recreations in blood; refresh not thy tired mind with spectacles of cruelty. Consider the rule which divines give about recreations, that we must not make God's judgments and punishments of sin, either upon man or beast, the matter and object of them. Now, the best divines hold, that enmity amongst themselves was a fruit of our rebellion against God, and more general judgment inflicted upon the creature after the fall. Which misery, coming upon them by our means, should rather break our hearts and make them bleed, than minister matter of glorying in our shame, and vexing those very vexations which our impiety hath put upon them. Alas, sinful man, what a heart hast thou, that canst take delight in the cruel tormenting of a dumb creature! Is it not too much for thee to behold with dry eyes that fearful brand which only thy sin hath impressed upon it; but thou must barbarously, also, press its oppressions, and make thyself merry with the bleeding miseries of that poor harmless thing, which, in its kind, is much more, and far better, serviceable to the Creator than thyself?

3. Engrossers of time. Thousands there are who plunge themselves over head and ears in courses of pleasure, which they call recreations, wherein they very unworthily and wofully waste the fat and marrow, as it were, of dear and precious time, the flower of their age, the strength of their bodies; melt the vigour of their spirits into effeminateness, sensuality, and lust; drown the fair and goodly

hopes of their education, the honour of their families, the expectation of the country, the improvement of their parts, in froth and folly; as though they were placed upon earth, as leviathan in the sea, only to take their sport and pastime therein. Lovers they are of pleasures, mirth-mongers, men of this world, sworn vassals to carnal looseness and riotous excess. They have their fool's paradise here, and therefore, in the equity of a just and holy proportion, must, with the rich man, look for their payment and torment hereafter. But God's children must make conscience of meddling at any time with recreations, without true cause and a just calling thereunto, and hold them of the same account and consequence with sleep and other temperate refreshings, which serve only to quicken the mind, revive the body, enlarge the breath, that we may return with more lightsomeness and alacrity to our work and callings. The season, then, of comfortable recourse unto these repairs and restoratives is, when we have truly wearied our bodies with some honest employment, or tired our minds in worthy and noble exercises, or both. And as we must not press upon them at our pleasure and prevent true need, out of an hankering humour after sportful vanities, old haunts, good-fellow meetings, conformity to the times, or some such sensual and inordinate attraction; so in the entertainment of them we must receive them as men do honey, with the tip of the finger, not with a full hand. By no means ought we to engage, and, as it were, to ingulf our affections into their excesses and immoderation; not suffer them so to insinuate as to steal away our hearts into a pleasing, insensible thraldom, so creating necessities of recreations; which is an extreme misery and intolerable slavery; which, notwithstanding many truly unworthy and unnoble gallants miserably languish and come to nothing, prove only unprofitable burdens of the earth, and, instead of a blessing, the very bane of the country that bred them.

Let such considerations as the following serve as so many curbs to restrain us from an unseasonable intrusion upon them, and so many keen spurs to post us out of them before we be limed and entangled by them.

(1.) Time is short: our life is but a span long, a bubble, a thought, a smoke, a shadow, a dream, the very dream of a shadow, or if you can name anything more fading and frail; and yet upon this moment depends eternity. As we behave ourselves here upon earth, either in conformity to the ways of God, walking with him, in self-denial, or in fashionableness to the world, in serving the times and our own turns, so shall we fare everlastingly in another life, and either become most glorious and happy creatures, crowned with an exquisite confluence and quintessence, as it were, of sweetest, unmixed, eternal pleasures,—a very shadow whereof, not the largest natural hearts of deepest understanding men, from the creation to the last day, were they all united into one exactest height and excellency of conceit, could possibly comprehend; nay, in this one circumstance, at the least, the saints shall surpass even angelical felicity; they shall behold, with incredible joy, their own nature, in that respect, honoured and advanced above the brightest cherub, shining for ever with infinite beauty and glorified splendour, in the sacred Person of the Son of God,—or else fall irrecoverably into the mouth of inexplicable and remediless horror, and so become the forlorn and woful objects upon which shall be exercised and executed the unquenchable wrath of God and fiercest torments in hell, with extremity and everlastingness; nay, and in this point more unhappy than the very devils: for, since their apostacy, there were no means nor possibility vouchsafed unto them of recovery and return to those everlasting mansions of glory; but the sons and daughters of Adam, since their fall, have had the very Son of God himself, with the dear and invaluable cry of his own heart's blood, to mediate unto, and solicit the Father of all compassions and mercy, for restitution into favour and plantation into the angels' room. And, therefore, as this thought, Oh what unhappy and accursed creatures were we, who, being crowned with the matchless transcendency of all felicities and glory, would not hold our station, and have shined still! I say, as this thought will endlessly haunt the damned angels with inconceivable biting and anguish, so, not only a corresponding self-fretting torture from this conceit, Alas, that we kept not paradise! will rend and tear the woful hearts of the wicked in hell, but also a further sting of that never-dying worm, not incident to the apostate angels, will extremely enrage them with restless gnawings of conscience and gnashing of teeth; when, out of the horror of their hideous woful yellings, they shall cry out against themselves, What wretches! what beasts! what maddened devils were we! who, when the glorious blood of Christ Jesus was so mercifully tendered unto us in the ministry of the word all our life long, we turned our backs against such blessed and bleeding embracements, and cruelly destroyed our own poor souls by impenitent continuance in sin; so losing, for a few bitter-sweet pleasures in this vale of tears for an inch of time, fulness of joy at God's right hand through all eternity.

(2.) Time is precious. If all this great massive body of the whole earth whereupon we tread were turned into a lump of gold, it were not able to purchase one minute of time. And were there no other circumstance to set an impression of high valuation upon it, yet this very one doth much ennoble it, that all those fair and shining bodies above our heads, and principally the prince of all the lights of heaven, that glorious and mighty giant, the prime and crown of all corporeal creatures, do tire and waste, as it were, their celestial vigours with the incredible swiftness of endless revolutions, to beget and give us time; I say us, who for the sin of every moment in it deserve eternity of punishment. But, that our hearts may be more sensibly wrought upon, and more effectually affected with the dearness and preciousness of it, let us suppose that the Lord, by divine and extraordinary dispensation, should give leave to a damned soul to come into this life again, and would vouchsafe him but one hour of a new trial, as it were, and a second time of gracious visitation; oh how highly would he prize, how eagerly would he apprehend, with what infinite watchfulness, endeavour, and diligence, would he improve that little short golden season! And, if therein he might have but the happiness to hear a sermon, oh with what affectionate inflamed attention would he listen unto the word of life! How would his heart break and bleed within him, and fall asunder in his breast like drops of water, to hear God's just wrath and holy indignation thundered out and threatened against sin! With what insatiable grasping and dear embracement would he labour to lay hold upon Christ Jesus and his gracious promises! In a word, he would think that, in demonstration of thankfulness for God's favour, might he be so happy as to have it, the spending of every moment of all that great body of time which lies between the creation and the world's end, if he might live so long, in as holy, pure, strict, precise, heavenly manner, as ever did the most mortified martyr upon earth, were far too little. Shall we, then, triflingly pass and play away the time that is so precious? And, in my supposition, the damned soul should be sure of an hour; but none of us can possibly purchase security for only one moment after I have spoken this word.

The time present is our only time; we have no more power and command over the time to come than over the time past. Even the next minute thou mayest be cut off by the stroke of death from all further time of repentance, acceptation, and grace for ever. Nay, yet further, were it possible that any uncomfortable passion were incident to a glorified saint in heaven, he would be sorry, and transported with extreme anger and indignation against himself, that he was not a more greedy engrosser, as it were, and improver of time, for doing excellently upon earth; and that every hour after his conversion was not crowned with some rarer and more remarkable exploit; with some more special and noble service for the glorifying of that most bountiful and ever-blessed God, who hath now honoured him with such unspeakable glory, and crown of joys, so infinitely transcendent to the utmost expectation of the most enlarged heart. Howsoever, therefore, men of this world, for the most part, except they be continually exercised in variety of pleasing employments, and still entertained with fresh successions of new pleasures, are sore troubled with time, and tediously perplexed how to pass it; which is the reason that they devise so many pastimes, with much solicitous and sensual forecast plot and project to themselves aforehand many and many a merry meeting, idle visitations, feastings, mutual entertainments of mere compliment and vanity, and jovial revellings, as they call them; that they chain together, as it were, by the art of epicurism and with links of liberty, continued occasions of company-keeping and good-fellow meetings, from the one end of the week to the other. (For solitariness and self-conversing is a very torturing rack, and the tide-time of melancholy, to the waking consciences of graceless and guilty men.) Though, I say, this be the custom and carriage of Satan's revellers, yet all christians ought to have time in dear and high esteem; in every moment whereof, should they lay down ten thousand lives for His sake that pardons their sins, and also do Him all the glorious service of both the militant and triumphant saints, it were infinitely too little for his love. Wherefore no marvel, though well-advised and watchful, they feel themselves rather pinched with want than pressed with plenty of her golden offers and opportunities to do good, and are ever addressed to entertain and welcome every hour with special attendance, as a gracious indulgence of God's patient love and long-suffering, and suffering them to do him yet more honour, (for which cause alone they long to live,) before they go down into the pit, and be seen no more. And they should be so far from being afraid of solitariness, as to hold their time alone the only time for sweetest contemplations, heavenly commerce, nearer conversing and communion with God.

(3.) We that are earthly angels by the nobleness of creation, though by voluntary degeneration incarnate devils, were put into and planted within the compass and comforts of this great and curious frame around us, the goodly workmanship of God's own almighty hand, wherein we have the sun to serve us; and we of this kingdom, by matchless and incomparable favour, the heavenly and healing beams of the Sun of righteousness to shine upon us through his glorious gospel,—I say, we were placed in this world, not to serve our own turns, to please our own hearts, to follow our own ways, to eat, drink, and sleep; to temporize, revel, or root in the earth; to play the epicure, libertine, or Machiavelian; to climb into high rooms by all means, lawful and unlawful; by bribery, simony, flattery, base insinuations, following the times, or some fouler means, and thereto domineer and tyrannize; in a word, to serve the devil for a few and evil days, to die, and so to be damned. No, no; a nobler task and more excellent end is appointed and apportioned for the prince and principal of all earthly creatures. Our being upon earth this little inch of time is for business of another nature, and for a far more important affair, and of dearest consequence; even with humbleness and truth to know and obey our God, to serve our brethren in love, and to save our own poor souls in the day of Christ. This is that one necessary thing, in respect of which all other things, though otherwise honest and excellent, are but respectively necessary, and so far as they further and are warrantably and comfortably subordinate and contributary to this end: nay, to this the exquisite quintessence and concurrence of all others, the dearest and most desirable things under the sun, are to be accounted but dross and dung. And yet, for all this, many of us while we yet abode in the darkness and damnation of our natural state spent many years, some twenty, some thirty, some perhaps forty, wholly upon hell, in base and unblessed courses, quite cross to the end of our creation. All that time (a misery to be lamented even with tears of blood) was utterly cast away upon the kingdom of darkness, fearfully lost upon our own lusts, sinful fashions, and pride of life, slavishly and wofully wasted in the devil's service. Nay, all that while, abominable and beastly sinners that we were, we set ourselves with sensual rage against the very face of Heaven, lay in actual high treason, and bore arms in open rebellion, against that dreadful Majesty, which might most justly every moment of that woful time have arrested us with death, arraigned us at the bar of his justice, and thrown us down into hell.

What manner of persons, then, I pray you, ought we to be in the short remainder of those few and evil days which are behind? Even to employ and improve the utmost possibility of all our natural acquired and gracious parts, our credit, calling, outward state, all our power, means, occasions, advantages, to win and work out glory unto God, enlargement of Christ's kingdom, confusion to the devil's dominion, conversion of others, comfort unto our own poor souls against our ending hour. A servant that hath loitered a great part of the day in his journey or business, and yet must needs reach home and finish his task, will toil at it towards night, double his pains, and put all his strength unto it; so we, having not only been slack in our business about God's service, and slow in the way to heaven, but even for many years, perhaps, run in a quite contrary course, and done the devil's work, must now towards the night of our natural life, and the conclusion of the short span thereof, spare no pains, double our diligence, press hard to the prize of the high calling, quit ourselves like men and be strong, with a holy violence lay hold upon the kingdom of heaven, with all zeal, courage, and resolution, labour to redeem the time past, for the days are evil; and our particular doom for eternity, of joys or woes, pleasures or pains, draws on apace, and is even at the door.

And as consideration of former time mispent, so a foresight also of dreadful times to come, may justly cause us to make much of, and husband well every moment we have now in our hands, for treasuring up a heavenly hoard of grace, comfort, patience, and courage against the evil day. Though the times, as yet, be fair and calm, and the candle of God shines still upon this kingdom with extraordinary prosperity and peace, there is no carrying into captivity nor crying in our streets, but every man is quietly reposed under his own vine, and there refresheth himself with the riches and comforts of a good and pleasant land; yet, as sure as the night follows the day, a change will come. If the glorious and triumphant times of the daughter of Jerusalem, that men called "The perfection of beauty, the joy of the whole earth, the glory of all lands," were turned into "a day of trouble, and of treading down, and of perplexity by the Lord God of hosts in the valley of vision, breaking down the walls, and of crying to the mountains," Isa. xxii. 5, what may we of this land look for, if we still turn the grace of God into wantonness, but at length to be turned out of our houses of peace as the unthankfullest and unworthiest people that ever the sun of heaven saw, or the sun of Christ's glorious gospel did shine upon so fair and so long? But, howsoever the kingdom fare, and God deal with us in public, (only let me tell you, by the way, that in the mean time we stand by a miracle of God's mercy, and a prop of his extraordinary patience,) yet every one of our particular day and doom cannot be far off. As yet, perhaps, the Almighty is with us, his providence protects our habitations, no remarkable affliction hath taken hold upon us, so that there is no mourning nor spectacles of miseries in our families; no crying, O my father Abraham, and O my son Isaac; O my son Absalom, my son, my son, Absalom! O Absalom, my son, my son! And these houses of flesh, it may be, wherein we dwell for a few and evil days, are as yet in reasonable good repair; and it is every way with us as it was with Job in the days of his youth, when he washed his steps with butter, and the rocks poured him out rivers of oil; yet we may build upon it as a principle which never failed sinful mortality, that days of danger and distress will have their turn and time also. Sorrow and sickness, perplexity and fear, temptation, desertion, trouble of conscience, the destroying sword, a fiery trial, striving unto blood, Marian times of most abhorred memory, or some dreadful visitations of one kind or other, may seize upon us, we know not how soon. But, howsoever we escape in the mean time, sure I am these frail bodies of ours, after a short while, will fall in sunder and moulder away into rottenness and dust; and our naked souls must stand at the just tribunal of the ever-living God, accountable with exactness and truth for all things done in the body. Far be it from us, then, and every one that at that last and great day would not cry to this rock and that mountain to cover him, like sons and daughters of confusion to trifle away time in this heat of our spiritual harvest; but rather, with redoubled and extraordinary resolution, let us gird up the loins of our minds, and with all fruitfulness and power improve every hour of this fair day of our gracious visitation, to treasure up peace to our poor souls against the stormy winter night of death, towards which every wind drives us, and both sleeping and waking we are posting apace, though we perceive it not.

(4.) We must be accountable for time. At the dreadful bar of that last tribunal, as we must be exactly answerable even for wandering, vain imaginations, idle words, and every the very least error of our whole life; nay, for not improving all our gifts, goods, and graces to the best advantage for God's glory; for misemployment of our wit, understanding, memory, affections, health, strength, courage, learning, liberty, authority, policy, or any other power or possibility which God hath put into our hands; so must we also give up a strict account for the expense of every moment of time. Now, tell me, at that great and general audit, whether of these two sums will sound more sweetly in our ears? Item, so many days in recreation, or so many days in humiliation? so many hours in prayer, or so many hours in playing at cards? so many weeks in jovial revellings and merry meetings, or so many weeks in watching over our ways and walking with God, &c.? A serious foresight of the inconceivable comfort of the one, and how cold the other will strike unto our hearts, might make us easily grow into blessed Bradford's care and practice this way, of whom it is reported, that he counted that hour not well spent wherein he did not some good, either with his pen, study, or in exhorting others; and not to rush upon recreations unseasonably, without necessity and warrantable calling.

(5.) The holiest hearts of the most worthy saints are wofully haunted with too many distractions and violent intrusions of idle, vain, and impertinent thoughts even in holy duties, religious exercises, and solemn use of the ordinances; which, without extraordinary watchfulness and wrestling on their parts, would utterly bereave and rob them of all the sweetness, power, and profit of those blessed means, and by little and little quite transform them into form and neglect. If in the best, then, and heavenliest businesses, the vanity of our own minds and malice of the devil press upon us with such importunity and restless assaults, with what furious and impetuous incursions and devastations of conscience are they like to oppress us in our idle hours, ill spent time, and pursuit of pleasures! Consideration whereof, methinks, should cause christians (who alone are truly sensible of the interruption and discontinuance of their sweet communion and society with Christ, and smart many times for the estrangement of their thoughts and affections from God) only to have recourse to recreations in case of true need; for necessity, I say, and seasonably, even as they use physic; so may they expect God's gracious protection from the hurtful prevailing of those sensual distempers and licentious ranging of their thoughts, which are wont to enrage and impoison the minds and affections of carnal men all the while. And these considerations should guard them, as often as they are hailed by the cunning ensnarement of old companions, the tyranny of former custom, or unmortified yieldingness of their own deceitful hearts to immoderation and excess in this kind, not to expose their hearts as a prey to temptation and vanity. Whereby they may be in continual danger, either by little and little to be drawn back and drowned again in the froth and fooleries of their disavowed pleasures, which were a horrible thing; or else, at least, to bring upon themselves, from time to time, as they transgress in this kind, much unnecessary discomfort and unsettledness in their christian course, disrelish in religious exercises, deadness of heart, disacquaintance with heavenly comforts, loss of that dearest thing and earthly paradise—peace of conscience, which, perhaps, they shall hardly with much ado recover a long time after.

(6.) Consider Chrysostom's preciseness against wasting time this way. "The present time," saith he, "is not for melting into mirth, but for lamentation and mourning; and yet dost thou vainly misspend it in merry conceits? The devil gnasheth the teeth, roars and foams, and flashes out fire against thy salvation; and dost thou sit still and jovially jest it out? Do we play and sport ourselves, beloved? Wilt thou learn the conversation of the saints? Hear what Paul says, 'By the space of three years I ceased not to warn every one, night and day, with tears,' Acts xx. 31. 'Out of much affliction and anguish of heart, I wrote unto you with many tears,' 2 Cor. ii. 4. 'Who is weak and I am not weak? who is offended, and I burn not?' 2 Cor. xi. 29.

'For we that are in this tabernacle do groan, being burdened,' 2 Cor. v. 4. And the apostle desiring, that I may so speak, every day to depart this life; dost thou laugh and play? Our time here is a time of war, of fight, of watch and ward, of harnessing, of standing in the face and fury of the enemy; and dost thou demean thyself like a dancer? Dost thou not see the faces of soldiers in the fight, how sad they are, how contracted, how terrible with frowns, how full of horror? Dost thou not behold the austere piercing intention of their eyes, and extraordinary excitation of heart, leaping and panting in their breasts?" His meaning imports thus much:— Doth an ordinary soldier in the field, against a mortal man and earthly enemy, recollect and unite all the spirit and powers of body and soul with all efficacy and earnestness for the encounter? and shall a christian soldier, that "wrestles not against flesh and blood, but against principalities, against powers, against the rulers of the darkness of this world, against spiritual wickednesses in high places," who is every moment furiously assaulted and hunted even like a partridge on the mountains, by the devil's open rage, the ambushment of the world, and the endless treacheries of his own false heart, trifle away his time and turn aside to toys?

4. I now proceed to advise, that recreations be no encroachers upon heavenly comforts; no diminishers of our delight in God; no devourers of spiritual joy. For this is a very divine thing, to be prized and preserved as a celestial jewel, far more worth than heaven and earth, which the world can neither give nor take from us, neither must any stranger meddle with it. We may take an estimate of its excellency by casting our eyes upon—

(1.) The intolerable bitterness of the contrary; I mean spiritual horror, which we see sometimes, by woful experience, doth enrage the guilty consciences of some forlorn sinners with such restless fury and unutterable anguish, that at length (extremest, I know not whether madness or cruelty) they lay violent and villanous hands upon themselves. In which case, such a hell upon earth is horror of conscience, they care not in the least for the sweetness of life, the rueful cries of their own dear children, the heavy looks of their yokefellows, the abhorred infamy they bring upon their own names, families, kindred, burial, posterity. Oh, how they spurn at, with a vile, disdainful contempt, pleasures, riches, honours, crowns, kingdoms, worlds of gold, anything, everything, as miserable comforters! Nay, it is so stinging, that they will rather venture upon that other hell, to which they are posting in a coffin of blood, a thousand thousand times more horrible, than endure it any longer. If sense, then, of Divine indignation, taking secret vengeance upon the guilty conscience of an impenitent rebel, puts him, as it were, into hellish flames above ground; what a heaven upon earth is a sweet feeling of God's reconciled face, and his everlasting mercies through Christ, sealed and set on by the Holy Ghost, and the testimony of a good conscience! And how deliciously doth an humble soul, so honoured with a foretaste and first fruits, as it were, of eternal joys, grasp the Lord Jesus in his ordinances, and blissfully sun itself in the love and light of his countenance!

(2.) The practice of the profane in their insatiable, restless pursuit of false joys and painful pleasures, which at best are but as crackling of thorns under a pot, and flashes of lightning before everlasting fire.

They hunt after them even into hell, and light a candle at the devil for lightsomeness of heart, by haunting alehouses, taverns, houses of ill-fame, playhouses, conventicles of good-fellowship, sinful and unseasonable sports, a thousand kinds of vanities and fooleries, which are nothing but the devil's wakes and revellings of hell. And all this little, poor carnal mirth is purchased many times with much shame, loss, misery, beggary, rottenness of body, discredit, damnation. At what a high rate, then, and with what eagerness and thirst, is that true, sweet, unmixed, glorious joy, springing out of the fountain of comfort in an honest and holy heart, to be sought after!

(3.) The differences between spiritual and carnal joy: in respect—

[1.] Of lastingness. A spiritually merry heart is a continual feast, saith Solomon; whereas "the joy of the hypocrite is but for a moment," Job xx. 5. Carnal joy is like lightning; spiritual, like the light of the sun. While the play lasts the sensualist laughs, but he falls into melancholy when all is done. The drunkard is merry whilst he revels it amongst his pot-companions in the alehouse, but when he comes home there is many times woful work. Whilst the gamester is at play he is well enough pleased, but, when he hath made away with all, he is ready to make away with himself also. A cunning and prosperous worldling, I confess, by God's permission, may patch together his pleasures all his life long; but, at furthest, at death comes the deadly and everlasting damp: whereas he that walks with God is contented and comfortable all the day, and death is the daybreak to him of everlasting brightness. Carnal joy, I say, is like lightning, a flash and away; leaves the mind in more extreme and deeper darkness; blasts the heart and affections with all spiritual deadness and desolations, with many boiling distempers, much raging wildfire, and unquenchable thirst after sensuality, earthliness, and epicurism; and, first or last, it is ever certainly followed with rending and roaring of the spirit, spiritual terrors, thunders, darkness, and damnation. But godly joy is like the light of the sun, which, though it may for a time be overcast with clouds of temptations, mists of troubles and persecutions, darkness of melancholy, yet it ordinarily breaks out again with more sweetness and splendour when the storm is over; but howsoever it hath ever the Sun of righteousness and fountain of all comfort so resident and rooted in the heart, that not all the darkness and gates of hell shall ever be able to uproot or stain it, no more than a mortal man can pull the sun out of his sphere, or put out his glorious light.

[2.] Of purity. The edge and relish of carnal joy is ever much abated and embittered with many sour sauces and envenomed mixtures; impatience of delay, difficulty and danger in attainment, unanswerableness to expectations, many secret terrors, fretting jealousies, discontented indignations against their discontinuance and vanishing, &c. And, besides, those three ensuing individual stings, which to an enlightened conscience inseparably and sensibly follow them at the heels, as a shadow the body in the sunshine, cut the very throat, and burst the heart of all worldly pleasures. 1. One of them is, as it were, natural, immediately attending all earthly mirth,—more melancholy and heavy-heartedness afterward. For as the rivers of sweet water run their course to die in the salt sea, so the honey of all earthly pleasure ever endeth in the gall of grief. Voluptuousness, even in her dearest minions, ordinarily expires with anguish and anger that it is gone. The transitory flashes of sensual delight are like the light of a candle, which leave at the close a noisome, vexing snuff behind. And that sweetness which sensualists swallow down so greedily, turns to gravel within them, and at farewell fills their spirit with the return of a more heavy melancholic humour than before the receipt. 2. The other I call a temporary sting, for all the ways of worldly pleasure are strewed also with needles and nettles, that I may so speak, which ever and anon prick and sting her darlings, as they pluck her fading flowers. So that, at best, they are but like bears robbing a wasp's nest, who ravenously rifle the combs, and with much ado suck out a little honey, but in the mean time are soundly stung and swollen about the head for their painful pleasure. In their several walks of a fool's paradise, they hunt both unreasonably and unseasonably after transitory delights; but they are even pained, and paid home, with a witness, in the very pursuit. For instance, the covetous man accounts worldly wealth and a hoard of gold his heaven upon earth; but, in heaping it together, his heart is wofully rent and torn asunder with carking thoughtfulness, restless rooting in the earth, anxious and endless casting about and forecasting: in a word, with much care in gathering, more fear in keeping, and most grief in parting from it. So that, for feeding his greedy eye upon a little vanishing heap of yellow earth, his heart is continually haunted with such vexing harpies—I mean wasting cares and false fears—that dry up even his vital moisture, and cut his very heartstrings in pieces. Good-fellow meetings and alehouse revellings are the drunkard's delight; but all the while he sits, he is, perhaps, in bodily fear of the constable: when towards night he goes grunting homewards, he becomes a gazing and laughing-stock to children in the streets; no sooner comes he reeling into his own house but he wrings fresh cries and tears of shame and grief from his wife and family, for the reproach, beggary, and misery he brings upon them. And as he goes on in this drunken good-fellowship, and takes a pride and pleasure in pouring in of strong drink, there many times insensibly grow upon him many loathsome diseases and deformities of body, rheums, dropsies, palsies, a fearful face, falling and never rising again, sometimes not even out of a little gutter that would scarce choke a child. The lascivious wanton that wanders in the twilight, in the evening, in the black and dark night, after the strange woman, besides the dart which sticks fast and rankles in his liver, meets in the mean time with rottenness in his bones, a consumption of his marrow, a wound, and dishonour, and reproach that shall not be wiped away. The boisterous aspiring Nimrod, out of a gluttonous desire of grasping offices and honours, screws himself into some high place as his only paradise, and, when he has gotten up, dances full merrily in golden fetters upon his slippery standing; but, couldst thou see into his inside, thou shouldst behold his heart miserably fretting and vexing itself, raging with many passionate distempers for the indignation of good men, contempt of inferiors, thwarting of competitors, envy of compeers, underminings of counter-factionists, jealousies of princes, &c. How many great men's hearts have burst with the blasting frowns of a king's forehead! Nay, and which is a bedlam misery upon the ambitious man, he is many times more grieved for an affront of some grandee opposite, because he cannot have his will of this or that man that stands in his way, or for the neglect of some expected complimental respect and observance, than pleased with all the other bravery and jollity of his high station. This is clear in Haman, though he was encompassed and crowned with much undeserved and extraordinary precedency and pomp, yet this one little thing, to wit, because Mordecai would not bow the knee and do reverence unto him at the king's gate, did utterly mar and dissweeten all the other excellences and extraordinariness of the king's favour: see Esther, chap. v. ver. 10—13, "And Haman told his friends and wife of the glory of his riches, &c. Yet all this," saith he, " availeth me nothing, so long as I see Mordecai the jew sitting at the king's gate." 3. The third is an eternal sting, which to a waking and working conscience ariseth out of a serious consideration and sense of God's casual, just, and holy indignation revealed in his book against impenitents in such kinds. Whereupon it is no marvel, though many times their hearts, hating to be reformed, and hearing their several dooms denounced against them from God's own mouth, in that word by which they shall be judged at the last day, be full sorely smitten with inward bitter gripings and secret guilty stings, the very hellish flashings and foretastes of that never-dying worm, which hereafter, without timely repentance, will gnaw upon their consciences with full rage and unquenchable horror, world without end. The worldling, therefore, may justly tremble and roar when he reads that cutting commination, " Go to now, ye rich men, weep and howl for your miseries that shall come upon you. Your riches are corrupted, and your garments are moth-eaten. Your gold and silver is cankered, and the rust of them shall be a witness against you, and shall eat your flesh as it were fire: ye have heaped treasure together for the last days," Jam. v. 1, 2. The wanton, when he well weighs that flaming place so full of vengeance against him, "But whoremongers and adulterers God will judge," Heb. xiii. 14. The drunkard, when he finds himself in the cursed catalogue of that damned crew, "Be not deceived; neither fornicators, nor idolators, nor drunkards, &c., shall inherit the kingdom of God," 1 Cor. vi. 9. The ambitionist, when he casts his eye from the top of his usurped honours upon that dreadful downfal, "Though thou exalt thyself as the eagle, and though thou set thy nest among the stars, thence will I bring thee down, saith the Lord," Obad. 4.

But now, on the other side, spiritual joy, which springs out of the wells of salvation, and is a ray and representation, as it were, of the Sun of righteousness, and that eternal fountain of soundest and lasting comfort, is all sweet, pure, shining, calm, hearty, unspeakable, utterly free from those sore grumblings and reluctations of conscience; envenomed mixtures and slavish apprehensions; after-repentings, stings, and melancholy horrors; though it may be assaulted, and something dimmed with some doubts, distrusts, and weakness of degree, by reason of our unglorified state of mortality; yet in respect of its creation, substance, truth, and blissful issue, it is a very glimpse of heavenly glory, a pure taste of the rivers of life and firstfruits of everlasting joys. Thus the blessing of the Lord maketh the heart spiritually merry with incomparable sweetness, and he addeth no sorrow with it.

[3.] Of dignity and divine temper. Carnal joys have for their foundation the fading arm of flesh and the fashion of this world, frail and fleeting as themselves; earthly power and policy for their prop and support; for their object, the garbage of the earth, gold and silver, food for swinish worldlings, noble captivities, gilded fetters; I mean, undeserved dignities, honours, offices, greatness, and high stations, the only aim of ambitious Shebnas; the filth and froth of brutish pleasures, fuel for the flames, and such like trash, pelf, and vanity; for their companions, fears, jealousies, guilty gripings; the senses for their seat, time for their limit, for their end endless grief and horror of heart: for all earthly pleasure determines in heaviness, as the sun sets in darkness.

But now, on the other side, spiritual joy is the blessed Spirit's sweet and lovely babe, grounded upon the sure covenant of everlasting love, mercy, and peace in Jesus Christ. The matter of it is the light of God's countenance, the garments of salvation, the precious robe of Christ's righteousness, interest in his dearest blood, and all the rich purchases of his passion; looking upon our names in heaven through the glass of sanctification, God's holy image renewed upon our souls, and the illustrious beams of heavenly graces shed from the throne of grace and shining there; every sweet promise in his blessed book; in a word, Jehovah, Isa. lxi. 10; Hab. iii. 18; Phil. iv. 4. And that glorious name proclaimed, Exod. xxxiv. 6, 7, a wellspring of unspeakable refreshing to every truly broken and bleeding heart, being well opened by a feeling and a fruitful mediation. For measure, it is immeasurable, without bound or stint, and passeth all understanding; no stranger doth intermeddle with it, neither can any man possibly conceive it, but he that enjoys it. It is, as it were, the amiable splendour and sparkle of that white stone in the Revelation, chap. ii. 27, which only shines upon heavenly hearts, with delight unspeakable and glorious; for seat and certainty, it is engraven by the finger of God with a heavenly sunbeam, as it were, shining from the face of Christ in the very centre of the heart; which not all the powers of darkness or hellish mists can finally dim or dispel, the world neither give nor take from us, neither man, nor devil, nor shadow of death ever raze or root out. It is honoured with that supernatural singularity and sacred temper, that, utterly against nature and all natural possibility, it extracts sweetness and life out of ordinary causes of dejection and sinking. Troubles, persecutions, and reproaches do fortify it, and serve as fuel to enlarge its lightsomeness. See Acts v. 41; xvi. 25. See Fox's Acts and Monuments, where the glorious martyr Woodman speaks thus:—" When I have been in prison, wearing otherwhile bolts, otherwhile shackles, otherwhile lying on the bare ground; sometimes sitting in the stocks, sometimes bound with cords, that all my body hath been swollen; much like to be overcome for the pain that hath been in my flesh; sometimes fain to lie without in the woods and fields, wandering to and fro; few, I say, that durst to keep my company for fear of the rulers; sometimes brought before the justices, sheriffs, lords, doctors, and bishops; sometimes called dog, sometimes devil, heretic, whoremonger, traitor, thief, deceiver, with divers others such like; yea, and even they that did eat of my bread, that should have been most my friends by nature, have betrayed me: yet for all this, I praise my Lord God, that hath separated me from my mother's womb, that all this that hath happened to me hath been easy, light, and most delectable and joyful of any treasure that ever I possessed." For duration, it is a very glimpse of heavenly glory, which, springing up in a sanctified heart, out of the wells of salvation, and carried along with addition of the fresh comforts from the word and sacraments, through a fruitful current and course of a christian life, is at last entertained into the boundless and bottomless ocean of the endless joys of heaven.

(4.) Of unconquerableness against all created oppositions and assaults of earthly discomforts. An ounce of sorrow mars a whole sea of worldly mirth. The boisterousness and bravery of all carnal joy vanisheth quite away and expires, even as a flower when the heat riseth that is sent upon it, upon the very first approach or presence of any either outward trouble or inward terror. A prick of a needle, much more a pang of the stone, or fit of the gout, is able to deprive a man of the pleasure of the world's monarchy. One serious thought of death, or the sight of one sin armed with God's anger, will put the proudest Nimrod, the greediest engrosser of all earthly delights, into Belshazzar's shivering. But now, let the christian, whose heart is sweetly reposed upon the rock of eternity, be utterly stripped of all outward comforts; let heavy accidents fall upon him as thick as one wave on the neck of another—which befel blessed Job; yet he is still where he was; he hath made God his portion, his only jewel and joy which he hath in heaven or on earth; his heart is fixed, trusting in the Lord; and therefore, when all earthly stays and staves of reed shrink in the wetting, and are shattered to nothing, he cleaves with an unshaken and triumphant tranquillity of mind to his "Sun and Shield," Psa. lxxxiv. 11. To his "Light and Life," John viii. 12. To his "Shield and exceeding great reward," Gen. xv. 1. Hear his sweet and noble resolution in this case, "Although the fig-tree shall not blossom, neither shall fruit be in the vines; the labour of the olive shall fail, and the field shall yield no meat; the flocks shall be cut off from the fold, and there shall be no herd in the stalls: yet I will rejoice in the Lord, I will joy in the God of my salvation," Hab. iii. 17, 18. While Jehovah is in heaven, his heart is in the haven, though ever so many storms or tempests of the troublesome sea of this world beat upon his house of clay. Rob him of all earthly refreshments and lightsomeness of this life, and let but the light of God's countenance shine upon him, which no darkness, nor dungeon, nor devil in hell can intercept, and he is incomparably more happy than the world's choicest minion, pleasure's dearest favourite, or the bravest Belshazzar upon earth, in the very top of his most jovial revellings and swaggering sensuality. But it is not so with the earthly-minded man; for, howsoever he may digest with reasonable patience, and carry well enough away all crosses and contradictions to his other worldly comforts, while he doth yet wallow without interruption and disquiet in the sinful pleasures of that selected way of death upon which the more headstrong current of his corrupt nature hath cast him, and the natural bent of his carnal affections hath singled out and made special choice of, to follow and feed upon with greatest delight,—which the fathers call a man's bosom sin,—yet cut him once short of the free and full enjoyment of this his sensual idol and earthly god, and you kill his heart quite, and plunge him presently into desperate distractions. For instance,—the covetous man, while his heart may nestle securely upon his golden heap, will pass by, without any great wound or passion, the curses of the poor, the grumblings of his conscience, the comminations of the ministry, the cry of the whole country against his oppressions, usury, sacrilege, and sinful ways of hoarding. When he comes home, and finds his bags and bonds safe, he blesseth himself in his heart against all threatened judgments, horrors, curses, confusions. Though Jesus Christ himself should preach and press them upon him, with his golden wedge he easily cuts asunder all scruples, doubts, exceptions, reasons, arguments, objections, which any ways oppose his covetous and cruel courses. He pleases and applauds himself against all censures and contradictions whatsoever to the contrary. But let God's angry hand, in his just judgment, by fire, robbery, or some secret consumption, snatch away his wealth, and he is likely enough to go out of his wits, and in great hazard of hanging himself. While the ambitious man is proudly mounted, sits fast upon the seat of honour, and is idolized, as it were, and adored above others, he can easily enough overlook with an imperious disdain the indignation of good men, emulation of great ones, the reproaches of the multitude, and all other petty and private crosses: but throw him down from his high place, turn him out of his offices and honours, and how weary is he of the world; how irksome to himself; how prodigal of his life; how impatient of the company of men! While the wanton wallows in the brutish pleasures of his abominable filth, he bears well enough away the weakening of his body, the wasting of his goods, the shame of his sin, loss of friends, stain of reputation; but beat him back, and bar him from the house of the strange woman, and you break his heart; banish him from his minion, and he is ready to make away with himself. Woe, sorrow, contentions, wounds without cause, redness of eyes, undoing of wife and children, hooting at in the streets, will well enough pass off with the drunkard, while he may domineer upon the ale-bench; but cut off the new wine and strong drink from his mouth, cross him in his swaggering course, confine him from his good-fellow meetings, and you take away the very life of his life. Thus every unregenerate man secures himself in some one sensual hold or other, wherein the crown of his carnal joy consists; of which bereave him, and you leave him joyless, heartless, hopeless, and helpless. But take from the true christian, if it were possible, both heaven and earth, and all the creatures and comforts of both; yet you cannot take away his joy. God is the strength of his heart, and his portion for ever. Surely he shall never be moved; his heart is fixed, trusting in the Lord.

Which, since it is so, that spiritual joy is such an invaluable jewel, and carnal so cursed a vanity, let every christian be exceedingly careful not to suffer the froth and filth of this to stain or lessen the glory and sweetness of the other. But, if he once perceive any company or kind of recreation begin to steal away his heart from communion and comfort in his God, let him abandon it as a canker and cutthroat of his spiritual happiness, and ever prize and prefer the joy of the soul, delights of grace, refreshings of the Holy Ghost, infinitely before all worldly pleasures, carnal contentments, ease, or any earthly thing.

II. VISITS TO UNSANCTIFIED GREAT MEN.

Complimental visitations of unsanctified great ones, without just occasion and a warrantable calling, besides sinful expense of precious time, are many times unhappy occasions to embark, especially by yielding natures, in some base and scandalous businesses; and to entangle them in those wicked services, or some uncomfortable inconvenience, which afterward in cold blood wofully wound their consciences, and perhaps much weaken their christian reputation.

Jehoshaphat may serve as a remarkable instance for this purpose. Upon a time he came down to see Ahab, king of Israel, by way of courtly visitation. And, though he was equal unto him in the crowned majesty of a king and a good man, yet trains and insinuations by royal entertainments, and a princely feast premised, as it appears in the story, he was cunningly caught and cast into the confederation and society of an unhappy war; whereby, with a dishonourable precipitation, he plunged himself both into spiritual miseries and temporal mischief, both hurt his conscience, and hazarded his life. For the first—1. He suddenly and rashly promised aid unto Ahab, whom the Lord hated, before he knew God's will in the point from the mouth of the prophet. 2. When faithful Michaiah had delivered the truth, and acquainted them with the mind of God, he, notwithstanding, went on with the business. 3. He did not appear on the prophet's side, and in his defence against the imperious insolence of that false flattering Zedekiah, or the merciless tyranny of Ahab, who sent him to prison for telling him the truth. For the second, by the cruel cunning of hollow-hearted Ahab, he exposed himself both to the fury of the whole Syrian army, (only upon a penitent ejaculation his life was rescued miraculously from that extremest danger,) and also to the wrath of God for helping the ungodly, and loving them that hated the Lord as the prophet told him, 2 Chron. xix. 2.

Mistake me not; I purpose not in this passage to censure or disgrace any warrantable ceremony and solemnities of state, mutual intercourse of noble deportment amongst compeers, civil exchange of fair and amiable behaviour one towards another, any charitable offices of humanity, or christian expressions of courtesy and love; but the idle, formal, flattering vanities, hypocrisies, disguisements of those many needless, fruitless, and endless salutations, compliments, visitations, entertainments, affected and acted by such vain people as are extremely troubled how to be rid of time,—a commodity of high account with all those who are sensible and mindful of their last account; every moment whereof ought in the mean time to be crowned with fruitful improvement by all those that truly fear God. I could wish that a gracious concurrence of goodness and greatness, true nobleness indeed, where God himself is the top, and religion the root, (in respect whereof those other, by birth, by riches, by mere moral virtue, by valour, by learning, by favour of princes, are but shadows and shapes of nobleness,) were honoured with all due attributions, highest respect, and best observance. In such a case, it is not uncomely for Paul to travel from Arabia to Jerusalem to visit Peter, Gal. i. 18; or the queen of the South, from the uttermost parts of the earth, to see Solomon, 1 Kings x. 1. But I would not have glittering folly, gilded rottenness, sacrificed unto with so much flattery and counterfeit crouching. For why should silken dung be so adored, and golden damnation deified? Now, the reasons why such visitations, as well as recreations, may many times prove snares to entangle us in sin, damps to dull our forwardness, or one way or other breed and bring upon us some spiritual miseries, are such as these:—

1. Great men without grace ordinarily make use of all others for their own advantage. With an imperious policy and a kind of crafty alchymy, they secretly and invisibly convert, dispose, and manage the agency, abilities, and serviceableness of their followers, visitants, adherents, and dependants, to serve their own turns, to feed their humours, further their private ends of profit, pleasure, rising, reputation, or some other choice carnal contentment and predominant worldly delight. They have their portion in this life, and their heaven here; therefore they labour to make their earthly paradise as full of pleasures as possibly they can. Their own sensual, covetous, and ambitious hearts are the centres wherein the lines and level of all their plots, policies, and projects do concur and meet; and to which they conduct and direct the officiousness, pliable-

ness, and several services of all those with whom they hold any kind of correspondence or intercourse.

2. Such exercises of courtly vanities, needless errands, idle business, are Satan's chief and choicest seasons for the suggestion of temptations, and too successful discharge of his fiery darts. He hath ordinarily more power over men, and is much likelier to prevail, when he finds them idle or ill occupied, than when they are busied with humbleness and sincerity in religious duties, or the necessary works of a lawful calling. In our best and holiest employments he is indeed most eager against us; but at times of idleness and exercises of vanity he is commonly most successful. In God's business, the honest executions of our calling, and seasonable christian recreations, we may expect, upon good ground, and with hopeful comfort, God's protection, the ordinary assistance of his blessed Spirit, harmlessness from the creatures, Satan's restraint, some good measure of mortifying help against the rebellious stirrings of our own corruptions, and such other blessings promised in such cases. But if men will needs be idle or employed in vanity, they justly bereave themselves of all these comfortable protections and privileges. For it is just with God, at such times, that he should withdraw from them his own protecting hand, restrain the gracious influences of the Holy Spirit, and let loose against them, with indignation, Satan, the creatures, and their own corruptions, which is a very grievous cut to a tender and waking conscience.

3. The presence and protestations, the intimations and motions, of men in high place, mingled with an affected familiar communication of them-

selves, and plausible neglect of all formal solemnities and austerities of state, upon purpose to insinuate sooner and more subtlely, are many times very potent to prevail with and persuade, especially inferiors. For they are apt, when they are so assaulted, 1. To conceive themselves highly honoured, when those condescend and vouchsafe to entreat and be beholding, who might, in other cases, command, nay, and perhaps upon a point of advantage and pang of displeasure, quite crush and cashier them. 2. To hold it a convenient policy in these days of the reign of iniquity and self-love, when "judgment is turned away backward, and justice standeth afar off; for truth is fallen in the street, and equity cannot enter," Isa. lix. 14, to gratify and demerit such mighty ones as may shelter and protect them from all storms of violence, oppressions, and wrong; nay, and perhaps by their countenance procure them a great deal of credit and esteem, if not observance and respect, from those amongst whom they live. 3. To call to mind, out of too many woful experiences, that in the frowns and angry foreheads of great men are infolded many times many secret plots of cunning cruelty and plausible malice; which, when time serves, fall full heavy upon the hearts and heads of inferiors, which are not in all points pliable to their humours. And out of such carnal considerations as these, by a rash, unadvised yieldingness, they too often plunge themselves hand over head into unworthy engagements, and become instruments of ill offices; the baseness and iniquity whereof doth afterward strike full cold unto their hearts, and leave a gash and grievous wound in their consciences, comforts, and christian reputations.

4. At such entertainments and tables of great men, not friends to the truth, thou wilt be ready to vomit thy morsels, and shalt lose thy sweet words, Prov. xxiii. 8. Thy dainty fare may be sauced, perhaps, with many bitters, with much rotten talk; if not empoisoned with blasphemies, obscenities, and horrible oaths. Thy music will be merry lies, feigned jests, scoffs, and scurrilities, against God's best servants, and the king's best subjects, commonly calumniated as pestilent fellows. For so the church complains, "I am their music," Lam. iii. 63. Few feasts, where the founder is not God's friend, but after his good-fellow guests are well heated with variety of dishes and strong drink, as their faces are inflamed with fiery reflections one from another, so their hearts will be enraged with mutual infection of furious malice, to cast out most prodigious villanous lies, hammered by the very foulest fiend in the darkest nook of hell, against those that are true of heart. The complimental forms and flourishes of thy welcome may prove as a pitfall, to plunge thee into some dishonourable employment, or one way or other to betray thee to an uncomfortable entanglement of thy conscience. So that if thy generous spirit will nobly rise against such froth and folly, ribaldry and railing—the unworthy degenerations of these worst times,—if it be sensible of God's dishonour, the disgrace of the saints, and thine own danger, thou canst not fail to be weary of such sinful cheer. Nay, besides the resolution of thy judgment, that in such a case thou wouldest far rather have staid at home with a dinner of green herbs, than to have thine ears so grated, and heart grieved, all the while at a great table; even in nature thou shalt fare worse. For

thy just indignation, discontentment, and sadness upon such ground will naturally contract thine heart, thicken thy blood, chill thy spirits, so that natural heat will faint and fail in the ordinary current and course of concoction. No marvel, then, that thou art readier to vomit thy morsels than to rejoice in those high entertainments or variety of messes, which are dissweetened with such distasteful and bitter mixtures. And thou shalt lose thy sweet words, both of humanity and christianity. For the first, out of the ingenuous simplicity and honesty of thy heart thou wilt return real, sincere, affectionate demonstrations of thankfulness for mere dissembled, formal ceremonies of entertainment and welcome. For the other, thou shalt be so far from finding a free and comfortable vent and entertainment to any good talk, that, if thou meddle that way, thou marrest all the mirth. Mention of heavenly things, our last account, the life to come, judgments against sin, privileges of the saints, and happiness of the pious ones, which might sweetly season, and, as it were, sanctify their meeting, and those good creatures of God they so plentifully enjoy, would presently cast all the company into deep melancholy. The word of God writ upon the wall, in the very height of the greatest jollity and revelling, did make the heart, joints, and knees of the mighty king Belshazzar to tremble, as the leaves of the forest when they are shaken with the wind. How often may we observe many goodly and gracious discourses buried in the bosoms of men of understanding and worth, placed below, by reason of the domineering talkativeness, and imperious ignorance, of some silken idol sitting at the head of the table! Horses, and hounds, and hawks, devour full often and eat up not only spiritual and holy, but even all moral and manly talk.

For the more convenient declining and prevention of any ensnarement and inconvenience in this kind, let me commend to the christian such cautions and considerations as these:—

(1.) Ever before thou go out of thy doors upon any occasion, business, journey, visitation, weigh well, with due deliberation, in the balance of a holy wisdom, all circumstances, concurrents, company, probability of all events, and consequences on both sides; of staying at home, or going abroad; visiting this or that friend; undertaking that or the other business; and ever constantly incline and resolve that way, which in all likelihood will bring most glory unto God, good unto others, and comfort unto thine own conscience. Let it only be the sinful liberty of hopeless worldlings to waste their time and labour (for the needless expense of every moment of the one, and motion of the other, they must very shortly be full dearly accountable at God's strict tribunal) in those impertinent vagaries and idle visitations, which have no other motive but a desire to be rid of time, and to feed a gadding and restless humour; no other end but vanity or vainglory; no issue but temptation, and greater disability to good duties. But let every wisely resolute and truly judicious christian disdain, however worldly wisdom derides it, to step over his threshold without a warrantable calling, aim at some honest end, probable foresight of some good to come thereon, honour to God, furtherance of some good cause, good unto our brethren, discharge of some duty of our calling, performance of christian offices, of charity, humanity, natural affection, mutual comforting, confirming, refreshing, and building up one another in our most holy faith, and the like. Otherwise he shall be in great danger of returning home far worse than when he went out; laden both with more personal guiltiness, and accessariness to other's sin; bleeding with some fresh bruise of conscience, by falling scandalously, or failing in some christian duty; grown into a further disacquaintance and estrangement from God; more deeply sunk, perhaps, into some sinful society, and sensual conformities with men of this world.

Some actions, I confess, and undertakings in their own nature, and in respect of the object, as the schoolmen speak, are indifferent; but clothed with circumstances and by the actual working of a particular agent, are not so, but necessarily become morally good or evil to the doer. And therefore, the assertion of Catarinus, in the council of Trent, to this purpose was consonant to the opinion of the greater part of the schoolmen: "Every particular action," said he, "is good or evil, neither is there to be found any one indifferent:" he means in the singular and actual existence; in the general there may. Recreation is, of itself and in its own nature, indifferent; but drawn into existence and exercise, put in practice, and putting on circumstances, it will ever become unto thee either sinful or sanctified. If rectified by such rules as I have formerly delivered for that purpose, it may prove comfortable; but stained with profane company, a sensual end, immoderate delight, no necessity in respect of weariedness of body, or tiredness of mind, vain expense of precious time due to holy duties or discharge of our calling, it may prove cursed. It is so also in the present point of visitations.

(2.) Although the apostle in these words, "And ye be disposed to go," 1 Cor. x. 27, seems to intimate that it is not utterly and absolutely unlawful upon any occasion for a christian, especially if invited, to visit an irreligious man, yet let none who desires to preserve peace at home in his own bosom, presume hereupon to plunge himself hand over head into any unwarrantable engagements and correspondences with worldly men, or build hence a licentious conceit of any allowance to communicate himself promiscuously with familiarity or content, either by way of invitation or visitation, to all comers, all company. It is a foul sign of a false heart, and of a professor that at length will certainly fall away, to expect, entertain, and enjoy with equal portion and delight the world's favourites and God's friends ; to be as open-hearted, open-handed, and open-housed to a wicked man as to a gracious man. Every true-hearted Nathanael, rightly informed and well advised, cannot fail to apprehend, acknowledge, and feel a vast and unprofitable difference between the sweet heavenly communion and confident communication of heart-secrets with faithful fruitful christians, and the irksome intrusions, vexing vain-glorious tediousness, and frothy conferences of carnal men. If any of God's children, therefore, at any time be disposed to take any allowance and encouragement from this place, to invite or visit known enemies to the purity of religion or power of godliness, let him cast his eye also upon those cases and cautions which may make it comfortable. They are such as these : 1. Their salvation. 2. Thine own safety.

[1.] For the first, be sure to propose unto thyself their spiritual good as thine only aim, or at least principal end : and in the sincerity and singleness of thine heart to seek indeed the salvation of their souls. We have Christ Jesus himself a precedent in this case, Matt. ix. 10—12. He suffered with patience publicans and sinners to press into his company, and did eat and drink with them upon purpose to heal their souls, and help them out of hell. But his pure and sacred soul was endowed with an infinite impossibility of receiving any touch or taint from those wicked ones with whom he conversed; whereas, worms and sinners that we are, if we watch not extraordinarily, and stand stoutly upon our guard, we are far likelier to be perverted by them, than they converted by us: and, therefore, at such times it concerns us much to recollect and quicken up all the powers of our souls and spiritual forces, with special address and resolution to preserve and vindicate all we can the honour, truth, and servants of God from all stain, disparagement, and unworthy censure. Let us labour and look to bring as much wisdom and courage to confront and countermine, as the devil's proctors do cunning and malice to undermine and affront the kingdom of Christ Jesus, and glory of christianity. It is lawful and laudable for the physicians of the body to visit sometimes such patients as are infected with contagious diseases to cure and recover them, so that, according to the rules of their art, they arm themselves with preservatives and counterpoisons to prevent and repel the noisomeness of the air and noxious vapours: so it may not prove unseasonable for spiritual physicians to be drawn sometimes, out of a desire of doing good, into the company of those who are wofully overrun with the leprosy of sin, and have, as it were, the plague-sore of scandalous life running upon them, so that they be fore-armed with prayer, premeditation, and watchfulness, to purify and preserve their own souls from spiritual infection.

[2.] In case of thine own safety; but so that in so doing thy sincere heart be not conscious unto itself of slavish distrust, false fears, prejudice of God's providence, or reliance upon the arm of flesh, but that it apprehend and approve upon good ground, and out of a holy wisdom, the present occasion, whether of invitation or visitation, as a comfortable means offered by God's good hand to mitigate the malice and mollify the hearts of those who might do thee a mischief. It was the saying of a wise man, that he would rather have a dog to fawn upon him than bark at him, and bark at him rather than bite him. Whereby he intimated thus much, as I conceive, that God's children should not, out of an austere, sour, unwarrantable retiredness, exasperate and enrage unnecessarily the too much already alienated affections of the contrary-minded; but so far as they may, without wound of conscience, stain of their character, or imputation of spiritual cowardliness, observe them with such common offices of humanity, which may disarm them and keep them, if not hearty friends, yet at least (which in these corrupt and angry times we hold a degree of happiness) moderate, and win their enemies. Isaac may be an instance in this second case, who, for a more confident securing of himself and comfortable settling of his peace, invited Abimelech and his followers to a feast, Gen. xxvi. 30. To the same purpose Jacob sent a present to Esau, Gen. xxxii. 20, and promised to visit him at Seir, Gen. xxxiii. 14. But at such times and in such company thou hadst need put on a great deal of courage and patience, wisdom and watchfulness, and warily decline two obvious errors and dangerous extremes, furious zeal and faint-hearted silence; of which see before, pages 135, 136.

(3.) Do not so stain thy worth and worthy hopes; discover not such extreme weakness and true baseness of mind; resemble not so near the fearful folly of obnoxious and vain-glorious worldlings, as to suffer the eye and excellency of thine heavenly spirit to be any whit dazzled or dulled with formal affected glistening of outward glory, as to hunt with fawning terror after the transitory favour of worldly greatness, to adore the worthless great and the world's minions with undeserved flattering attributions, and, with ambitious affectation, to contend for their countenance and uncomfortable correspondence with them. The greatest man, without virtue and grace, though ever so gloriously enriched with human felicities, is but as a dead carcass hung over with jewels—a very spectacle of commiseration to every spiritual eye; even as that body is, which adorned with goodly features and many other admirable beauties, yet wanteth eyesight, the comfort of life, whereby it walks in perpetual darkness and desperate danger. Goodness, though attended with contempt and disgrace, is incomparably more amiable in the eye of an honest Cato, much more in a holy christian, than all the vainglorious boisterous representations of any greatness or pomp. Memorable and remarkable to this purpose was the magnanimity and resolution of that holy prophet, "As the Lord of hosts liveth, before whom I stand, surely, were it not that I regard the presence of Jehoshaphat the king of Judah, I would not look toward thee nor see thee," 2 Kings iii. 14.

Miserable, then, is the vanity and vain-glorious slavery of such as with great eagerness and impotency hunt so ambitiously after high dependencies, and hold it a strange happiness to insinuate themselves into the bosom of the world's favourites, though it be by baseness, bribery, a universal obsequiousness, and vile accommodations. They, many times, with vaunting intimation also to others, proudly applaud and please themselves for their access, countenance, and entertainment with great men, as though it argued in them some rare extraordinary sufficiency and worth, whereas, perhaps, it is their own flattering insinuations and intrusions, their instrumental agency and employment in some ill offices, lewd services, which brings them into such request and acceptation. But let such know, it is a thousand times more comfort and true credit to be received with christian love and arms of grace into the heart and affections of a godly man, than to be entertained with greatest glory and worldly applause into grace and favour with the greatest graceless one upon earth. For, alas! when a man hath done all he can to please the humours of ungodly great ones, by an unconscionable satisfying of their carnal desires, and, to gratify them, hath unhappily grieved his own conscience, he can at last, when God's dreadful visitation and flaming vengeance shall seize upon him for that sin, look for no better reward and reply than that cold comfort and cutting answer which Judas, in the extremity of his anguish and horror, received from the high priests and elders. That cursed man came unto them out of the rage of his vexed conscience, ready to tear his traitorous heart out of his body with his own hands, and threw the thirty pieces of silver amongst them, and cried out, " I have sinned, in that I have betrayed the innocent blood." But what recompense do they return for his employment in villany to serve their turn? Their reply is, "What is that to us? see thou to that," Matt. xxvii. 4. And such a man shall certainly, in the day of distress, be enforced to take up some rueful complaint, proportionable to Wolsey's heavy groan, " Had I been as careful to serve the God of heaven as my great master on earth, he had never left me in my grey hairs." And we see, in the meantime, favour is deceitful and transitory even in private men, much more in great personages; the volubility of whose nature is soon glutted, and very variable for kinds of satisfaction. A thousand experiences in all histories and times teach us how irregular, and many times retrograde, the revolutions of highest favours run. They have their paroxysms and declinations, and ever at length their most certain expiration and everlasting period.

But, on the other side, consciousness of having held an unfeigned fruitful correspondence and communion with God's people, the only excellent ones, by all nearest and dearest engagements and obligations of a profitable and comfortable fellowship in the gospel, and mutual intercourse of godly conference, heavenly counsel, spiritual encouragements, consideration one of another, confirmation in grace, and well-grounded hopes of meeting together in heaven, will incomparably more refresh the trembling heart of a dying man, than if he had been crowned all his life long with the imperial glory of all earthly kingdoms. And, in the meantime, there is nothing in this world to be admired but the illustrious splendour of heavenly graces, shed and shining from God's merciful throne by his sanctifying Spirit into the souls of the saints. Neither anything so to be desired, no such prerogative and paradise in this vale of tears, as a mutual communicating of their divine brightness, and the sweet joy issuing from thence, a very glimpse and earnest of everlasting glory to the humble hearts one of another.

(4.) When thou visitest others, or thyself invitest them, take notice ever beforehand, with as punctual and special survey as thou possibly canst, of their humours, dispositions, opinions, and behaviour, and thereupon premeditate and prepare convenient and seasonable matter, whereby thou mayest more successfully address and apply thyself, with all meekness of wisdom and patient discretion, to insinuate, interpose, argue, answer, reprove, reply, and so demean thyself in thy whole discourse, that through thy default neither the glory of God, the honour of his truth, the reputation of christianity, nor thine own conscience, receive any indignity, disgrace, diminution, or wound. Would christians take this counsel, hold this course, they would, at such times, not so often depart with spiritual discontent, and so smitten with consciousness afterward of their silence, omissions, cowardliness, and unprofitableness in company. For want of care and conscience in this point, country people meet many times in their assemblies of good-fellowship, at ale-houses, bakehouses, gossippings as they call them, &c., as at a common mart of tale-telling, backbiting, disgracing their neighbours, raging against professors, saucily and unseasonably meddling with and falsely censuring other men's matters; yea, and sometimes reviling the christian ministry, especially is managed with manifestation of the Spirit, and a holy impatience to see the devil domineer and revel in the blood of the people's souls without contradiction. When they come together at such times, every one opens his pack of tales; for a tale-bearer is compared to a pedlar, as the word in the original clearly intimates,* who, having furnished himself, and filled his pack with a variety of peddling and petty stuffs, trots up and down for vent from house to house, where he finds best custom and special entertainment; I say, at such meetings it is their manner to open every one his pack of false and slanderous tales, which they have raked and scraped together by their own malicious surmises, listenings, whisperings, pragmatical inquisitiveness into other men's businesses, or some odd idle intelligencers, whom they entertain for that purpose; and there, out of a restless humour of talkativeness and tattling, they lay abroad such rotten wares to the impoisoning of the ears of those that hear them, the defaming of their brethren far better than themselves, and certain demonstration to their own consciences that they are as yet the children of the devil, that father of lies and slanders, and have of him already learned the very language of hell. Were such meetings mingled and seasoned with gracious talk, (and all our talk ought "to be always with grace," Col. iv. 6,) with holy conferences, and helping one another towards heaven; with planting and preserving christian love and kind affections one towards another, it were a happy thing: but, while there is nothing but ribald and rotten communications, sowing many times much seed of

* לא תלך רכיל "Thou shalt not go up and down as a tale-bearer," Lev. xix. 16. Of רכל mercari, see Pagnin.

bitterness and heart-burning against their brethren in the ears of one another, and a cursed sacrifice, as it were, of spiteful and slanderous tongues offered up unto Satan, such miserable meetings are fitter for pagans, than professors of religion; for the consistory of hell, than for the communion of saints. Neither are higher places and great feasts free from such froth and transcendent villanies of the tongue; because there the most hold it a point of preciseness to make conscience of their conference, and say to themselves, "Our lips are our own, who is Lord over us?" Psa. xii. 4. They labour more to furnish themselves beforehand with complimental phrases, forms of flattery, flourishes of wit, variety of jests, and other vain-glorious ostentations of courtly ornaments, than with any one word of the Scriptures, the world to come, or the way to heaven. They, I say, therefore, too often unworthily dishonour such meetings with much ignoble deportment in their discourse. Besides other deformities and indignities, how seldom shall we find great tables and solemn feasts without that cursed music, mentioned Lam. iii. 63? But oh, how infinitely unworthy is it for a man of honour and worth to suffer with patience a roguish fiddler, scurrilous jester, or stigmatical son of Belial, to fall foul upon those men, the truest nobles, upon earth! Of whom, and the time is at hand, even the proudest of them all, repenting and groaning for anguish of spirit, will say, nay, with hideous yellings will roar out, "These were those whom we had sometimes in derision and a proverb of reproach. We fools accounted their life madness, and their end to be without honour; but how are they now numbered amongst the children of God, and their lot is among the saints? Therefore have we erred from the way of truth. Where now is the bravery and pomp of our high places? the earthly paradise of our dearest pleasures? the rose-buds with which we crowned ourselves in the spring of youth? They are all withered, vanished, and come to nothing; they are passed away like a shadow, as the remembrance of a guest that tarrieth but a day, nay, as a post that hasted by."

III. NATURAL ACTIONS.

Concerning natural actions, as meat, drink, sleep, &c., I shall not say much. For were it not that through the course of nature we wofully besot even common sense, and infatuate our reason with sensuality and wilful blindness, every man might be a rule unto himself for temperance and moderation this way. Hence that proverb hath its probability, "Every man is either a fool or a physician." Either he hath learned by manifold experience and observation of the state, exigency, and ability of his own body, what seasons and proportions of such natural helps may be fittest for his temperament and constitution; or else he is most unworthy of that noble thing, an understanding soul, which he bears in his bosom.

1. For the first, gluttony, and fulness of bread, which, as the schoolmen say out of Gregory, consists in these five points, 1. In an over burdening of nature with new matter and more meat, before the perfection and period of concoction have raised a kindly appetite. 2. In a curious hunting after costliness, variety, and daintiness of fare. 3. In a luxurious affectation of too much art, and

exactness in dressing and preparing it. 4. In excess and immoderation in respect of the quantity. 5. In a sensual fury of the appetite after good cheer. I say, this unmanly monster and tyrant of the belly, as Chrysostom calls it, doth at this day reign as generally, and cry as loud, as any sin I can upon the sudden remember. And yet there are many foul and scarlet abominations, contempt of godliness, unworthy coming to the sacrament, usury, idleness, many hateful baits and enticements to lust, monstrous fashions, &c., which are not taken to heart in any proportion to their execrableness; against which pulpits are too silent, and the times digest without any great remorse and reclamation.

We lift up our voices loud against drunkenness, and it is high time; for it grows towards a high tide, and threatens, without timely and resolute opposition, a lamentable inundation to the whole kingdom. Whereas his foul fellow fiend, gluttonous revelling, eats up God's creatures with abominable excess, far more unobservedly and uncensured, and yet it is a work of darkness, and damns as well as drunkenness, Gal. v. 21; nay, and that more dangerously, because more insensibly. To preserve thee fair and free, not only from wallowing in this beastly sin, which is proper to belials, but even from any touch and all appearance of it, take notice,— nay, to fire the most ravenous sensualist out of this swinish filth, let him also consider:—

(1.) That even that sinful superfluity by which he slayeth his own body, "For by surfeiting," saith the wise man, "have many perished," might very comfortably revive the hungry faintings, and sustain the languishing life of many made of the same mould, and far better than himself. So that upon the matter there is, as it were, a double murder. How then are such good creatures of God sanctified by the word and prayer, 1 Tim. iv. 5, to such luxurious fratricides, unmercifully mindless of Joseph's afflictions? or how do they eat to the glory of God? 1 Cor. x. 31.

(2.) Whereas thou mightest enjoy an active, able, healthful, and lightsome body, which is a happiness to be prized above gold, riches, and infinite wealth, by thine intemperance this way thou fillest it with crudities, obstructions, and many woful distempers. "The pains of watching, and choler, and pangs of the belly, are with an insatiable man," saith the wise man. The stomach surcharged above the sphere of its activity, (as they say,) and power of natural heat, by immoderate cramming or heaping upon it more meat before the former be concocted, like a fire, laden with green wood beginning to burn, engenders many smoky clouds, as it were, of raw superfluous fumes, which, ascending into the brain, are the source of various sicknesses, distempers, and diseases. As, therefore, thou wouldest not with a dram of swinish pleasures purchase a pound of exquisite pain, always rise from the table with an appetite.

(3.) Continuance of life is a precious indulgence from God, and to be highly prized, both of the unregenerate, that he may yet repent and seek peace with God before the pit of destruction hath shut her mouth irrecoverably upon him; and also of the christian, that he may do more nobly yet, make his election sure, with fuller conquest trample upon his bosom lust and body of death, grow into a nearer fellowship and communion with his God, and look back upon as much time as he can possibly get sincerely spent in his service, before he look his Captain, Christ Jesus, in the face, who hath so dearly bought him, and will so gloriously crown him. Now, this foul excess and fulness of feeding robs us of this jewel before our time, and shorteneth yet more our already short span of living in the world. "He that dieteth himself, prolongeth his life," saith the wise man; therefore it follows, by a consequence of contrariety, "he that is greedy upon meats, puts a knife unto his throat." Whereupon, saith one, many, by overmuch eating, and continual feasts, stifle nature, and choke up themselves; which, had they fed coarsely, or like galley slaves been tied to an oar, might have happily prolonged many fair years.

As therefore thou wouldest not drown and dull the powers of thy soul in the sottishness of such dunghill excess, but have them at command for the ready exercise and improvement of their best abilities in time of need, and for a comfortable discharge of both thy callings, eat moderately. "Sound sleep cometh of moderate eating," saith the wise man, "he riseth early, and his wits are with him;" he is able, active, and strong for any undertaking. For as the soul ought not, with carking thoughtfulness, false fears, unnecessary dejection, to afflict and waste the body, so neither ought the body, by any sensual indulgence and intemperance, to weaken the soul; but both body and soul should serve one another in sobriety and moderation, that the whole man may be more sufficiently and cheerfully serviceable to Him that created both body and soul for that purpose.

The very heathen, by the light of reason, did

abominate with much moral indignation the superfluous vanities and curiosities of this swinish sin. "A bull," saith Seneca, "will be filled with a pasture of a few acres; one forest will suffice many elephants: but scarce the air with all her fowl, the sea with all her fish, the earth with all her roots and riches, will satisfy the insatiable appetite of a gluttonous epicure. And therefore," saith he, "we may well rank and reckon men given to the belly amongst brute beasts, not reasonable creatures; nay, some of them not so much as amongst living creatures, but rather loathsome dead carrion."

2. Now in a second place, concerning excess in drink, it is not possible that any who hath given his name to the purity and power of godliness would plunge himself into the hateful and abhorred dungeon of drunkenness, which Augustine compares to the pit of hell.

3. Now in the third place, concerning sleep, I have little to say; no constant rules of and certain measure can possibly be prescribed; because it is much diversified, and necessarily receives great variation by health and sickness, by age, by time of the year, by emptiness or fulness of the body, by variety of natural constitutions; only let me counsel christians, who only make conscience of expense of time, and are sensible of its preciousness expressed before, to take notice, that they may surfeit and sin in sleeping, as well as in eating and drinking. That it ought only, as other of God's good creatures, to serve the strengthening and refreshing of our bodies, not to satisfy ease, sloth, and a sluggish humour; and therefore to beware, and diligently to watch, lest that great devourer and waster of time rob and

bereave them of the very marrow of time, the flower and firstfruits, as it were, of the day; I mean many precious and golden hours in the morning, freshest, and fittest to converse most fruitfully with God, to examine our spiritual state, to offer up an acceptable sacrifice of prayers and praises, to buckle fast unto us the christian armour, and to prepare with resolution and life to hold a sweet and blessed communion with his holy Majesty all the day after. And let them often remember, when they see the sun up before them, that saying of Austin, "It is an uncomely thing for a christian to have a sunbeam find him in bed; and if the sun could speak, it might say, I have laboured more than thou, yesterday, and yet I am risen, and thou art still at rest."

For conclusion, let me advise and forewarn, with as great earnestness and heartiness as I possibly can, all God's children, that as they infinitely value and prefer a pure heart, a heavenly mind, that invaluable jewel of a peaceable conscience, and that sweetest life of walking with their God, before a world of gold, that they would watch over themselves very extraordinarily, and with singular care and heedfulness, in the use and enjoyment of things lawful in their own nature, yet by our corruption capable of inordinateness and excess, such as are meat, drink, sleep, apparel, visitations, recreations, "for more," saith a worthy divine, "perish with preposterous following of lawful things, than by unlawful courses." Soft sands swallow more ships than hard rocks split asunder. However, sure I am, christians are in more danger of being spiritually undone by a sly insinuation and ensnarement of licentiousness and immoderation in such lawful things, than by the gross assault of foul sins and temptations to do notoriously. For,

(1.) A sanctified heart will generously rise, and resist with resolution against the invasion and power of any work of darkness, which by its enormity wastes the conscience,—as adultery, murder, swearing, profaning of the Lord's day, usury, bribery, speculative wantonness, and idleness, which it may too often be insensibly seized upon, and surprised by an excessive sinful delight, in things unsinful in themselves, yet empoisoned unto us by the venom of our own over-eager, unmortified affections, and that without any great remorse or reclamation.

(2.) We often find too, by woful experience, that some, who having given their names to religion at first with great forwardness and heat, yet afterward are not so much foiled by gross relapse into notorious sins, as by surfeiting with licentious excess in the abuse of lawful things, and drinking too deep of worldly pleasures, under a colour of christian liberty and convenient recreations, if they fall not quite away, yet fall fearfully into a dead sleep of carnal security and cursed forgetfulness of God, at least for a time, until they be revived and quickened by the inquisitive hand of some piercing ministry, the smart of some outward heavy cross, or wrath of God upon their consciences.

(3.) Things not sinful in their right use, and offering themselves with unsuspected representation of harmlessness and allowance, without extraordinary watchfulness and heed, do more easily lime our earthly ravenous affections, far sooner ensnare and deceive, insensibly draw and drown us in many scandalous excesses and estrangements from God, before we are aware.

IV. CIVIL AFFAIRS.

Now concerning civil affairs and dealings in the world, that thou mayest settle and keep thine heart and hands in a holy temper, and untainted, without wound, wrong-doing, or any uncomfortable entanglement:

1. Ever, in all thy bargains, contracts, covenants, dealings, negotiations, mutual intercourse of any kind of commerce with others, represent seriously and solemnly to the eye of thy best judgment and deepest consideration that royal principle, "Do as thou wouldest be done by." With real fellow-feeling put thyself into the place, and impartially put on the person of the party with whom thou art to deal. Weigh well all the circumstances, conditions, covenants, inconveniences, consequents, and passages of the whole business, and then, returning to thyself, deal out and proportion unto him that measure, in every particular, which thou wouldest be willing, upon good ground and sound reason, to receive at the hands of another, if thou wert in his case. This is the sum of the law and the prophets, for serving our brethren in love, pressed upon us by the Lord Jesus himself; "All things whatsoever ye would that men should do to you, do ye even so to them," Matt. vii. 12. Which, if it were as effectually and feelingly taken to heart and practised, as it is ordinarily talked of and pretended, it would not only cut off and prevent all cruelties, oppressions, grinding the faces of the poor, all cozening, undermining, over-reaching, defrauding, and

defaming, but also stir up and quicken our affections with a compassionate lively touch, to a mutual exercise and exchange of all offices of humanity, kindness, and love of all kinds.

But that you may understand this rule aright, conceive that, when we counsel men to do unto others as they would be dealt with themselves, it is not to be understood of any irregular, passionate, exorbitant will, but that which is grounded upon right reason, guided by a rectified conscience, ordered and enlightened by grace and God's truth.

And I the rather refresh your memories with the true apprehension of this point, that you may clearly see the rottenness and vanity of the usurer's cunning cavil, but of cruel consequence.

Objection.—I deal, saith the usurer, as I would be dealt with, and do as I would be done by, and therefore all that while I hope I do no wrong; I would willingly pay ten in the hundred if I had need, and then why may I not take so? To which I answer:

(1.) That royal rule, Do as thou wouldest be done by, must be understood and expounded, as I intimated before, according to the grounds of a good conscience, dictates of right reason, and directions of a just and rectified will, not out of the mists and miseries of a depraved and exorbitant judgment. Otherwise, Abimelech, Saul, and others of that desperate rank and resolution, might conclude that it were lawful for them to kill other men, because they were willing to be killed themselves. See Judges ix. 54; 1 Sam. xxxi. 4; for they might say, they did but as they would be done by. It would also very absurdly follow, the magistrate being in the malefactor's case would gladly be pardoned, therefore he must pardon the malefactor. These, and the like abominable and absurd consequences, demonstrate the vanity of the usurer's inference, and that Christ's rule is not so general, but restrainable to that will, which is orderly and honestly guided by the light of nature and God's law.

(2.) We must then have recourse to this general fountain of the second table, and fetch light and direction thence, when we have no express and special word in God's book; but the Scriptures have clearly and directly determined and resolved the point of usury.

(3.) If the usurer were in the borrower's case, he would not willingly, as he pretends, give ten in the hundred. I mean, with an absolute and free will, but of force and constraint, because without paying at that rate he could not have it. If a man would borrow upon usury, to buy land, engross, forestal, or compass some unlawful matter, that were a corrupt will, and no rule; but if his desire so to borrow were just and lawful, as in some cases it may be, then it is no entire will, but mixed and forced by some necessity for the avoiding of a greater evil, and therefore denied in the eye both of law and reason to be any will at all. He that would borrow should have need to borrow, for a needless desire is unlawful; and an ingenuous man who hath need to borrow, would not willingly borrow but for need, much less would he pay usury. Therefore, the will of the borrower in this case is either corrupt, or no will at all, and so consequently without the compass of Christ's rule.

The will of the borrower in this case is like the will of an honest traveller, in giving his purse to an arrant thief, for fear he should lose both purse and life. Is such a man willing, think you, to lose his money? Or like the will of a man whose house being on fire, plucks down part thereof to save the rest,—willingly indeed, as the case stands with him, yet not simply, but upon necessity. So the borrower's will is not free, but forced, and so a will against will.

2. With an infinite disdain and resolute contempt abhor to get so much as one farthing all the days of thy life, by any wicked means or wrong doing. Do not plague thy present outward state, be it little or much, neither empoison it to thy posterity by any addition unto it by usury, bribery, simony, sacrilege, stealing, grinding the faces of the poor, oppression, lying, falsehoods, forswearings, overreaching tricks of wit, cozening, cunning conveyances, &c.

Thereby thou shalt desperately fall into the revenging hands of an angry God; Divine vengeance will pursue thee hard, and continually at the heels, for thy destruction; which is incomparably a greater plague than extremest beggary, and the bitterest confluence of all the most vexing outward miseries in the world. "Let no man," saith Paul, "go beyond and defraud his brother in any matter: because that the Lord is the avenger of all such," 1 Thess. iv. 6.

Again: a little ill got, naturally accompanied with God's curse, may so empoison thy whole inheritance, and all the rest of thy goods, that it may prove like a dead fly in a box of precious ointment, a spark of fire in the thatch; a strong incentive to Divine justice, not only to eat up all honest comfort in outward things, but also to consume and waste all thy wealth: nay, and since immoderate desire of enriching and raising his posterity is the keenest spur to a man's unconscionable hoarding, even to cut off also many times the cruel worldling himself, and cast him out of the world without stock or seed. And therefore, though the covetous wretch, out of the hardness of his heart, and searedness of conscience, be fearless and senseless of the wrath of God, the wrong of his neighbour, and the wretchedness of his own soul; yet if he desire, as he doth, with a raging unsatiableness, like the grave or hell, to thrive in his outward state and prosper in the world, let him not meddle so much as with a stick, or a straw, or a pin of another man's; neither at any time put his hand to any wicked way of getting, lest, beside the loss of his soul at last, and a world of miseries in the mean time, he miss the very mark so eagerly aimed at, of making him and his great in the world, For hope of which he is cursedly content to part with all true contentment in this life, and a crown of bliss in the kingdom of heaven.

For this purpose, and to persuade and press this point unanswerably, let us take a view in God's book of the divers ways how he is wont in wrath to deal with wrong doers and unconscionable dealers.

It comes to pass sometimes, that the wicked worldling, insatiable earth-worm, God cursing his covetousness and cruelty, may see an end of his wealth even in this world, according to that text, "As the partridge sitteth on eggs, and hatcheth them not: so he that getteth riches, and not by right, shall leave them in the midst of his days, and at his end shall be a fool," Jer. xvii. 11; "He hath swallowed down riches, and he shall vomit them up again; God shall cast them out of his belly. The increase of his house shall depart and his goods shall flow away in the day of his wrath," Job xx. 15, 28.

Or it is no strange thing to see him prosper by unconscionableness and craft, usurious and other injurious practices, all his life long, but then having scraped together his hoard of iniquity with a great deal of carking thoughtfulness, and self vexation; kept it with extreme fear, slavish distrust, and heart-gnawing jealousies; parted from it with much anguish, horror, and almost with as painful divorce as that of the soul from the body,—at last, after the loss of it, with his soul and all,—1. He either leaves it to those who will liberally let fly abroad, and enlarge those golden heaps which greediness had formerly confined and strongly guarded with bolts and bars, according to that text, "He that by usury and unjust gain increaseth his substance, he shall gather it for him that will pity the poor," Prov. xxviii. 8. See also Prov. xiii. 22; Job xxvii. 16, 17. 2. Or it may be wholly scattered amongst mere strangers, according to that text, "A stranger eateth it," Eccles. vi. 2. See also Psa. xxxix. 6; Eccles. iv. 8, and ii. 18, 19. 3. Or being bequeathed to his own children, and blasted by God's secret curse, it may melt away in their hands, as snow before the sun, according to that text, "There is a sore evil which I have seen under the sun, namely, riches kept for the owners thereof to their hurt. But those riches perish by evil travail; and he begetteth a son, and there is nothing in his hand," Eccles. v. 13, 14.

But, however, whether ill-gotten goods perish or prosper in the owner's hands, or his posterity, sure I am, the inevitable plague and just vengeance of God cleaves inseparably unto his soul, and hunts that man to destruction whosoever he be, that enricheth himself by wicked and wrongful means, without timely repentance, and true restitution, if he be able.

"He that hath oppressed the poor and needy, hath spoiled by violence, hath given upon usury, and hath taken increase," and the same reason is also of all indirect and unlawful getting, "shall he then live? He shall not live: he hath done all these abominations; he shall surely die; his blood shall be upon him." Ezek. xviii. 12, 13.

And marvel not, neither be misled, though thou observe sometimes wicked worldlings themselves, their heirs, and heirs' heirs, to wallow also in that wealth which their grandfathers got wrongfully. For they are for all this but as so many sensual earth-rooting hogs, fatted for the knife, Psa. xci. 7; and have this woeful brand set upon them by the Spirit of God, they are "men of the world, which have their portion in this life," Psa. xvii. 14. But ever hold this as a terrible and true principle,—it is one of the greatest curses under the sun, to prosper in our ways, and be out of the way to heaven.

Further: it is a ruled case, and concurrent resolution amongst divines, that if thou dost not restore, being able, whatsoever thou hast any ways got wrongfully and wickedly, thou canst have neither well-grounded assurance of unfeigned repentance, nor true comfort of the pardon of that sin. A cutting conclusion against all usurers, simonists, sacrilegians, bribe takers, grinders of poor men's faces, hoarders by fraud, oppressors of all under them of the same trade by some machiavellian trick, and the rest of that cruel crew.

How can he be said to repent soundly, who lies

still soaking in his sin, wittingly and willingly? Now, whoever keeps still in his hands anything wickedly got, continues a wrong-doer still, and therefore doth it not faithfully, but only feigneth repentance. Whereupon, saith Austin, "If a man restore not ill-gotten goods, being able, his repentance is not comfortable, but counterfeit." Dreadful also is the doom of the said father upon all wrong-doers, "The sin is not remitted, except that which hath been unjustly taken be restored; either in act, if thou be able, or at least in unfeigned affection, if thy state be wasted."

What a mad folly is it then, and cursed cruelty to thine own soul, to heap up those riches of iniquity by baseness and wrong, which thou must afterward restore in the sense I have said, or else never enjoy any comfortable assurance of a true conversion or pardon of sin! Were he not a foolish thief that would keep his stolen goods both in the face of his accuser and judge? Though in the mean time thou conceal thy cunning conveyances from the discovery and doom of human justice, yet assure thyself, besides the secret grumbling of thy self-accusing conscience, the angry eye of God also sees clearly and will shortly most certainly revenge.

Once more: alms-deeds, charitable erections of colleges, hospitals, free schools, and other inferior bountiful contributions, when God enables by good means, when the necessities of his poor cry for relief, and the sanctified heart with affectionate sincerity aims at God's glory, are sweet-smelling sacrifices with which God is well-pleased, Phil. iv. 18; Heb. xiii. 16. But if his slavish gifts and good deeds, largesses, and liberalities in this kind, be empoisoned with former fraud, oppression and wrong, though the poor be better thereby, yet to the impenitent and not restoring usurer himself, or any other wicked dealer, in respect of acceptation with God, and true comfort to his own heart, they are no better than the cutting off of a dog's neck, or the sacrifice of a fool. Ill-gotten goods are for restitution, not for distribution. Lest any covetous caviller think the point too harsh and precise, hear what the ancient fathers say to this purpose. Bernard: "God receiveth not any alms at the hands of an oppressor or usurer." Jerome: "Significantly saith the prophet, 'his own bread,' lest men should turn bread gotten by oppression and usury into a work of mercy." Augustine: "When God shall begin to judge, those that now live by fraud, and give alms of the spoils of the oppressed, will say, Lord, we have kept thy commandments, and in thy name we have done works of mercy; we have fed the hungry, we have clothed the naked, and entertained strangers. To whom God will reply, You tell me what you have given, but you tell me not what you have taken away. You recount whom you have fed, but why remember you not whom you have undone? They rejoice whom you have clothed; but they lament whom you have spoiled. A man is filled with bread whom thou feedest with spoil, but the Lord will bless not thee, but him whom thou hast undone. Chrysostom: "But what is the excuse of many? I have indeed been an usurer, say they, but I have also been good to the poor. A sweet piece of matter, sure! But God accepts not such sacrifices. It were far better to give nothing to the poor at all, than give in that manner. That wealth which is won by thy just labours is many times quite marred with such wicked mixtures."

Even Pliny, a heathen, tells us, "That the poor are not to be fed like the whelps of wild beasts, with blood and murder, rapine and spoil, but that which is most acceptable to the receivers; they should know that that which is given unto them is not taken from any body else."

Nay, one of the bloodiest men that ever breathed, Selymus, a Turkish emperor, upon his bed of death replied thus to an attendant, moving him with the wealth taken from the Persian merchants to build an hospital for relief of the poor, "Wouldest thou, Pyrrhus, that I should bestow other men's goods, wrongfully taken from them, upon works of charity and devotion for mine own vainglory and praise? Assuredly I will never do it: nay, rather see they be again restored unto the right owners." Which was done forthwith accordingly, to the great shame, saith the author, of many christians; who, minding nothing less than restitution, but making an offering out of robbery, do, out of a world of evil-gotten goods, cull out some small fragments to build some poor hospital. A poor testimony of their hot charity. Wretchedly then do they delude the world, and deceive their own souls, who vainly think that some works of mercy at last, when they must needs leave all, will expiate and recompense the cruelties and unconscionable dealings of their whole life before. Zaccheus' penitent proclamation consisted of two branches, Luke xix. 8, as well for restitution, as distribution. He that would find the same mercy, must follow the same method.

3. Let thy desire and delight never fall, or be fastened immoderately upon any earthly thing, though ever so excellent, delicious, or amiable. For

exorbitancy and error this way brings many times, 1. A loss of the thing so doted upon. 2. Sometimes a cross. 3. Ever a curse.

(1.) For the first; our righteous and holy God, when he sees the current of his creatures' affections carried inordinately and preposterously from the fountain of living waters unto broken cisterns that can hold none,—from the bottomless treasury of all sweetest beauties, dearest excellences, amiable delights, unto painted shadows,—from the rock of eternity, unto a staff of reed,—I mean, from the Creator unto the creature, he wisely and seasonably, in the equity of his justice, and out of the jealousy of his own glory, takes away that earthly idol, that, the occasion of such irregular affection removed, he may draw the heart, in which he principally takes pleasure, to his own glorious self, the only loadstone of all sanctified love, and boundless ocean of happiness and bliss. Nay, it may be said, in the sweetness of his mercy also, when he sees us distracted, and as it were desperately mad with making too much of any transitory thing, so that our mind doth still run and rest upon it as our only heaven upon earth, he snatches the edge-tool out of our hands, lest we make away with ourselves spiritually, and withdraws the beloved vanity from before our eyes, lest we grow stark blind in the mysteries of faith and matters of heaven, by too much gazing upon the fading beauty of any baser earthly object.

Thus the immoderate partial affection of parents may become many times occasional and accessary to the untimely taking away of a sweet, fair, and towardly child. Whereby our gracious God justly intimates unto them their intolerable unthankfulness of his mercy, and extreme indignity to his majesty, in wickedly preferring in their love a creature before their Creator; and mercifully teaches them that the flower and fervour of their best and dearest affection is only due, and should be wholly devoted, to the greatest good, God himself, and those truest, unutterable, ever-during delights prepared for the blessed, in his word here, and in the world to come hereafter, 1 Cor. ii. 6.

Conceive proportionably of other things immeasurably desired and delighted in. If thou dotest upon a good understanding, thou mayest be stricken with distraction; if upon abundance of learning, or much worldly wisdom, thou mayest be infatuated, at least at some special times when thou wouldst gladly do the best, or in some important business which most concerns thee; if upon some high place, thou mayest with Haman, Shebna, and thousands more, be thrown down into the gulf of calamity and woe, contempt and scorn; if upon a fair house, it may be levelled with the ground by the flames of God's wrath; if upon a beautiful face, it may be disfigured with the small-pox, or other deformities; if upon a hoard of gold, it may be dispersed by fire, robbery, desolations of war; nay, even upon thy graces with an overweening conceit of self-excellency, self-opinion, self-sufficiency, if they be only general graces, thou mayest be quite stripped of them; if saving, thou mayest be cast into a damp and desertion for a time, in respect of all comfort, sense, use, and exercise.

(2.) For the second, though God may permit thee still to possess that outward worldly comfort upon which the fury of thine affections is so fastened, and thine heart grasps with such greediness and excess, yet in this case thou mayest justly expect a cross, either.

[1.] In the thing doated upon. With what a deal of cutting discomfort and gashes of bitter grief did Absalom, dandled in David's affections with too much indulgence, rend his father's royal heart, by imbruing his hands in his brother's blood, and with unnatural traitorous violence and villany snatching at the imperial crown upon David's head! Daily experience presents unto our eyes and ears the many woful discomforts, unkind requitals, and unnatural usages which parents receive at the hands of those children whom, in their younger years, they made wanton with their love, and indiscreetly doated upon them.

[2.] Or in some other kind; for example,—if thine heart be set upon riches, God may justly, and mercifully too, exercise and afflict thee with his heavy hand upon thy body with sickness, upon thy conscience with terror, upon thy reputation with disgrace, or the like, thereby to unglue thy noble spirit from the dust, and rend it from grovelling upon the earth. If thou be ambitiously enamoured of honours and high places, after wasting thy wealth, wounding thy conscience, wearying thyself with bribery, baseness, and irksome waiting, thou mayest be taken away untimely in the very pursuit, or presently after the attainment of them. Thus it is not strange or extraordinary with God to prevent, or take off our hearts from taking self-conceited pleasure or pride in anything we enjoy, by crossing and correcting us in other kinds. Even Paul, that blessed saint and servant of the Lord, lest his heart should be too much pleased and puffed up with abundance of revelations, was vexed and crossed with "a thorn in the flesh, the messenger of Satan to buffet him," 2 Cor. xii. 7.

(3.) For the third, however it fare with thee otherwise, if thou settle thine heart upon any earthly thing with inordinate desire and delight, thou shalt be sure to be haunted with a double curse :—The rage of insatiableness, unsatisfiableness; and that greatest plague, hardness of heart.

[1.] The Father of spirits hath inspired into our immortal souls a large capacity, and such an infinite appetite, that no finite excellency, created comfort, or earthly thing can possibly fill. Gold, silver, riches, honours, crowns, kingdoms, are no fit matter or adequate object for such an immaterial and heaven-born spirit to repose and feed upon, with final rest and full contentment. Nay, not this whole material world, were it beautified and set out with all the amiableness, splendour, and allurements which the devil, by his juggling alchemy, put upon it when he presented it to the eye of Christ Jesus, Matt. iv. 8, with the addition of the starry and empyrean heaven, shining with all their admirable beauty and glorious inhabitants, could by any means confine, satisfy, and content the irksome wanderings, unlimited desire, and vast comprehensiveness of the soul; but it would still be transported with the passionate disquietude of self-vexation, and tortured upon the rack of restless discontent, until it fasten and fix upon an object infinite both in excellency and endlessness, wherein is contained the whole latitude of being and goodness, the ever-blessed and only adored Trinity. Where, and when alone, it softly and sweetly, with the height and fulness of all desirable contentment, rests in the arms of God, and bosom of eternal bliss, which all blessed souls attain thus, and by these means:—

When it pleased God, by the merciful violence of his almighty hand, to turn the sensual bent and powerful current of the seduced soul from the creature to the Creator; from the painted bravery of this vain world to the heavenly beauty of his blessed word; from carking encumbrance about many things, to pursue and ply that one needful thing, by a sound and universal change of the whole man, and translation of him from the darkness of natural ignorance, death in sin, and power of the devil, to the light of saving knowledge, the life of sanctifying grace, and the living God: I say, then the restless wanderings of the unsatisfied soul begins first to settle with some sweet contentment upon the flowers of paradise, glimpses of heavenly glory, infallible earnests of everlasting bliss and saving graces; and its infinite appetite is well stayed, in the mean time, with that comfortable intercourse and blissful communion which it enjoys in part with the blessed Trinity, by the word, sacraments, and other his holy ordinances appointed and sanctified for that purpose, until it remove from a house of flesh into the empyrean heaven.

The *understanding* is first filled with final and everlasting contentment by a clear glorious sight of God, which is called beatifical vision; when we shall see him face to face, and know him as we are known, 1 Cor. xiii. 12; "see him as he is," 1 John iii. 2. For as the sun of this world, by his beams and brightness, enlighteneth the eye and the air, that we may see not only all other things, but also his own glorious face: so God, blessed for ever, the sun's Creator, the imperial Sun of the world above, in whose presence the united splendour of ten thousand of our suns would vanish away as a darksome mote and lump of vanity, doth, by the light of his holy Spirit, so irradiate the minds of all the blessed, that they are thereby enlarged and enabled not only to behold eminently in him the beauty, goodness, and excellency of all creatures in a far more admirable and orient manner than in their own beings, but also his own face, essence, wills and counsels, perfections and attributes, incomprehensible greatness and majesty.

The *will* also is then fully and for ever satisfied with a perfect, inward, eternal communion with God himself. Our glorified Saviour, being God and man, by his human nature assumed, uniteth us to God, and by his Divine nature assuming, uniteth God unto us; so that by this secret and sacred communion, we are made in an admirable and blessed manner partakers, and, as it were, possessors of God himself, and communicate with him in all his goodness, perfections, excellences, and happiness. Oh bottomless depth and dearest confluence of all joys, pleasures, sweetnesses, delights, inconceivable, unutterable, infinite! This is the supreme end of our creation and redemption; the very flower, quintessence, and sinew, as it were, of our sovereign good. By this act of blessedness we are filled with all the fulness of God; he becomes unto us all in all: so that thereby we live in his very life, in purity, eternity, sincerest pleasures, highest perfection, though not to the height of his infiniteness, for we are but creatures, yet in proportion to our capacity and utmost possibility, which is a felicity above measure and past imagination. In these two acts thus exercised about an infinite object, God himself, doth blessedness, essentially and formally consist; but principally in the fruition of God, by a full, immediate, and complete communion with him, and most blessed participation of all his glory and all-sufficiency. And therefore, Aquinas and all his followers come short in placing our highest bliss only in the act of the understanding,—the vision of God. I am wont to express and illustrate it thus, though there be an infinite distance and disproportion in the things compared: it would mightily delight a man, really and in person, with ease and safety, to pass over and view the circuit of the whole earth and all the wonders of the world; all the great cities, renowned men, magnificent courts, rich mines, spice islands, vast mountains, &c., of which geographers write, and travellers talk; but if, besides, as he passed along, he should have sure and everlasting possession given of them all, what an immeasurable material addition would it make unto his speculative delight! And with what strange amazement and admiration of his making for ever and marvellous happiness would it fill his heart! Even so proportionably, but above all degrees of comparison; though a boundless ocean of endless sweetness and inexplicable joy arise in the soul from the sight of God, yet this blissful communion, whereby we possess and enjoy him in a near, excellent, unspeakable manner, and partake with him in all his excellences, perfections, and felicities, doth crown, as it were, our crown of glory, and actuate that heart-ravishing contemplation with the very life of everlasting life, and soul of heavenly joys and highest bliss.

Thus, and in this manner, do the restless wanderings and infinite appetite of these aspiring sparks of heaven, our immaterial and immortal spirits, come to final rest and everlasting repose, when at last they shall grasp in the arms of their desire that chiefest good, the most glorious Deity, and bathe themselves freely and fully in that ever during wellspring of immortality and life. But now, set aside the fruition of this object, infinite both in excellency and endlessness, the only aim and end of the soul's endless aspirations, and though thou shouldest crown a man completely with the worth of this whole world, the admirable splendour of the empyrean heaven, the beauty of a shining sun-like body, the rich and royal endowments inherent in a glorified soul, the sweetest company of saints and angels, the comfort of eternity, yet his soul would still be full of emptiness and appetite, and utterly fail to gain the surest sanctuary and supremest solace to settle her unsatisfied longings upon. Only once admit it to the face of God, by beatifical vision, and to fruition of the most glorious and ever-blessed Trinity, by immediate communion, and so consequently to those torrents of pleasures and fulness of joy flowing from thence, and then presently, and never before, its infinite desire expires in the bosom of God, and it lies, as it were, down softly, with sweetest peace and full contentment, in the embracements of everlasting bliss. The other innumerable, inestimable joys in heaven are, I deny not, transcendent and rapturous, but they are all only accessories to this principal, drops to the ocean, glimpses to the sun. Well then, if this be the only way to the soul's eternal welfare, then those unhappy souls, which run a contrary course, and seek for satisfaction in any creature or created comfort, stand deservedly still upon the rack of restless discontentment, and are justly cursed with the gnawing rage of unsatiableness, and must needs be so. For besides, 1. That the furious torrent of our sensual corruption, being once on foot after worldly pleasures, and swelling by a continual infusion of hellish poison, doth, with an impetuous headstrongness, bear and break down all bonds and banks of moderation and stint, and will never be restrained from its insatiable rage, if God help not, until it be swallowed up in the bottomless gulf of misery and horror; for it is the native property, or rather, poison of inordinate affection, not only to drink deep of sinful delights, but to carouse, to be drunk, nay, to add unquenchable thirst unto drunkenness, sucking them in with fresh supply of endless greediness, as the horse-leech sucks corrupt blood till it burst again. 2. That the infinite desire of the soul confined to a creature, or any worldly comfort, is pained and pinched as a foot wedged in a strait shoe, it being no competent and proportionable satisfaction to its expectation and large capacity. Hence it is, that give Rome to Cæsar, as they say, and he will ambitiously pursue the sovereignty of the whole earth. Let Alexander conquer the world, and he will ask for more; let those be subdued, he would climb up the stairs of his vast desires towards the stars; if he could aspire thither, he would peep beyond the heavens. There is no rest unto man's soul but in God's eternal rest. 3. That there being no proportion between spirits and bodies, thou mayest as well undertake to fill a bag with wisdom, a chest with virtue, as thine immortal soul with gold, silver, riches, high places, this whole material world, or any earthly thing: see Eccles. v. 10. 4. I say, besides these three causes of unsatisfiableness, God himself doth justly put that property and poison into all worldly things doated upon and desired immoderately, that they shall plague the heart that pursues them, by filling it still with a furious and fresh supply of more greediness, longings, jealousies, and many miserable discontentments, so that they become unto it as drink unto a drunkard, a man in a dropsy or burning fever, and serve only to inflame it with new heat and fiery additions of insatiable thirst and inordinate lust. No marvel then, that the workings of the heart of every natural man unreconciled to God be like the raging sea that cannot rest. That roaring element, to which the Spirit of God compares a wicked man, must needs be a much troubled and very restive creature, since it is continually tossed and turmoiled with a variety of contrary and confused motions. If thou couldest see the inside of the greatest graceless monopolist and ingrosser of all the most desirable excellences under the sun, glistening in the highest imperial throne upon the earth, thou shouldest behold his heart, for all that, rent asunder with many raging distempers and tempestuous whirlwinds of contrary lusts,—a very hive of unnumbered cares, sorrows, and passions; boiling incessantly with irksome suspicions, false fears, insatiable longings, secret grumblings of conscience, torturing distractions, and tumultations of hell.

By the way, let me tell you, that these immoderate desires and inordinate delights which I speak of, glued to some special sensual object which natural corruption singles out, and makes chiefest choice of to follow and feed upon with greatest contentment and carnal sweetness, become the parents of every man's bosom sin.

If it fall in love with *honours and greatness*, it breeds and brings forth ambition, which is an unquenchable thirst after visible glory, and a gluttonous hunting after high places. As it inhabiteth the highest and haughtiest spirits, and is superlative and transcendent in its object and aspirations, so of all the stormy perturbations which rend and rage in the heart of man, it is most tempestuous and desperate. Venturous it is to climb up any heights of baseness, bribery, blood; to tread upon the ruins of the noblest innocency, upon the merciless desolations of dearest friends and nearest kindred, to domineer for a while, though it be damned everlastingly afterwards, as it is too clear in the Turkish emperors, and in that great master of mischief and machiavelism, Richard III. of this kingdom, who with a bloody hand pressed out the breath of those two orient princes in the Tower, his nephews and natural lords. It is victorious over all other affections, and masters even the sensuality of lustful pleasures, as appears in the greatest warriors and ancient worthies amongst the heathen, who, tempted with the exquisiteness and vanity of choicest beauties, yet forbore that villany, not for conscience' sake and fear of God, whom they knew not, but lest they should interrupt the course and stop the current of their warlike reputation, ambitious designs, and achievements of state. But whatever other pestilential properties empoison it, it never fails to engender in the heart which harbours it, as its proper thunderbolt, blasting, fears, cares, jealousies, envies, enraged thirst of still rising, impatiency of competition, and dissatisfaction. For the proud and ambitious man "enlargeth his desire as hell, and is as death, and cannot be satisfied," Hab. ii. 5. Who an fill the bottomless pit of hell, or stop the unsatiable jaws of death? Neither can the greedy humour of a haughty spirit, the aspiring insolency of a boisterous Nimrod, be possibly stayed or stinted; no, not with the top and variety of highest honours, though he should alone and absolutely be crowned with the sovereignty of the whole earth, and command the felicities of this wide world.

If it fall in love with *riches*, it breeds and brings forth covetousness, the vilest and basest of all the infections of the soul, in the most contemptible and dunghill disposition. For this kite-footed corruption, wheresoever it seizeth and domineers, blasts and banisheth all nobleness of spirit, natural affection, humanity, discretion, reason, wisdom, manliness, mutual entertainments, intercourse of kindness and love, and turns all, even the soul itself, into earth and mud. It draws, by a cunning reserved baseness, all occasions, circumstances, advantages, wit, policy, even friends and acquaintance, nay, religion, conscience, and all to be serviceable and contributory to a greedy wolf and raging gangrene of hoarding up gold and worldly pelf. In a word, it makes a man, with a bedlam cruelty, to contemn himself, body and soul, for a little transitory trash; wilfully to abandon both the comfortable enjoyment of the short time of this present mortality, and all hope of the length of that blessed eternity to come. And as the object of it is most earthly, base, and incompetent, so of all other vile affections it is most sottishly and senselessly insatiable. For how is it possible that earth should feed or fill the immaterial and heaven-born spirit of a man? It cannot be; and the Spirit of God hath said it shall not be: " He that loveth silver shall not be satisfied with silver. His eye is not satisfied with riches," Eccles. v. 10; iv. 8. Hence it is, that the more deeply and more eagerly the dropsy heart of the covetous man doth drink deep of the golden stream, the more furiously still it is inflamed with insatiable thirst; nay, certain it is, that if he could purchase and possess a monopoly of all the wealth in the world, were he able to empty the western parts of gold, and the east of all her spices and precious things, should he inclose the whole face of the earth from one end of heaven to another and heap up his hoard to the stars, yet his heart would be as hungry after more riches as if he had never a penny, and much more.

If it fall in love with *beauty, and the swaggering bravery of good-fellowship,* it begets lust and sensuality, which make their minions mad with bitterness and malice against the very least glimpse of holiness or any religious restraint; enrages them with mutual fury to engulf themselves into the bottomless whirlpool of sensual pleasures, and so empoisons their hearts with a furious unquenchable thirst after them, that they will never leave their hold and haunt, until they either be broken with the hammer of the word, or burst with the horror of despair. You may trace these pestilent properties in the practice of those voluptuous gallants mentioned in the Book of Wisdom, ch. ii. (A book though not of Divine authority, yet profitable for precepts of morality.) In which chapter you may find, as I have ever conceived, a description to the life and most exact character of the good-fellows of our times, who are transported equally with a desperate insatiable humour of ravenous feeding upon the froth and filth of their impure delights, as greedily as the ox sucks in water; and with an implacable enmity against the purity and power of godliness. For the first, hear their cry unto their companions, verse 6, &c., "Come on, therefore, let us enjoy the good things that are present, and let us speedily use the creatures like as in youth. Let us fill ourselves with costly wine and ointments, and let no flower of the spring pass by us. Let us crown ourselves with rose-buds before they be withered. Let none of us go without his part of our voluptuousness; let us leave tokens of our joyfulness in every place; for this is our portion, and our lot is this." For the other: take notice of their boisterous swaggering combination to become goads in the sides, and cruel pricks in the eyes, of God's people. For, proportionably to their impatience of being crossed in their course of pleasures, is their rage in persecuting the godly. And therefore being resolute to live and die good-fellows, they also resolve, upon the same ground, to hold an everlasting irreconcilable opposition to the way which is called holy, especially since everywhere it is so spoken against. Whence, I say, they grow and glue themselves together in this combination, verse 10, &c. "Let us oppress the poor righteous man; let our strength be the law of justice; for that which is feeble is found to be nothing worth. Therefore let us lie in wait for the righteous, because he is not for our turn, and he is clean contrary to our doings; he upbraideth us with our offending the law, and objecteth to our infamy, the transgressing of our education. He professeth to have the knowledge of God, and he calleth himself the child of the Lord. He was made to reprove our thoughts: he is grievous unto us, even to behold; for his life is not like other men's, his ways are of another fashion. We are esteemed of him as counterfeits: he abstaineth from our ways as from filthiness; he pronounceth the end of the just to be blessed, and maketh his boasts that God is his father. Such things they did imagine, and were deceived; for their own wickedness hath blinded them. As for the mysteries of God, they know them not; neither hoped they for the wages of righteousness, nor discerned a reward for blameless souls."

If it *edge and enrage malice*, it breeds revenge, a wolfish and unnatural thirst after blood, which haunts most the weak, fearful, and cowardly spirits; for we ever see the basest and most worthless men to be most malicious and revengeful. Seldom doth it find any harbour in a well-bred and a generous mind. As thunders, tempests, and other terrible agitations in the air trouble only and disquiet these weaker frail bodies below, but never disturb or dismay those glorious heavenly ones above; so scurrilous sneers, imperious doggedness, disgraces, and wrongs, vex and distemper men of baser temper; but the nettling disposition, causeless spite, and childish brawlings of hasty fools, wound not great and noble spirits. Now, this boiling and biting distemper, though, against nature, it fed upon blood, yet so true is the point I pursue, (but would you think it?) is also insatiable. Witness that monster who, as Bodin reporteth, when he had surprised upon the sudden one whom he mortally hated, he presently overthrew him, and, setting his dagger to his breast, told him he would certainly have his blood except he would renounce, abjure, forswear, and blaspheme the God of heaven. Which when that fearful man, too sinfully greedy of a miserable life, had done in a most horrible manner, he immediately despatched him as soon as those prodigious blasphemies were out of his mouth; and in an awful triumph, insulting over his murdered adversary, as though whole hell had dwelt in his heart, he added this most abhorred speech,—" Oh," said he, " this is right noble and heroical revenge, which doth not only deprive the body of a temporary life, but brings also the never-dying soul into everlasting flames." Witness the cruellest of men, Mohammed, who, as the story reports, was in his time the death of eight hundred thousand men. But, above all, that beast of Rome carries away the bell for insatiableness in blood-sucking, who, though he was long since drunk with the blood of the saints as with new wine, in his drunken humour hath furiously spilt and poured out upon the face of Christendom a world of blood. Witness the incredible deal of christian blood which that merciless monster, the popish inquisition, swallowed down in secret; witness the horrible butcheries executed upon professors in the Low Countries : guess the rest by that cruel confession of Alva,* who, boasting in the bloodshed of the saints, said on a time at his table, that he had been diligent in rooting out of heresy, (so the antichristians call the right way to heaven), for, besides those that were slain in war and secret massacres, he had put into the hand of the hangman eighteen thousand in the space of six years. Witness Farnesius's resolution at his departure out of Italy,—to make his horse swim in the blood of the Lutherans. Witness that most abhorred prodigious villany that ever the sun saw,—the massacre at Paris; when in divers places of France

* Metran. Belg. Hist. lib. 4. p. 127.

about threescore thousand persons were murdered, and the streets of that city, as the story tells us, strewed with carcasses—the pavements, market-places, and river dyed with blood. Witness, besides other cruelties and bloody afflictions, three hundred faithful servants of Christ burned to ashes in this kingdom, within less than five years. Witness that horrible parricide perpetrated upon the royal persons of two French kings, Henry III. and Henry IV., who were successively butchered in a most barbarous manner by two popish assassins, Clement, and Ravilliac. Nay, in the late civil wars of France, twelve hundred thousand natural French are said to have been slain, this Romish beast being the bellows and incendiary. Yet, I say, though he hath already drunk up such a deal of blood, as insatiably as Behemoth, he is yet still like a she-wolf in the evening; and at this very time* carousing almost in all corners of the christian world with the blood of the martyrs of Jesus, as greedily and with as furious a thirst as ever he did since the dragon first gave him his power, Rev. xiii. 4. But I hope, in the strong God of our salvation, (for strong is the Lord God who judgeth, Rev. xviii. 3,) that this is the last draught, and that upon his next health, as it were, begun to the devil in this cup of fiery cruelty against the servants of Christ, the vial of God's unquenchable wrath will choke him for ever. Blood he shall have enough, but from the revenging hand of the Lord God of recompenses, in fury and jealousy.

[2.] Besides that thus the rage of insatiableness and restlessness of pursuit doth still boil in every carnal heart that is carried immoderately after its

* About A.D. 1626.

own ways, or inordinately upon any earthly thing, it is also thereby, in God's just judgment, extraordinarily hardened and estranged from God. For the more deeply our affections are drowned in the world and endeared to any sensual delight, the more desperately are they divorced from God and deadened to heavenly things. It is just with God to suffer that heart to be turned first into earth and mud, and afterwards to freeze and congeal into steel and adamant, which prefers earth before heaven, a dunghill before paradise, broken cisterns which can hold no water before the ever-springing fountain of glory and bliss; a few bitter-sweet pleasures of an inch of time in this vale of tears, before unmixed and immeasurable joys through all eternity in the glorious mansions above. Our hearts are originally hard by the curse of nature, Ezek. xi. 19; afterwards by a wilful course and continuance in sin we add adamant of our own, Isa. xlviii. 4; Zech. vii. 12; and by not suffering the sword of the Spirit to search and sunder our minion delights from our bosoms, Heb. iv. 7. Then Satan is let loose to put to his iron sinews, Luke xxii 3. Lastly, God himself hardeneth by an act of justice, as we may see, Exod. ix. 12. Thus the heart which hates to be reformed, being glued to a sensual object or worldly lust by its own inbred corruption, infusion of hellish poison, and just curse of God, grows into such a prodigious rock, that no created power, not the softest eloquence or severest curse, nay, not the weight of the whole world, were it all pressed upon it, can possibly mollify or reclaim it. It will never yield or relent, or be rent from its darling delight, but die in its deadness, and be desperately hardened for the very depth of hell, except the Almighty

Spirit take the hammer of the word into his own hand, that, by his special irresistible power and merciful violence, he may first break it in pieces with legal remorse, and afterwards, by the sprinkling and powerful application of Christ's blood, resolve it into tears of true evangelical repentance, that so only by a gracious miracle of Divine mercy it may be softened, sanctified, and saved. The stubborn Jews were heavily laden with an extraordinary variety of most grievous crosses and afflictions. There was nothing wanting to make them outwardly miserable; and no misery inflicted upon them but upon purpose to humble and take down their rebellious hearts. The prophet Isaiah, chap. i. 5, paints out to the life the rueful state of their fresh bleeding desolations: "The whole head," saith he, "is sick, and the whole heart faint;" (for the place is meant, not as some take it, of their sins, but of their sorrows.) But all these blows and pressures were so far from melting them, that they made them harder: "Why should ye be stricken any more? ye will revolt more and more." What created power can possibly have more power upon the souls of men than the sacred sermons of the Son of God, who spake as never man spake? and yet his dear entreaties and melting invitations, which sweetly and tenderly flowed from that heart which was resolved to spill its warmest and inmost blood for their sakes, moved those stiff-necked Jews never a jot. "Jerusalem, Jerusalem, how often would I,—and ye would not!" Matt. xxiii. 37. Isaiah, that noble prophet, whose matchless style incomparably surpasseth the utmost possibility of all human invention, and to which the choicest elegances of profane writers are pure barbarism, shed many and many a gracious shower of most heavenly, piercing, sweetest eloquence upon a sinful nation and rebellious people, which were fruitlessly spilled as water upon the ground, or lost as upon the hardest flint. His many heavenly soul-searching sermons, which breathed nothing but spirit and life, yet to them, hardened in their sins and hating to be reformed, were but as an idle and empty breath, vanishing into nothing, and scattered in the air. "The Lord" (as he saith) "made my mouth like a sharp sword, and me as a polished shaft," Isa. xlix. 2; and yet that two-edged sword was full often blunted upon their hard hearts, and his keen arrows, discharged by a skilful hand, rebounded from their flinty bosoms as shafts shot against a stone wall; which made that seraphical orator cry out, "I have laboured in vain, I have spent my strength for nought, and in vain," ver. 4. A course of extraordinary severity and terror was taken with the tyrant Pharaoh; he was not only chastised with rods, but even scourged with scorpions; and yet all the plagues of Egypt were so far from taming and taking down his proud heart, that every particular plague added unto it a several iron sinew; so far they were from softening it, that they seared it the more. No material weight can more crush the heart of a man into pieces than braying in a mortar; and yet, saith Solomon, "Though thou shouldest bray a fool," an old obstinate sinner, "in a mortar among wheat with a pestle, yet will not his foolishness," his wilful cruelty in killing his own soul, and extreme madness in exchanging a little transitory pleasure with endless pain, "depart from him," Prov. xxvii. 22. Now what a horrible hardness and hellish stone is that which no ministry or misery, nay, nor miracles, see Exod x. 27; 1 Kings xiii. 33; 2 Kings i. 11; nor mercies, Isa. xxvi. 10, can possibly mollify.

Here now I should have passed out of this point, did I not conceive that of all the weightiest civil affairs incident to human deliberation, there is none more material, important, or of greater consequence, either for extremest outward vexation and heart's grief, or extraordinary sweet contentment and continual peace, than matter of marriage. A word or two therefore concerning a convenient entrance into, and a comfortable enjoyment of that honourable estate.

1. For the first point: let thy choice be in the Lord, according to blessed St. Paul's rule, "only in the Lord," 1 Cor. vii. 39. Let piety be the first mover of thine affection, the prime and principal consideration in this greatest affair : and then conceive of personage, parentage, and portion, and such outward things and worldly additions, as a comfortable accessary, considerable only in a second place. Let the world say what it will, to a mind truly generous and ennobled with grace, the most absolute concurrence and greatest exquisiteness of beauty, gold, birth, wit, or what else besides may be found most remarkable and matchless in that sex, should be nothing, nor hold scale with the lightest feather upon any lady's head, compared with a gracious disposition and godly heart. Religion or the fear of God, as it is generally the foundation of all human felicity, so must it specially be accounted the ground of all comfort and bliss, which man and wife desire to find in the enjoying of each other. There was never any gold, or great friends, any beauty, or outward bravery, which tied truly fast and comfortably any marriage

knot. It is only the golden link and noble tie of christianity and grace, which hath the power and privilege to make so dear a bond lovely and everlasting, which can season and strengthen that nearest inseparable society with true sweetness and immortality.

Again: let conjugal love warm thine heart, at least in some measure with affectionate contentment, and some more special repose upon the party, as one with whom thou canst heartily and comfortably consort: for the husband, all concurrents and ordinary possibilities considered, ought to settle his affections upon his wife as the fittest that the world could have afforded him; and the wife should rest her heart upon her husband, as the meetest for her that could have been found under the sun. By a constant intercourse of which mutual contentment in each other, the husband will be to the wife as a covering of her eyes, Gen. xx. 16, that she lift them not up on any man; and the wife to the husband, the pleasure of his eyes, that he may still look upon her with sober and singular delight. Otherwise, they will find but cold comfort in that counsel and commandment of Solomon, " Rejoice with the wife of thy youth. Let her be as the loving hind, and pleasant roe," Prov. v. 18, 19. Without this mutual complacency, if I may so speak, and loving contentment in each other, I doubt whether I should encourage any to proceed. And yet why should not a comfortable concurrence of grace on both sides, consent of parents, meetness in condition, years, and all other requisites besides, create in a mortified heart, matrimonial affection?

Further, in going about such an important business, ply the throne of grace with extraordinary importunity and fervency of prayer; press upon, and wrestle, as it were, with God in days of more secret and solemn humiliation for a blessing in this kind, and with that sincerity, that thou do heartily desire him, whatsoever thy conceits and expectation of future comforts and conveniences may be, yet if it be not with his liking and to his glory, he would be pleased to dash it quite. A good wife is a more immediate gift of God; "House and riches," saith Solomon, "are the inheritance of fathers; and a prudent wife is from the Lord," Prov. xix. 14. And therefore such a rare and precious jewel is to be sued and sought for at God's mercy-seat with more extraordinary earnestness, importunity, and zeal. And methinks, that wife, child, or what other good thing is procured at God's merciful hand by prayer, should bring with it, even in our sense and thankful acknowledgment, a thousand times more sweetness and comfort than that which is cast upon us by God's ordinary providence, without any suit at all unto his heavenly highness.

Once more: let the parties deal plainly and faithfully one with the other, in respect of their bodies, souls, and outward state. I mean it thus: that they should not deceive and cozen one the other by a crafty concealment of disease, special deformity, natural defect, &c., in body; especially, which they think in their consciences and impartial consideration, if it were their case, would breed intolerable distaste and discontentment; or of some secret maim and crack in their outward state, which neither the other party or friends do either expect or suspect, for so they may bring a great deal of after-misery and too late repentance upon the match. For naturally we hate those who beguile us. And a man or woman is most impatient of failing, and being disappointed of their hopes and expectations, in so great and weighty affair as marriage is. And, therefore, it were very convenient and much better to disclose, the one unto the other, the material infirmities and wants in either of their bodies or goods, though with hazard of missing the match, rather than the one to obtain the other with guile, cunning, and after-discomfort. I said also, in respect of their souls; by which I mean, that for the time of wooing only as they call it, they should not put on a vizor, flourish, and show of religion, conversion, and grace, when in deed and truth there is no such matter. For this execrable imposture also is sometimes villainously practised, to the infinite prejudice and perpetual heart's grief of the deluded party. And not only some parties are cunning, reserved, and faulty this way, but even christian friends are too often too forward, peremptory, and audacious, in giving testimonies and assurances in such cases. Now, this is the greatest guile, and most cursed cozenage of all, when one conceives by the present cunning carriage of the party, and partial information of friends, that he or she hath met with a soul beautified by grace, whereas, when it comes to the trial, the person hath just none acquaintance with God at all.

2. Now I come unto the second point: a religious and comfortable continuance in the marriage state. For the happy attainment whereof, let us take notice of, and to heart, first, some common duties which are mutually to be performed on both sides.

Lovingness, which is a drawing into action, and keeping in exercise, that habit of conjugal affection and matrimonial love mentioned before. It is a sweet, loving, and tender-hearted pouring out of their hearts with much affectionate dearness into each other's bosoms, in all behaviour one towards another. This mutual melting-heartedness, being practised fresh and fruitful, will sweeten and beautify the marriage state.

For an uninterrupted preservation of this amiable deportment on both sides, let them consider,

(1.) The wise hand of God's gracious providence guided all the business and brought it to pass. And he commands constancy in this loving and lightsome carriage. "Rejoice with the wife of thy youth. Let her be as the loving hind, and pleasant roe," Prov. v. 18, 19; see also Eph. v. 25. Methinks this charge from the Holy Ghost, being often reverently remembered, should ever beat back and banish from both their hearts all heart-rising and bitterness, distaste and disaffection; all wicked wishes, that they had never met together, that they had never seen one another's faces, &c. When the knot is once tied, every man should think his wife, and every wife her husband, the fittest of any in the world. Otherwise, so often as he sees a better, he will wish that his choice were to make again, and so fall off from respect to this commandment, and from kindness and love to his own. Which is an unpardonable disparagement to God's providence, and an execrable impoisoner of marriage comforts.

(2.) That by the power of the honourable ordinance of marriage, the two are made one. And therefore, they ought to be as lovingly and tenderly affected one unto the other as they would be to their own flesh.

(3.) The compassionate and melting compellations which Christ and his spouse exchange in the Canticles: "My fair one, my sister, my love, my dove, my undefiled, my wellbeloved, the chief of ten thousand," &c.; whose chaste and fervent love that of married couples should resemble and imitate.

(4.) That these mutual expressions, and exercise of this matrimonial love, are very powerful to preserve chastity and pureness in body and spirit on both sides. It is noted of Isaac that he loved Rebekah dearly; and this was a special preservative that he fell not to polygamy or concubines, as many of the patriarchs did.

Faithfulness.

(1.) In respect of the marriage bed, which they ought on both sides to keep inviolable, undefiled, and honourable. Wherein, if they transgress, besides a whole hell of spiritual miseries, they strike at the very sinew, heart, and life of the marriage knot.

(2.) In respect of domestic affairs and businesses of the family, the care and burden whereof is common to them both. The husband that hath a prodigal and slothful wife doth but draw water with a sieve, as an heathen said, and casts his labours into a bottomless sack; and the wife that is matched with an idle unthrifty husband draws a cart heavy laden through a sandy way without a horse. By which is intimated an impossibility of thriving in the world, and prospering in their outward state.

(3.) In the concealment of each other's secrets. It is a very unnatural and monstrous treachery to publish one another's faults and frailties, or anything which, in hope of keeping counsel, they have communicated one to another.

Patience, which is as precious and needful a holy duty as I can possibly commend in this case, for comfortable conversing together. For a more prepared and constant exercise whereof, consider,

(1.) That two angels are not met together in a matrimonial state, but a son and daughter of Adam; and therefore they must look for infirmities, frailties, imperfections, passions, and provocations, on both sides.

(2.) That it is a charge given to all,—"That the sun must not go down upon their wrath," much more to man and wife linked together in the nearest bond.

(3.) That there never did, nor ever will come any good by the falling out of man and wife. Well may they thereby become ridiculous to their servants, a by-word to their neighbours, table-talk to the country, troublers of their own house, and as a continual dropping one unto another: but they shall never gain by their mutual hastiness, passions, and impatiency. What good can come by a man's anger and indignation against his own flesh? What prodigious madness is it for those to grow strange, whom so many and perpetual bands have tied so fast; and who, without dearest and most intimate familiarity, can neither enjoy civil contentment nor peace of conscience? Suppose that the heart should fall out with the head, and deny unto it those spirits which supply the brain, and serve for exercise both of sense, and consequently of the higher part of the soul; what would follow, but distemper, distraction, and madness? Or that the head should fall out with the body, and thereupon restrain from it the influence of animal spirits, the instruments of the quickening and moving it; what would become of the head, when the body were dead? Proportionable mischiefs and miseries fall out upon the marriage state, by falling out, strangeness, bitterness, and angry reservedness between the parties.

This grace then will be of excellent use, and must be exercised many ways:

[1.] In bearing with the wants and weaknesses, infirmities and deformities of each other. And let the man (for the woman is the weaker vessel) remember for this purpose how many faults, frailties, and falls, and how many times Christ remits and pardons his spouse the church. And he ought to love his wife, as Christ doth the church, Eph. v. 25. The body doth not reject the head because it is bald, or but one-eyed; the head rageth not against the body because it is deformed or diseased, but doth rather condole and sympathize.

[2.] About cross accidents in the family, losses in their outward state, going backward of businesses, &c., they must not lay the fault one upon another to the breaking out into choler, impatience, and stamping, but both join with blessed Job in that sweet and meek submission to God's pleasure, "The Lord gave, and the Lord hath taken away: blessed be the name of the Lord," Job. i. 21.

[3.] In waiting for the conversion of one another, if either prove unconverted. In which case, be patient, pray, and expect God's good time. We have God himself a sweet pattern for this purpose. Or, if the one be but a babe in Christ, weak in christianity, deal fairly, lovingly, and meekly. Let our Lord Jesus' tender-heartedness to spiritual babes teach us mercy this way. See Isa. xl. 11.

A *holy care* and *conscience* to preserve between themselves the marriage bed undefiled, and in all honour and christian purity.

In the next place, let us take a view of, and

to heart, duties peculiar and proper to each severally.

To the husband.

1. Let him behave himself as the head to the body, 1 Cor. ii. 3; Eph. v. 23.

(1.) The head is, as it were, the crown and glory of the body; so let the husband shine and show himself in a kind of eminency, excellency, and authority over the wife. To be a head, implies and imports a pre-eminence, superiority, and sovereignty, as appears by the apostle's gradation, 1 Cor. ii. 3. Man is the woman's head, Christ is man's head, God is Christ's head. For procuring and preserving which, let the husband be manly, grave, worthy, not light, vain, contemptible. Let him not be bitter, wayward, passionate; let him not be base-minded, vicious, vain-glorious; let him not be a drunkard, a gamester, a good-fellow. Dissoluteness and a disordered life in the man do much abate and diminish the wife's respectfulness and reverence unto him. Majesty, authority, venerableness in any superior, is not any ways more lessened or sooner lost than by light behaviour, personal worthlessness, or unworthy deportment in his place. Whereas true worth, goodness, grace, shining from within, do beget a more loving reverence and reverent love, than all outward forms of pomp and state, than any boisterousness or big looks, can possibly produce.

(2.) The head is the seat of understanding, wisdom, discretion, forecast. Out of which consideration, let the husband stir up, quicken, and enlarge his manly spirit to comprehend and rightly conceive all affairs, provisions, occasions, offers, ingenuous deportment, and worthy usages, which may any ways procure and promote his wife's true contentment, honour, and happiness. It is his necessary and noble charge, with a special and punctual care and casting about to provide for her soul, body, comfort, and credit; with all meekness and love to instruct and inform her in all passages of her duty, and procurements of her good.

(3.) The head, indeed, hath the precedency and prerogative of noblest operations and the soul's divinest acts, by the benefit of its native temper and constitutions, it being the seat of the senses, and of other proper instruments fitted for such high employments; yet, notwithstanding the body and other parts are animated and enlivened with the very same soul, both for substance, faculties, immortality, activeness in every way; so that if the foot, for instance, had an ear, an eye, an animal spirit, and an organization, as the philosophers speak, adapted for such functions, it would hear, and see, and understand as well as the head. And therefore the head, by a natural instinct, as it were, and sympathy, doth continually and tenderly, with fresh successions of a lively and quickening influence, cherish and refresh other parts as well as itself. The husband, by the benefit of a more manly body, tempered with natural fitness for the soul to work more nobly in, doth, or ought, ordinarily outgo the wife in largeness of understanding, height of courage, steadiness of resolution, moderation of his passions, dexterity to manage businesses, and other natural inclinations and abilities to do more excellently; yet, notwithstanding, let him know that his wife hath as noble a soul as himself. "Souls have no sexes," as Ambrose saith. In the better part they are both men. And if thy wife's soul were freed from the frailty of her sex, it were as manly, as noble, as understanding, and every way as excellent, as thine own : nay, and if it were possible for you to change bodies, hers would work as manfully in thine, and thine as womanly in hers. Let the husband, then, be so far from insulting, contemning, or undervaluing his wife's worth, for the weakness of her sex, that, out of consideration that her soul is naturally every way as good as his own, only the excellency of its native operations something damped and disabled, as it were, by the frailty of that weaker body with which God's wise providence hath clothed it for a more convenient and comfortable, but ingenuous serviceableness to his good, —that, I say, he labour the more to entertain and entreat her with all tenderness and honour; to recompense, as it were, her suffering in this kind for his sake.

(4.) The head is the well-spring of all quickening motion and sense, liveliness and lightsomeness to the body. If the derivation of animal spirits from the brain were restrained and intercepted for a while, the body would be presently surprised with a senseless damp and dead palsy. The wife, for the husband's sake, hath forsaken her native home, father's house, parents, and many comforts of that kind, and therefore has good reason to expect now, and receive from her head, new matter, and a continued influence of light-heartedness, comfortable enjoying herself, and cheerful walking. If he, to whose company and conditions she is now so nearly and necessarily confined, and, as it were, enchained, prove unkind, she holds herself utterly undone for any outward contentment.

2. Let him dwell with her, according to knowledge, 1 Pet. iii. 7.

(1.) By a wise discovery at the first, and timely acquainting himself with her disposition, affections, infirmities, passions, imperfections; and thereupon, with all holy discretion, apply and address himself in a fair and loving manner to rectify and reform all he can, and to bear the rest with patience, passing by it without passion and impatiency, still waiting upon God by prayer, in his good time, for a further and more full redress and conformity. One of the rankest roots of distaste and discontentment in the marriage state is, the neglect of a punctual observation of each other's properties; of taking the right measure of each other's manners, upon purpose, that with mutual patience and forbearance they may support each other in love, and lovingly bear one another's burdens. Memorable is that speech, and may be a fit medicine against marriage jars, which a reverend man received from a husband, who being asked how such a choleric couple could so consort together: "Thus," saith he, "when her fit is upon her, I yield to her, as Abraham did to Sarah; and when my fit is upon me, she yields to me, and so we never strive together, but asunder."

(2.) By a provident, discreet, and patient ordering, guiding, and managing businesses abroad, and family affairs at home; without that carking impatience, and distrust of God's providence, without that clamour, boisterousness, and confusion, with which worldlings are wont to trouble their own houses. It is incredible to consider the vast and invaluable difference between the comforts, calmness, and many sweet contentments of a household governed by the patient wisdom of a heavenly-minded man, and the endless brawlings, bitter contests about trifles, disorders, and domestic quarrels, which haunt that family where a choleric, covetous, and hare-brained husband doth domineer. This latter is like the middle region of the air, continually torn and rent with fresh commotions, thunders, and many tumultuous stirs, which rise at first from a thing of nothing, a thin invisible fume drawn out of the earth: so earthly things, vainer than the most vanishing vapour, do ordinarily rise in such nurseries of disquietness and noise, a world of needless troubles, passionate distempers, and self-vexations. But the former is like the highest part of the air, full of calmness, tranquillity, and constant light; the Sun of righteousness, shining still upon it with the blessed beams of patience, contentment, and spiritual nobleness of mind, doth from time to time dissolve and drive away all mists of worldly mourning, storms of bitterness and brawling, matter of such senseless and brainless molesting one another, and doth with a sweet and kindly heat refresh and support the heart against all choleric encounters and cross accidents, by virtue of such heavenly and healing cordials as those which were wont to calm and repel the most tempestuous assaults upon the afflicted saints, Job i. 21; 1 Sam. iii. 18.

(3.) But, above all, by leading his wife in the way of life, and in the path of holiness. This is the flower and crown of all his skill, to be a blessed and manly guide unto her towards everlasting happiness. For want of this wisdom and will, many a poor soul lies bleeding unto eternal death, under the bloody and merciless hand of an ignorant, profane, or pharisaical husband, who, perhaps, may have knowledge enough and too much to thrive in the world, to prosper in his outward state, to provide for posterity, nay, to oppress, over-reach and defraud his brother, but no wit, no understanding at all, to teach and tell his wife one foot of the right way to heaven; "wise to do evil," as the prophet speaks, "but to do good they have no knowledge," Jer. iv. 22; no holy habit or heart to pray with her, to instruct and encourage her in the great mystery and practice of godliness, to keep the sabbath holy, and days of humiliation; to read the Scriptures, repeat sermons, and confer of good things with her; from which he is so far, that, although it be the strongest bar to keep her from grace, and the destroyer of both their souls, he will needs persuade her that all this is too much preciseness. And yet hear Chrysostom: "Let them both go to the house of God, and afterward at home let the husband require of the wife, and the wife of the husband, those things which were there spoken and read, or at least some of them." And in the same sermon, "Teach her," saith he, "the fear of God, and all things will flow in abundantly, as out of a fountain, and thine house will be replenished with innumerable good things."

(4.) By a conscientious and constant care also for the conversion and salvation of their children and servants. Every husband and head of a family is, as it were, a priest and pastor in his own house; and, therefore, if he take not a course to catechise them, pray with them, prepare them for the sacrament, and to "bring them up in the nurture and admonition of the Lord," as the apostle counsels, Eph. vi. 4; to restrain them all he can from lewd courses, ill company, and the corruptions of the times; but suffers them to have their swing in their youthful rebellions, unhallowing the Lord's day, ale-house hauntings, and stubbornness against the ministry;

let them then know, that all those sins they so run into by such gross neglect and default, are set upon his score, and he must be exactly accountable, and full dearly answer for them at the great and last day. Nay, let me further tell him that which will make his ears to tingle, and heart to tremble, if it be not of adamant, and his heart-strings turned into iron sinews; those his children and servants, who, by his impenitent omissions, have perished in their sins, will curse him for ever hereafter amongst the fiends in hell. They will follow thee up and down in that ever-burning lake with direful curses and hideous outcries, crying out continually, "Woe unto us, that ever we served such a wicked and wretched master, that had no care of the salvation of our souls, took no course to save us out of these fiery torments!" Even thine own dear children, in this case, will yell in thine ears, world without end, " Woe, and alas, that ever we were born of such accursed parents, who had not the grace to teach us betimes the ways of God, to keep us from our youthful vanities, and to train us up in the paths of godliness! Had they done so, we might have lived in the endless joys of heaven; whereas now we must lie irrecoverably in these everlasting flames. Oh! it was the fault of our own parents' unconscionable and cruel negligence, that all our life long stuck full deep in our souls, and hath now strangled them with everlasting horror." That this must needs be so, ordinary observation and common experience doth too often confirm. We hear, many times, many miserable malefactors bitterly complain at the place of execution against parents and masters, saying, " If they had taken care and conscience to have taught and restrained us betimes, we had never come to this shameful end." How much more will they cry out against them with endless yellings, when they shall feel the flames of hell!

To the wife.

1. Let her be in subjection to her head,

(1.) By a reverent and humble persuasion of his precedency and authority over her, grounded and engraven in her resolution principally, 1. By virtue of Divine ordination, Gen. iii. 16, Eph. v. 24; 2. The very law of nature; 3. Her husband's headship; 4. Womanly infirmity may also be a powerful motive to this purpose. For, if her heart begin to swell, and be lifted up with an overweening conceit of a sufficiency above her sex, so that she grow discontented, and impatient of contradiction and command, she brings a world of unnecessary misery and molestation into her own house, and lies in a grand transgression and grievous sin against the institution of the marriage state. It is no nobleness of birth, greatness of portion, nimbleness of tongue, fulness of wit, or any other excellency incident to her sex, which can give her any right or privilege to seize upon the sovereignty, and take the reins into her own hands. Some servants also may be wiser than their masters, some subjects more politic than their prince; but that gives them no warrant: nay, for all that, it were monstrous and unnatural villany for any servant thereupon to domineer, or private man to rush into a royal throne. No sufficiency of gifts or singularity of worth must justle us out of that rank and station wherein God's wise providence and all-seeing wisdom hath placed us. A man may be a superior in power and place to his superior in parts and personal endowments.

No pretence then, or plea on the woman's part, can possibly procure any dispensation, against God and nature, of unwomanly domineering and deposing her head.

(2.) By a hearty and cheerful submission. 1. To all his lawful and honest dictates and directions in respect to her personal behaviour; that it may be fashioned and addressed with an ingenuous and loving accommodation of herself to do him all the honour, and give him all the contentment, she can possibly with good conscience. Also for educating, ordering, and disposing her children, servants, and other domestic affairs (wherein, notwithstanding, there are some passages more proper and native to her sex, in which, except she be senseless, graceless, and strangely weak, it will be very unmanly, dishonourable, and unworthy for him to be too meddling, prying and pragmatical.) But, above all, for guiding her aright in the sweet and glorious path of christianity, that after their nearest and dearest comfort, and communion in the best things and spiritual blessings, which only can allay the smart of all cross accidents, and sweeten the bitterness of a few and evil days in this vale of tears, they may for ever be crowned together in heaven. 2. To all his reasonable and religious restraints, not only from wicked haunts and customs, sinful fashions, and passions, but in case of inconvenience, dishonour, or just displeasure; for the abridging or abandoning her ease, will, desires, delights, this or that company, and conformity to the times in her attire. For the spouse, for Christ's sake, sovereignty, and love, doth deny herself, her own reason and wisdom, her natural wit and wilfulness, her passions, pleasures, and profits, her ease, and liberty. And the wife is charged by blessed Paul to be subject to her husband, as the church is to Christ, Eph. v. 24. 3. To all his motions, admonitions, counsels, comforts, reproofs, commands, countermands, even in every thing, only in the Lord. So we see the body to rest upon the head's motion, either for rest or motion. In a word, she ought, like a true looking-glass, faithfully to represent and return to her husband's heart, with a sweet and pleasing pliableness, the exact lineaments and proportions of all his honest desires and demands, and that without discontent, thwarting, or sourness. For her subjection in this kind should be as to Christ, sincere, hearty, and free.

2. Let her be a helper, Gen. ii. 18, and do him good all the days of her life, at all times, upon all occasions, in all conditions; in adversity or prosperity, acceptation or disgrace, sickness or health, youth or old age; and that with kindness and constancy.

Helpfulness to her husband must be universal; apprehending and improving, with all readiness and love, all opportunities to do him any good in soul or body, name or estate. In a special manner she must learn and labour, with all meekness of wisdom and patient discretion, to forecast, contrive, and manage, as her more proper and particular charge, household affairs and businesses within doors. For which, see a right noble glorious pattern, Prov. xxxi. For the pride, vanity, idleness, and luxury of these last times, wherein there is so much hell upon earth; such an impetuous reign and rage of sin in all sorts, hath transported also that sex into many monstrous degenerations; so that our great women in these days would be very loth to work after this sample, though set by the Holy Ghost himself; yet heretofore right noble princesses and daughters of mighty kings made conscience of a particular calling, and disdained not to put their hands to housewifery. See Gen. xviii. 6; xxvii. 14; 2 Sam. xiii. 8.

But, above all, let her be assistant to him in setting up and forwarding the rich and royal trade of grace, in erecting and establishing Christ's glorious kingdom, both in their own hearts and in their house. This is that one necessary thing, without which their family is but Satan's seminary, and a nursery for hell. And, therefore, let her be so far from drawing a contrary way, (a cursed villany of some wicked wives abroad in the world,) or dead-heartedness this way, which is the grave of all spiritual graces, that in case of negligence and slackness she should labour by all wise, modest, seasonable insinuations, to stir up and quicken her husband to constancy and fervency in religious exercises of prayer, reading, catechising, conference, days of humiliation, and other household holy duties. As the two greater lights of heaven do govern this great world with their natural, so let the husband and wife guide the little world of their family with the spiritual light of divine knowledge and discretion. When the sun is present in our firmament, the moon, out of a sense, as it were, of a natural reverence to the fountain of all her beauty and light, doth veil her splendour, and withdraw her beams. But when he is departed to the other hemisphere, she shows herself, and shines as a princess amongst the lesser lights. When the husband is at home, let the wife only, if need be, serve as a loving remembrancer to him, to keep his turns and times of enlightening and informing the ignorant, dark, and earthly hearts of their people. But in his absence comes her course, when her graces of knowledge and prayer ought to show forth themselves, and shine upon them, to preserve them from coldness, and that dreadful curse which hangs over the head of those that know not God, and shall certainly fall upon those families that call not on his name. See Jer. x. 25.

For conclusion of the point, and crowning of the marriage state with sound and lasting comfort in the present time, and with everlasting peace and pleasures at last, let man and wife jointly labour to sweeten and sanctify their mutual carriages, both common and several duties each to the other, with often and constant meeting together in prayer. For persuasion to which practice, consider such places as these, Gen. xxv. 21; 1 Cor. vii. 5; 1 Pet. iii. 7. Continually, saith Chrysostom, teach her profitable things, and pray together.

If besides family prayers, wherein the more general affairs of the household are to be commended unto God, man and wife make conscience also of this more private duty between themselves, wherein many particulars are to be petitioned only proper and individual to that near society; I say, if they set themselves unto it with sincerity of heart, it may be a notable help, and, by God's blessing, prove a sovereign antidote against any root of bitterness, heart-rising, dissension, or discontent between them; (for wrath and ill will lurking in the heart towards any, doth utterly damp and impoison the power and comfort of prayer, much more towards those who are united with so many dear and perpetual bonds; so that praying together will make them leave jarring, or jarring will make them leave praying;) against all dishonours and defilements of the marriage-bed; against want, monstrousness, and miscarriage of children; against weariness and light esteem one of another; against plunging themselves insensibly into the gulf of worldly-mindedness, the canker and cut-throat of all grace, comfort, and nobleness of mind. This private morning and evening sacrifice offered to the throne of grace with heartiness and life, will spiritualize (if I may so speak) their love, and renew it daily upon their hearts with fresh, ardent, and heavenly embracements. It will marvellously sweeten all reproaches and contumelies cast upon them by envenomed tongues for their profession, when they shall come together in private and complain unto God, and beg, at his merciful hands, patience and christian fortitude to take them, in submission to his will and conformity to his Son, as so many crowns of glory to their heads, and of joy unto their hearts, Acts v. 41; 1 Pet. iv. 14; Job xxxi. 36. It will sweetly seal unto them, in the mean time, their assurance of meeting together hereafter in heaven; and when the time of sorrow shall come, and the stroke of death divorce them for a time, consciousness of their former blessed communion in prayer will not only serve as a counter poison against all slavish bitterness of immoderate grief, incident to hopeless worldlings, but crown their hearts at parting (which is a precious thing) with incomparably more true, inward, lasting contentment, than if they two had covetously hoarded and heaped together all the wealth of this world.

WORKS OF MERCY.

Now, concerning works of mercy, which, springing from a heart melting with a sense of God's everlasting mercy to itself, quickened with a lively faith in the Lord Jesus, and shining with saving graces, are "an odour of a sweet smell, a sacrifice acceptable, wellpleasing to God," Phil. iv. 18; Heb. xiii. 16.

Conceive first there are two sorts of them; 1. Spiritual; 2. Corporeal.

Spiritual flow from the fountain of truest mercy, and compassion of greatest tenderness and consequence, even to relieve, repair, and refresh the poverty, wants, and miseries of the soul. 1. By instructing the ignorant, Prov. x. 21, and xv. 7. 2. By giving counsel to them that need or seek it, Exod. xviii. 19—23; Ruth iii. 1. 3. By recovering the erroneous, Exod. xxiii. 4. 4. By labouring for the conversion of others, Psa. li. 13; Luke xxii. 23. 5. By exhorting one another, Heb. iii. 13. 6. By reproving the offender, Lev. xix. 17. 7. By admonishing them that are out of order, 1 Thess. v. 14. 8. By considering one another, to provoke unto love and to good works, Heb. x. 24. 9. By comforting the heavy heart and afflicted spirit, 1 Thess. v. 14. 10. By forgiving from the heart our brethren their trespasses, Matt. xviii. 35. 11. By correcting children when necessary, Prov. xxii. 15. 12. By raising those who are fallen by infirmity, with much meekness and tenderness of heart, Gal. vi. 1. 13. By mutual encouragements against the cruelty and confusions of the times, and in the way to heaven, Mal. iii. 16. 14. By supporting and mercifully making much of weak christians, 1 Thess. v. 11. 15. By patience towards all men, 1 Thess. v. 14. 16. By praying one for another, James v. 16.

Corporeal, spring from a compassionate heart and fellow feeling, affectionately yearning over the temporal wants and necessities of our brethren, whereby we are stirred up, as occasion is offered, according to our ability, to succour and support their outward extremities and distresses; to feed the hungry; to give drink to the thirsty; to clothe the naked; to entertain the stranger; to visit the sick; to go to those that are in prison, Matt. xxv. 36; to give a helping hand for raising our brethren fallen into decay, Lev. xxv. 35; to lend, hoping for nothing again, Luke vi. 35.

Thus christians ought to be ready to distribute, willing to communicate in all kinds to the outward necessities also: 1. Of those of the household of faith, the principal and most moving object to draw bounty from a truly charitable heart, Gal. vi. 10. 2. In the next place, of the lame, the blind, the sick, the aged, the trembling hand, or any that God hath made poor. 3. Of any whosoever in a case of true necessity and extremity, whatsoever the party hath been before; for there thou relievest not his notoriousness, but his nature; though thou abhor the man for his former wickedness, yet, he being upon point of perishing, do good unto the common state of humanity.

Now of these two kinds, fathers, schoolmen, casuists, all concur and conclude that spiritual alms, all other things being equal, are more excellent and acceptable than corporeal; because, 1. The gift is more noble in its own nature. 2. The object more illustrious,— man's immortal soul. 3. The manner transcendent, being spiritual. 4. The charity more heavenly, which aims at our brother's endless salvation.

Let then every christian conscionably and constantly endeavour to improve to the utmost, upon all occasions and seasonable offers, all his spiritual abilities, heavenly endowments, illuminations of learning, moral wisdom, providence, and discretion; all his skill in the mystery of Christ, word and ways of God; all his experience in temptations, cases of conscience, spiritual distempers; his spirit of counsel, comfort, courage, or whatever other gift or grace soever he is enlightened and endowed with, to relieve and refresh every way the souls, to procure and promote by all means the eternal salvation of others.

Let the saving light of thy divine knowledge, spiritual wisdom, heavenly understanding, or what other excellences and perfections shine in thy soul, resemble in all fruitful improvement and free communication that bountiful light in the body of the sun; which, 1. Enlighteneth that goodly sphere wherein it originally dwells, and makes it the fairest and most beautiful thing in the world. 2. Next, it illuminates and beautifies all the orbs and heavenly bodies about it. 3. By the projection of his beams it begets all the beauty, glory, sweetness, we have here below on the earth. 4. It insinuates into every chink and cranny of the earth. 5. His beams glide by the sides of the earth, and enlighten even the opposite part of heaven, with all those glorious stars we see shining in the night. 6. It is so communicative and eager in doing good in its kind, that it strikes through the firmament in the transparent parts, and seeks to bestow its brightness and beauty even beyond the heavens; and never restrains the free communication of its influence and glory, until it determine by natural and necessary expiration. Even so proportionably let the fruitful light of thy divine knowledge and heavenly counsel especially be still working, shining, spreading to do all possible good. 1. Let it make thine own soul all glorious within; fairly enlighten it with an humble reflection of self-knowledge, with purity, peace, and spiritual prudence, to guide constantly thine own feet with all uprightness and patience in the path that is called holy. 2. Let it shine upon thy family, and those that are next about thee, with all seasonable instructions in convincing them of the truth and goodness of the ways of God, either for their conversion or inexcusableness. 3. Let it be spent and employed upon thy neighbours, kindred, friends, acquaintance, visitors of all sorts, when they come towards thee; to warm their hearts all thou canst with heavenly talk, and to win their love to the life of grace. 4. Let it insinuate also amongst strangers, and into other companies upon which any warrantable calling shall cast thee; and especially, if it find acceptation and entertainment, let them know "that one thing is necessary; that all impenitents shall be certainly damned; that upon this moment dependeth eternity, &c." 5. Nay, let it offer itself, with all meekness of wisdom and patient discretion, even to opposites; and labour to conquer, if it be possible, the contrary-minded, if their scornful carriage and furious visible hate against the mystery of Christ hath not set a brand of dogs and swine upon them. 6. When upon all occasions, in all companies, by all means, it hath done all the good it can, yet let it still retain that constant property of all heavenly graces, an edge, an eagerness to do more good still, and rather want matter and means, than readiness and resolution to propagate itself. And this way may the poorest christians be plentiful in works of mercy, and enrich the richest with spiritual alms, which, in the mean time, may comfort the bountiful hearts of those who are true of heart, to whom the Lord, out of his best wisdom, hath denied this earthly dross. But yet for all this I would have you know, that I know none, not the poorest, excepted or exempted from seasonable ministering to the corporeal necessities also of their brethren. We have a precept from St. Paul, "That we must work with our own hands, that we may have to give to him that needeth," Eph. iv. 28: and a noble precedent in the poor widow, who cast her two mites into the treasury, which was "all she had, even all her living," Mark xii. 44. And if any here make a counterplea of their poverty, I would know if there be any so poor, that is not able to give a cup of cold water only; and yet this from a sincere heart shall be both graciously accepted and certainly rewarded, Matt. x. 42.

And therefore, in a second place, I infinitely desire and entreat, (and this is that which in this point I would especially press and persuade with deepest impression,) that every one who hath given his name unto Christ, rich or poor, according to his power and proportion, would with singular care and conscience address himself to a fruitful, affectionate, and constant discharge of this much-honoured duty of almsgiving, in this kind also, properly so called.

1. For we are bound to abound in this grace also. Therefore saith Paul, "As ye abound in every thing, in faith, &c., see that ye abound in this grace also," 2 Cor. viii. 7. There is no religious professor of any reputation, upon good ground with the church of God, but takes to heart, and desires to be exact in all commanded christian duties every day, as prayer

and reading Scriptures. Upon thy secret, and solitary review of the day past, call thyself to a strict account; as for others, so concerning this duty also, of doing good "unto all men, especially unto them who are of the household of faith," Gal. vi. 10; for the discharge of this duty ought also to be daily, if thy ability will bear, and the necessities of the poor shall require: "In the morning sow thy seed, and in the evening withhold not thy hand. Give a portion to seven, and also to eight," Eccles. xi. 6. 2. Let the sense and consciousness of any omission, neglect, or sloth in performing it, wound thy conscience, humble thy soul, and quicken thine heart with new life of resolution, and more lively endeavour to mend every morning, and perfume, as it were, thine every day's walking with God, with this sweet-smelling sacrifice of mercifulness, bounty, and love, Phil. iv. 18. Let this duty, likewise, with the rest, fall within the compass of thy severest search; penitent melting, renewed vows, in all thy more solemn self-examinations before the sabbath, sacraments, and upon days of humiliation. It is a profitable consideration to think, that a customary gross neglect of any one christian duty, in its season, of which the conscience is or may be convinced, may justly damp and deaden the lightsome and fruitful performance of all the rest. For example: a willing known omission of private prayer, or reading the word every day, may intercept and restrain the sweet influence of God's wonted refreshing mercy, and the fructifying beams of his pleased countenance from thine heart, in the use of all the other ordinances. An affected idleness and neglect to employ any one grace in the soul, when seasonable occasion calleth for improvement, may blast the comfortable exercise and sensible comfort of all the rest. For example: if thou suffer thy patience ordinarily to sleep, when thy passions begin to break in upon thee like a torrent, and heat thine heart with their swelling poison, or when some cross doth nettle thy desire of ease, no marvel that thou find a faintness also to seize upon thy faith, brotherly kindness, love, zeal, joy, and peace in believing. Why then, when thou feelest thine inward man to begin to languish, and the whole body of christianity to grow, as it were, towards a consumption; amongst other inquisitions, why dost thou not also fear out of a godly jealousy, and labour to find out whether the coldness of thy charity, and too much neglect of relieving the poor members of Jesus Christ, may occasion thy spiritual damp? It is the duty and property of every true-hearted Nathanael to have respect to all God's commandments, Psa. cxix. 6; so, though they cannot in perfection and height fulfil them, yet with truth and sincere endeavour to have respect to a conscionable use of all the ordinances, to the performance of all holy duties, and exercise of all spiritual graces in their due seasons.

2. If the world hath locked up thine heart, and congealed the bowels of thy compassions towards the poor, let the blaze of thine outward profession shine ever so fair, manage the heartless representations of external holiness ever so demurely, keep the times and tasks of daily duties with ever such great austerity; nay, though thou be able to amuse weaker christians with some affected strains and artificial fervency in prayer, (for by the mere power, or rather poison of hypocrisy and vain glory, a man may pray sometimes to the admiration of others, especially less judicious christians, having cunningly

collected the most moving passages for that purpose from the best gifted in that kind, and then giving an enforced action and life unto them in the delivery, as some, in other cases, act other men's inventions to the life,)—I say, for all this, if the holy heat of brotherly love doth not warm thine heart, and upon occasion work affectionately and effectually, I dare to say, that thou art rotten at the heart-root, there is no true love of God in thee, no grace, no hope of salvation. Let that terrible and flaming place against all covetous pharisees dissolve thy frozen-heartedness this way, and enlarge the bowels of pity towards the poor brethren of Christ Jesus, or else never think hereafter to look him in the face with comfort, or to find mercy at that day. Mark it well, and meditate upon it: "Whoso hath this world's good, and seeth his brother have need, and shutteth up his bowels of compassion from him, how dwelleth the love of God in him?" 1 John iii. 17.

3. But, above all other motives of mercifulness to the poor, which in the book of God are very many, and most quickening, methinks that argument which Paul presseth to this purpose should melt the most flinty heart; "For ye know," saith he, "the grace of our Lord Jesus Christ, that, though he was rich, yet for your sakes he became poor, that ye through his poverty might be rich," 2 Cor. viii. 9. Shall the only and innocent Son of the all-powerful and ever-blessed Lord, and King of heaven and earth, empty, as it were, and disrobe his heavenly highness of that royalty and majesty above, and become so poor, that whereas "the foxes have holes, and the birds of the air have nests, the Son of man hath not where to lay his head," Matt. viii. 20;

that through his poverty and pouring out his heart's blood he might crown us with the inestimable riches of heavenly glory; with joys and pleasures more than the stars of the firmament, even for ever and ever; and shall not we, worms and guilty creatures, most unworthy the least bit of bread we put into our mouths, part with our superfluities sometimes, both in respect of the necessity of nature and exigency of estate, as the schoolmen speak, to relieve the fainting soul of him for whom Christ died, and which he would take as done unto himself, Matt. xxv. 40, were it but a cup of cold water only? Mark ix. 41. Monstrous unthankful cruelty! mercilessness, that merits the fiercest flame in the dungeon of fire and brimstone!

4. The last and everlasting doom, at that great and dreadful day, must pass upon us according to our conduct in this kind. Then shall there be a severe and sincere search and inquiry made after works, as the signs, evidences, and outward demonstrations of faith, and the root of grace in the heart; or of unbelief and rottenness at the heart-root; and consequently as arguments of a righteous doom passed upon the sheep and goats. That glorious sentence of absolution, " Come, ye blessed of my Father, inherit the kingdom prepared for you from the foundation of the world," Matt. xxv. 34, which sounds out nothing but pleasures, joys, delights, glories, beauties, felicities, crowns, kingdoms, angelical entertainments, beatifical visions, spiritual raptures, highest perfections, unutterable exultations of spirit, sweetest varieties, eternities, shall be pronounced upon the godly, according to the effects and fruits of their faith; to teach us, in the mean time, what faith to trust unto and rest upon for justification,

even that which works by love; and also at that day to let all the world see, angels, men, and devils, that the kingdom of heaven is given only to true-hearted Nathanaels, honest professors, working believers. Now, in the text for this purpose, there is singled out with special choice, an eminent synecdochial instance in one of the worthiest effects of faith and noblest fruit of grace, even the point I now press and labour to persuade, namely, an open-hearted, real, fruitful bounty and love to God's people and distressed members of Christ Jesus, for Christ's and their goodness' sake.

But that other doom of damnation, "Depart from me ye cursed into everlasting fire prepared for the devil and his angels," Matt. xxv. 41, which breathes out nothing but fire and brimstone, stings and horrors, woe, flames of wrath, and the worm that never dieth, trembling and gnashing of teeth, seas of vengeance, torments without end, and past imagination, shall pass upon the reprobates for omission and neglect of this noble duty. For mercilessness to the poor members of Christ, unkindness to christians, hard-heartedness towards the household of faith, is one of the rankest, bitterest weeds which grows out of a graceless heart; a clear and full evidence that all was naught, and a notable remembrancer, as it were, to that high and everlasting Judge that his blessed Spirit never dwelt there. How deeply then doth it concern every christian to practise and ply upon all opportunities that most gainful art of almsgiving, which shall be so highly honoured at that great day, before that glorious universal presence, when every merciless man shall cry to the rocks and mountains, to fall upon him, and hide him from the wrath of the just

God, who will flame unquenchably and everlastingly against all those who, in this life, have shut up their bowels of pity against his poor, and been unkind towards the dearly beloved of his soul! Jer. xii. 7.

I know Bellarmine labours to impoison this last passage with his false gloss and popish sophistry, asserting that the causal conjunction, "for," Matt. xxv. 35, intimates and implies works meritoriousness. I say, No: "for" is there a note of consequence and order, not of the cause, or any meritorious causality. The causal conjunction, in grammar, doth indeed serve to show the reason of a former sentence, but it doth not necessarily show a reason from the cause of a thing, but many times also from the effect and other kind of arguments. And logic also teacheth, that there be divers kinds of causes, principal and less principal, &c.

Bellarmine replies: Doth not Christ there speak in the same manner of the rewards of the godly and of the punishments of the wicked? But no man can say that in these words, "Depart ye cursed," &c., that the cause is not rendered, but only the order and consequence implied; "For the wages of sin is death," Rom. vi. 23.

I answer: By the like fallacy also do the popish impostors plead for justification by works :— evil works damn, therefore good works save. Most falsely, as appears by that rule in arguing, "The consequence is of no validity where there is not a perfect contrariety." Now, between good and evil works there is no perfect contrariety, for evil works are perfectly evil against the law of God; but good works are not perfectly good according to the law of God. By the same reason, neither doth it follow, that eternal death is the wages of sin, or that eternal life is the wages of good works.

5. If thou lay out to the poor cheerfully, seasonably, liberally, and yet but according to thy ability, thou shalt become (which, besides the only course of growing comfortably rich, is also a crown of infinite honour) creditor even to thy Creator. "He that hath pity upon the poor, lendeth unto the Lord; and that which he hath given will he pay him again," Prov. xix. 17. And in the mean time, for repayment in due time, thou hast security infinitely above all exception, a bill under his own hand, even his own blessed book; wherein to fail were to forfeit his Deity, if I may so speak, which is prodigious blasphemy to imagine. Now, what a keen spur and inflaming motive is this to be merciful, that we shall make God himself our debtor, even the ever springing Fountain of bliss, and Lord of all goodness, who doth all things like himself, omnipotently, bountifully, above all expectation, as becomes the mighty Sovereign of heaven and earth. If he work, he makes a world; if he be angry, he drowns the whole face of the earth; if he love, the heart's blood of his dearest Son is not too dear; if he stand upon his people's side, he makes the sun to stand still and the stars to fight; if he repay, he gives his own all-sufficient self, with the overflowing torrents of all pleasures and glory through all eternity.

6. Nay, the way to thrive and fare well in the world, if our most wise God think it fit, is to be compassionate this way. "If thou draw out thy soul to the hungry," saith the prophet, "and satisfy the afflicted soul, then shall thy light rise in obscurity and break forth as the morning, and thy darkness be as the noon-day; and thine health shall

spring forth speedily: the Lord shall guide thee continually, and satisfy thy soul in drought, and make fat thy bones: and thou shalt be like a watered garden, and like a spring of water whose waters fail not," Isa. lviii. 8, 10, 11. "Thine horn shall be exalted with honour, and thou shalt not want," Psa. cxii. 9; Prov. xxviii. 27. It will be then a profitable inquisition amongst others, when a man finds himself to go backward in his estate, God's secret displeasure to blow upon his wealth, or afflict his body with painful diseases, to examine well whether he was not ordinarily wont rather to shut up his bowels of compassion, than to pour out his soul to the poor, 1 John iii. 17.

Also, take notice of the order of those objects upon which thy christian love is regularly and seasonably to be directed, and thy works of mercy discharged. The catalogue of them runneth thus, as I conceive:

The public state wherein thou livest, and whereof thou art a member, challengeth the first place and precedency. In the next place stands thyself, then thy wife, then thy parents, then thy children and family, then the household of faith, then thy natural kindred sprung lately from the same progenitors, then thy nearest neighbours and common friends, then thy countrymen, then strangers, then thine enemies; for as thou wouldst be holden a "child of the highest," Luke vi. 35, thou must love thine enemies, and relieve them too, Prov. xxv. 21; Rom. xii. 20. And because our naughty hearts do naturally rise and swell against them with much enraged anger, disdain, and contempt, ponder seriously upon the following points, as counterpoisons, to keep out these foul fiends, and preserve thine affections ever calm and unstained this way, and in a holy charitable temper and disposition to do them good.

(1.) First, he that becomes a goad in thy side for thy blessed profession, and because thou followest goodness, is stark mad, and utterly besides himself in matters of salvation. He is as a dead man, without all sense of spiritual self-murder. Now, it is extreme weakness to level thy wit with a madman; and barbarous inhumanity to wreak thy spite upon the dead, and basely to vex a lifeless carcass with braving insults.

(2.) Thou wouldst most wilfully forsake thine own mercy, and judge thyself infinitely unworthy of everlasting life, of any part or portion in the rich, glorious, eternal purchases of the meritorious death of Christ, if thou couldst not frankly forgive the greatest wrong of thy greatest enemy, upon this ground only,—because Jesus Christ hath freely poured out the dearest and warmest blood in his heart, to purchase for thee, a sinful worm, and while thou wast yet his desperate enemy, pardon and salvation from the endless woes and damnations of hell.

(3.) The merciful patience of God himself, in forbearing and bearing with infinite wrongs and dishonours done unto his great majesty every day, may be a matchless pattern and precedent to us woful sinners, and teach us easily to pardon and patiently to pass by all the provocations of our fellow-creatures. How many blasphemous mouths are continually open against the Majesty of heaven! With what dreadful oaths do they tear and recrucify the precious body of his glorified Son, that sits at his own right hand! With what monstrous lies and hateful slanders do they disgrace his ambassadors, and vilify his chosen! Nay, where shall you find one of those who have sincerely given their names unto Christ, whose neglected innocency is not trampled upon with the feet of pride and contempt, and whose guiltless fame lies not bleeding under the merciless strokes of intemperate tongues? How many sons and daughters of Belial do horribly, and with a high hand profane his sabbaths, pollute his sacraments, and turn their backs upon his word! How many everywhere turn themselves into barrels and beasts, even into sinks, by drunkenness! How many Nimrods and machiavellian landlords grind the faces of the poor! In a word, how many incarnate devils walk up and down the earth, with hearts and hands as full as hell of all manner of mischief, lewdness, and rebellion! And yet we see, in the mean time, our gracious God bears patiently with these numerous and prodigious provocations. Though he be armed with his own irresistible omnipotence, have ever in a readiness all the angels of heaven, all the creatures upon earth, all the devils in hell, nay, the very hands and consciences of such stubborn rebels, to be the instruments and executioners of his just wrath upon their sins; yet doth he sweetly and fairly temper and moderate his indignation, to see if the riches of his goodness and forbearance, and longsuffering, will lead them to repentance. If almighty God, whose majesty, blessed and glorious for ever, is chiefly wronged, even by thy wrongs also, whose mildness and mercy are most shamefully abused with the horrible ingratitude and intolerable contempt of such as hate to be reformed, be so wonderfully patient, then be not thou perverse; but rather heap coals of fire upon thine enemy's head by kindness and love, that thou mayest be the charitable child of thy Father who is in heaven, who suffers his rain to fall as well upon heaths and weeds, as upon flowers and fruit trees.

(4.) By harbouring heart-burning and angry thoughts in thy breast against those thou art tempted to hate, thou wofully hardenest thine own heart, which is an unspeakable hurt, and deprivest thyself, all the while thou art so evil tempered, of the blessing, benefit, and comfort of all the ordinances, not only of the sacrament of the Lord's supper, as ignorant people suppose, but also of prayer, hearing the word, singing of psalms, and conference, 1 Tim. ii. 8; Matt. v. 23, 24. Now, what extreme madness is it, and foolish cruelty to thine own soul, by cherishing and keeping warm in thy bosom such a base dunghill viper as revengeful spite, to cast the whole frame of thy spiritual building into combustion, and to make God thine enemy, whereby thou hurtest thyself incomparably more than thou canst ever possibly harm thine enemy?

(5.) A great deal of spiritual good doth, by accident, accrue to the christian by the malice of his enemies. The raging and railing enemies of God's people serve as scullions to scour the Lord's vessels of honour; as shepherds' dogs to hunt Christ's sheep into order, and to purer pastures. 1. Their narrow watching over the ways of the believer to take him tripping, and prying into all passages of his life, upon purpose to disgrace his profession, should make him walk more precisely, and to hold a continual counterwatch over all his courses, that he give no just cause of offence, or any true matter of cavil or calumniation. Whence it is that David prayeth, "Lead me in a plain path, because of mine enemies," Psa. xxvii. 11, or those who observe me. 2. Their hitting him in the teeth with the reproach of his former sins should serve as a remembrancer unto him, to revise and renew more effectually and feelingly the great work of his first repentance, and to open afresh a fountain of penitential tears; or at least of new grief, that he can grieve no more for those particular sins which any cursing Shimei or slanderous Doeg brings into his mind upon such occasion. For it is the manner of ignorant enemies to God's holy ways, to charge upon his children, even with much bitterness and insult, the faults and follies of their unregenerate time. Though almighty God hath buried them for ever in his mercy, yet they will never suffer them to die out of their malice. Though the blood of Christ hath covered them everlastingly from the sight of God, and search of Satan, yet their base and dunghill spite will ever and anon rake into them again to their disgrace. Thus were Austin and Beza, two great lights of the church, in their times; and so are many other modern worthies and champions of Christ daily dealt with. In which case, learned Austin sweetly replied to the Donatists upbraiding him in such an unworthy fashion with the impiety and impurity of his former life; "Look," said he, "how much they blame my fault, so much I commend and praise my Physician." And blessed Beza, to a fellow objecting unto him his youthful poems; "This man vexeth himself because Christ hath vouchsafed me his grace." And king David, with whom I should have begun, when Shimei railed upon him and called him murderer, said, "Let him alone, and let him curse: for the

Lord hath bidden him," 2 Sam. xvi. 11. And yet besides this, I doubt not but upon these occasions David's heart bled afresh for his sin; Austin's, for his former heresy and sensuality; Beza's, for the vanity of his youth. 3. Their blazing abroad some special visible scandalous infirmity of his, and yet to which he is exposed, and, as it were, hurried by the impetuousness of some sudden passion or violent temptation, and which is one of his greatest griefs, and much matter of mourning in secret, should cause him to strengthen his watch, and improve all his spiritual valour against the assaults and insinuations of it. 4. Their malicious fathering upon him, by false reports, those faults he yet never fell into, and yet to which he may be naturally much inclinable, should furnish him with more than ordinary care and courage, wisdom and watchfulness, to prevent the scandal of any such guiltiness. 5. Their slanderous laying to his charge the things he never did, nor was ever like to do, which is also a hellish humour and devilish trick of profaneness against profession, should lead him to a strict inquiry into his heart and life, to find out some other sin of which, upon that occasion, God would have him take notice and mortify. It may be thou art falsely charged with hypocrisy, look that thou be not earthly-minded; with pride, look that thou be not passionate; with worldliness, look that thou be not lukewarm.

Thus have I somewhat insisted longer upon this point, on purpose to stir up and quicken the spirits of all God's people to a fruitful, constant exercise of christian charity and bounty towards their poor brethren; to be as well plentiful in works of mercy as precise in duties of piety; (God loves mercy as well as sacrifice, nay, in some cases, he prefers it;) to be so much more mindful and apprehensive of all opportunities for a sincere discharge of this much urged and honoured duty, as the wicked are malicious, and pharisees forward, to charge upon them the contrary.

For you know that carnal men are extremely greedy of casting aspersions and disgraces upon the innocency of religious professors. No excellency of parts, singularity, worth, eminency of zeal, height of holiness, integrity and purity of life, can possibly privilege the best man that ever breathed the life of grace in the bosom of the church, from the scourge of tongues. The only worthies upon earth, of whom the world was not worthy, were vexed with cruel mockings, Heb. xi. 36. Paul, that precious pillar of God's church, was called "a pestilent fellow," Acts xxiv. 5; nay, Christ Jesus himself, in whom the fulness of the Godhead dwelt bodily, was accused of having a devil, John vii. 20. And no marvel that they who daily blaspheme the mighty Lord of heaven and earth, blessed for ever, should deal thus with his children. Daily experience tracks them in five pestilent passages this way; it is their practice, with all their cunning, and upon all occasions, 1. To lessen, disgrace, and disparage all they can the graces, worth, and good parts of good men. 2. To report true things maliciously, and upon purpose to bring them into hatred and disesteem: so Doeg dealt with David. 3. To charge upon them, with much credulity and confidence, things they never did, never knew, never thought or dreamed of. 4. With lewd foreheads, and the very impudence of hell, to fasten upon them, by slanderous imputation, those sins and vices, in the contrary graces and virtues whereof they are many times very eminent and remarkable. Elijah was slandered to be a troubler of the state, 1 Kings xviii. 17; whereas, in truth, he was the strongest pillar of the kingdom, the very chariots and horsemen of Israel, 2 Kings ii. 12. 5. Nay, and which is yet more, to father upon them those faults wherein they themselves, hateful hypocrites! are grossly and notoriously guilty. Tertullus tells Felix that Paul was "a pestilent fellow," Acts xxiv. 5; or, as it is in the original, " a very plague;" whereas not only Paul was one of the best men upon earth, but Tertullus himself a cut-throat of all goodness, and furious opposer of the glorious gospel. Joseph was charged by his lewd mistress with an assault upon her chastity; whereas he was not only more free that way, but also she herself was notoriously naught. Ahab called Elijah a troubler of Israel, whereas not only that blessed prophet was the very strength of that state, but also himself, by his abominable, covetous, idolatrous villanies, brought confusion and misery upon the whole kingdom.

Now, out of this cunning, malicious humour, carnal men lie in wait, and are most eager to apprehend any shadow of occasion; or, rather than fail, to make matter in their own spiteful brains, or take it up from the lying oracle of some frothy ale-bench, whereby to stain the honour of profession with the unworthiest imputations of covetousness, hard-heartedness, and unmercifulness; whereas they themselves, mere men of this world, are as covetous as the skin will hold, fast nailed and glued unto the earth, never in their life lift up a joyful thought towards heaven, neither dare think seriously upon the world to come without a great deal of slavish sadness and secret terror. And in their grasping of worldly goods, they care not at all for conscience, make no account at all of that most certain strict account at God's dreadful tribunal, but only how to carry matters smoothly and plausibly in the eyes of men, and daub over their unjust dealings with close conveyances and tricks of wit.

I go not about here to apologize for any uncharitable counterfeits, or those most odious outside christians, who put on the glory of an angel in outward profession, that they may play the devil more unobservedly in usurious practices, oppressions, and unconscionable griping; wear a cloak of zeal, in conformity to the external forms of obedience to the first table, upon purpose to cover their cruelty and inhumanity, in undermining and overreaching their brethren, and to prey the more invisibly upon the simplicity of those whom they deceive by their appearance.

But yet, I must tell you, that many times even some of God's own best children are full falsely and foully charged by foul-mouthed worldlings themselves with worldliness, covetousness, and imputations of that nature, who, by God's mercy, are so far from doting upon earth and the fading glory thereof, that, in their retired and advised thoughts, they would not lose the love and light of God's countenance, and testimony of a good conscience, to win the whole world; they would not exchange their comforts of godliness and interests in a crown of life for ten thousand worlds, were they all turned into one invaluable pearl. They feel themselves incomparably more comforted and kindly refreshed at the heart root with one thought of heaven and that endless joyful rest above through all eternity, than with a world of earthly contemplations, though all composed of gold, pleasures, possessions, honours, diadems, and all the glorious and most desirable treasures under the sun. And who, in respect of any unconscionableness, wrongs, injustice, or wicked ways of getting, might with sincerity of heart, proportionably to their states and callings, take up Samuel's protestation, "Behold, here I am: witness against me before the Lord and before his anointed: whose ox have I taken? or whose ass have I taken? or whom have I defrauded? whom have I oppressed? or of whose hand have I received any bribe to blind mine eyes therewith? and I will restore it you?" 1 Sam. xii. 3. And sincere thoughts, resolutions, and protestations to this purpose, are clear evidences of unearthly-mindedness. Blessed Job pointedly illustrated this point: his own friend charged him with inhumanity, covetousness, and cruelty; and thereupon inferred that God's afflicting hand was heavy upon him. How much more think you would the children of fools and children of villains viler than the earth, of whom he elsewhere complains, vex him slanderously? "Is not thy wickedness great," said Eliphaz, "and thine iniquities infinite? For thou hast taken a pledge from thy brother for nought, and stripped the naked of their clothing. Thou hast not given water to the weary to drink, and thou hast withholden bread from the hungry. Thou hast sent widows away empty, and the arms of the fatherless have been broken. Therefore snares are round about thee, and sudden fear troubleth thee," Job xxii. 5—7, 9, 10. Whereas, in deed and truth, righteous Job was right nobly minded, tender-hearted, charitable, bountiful, as appears by his confident declaration to the contrary; "If I have withheld the poor from their desire, or have caused the eyes of the widow to fail, or have eaten my morsel myself alone, and the fatherless hath not eaten thereof; if I have seen any perish for want of clothing, or any poor without covering, if his loins have not blessed me, and if he were not warmed with the fleece of my sheep; if I have lifted up my hand against the fatherless, when I saw my help in the gate, then let mine arm fall from my shoulder blade, and mine arm be broken from the bone," Job xxxi. 16, 17, 19—22.

Thus, many times an imputation of worldliness, hard-heartedness, or unhospitality, is laid upon God's children, without any cause, truth, or conscience; occasioned, as I conceive, (for I desire to discover unto you a depth of Satan's malice in this point,) partly from the parties accusing and slandering: partly from the parties accused and slandered.

Occasions ministered by *profane men* are such as these:—

1. They many times, when they find their consciences disquieted, their former courses controlled, their carnal humours crossed and contradicted, and themselves much diseased and disturbed in the pursuit of their sensual pleasures, by the searching power of a conscionable ministry; or when they plainly see that their unzealousness, lukewarmness, and formality in religion, is censured and condemned by the forwardness and zealous carriage and conversation of the saints, they seek by all means, and labour might and main, to oppose those ministers that so vex them with their faithful preaching; and those godly christians which silently disgrace them with their gracious life and zealous exercise of christianity. And, therefore, since many times, by God's goodness, they

cannot find any visible or conspicuous matter or miscarriage to charge them with truly, because the saints practice not gross and notorious sins, such as swearing, drunkenness, lying, uncleanness, sabbath-breaking, idleness, and the vanities of good-fellowship, like themselves; therefore I say, they audaciously dive into their hearts with unhallowed censures, and lay unto their charges those invisible errors which none can see but God's all-seeing eye, and from which they cannot be cleared and acquitted but only by their own consciences and his highest tribunal. So that they take credit that such imputations, though groundless and false, yet will be sure to cleave to the good name of God's children, as certainly without redress or remedy, as they were devised without truth or charity. We may see this clearly in the present point, and the slander of hypocrisy, which is also the ordinary portion of the best, from men of the world. When profane opposers unto grace pry curiously into all the ways of a child of God, and can find nothing so faulty in his outward carriage, or reprovable in the ordinary course of his life, as they expect and desire, yet, lest they should not show themselves the real children of Satan, the accuser of the brethren, they will be meddling one way or other, they will be nibbling at his good name with some such speeches as these;—" Well, well, though he be an excellent pulpit man, or a zealous professor, yet is he not so and so; is not he as well given unto and greedy of the world as other men?" When they hear other men commend his zeal and forwardness in profession, they will be casting out such malicious doubts as these;—" Go to, my masters, I fear that all is not gold that glisters." Now, how is it possible, or by what outward witnesses can the christian clear and discharge himself of the imputations of worldliness and hypocrisy, since the one lies in the greedy affections of the mind, and the other lurks in the hidden corners of the heart; the purity and secrets of which none can truly see and censure but the Searcher of all hearts? Were a man accused of adultery, drunkenness, or such visible notoriousness, there might be means found for the manifestation of his innocency, by an exact scanning of time, place, and other circumstances. But this is the malicious and pestilent policy of Satan and his agents, when they see that the saints, by the mercy of God, are free from those gross sins and notorious corruptions which ordinarily reign in the children of darkness, they spitefully and cunningly lay unto their charge imputations of such a nature, from the which, though they be free, they cannot free themselves; and though they be clear, yet by reason of the malice of men and invisibleness of the matter, it will never so appear, until the brightness of Christ's coming bring forth their righteousness as the light, and their judgment as the noon-day; and of which the slanderers have none other ground in the world but this, because themselves are such. For put a profane worldling to prove the slander of worldliness and hypocrisy which he puts upon the christian, and he will be able to give you neither probable reason nor wise word to purpose. And no marvel: for let the matter come to be examined, and he shall find that man, whom he so miscensures, to be both faithful towards God, and conscientious towards man in all his ways. Not only innocent from oppression, corruption, wrongful dealings, and all unlawful ways of getting; but also, in a special manner, with a most compassionate tenderness and love, right dearly affected to every true-hearted Nathanael and the whole household of faith, (which no unregenerate man can possibly be, and which is the truest and noblest issue of sanctified charity.) Nay, and besides, not any ways wanting (though it stand not with the policy of profaneness to acknowledge it) in other charitable actions, with spiritual discretion, to any truly distressed and miserable. And, therefore, there is no ground in the world left for such graceless lies, but only this,— carnal worldlings carve conditions to other men out of the crookedness of their own nature, and cunningly put on the policy of cutpurses, who in throngs at fairs and markets call upon others to beware of cutpurses, that themselves, being truly so, may with less suspicion and observation dive into the pockets and purses of true men. Many there are, who, being themselves truly worldly and hypocrites indeed, call christians so, that the mask of their villanous hypocrisy may be less marked, and themselves root in earthliness until they reach the very bottom of hell, and no man regard them.

2. If a man would be irreligious and unconscionable, it is a very easy thing to grow rich and into reputation with the world. If once he so far harden his heart, sear his conscience, and abandon the fear of God, that he resolve, without remorse or shame, to defraud, dissemble, bribe, oppress, put to usury, serve the times, make use of all men for his own turn, to cloak cruelty with conscience, pretend friendship when he purposes to deal like a Turk; in a word, to plot and practise any lewd device or conscienceless course for his advantage and rising, I do not see how such a fellow, in these griping days and times of confusion, should escape wealth,

preferment, and respect in the world. And as it is easy for fellows of such ill conscience to thrive, and wicked men to grow wealthy, so methinks it is no great matter for such to make sometimes very goodly shows to the world of bountifulness and liberal profusions in feasts, entertainments, and larger gifts to the poor, out of their superfluities and heaps of ill-gotten goods. But herein (though it be well that such goods do good unto some) they are like unto thieves, who, having robbed some rich merchant, and taken hundreds from him, do scatter here and there by the way some small pieces of silver to the poor. But these are a very poor amends for their merciless bloodshed and lawless robberies; this is, as they say, to rob Peter, and clothe Paul. Thus many great men keep great houses, and that is well; it is fit greatness should be accompanied with liberality; but alas! they grind the faces of the poor and eat the flesh of God's people to uphold their hospitality. So some ministers heap living upon living, that so they may be enabled and furnished to purchase a great name by keeping a great house; but alas! they maintain their greatness and state with the price of the precious blood of souls, and feed the greedy humour of their pharisaical goodfellowship with the fearful gangrene of spiritual bloodshed. So others may be sometimes good unto the poor, and bountiful, as they say, in their own houses; but alas! they mar all their alms; giving by unlawful getting, and turn that, which of itself is one of those sacrifices with which God is well pleased, into abomination and sin unto themselves. A goodly matter, sure, to scatter here and there, now and then, some few drops of charitable devotions; whereas they have many huge and headlong torrents of gain and goods

coming in daily, by oppression, violence, mercilessness, devouring widows' houses, rackings, enhanc-
ings, gripings, usuries, immoderate takings, and
so forth.

3. Profane hypocrites are commonly pharisaical
in their alms-giving; they affect and pursue observation, singularity, vain-glorious ostentations in
their contributions of charity. Their forefathers,
the pharisees, when they gave their alms, made a
trumpet to be sounded before them; so these fellows,
their followers, and succeeding actors upon the
same stage of hypocrisy, lest their good deeds should
die in the distribution, and be obscurely buried
in the bellies of the poor, they also get unto themselves a kind of tale-bearing trumpeters too. They
cunningly observe those opportunities, and single
out such objects of their commiseration and charitable devotions, whereby they may soonest and most
compendiously purchase a name of being good to
the poor, and have their bountiful disposition blazed
abroad with most circumstances, best advantages,
and partial enlargements. And thus it is a very
easy thing for a pharisee to be famous in this way;
for since he gives more for commendation, than for
conscience, far more for praise amongst men, than
out of a true-hearted compassion to the party, he
dares dispense with a good conscience, and take
liberty unto himself to place his good turns there
where there is best possibility of being spoken of,
and greatest hope of the richest return of applause
and admiration. So that such an one ordinarily,
in his open-heartedness and charitable distributions,
hath a special eye and inclination to those that flatter him to his face, and are likely to prove the
loudest trumpets of his bountifulness abroad where

they come. And he is so far from a right and seasonable apprehension of due circumstances, difference of parties, and those spiritual discretions observable and necessary in such christian exercises of love, and from the practice of the apostle's precept, "Do good unto all men, especially unto them who are of the household of faith," Gal. vi. 10, that he would rather afford his helping hand for the relief and raising up of a decayed goodfellow than of a distressed christian.

4. Though carnal men be so covetous, and so hold fast earthly contentments, that they would rather lose their precious souls everlastingly, than leave them; yet, if it might be, if it were possibly compatible, they would give anything in the world, both to serve and satisfy themselves in the ways of vanity, and afterwards to save their souls in the day of wrath,—both to partake of the pleasures of the present life, and to be secured from the vengeance that is to come. What would not the great ones of the world give to purchase two heavens; one here, and another in the other world? What would not sensual worldlings part with, to redeem their sins, if they might have a dispensation to continue in sin? to live the life of vanity and lust here, and afterwards to die the death of the righteous, and to receive their crown? In such cases, in their sober considerations, (so that their present temporal happiness sustain no hazard or diminution, nor the delights of their sweet sin any disturbance,) they would not stand upon any worldly good; though it were "thousands of rams, or with ten thousands of rivers of oil;" nay, they would give their "first-born for their transgression, the fruit of the body for the

sin of the soul," Micah vi. 7. Many there are who may be easily persuaded, and can well find in their hearts to give anything towards the service of God, and salvation of their souls, save themselves; I mean, their hearts and affections, which the world and their darling pleasures have principally possessed. Hence it is that many rich ones and men of the world, being otherwise very guilty, and obnoxious in many respects, are very willing and well content many times to contribute bountifully to good uses, and to make good show of liberality towards the poor; that thereby less notice may be taken of their other notoriousness, and with some kind of hope so to cover and conceal many gross corruptions from the wrath of God, and the world's censure. For, I know not how, there is an inbred opinion and conceit seated in the hearts of natural men and papists, that alms-deeds, and such works of charity, make amends for other miscarriages, though foul and scandalous, and are pleasing to almighty God, though the parties from whom they proceed be polluted with secret impurities and reigning sins. Since, therefore, they persuade their hearts that charitable devotions and distributions have some power, as it were, somewhat to appease Divine wrath, and to satisfy for other sinful exorbitances and aberrations, and see plainly that it is the most compendious way to purchase a great deal of credit in these cold and compassionless times, and the only object to divert the eyes of the greater from the observation of their other faults, therefore, they open their hearts the more liberally, and enlarge their bowels to greater bountifulness, which otherwise their covetousness would keep shut

Thus many, to diminish the horror and remarkableness of their unmortified lusts and open lewdness, exercise a good art without a good heart.

Occasions from the *parties slandered* are such as these:

1. Christians, of all men in the world, are the special marks and ordinary objects upon which are discharged and exercised all kinds of malice and mischief; not only the impoisoned arrows of spiteful tongues, the swords of tyrants, the flames of cruelty, but also many lesser and less-marked vexations, as wrongs, oppressions, mercilessness, and many unconscionable usages. Profane men, being seated in high places, or besotted with the world's favours and flatteries, do many times, out of their pride and malice, very contemptuously roll down, as from aloft, indignities, insolences, many hard and heavy inhumanities and injustices upon God's children, as a number of neglected underlings. So that, as the prophet speaks, "He that departeth from evil, maketh himself a prey," Isa. lix. 15. He that by the mercy of God breaks out of the bonds of Satan, into the blessings and blessed state of grace, shall for ever after, not only be furiously persecuted by the rage of hell, and malice of profaneness, but also lie more open to the insults, wrongs, and oppressions of his adversaries, and treacherous insinuations of false friends. Since therefore christians, by reason of their patience, the world's discountenance, disaffection of great ones, their own resolute disallowance of all indirect courses, and of any base and unconscionable advantage, are many times mightily oppressed by the greedy policies, and encroachments of boisterous worldlings, and causeless opposers; and not only so, but

sometimes also cunningly and insensibly preyed upon even by professed friends. For there are a kind of men which putting on for the time the glory of an angel, mix themselves with God's people, and press into their company, only because they see and find them to be such as from whom, by reason of the singleness and simplicity of their hearts, the unsuspiciousness of their charity, the equity and conscionableness of their dealing, in these cozening, supplanting, and undermining days, they may the most fairly and easily suck out the greatest advantage. I say therefore, since God's children are most subject both to the wrongs of open enemies, and supplantation of seeming friends, they are many times not so enabled in outward things or strong in their worldly state, to make such a flourish in dispersing their superfluities as those men which get without conscience, and disburse without spiritual discretion.

2. A christian dare not, for his life, so far enlarge his conscience, as to gain by any unwarrantable means, or unconscionable course, as oppression, corruption, cozening, violence, lying, or unjust dealing; and therefore in this griping and greedy age, in the highest noontide of iniquity, or rather darkest midnight of the works of darkness, though outward want be infinitely countervailed with inward comfort, he doth not commonly come to that excess and superfluity of temporal things, which many times worldlings, with wider consciences, easily and immeasurably engross. The largest consciences, in these last and worst days, are the only devourers and swallowers down of worldly wealth. A religious resolution to save a man's soul is many times a notable curb to keep him from

growing rich and into reputation with the world. God's blessings, even in temporal things, I deny not, are sometimes very plentifully upon the right owners, God's own children; and both heavenly and earthly happiness have been wreathed together by the merciful hand of God, and set upon their heads; but if we look upon the common courses holden in the world that way, and in all forecast of carnal reason, he is likeliest to grow rich and rise who is resolved to damn his soul. In the ordinary conceit of profane policy, and apprehensions of worldly wisdom, Joseph missed a great deal of earthly contentment, and in a precise humour put from him much possibility of preferment, by not yielding to the solicitations of his mistress. Micaiah, in not joining with the four hundred false prophets, in their lying flattery to please the two kings. Jonathan, in not joining with his father Saul, for the destruction of David. Had a sensual worldling been in Joseph's case, an unsanctified minister in Micaiah's, an ambitious Absalom in Jonathan's, assuredly they had all yielded to the several temptations. The conscience of an unregenerate man will marvellously stretch itself, and grant out very large dispensations, especially when any special glory, profit, or pleasure of the world, is in pursuit and possibility. It was so in all ages; and at this day many a good man, many times, of great spirit, worth, and understanding, sits obscurely in a very low place, and is kept under in mean estate by the world's oppressions, because he dare not displease God, or enlarge his conscience proportionably to the vast gulf of the time's corruptions. This is the very true reason why folly is set in such great excellency, and sincerity seated in the lowest place; why so many servants are on horseback, and so many princes walking as servants on the ground. Since, therefore, the christian is happily restrained by the checks and tenderness of a good conscience, from all unwarrantable means, and unconscionable courses of getting; though his heart be most compassionate, his heart heated with true charity, and his desires enlarged to do good unto all, and all the good he can; yet he is many times kept short, by reason of his short pittance, from those outward real expressions and effects of charity, to which his tender-hearted zealous affection is inwardly truly inflamed; and from those more bountiful effusions and liberalities which rich worldlings may, out of the tithe, nay, the thousandth part of their ill-gotten goods, plentifully perform.

3. Christians know themselves bound in conscience to a careful provision for their families; to diligence and faithfulness in their callings; from all unnecessary expenses, and the prodigal effusions of good-fellowship, from ambitious affectation of applause and vainglory, by pharisaical ostentations: and therefore, to the greedy observation of carnal eyes, and undiscerning unregenerate men, who want no malice to mistake, or cunning to apprehend any shadow or show of any seeming advantage for the disgrace of good men; they seem, and are miscensured to hold upon the world, to feed upon earthly-mindedness, not to be so open-hearted, good-natured, and charitably affected as other good-fellows, as they call them, which make no such profession of purity and preciseness. And this misconceit of God's children is made more passable, by the profane plausibleness of vainglorious worldlings. It is

sooner, and more easily entertained, because unconscionable men take any compendious course of growing rich, which their covetous humour suggests unto them; and by allowance and exercise of unlawful means of getting, bring in many times great store of wealth with much ease; and therefore need not toil so in their trades, or follow the businesses of their proper callings with such attention and exactness. And if at any time they resolve to be more bountiful and liberal, they commonly make choice of those times, places, persons, and other circumstances, whereby (as they think) their good natures may be most noted, and their names grow greatest for extraordinary kindness and good-fellowship.

4. The christian doth incline and enlarge the tenderness of his special compassion towards the necessities of the saints, and conveys the noblest issues and effects of his inflamed charity into the bosoms of God's children. And indeed he is governed by the commandment; "Do good unto all men, especially unto them who are of the household of faith." And there was never more need, for however worldlings may be bountiful one to another, and exercise many mutual offices of kindness and carnal love among themselves, yet, for the most part, they are very uncompassionate, straitlaced, and hard-hearted towards distressed christians. Nay, ordinarily, they are rather ready to combine and contribute their malices, policies, and purses, to throw them down lower into outward want and misery, than to put forth their helping hands for their recovery, comfort, and enlargement; though it were in their sufferings for God's cause, and testimony of a good conscience. So that, as christian distresses are the

principal object of the christian's compassion and bounty, so worldlings are only heartily kind and openhearted to the men of the world. Now, that you may rightly understand the point, you must conceive, that the good deeds and commendable parts of an unregenerate man are ever carried more boisterously and with greater noise, are entertained by the world with a far more general applause and notice, than the godly actions and divine graces of God's children. "The world deals with men in this case," says Greenham, "as it deals with witches and physicians; the witch, though she fail in twenty things, yet if she do some one thing aright, though it be but small, the world loveth and commendeth her, for a good and wise woman. But the physician, if he work six hundred cures; yet if, through the waywardness of his patient, or for the punishment of his patient's sin, he fail but in one, that one failure doth more turn to his discredit, than his manifold goodly and notable cures do get him praise. In this manner," he continues, "doth the world deal with men: if a worldly man have but an outward gift of strength, of speech, or of comeliness, he shall be greatly praised, and counted a goodly man, though he be an idolater or a profane person; and though he swim and flow over in all manner of vices; but let the child of God be truly zealous in true religion, let him be honest and holy in conversation, yet if there be but one infirmity in him, or if he have through weakness fallen into some one sin, that one infirmity against which he striveth, or that one sin for which he is grieved, shall drown all the graces of God in him, be they ever so great, and the world will account him a most wicked man." It is just so in this particular: a profane man many times by some one special markable act of bounty and contribution, or for some few seasonable ostentations of good fellowship and kind nature, get the start and precedency in opinion and reputation with the world, before many a gracious christian, who bears in his bosom a constant habitual tender-heartedness to all true necessities, and as occasion offers opens his heart, his hands, and his house, most joyfully and compassionately, to refresh and comfort the needful exigencies of any true-hearted Nathanael. And the worldling doth the rather and more easily carry it, because, in the dispersing of his doles and largesses, he many times makes choice of tale-bearing trumpeters, who, knowing his pharisaical humour, are likely to blaze his bounty most abroad in the world; whereas the christian singles out specially for such purposes the distressed saints, from whom he expects no more than a secret and silent blessing of God in their hearts, for his goodness conveyed unto them by such an instrument.

Thus I have discovered unto you a mystery of Satan's malice, and the cunning despitefulness of profane men, who labour many times out of pure malice and wilful misunderstandings to fasten upon God's children imputations of worldliness, hardheartedness, cruel dealing, and such like.

The occasions, as I have thus fully told you, are such as these.

Upon the *worldling's* part : 1. His hearty desire to disgrace christians, whom since, by the grace of God, he finds free from open gross sins, presently grows to such speeches as these; " Why, but are not such and such given to the world, as well as other men ?" &c. 2. He dares enlarge his conscience to courses of unlawful getting; and therefore it is more easy for him to open his hand now and then to some boisterous flourishes of liberal-mindedness; especially, since thereby he hopes to repair his reputation for his other indiscretions. 3. He is commonly pharisaical in an ambitious exercise and more public acting of his deeds of charity, and therefore, whatsoever he doth that way, is for the most part carried abroad with special and remarkable noise and notice. 4. He would gladly still the cryings of his guilty conscience, and seem to himself to redeem the sins of his soul, by a more bountiful disbursement of outward things.

Upon the *christian's* part: 1. He is most subject to wrongs and weakenings in his outward state; both by the violent encroachments of professed opponents, and covetous insinuations of false friends. 2. He dare not, for any gold or good, undertake any unwarrantable and scandalous course of gaining. 3. He finds himself bound in conscience to faithful diligence in his calling, and christian provision for his family. 4. He spends the best and most of his bounty and charity upon the household of faith.

But, on this point, as I said before, I apologize for none but those, whom their own consciences, and the merciful tribunal of God, do acquit. Let christians look unto it; the world is very watchful, and greedy, with great curiosity and cunning, to apprehend the least shadow of any occasions for the blaspheming of the ways of God, and the disgracing of his children. And therefore ever and anon you shall hear the spirit of profaneness crying out, and complaining: "You see these fellows, which make such show of forwardness and purity, what they are: none so covetous; none so uncharitable; none so unmerciful, and cruel in their dealings as they; none so hard-hearted to the poor." Now, although such bitter speeches as these are often the mere evaporations of pure malice, and flow from no other ground in the world, but only from the gall of graceless men; yet let all those who truly fear God, take heed how they give just occasion thereunto. Assuredly it were far better for him, whosoever he be, that a millstone were hanged about his neck, and he were drowned in the depth of the sea; than that by the continuance of his cruel and unconscionable dealings in the world, he should minister just occasion to any railing Rabshakeh to revile the servants of the living God, or to slander their holy profession. Methinks, this one preservative should be powerful enough to keep the heart of every christian from doting upon the world, or suffering it to be possessed thereof. It is this,—every christian, by a fruitful faith, may be assured of a crown of life, either by assurance of adherence, or evidence, or both. Now, if but once a day he should take a serious survey of the glory, everlastingness, and unutterable excellences of that immortal crown, methinks it were able so to dull the edge, and dissolve the drossiness of all earthly desires, that they would never more be able to heat or harden his heart with immoderate or delightful repose upon the vexing vanities of any worldly thing. I say it again; methinks, if a man do but once a day cast the eye of his faith upon that crown of life, which our dear Redeemer holds for us in his hand, ready to set upon our heads when we shall be dissolved from this vale of tears; the goodly glory thereof should be able to dispel these mists of fading vanities, and hurtful fumes of honours, riches, and earthly pleasures; which this great dunghill of the world, heated by the fire of men's inordinate lusts, doth evaporate and interpose between the sight of their souls and the bliss of heaven.

Worldliness, earthly-mindedness, covetousness, are infinitely unbecoming an heir of heaven. Be fired then, and frightened from all inclinations and bent that way, by such considerations as these:

1. It is a most base and dunghill distemper, which eats up not only all religion and honesty, manliness and reason, natural affection and discretion, but even also humanity and friendliness; so that a man had almost as well converse with a cannibal for any ingenuous and conscionable dealing, as with a truly covetous wretch.

2. Shall the immortal comprehensiveness of the divine and excellent soul, which is able to peruse and pass over heaven and earth in a moment, and capable of beholding the mystery of Christ and the eternal vision of God, be unworthily confined to a piece of ground, a heap of white and yellow clay? a vile imprisonment, and inexpiable wrong to so noble a nature!

3. It is a devouring gangrene, an insatiable wolf, which the more it hath, ever the more hungry it is. It is as fire which increaseth by that nourishment which is given unto it. The horseleech's daughter, the grave, is nothing to this gulf, and it holds the heart continually upon the rack of self-accusation and carking; for three ravenous vultures seize upon it successively, and gnaw in their turns with incredible torment,—care in getting, fear in keeping, and grief in leaving.

4. All God's blessed ones, in all ages, embracing the promises of life in the armies of their faith,

willingly confessed themselves to be pilgrims and strangers here upon earth, looking for a city in another country, "which hath foundations, whose builder and maker is God." There are good reasons, besides religion, that they should go into such resolutions, for all things here below are full of transitoriness, mortality, and change: "vanity of vanities, all is vanity;" but above, is constancy and an eternity of all excellences, perfections, and pleasures. Besides, that thou shalt have there a body brighter than the sun, a soul replenished with unutterable delights, the glorious company of Christ Jesus, angels, saints, christian friends, the vision and fruition of God, blessed for ever, wherein consists the crown and life of all celestial joys; I say, to say nothing of these, but even the space of one foot upon the pavement of the empyrean heaven is incomparably more worth than the great body of the whole earth, were it all turned into gold, and beset with as many invaluable pearls as it is now with blades of grass.

5. Nature seemeth, saith a mere moralist, in the first birth of gold, and from the barren spots whence it proceedeth, to have presaged the misery of those that are in love with it; for it hath so ordered the matter, that in those places where it is found there grows with it neither grass nor plant, nor anything of worth; giving us to understand thereby, that in those minds where the desire of this metal grows, there cannot remain so much as a spark of true honour and virtue.

6. God is not only a Father, but also All-sufficient; why shouldst thou then fear want, that fearest him? He provides every day for millions of fowls; will he then be wanting to a man, to a chris-

tian, to his own child? Christ himself, pressing reasons to this purpose, tells us that our heavenly Father clothes the lily above Solomon's royalty, and feeds the fowls of the air, which neither sow nor reap, nor gather into barns. What a cursed veil, then, of base distrust darkens thine hard heart, that thou shouldst either cark or deal unconscionably?

7. Two hours of fire will disperse and consume the hoard of a hundred years' heaping together. And where art thou then? Thine heart then is seized upon at once with unutterable anguish, and the very horror of hell, for the loss of thine heaven upon earth; and with cries of blood and furies of conscience for thy covetous, cruel, usurious, injurious courses for many years. Thus many a worldling spins a strong thread to strangle himself both temporally and eternally.

8. The sun is a very glorious and contented creature, and yet it harbours no golden mine in its fair and refulgent body. The blessed angels are full of all felicities, and yet they have no silver; they want no happiness, and yet they want gold. Heaven, the chief and royal seat of blessedness, is empty of these treasures: there grow no minerals; the vein of silver and gold is not to be found there. The Son of God himself, infinitely the most happy creature, I speak in respect of his humanity, that ever issued out of the hands of God, were there any such great matter or excellency in riches, had never said of himself, "The foxes have holes, and the birds of the air have nests: but the Son of Man hath not where to lay his head," Matt. viii. 20. Could a bearing-mantle of cloth of gold, and impearled cradle, delicious fare every day, thousands a year, make a man

truly happy, the right and royal Heir of all things would never have chosen a stable for his birth-chamber, a manger for his cradle, barley-bread for the entertainment of his followers, a less fixed habitation for himself than the poorest bird.

9. The sun and moon are far more glistering and glorious than the burnished gold of Ophir; and the poorest man hath as large a prospect and part in them as the vastest encloser or most griping usurer; but much more benefit by them than the rich worldlings by their golden heaps. For he is comfortably warmed and refreshed with the influence of their heat and light; but they, if the devil did not hoodwink them, might see every time they look thereon, that rust cleaving to their unrighteous mammon which hereafter "shall eat their flesh as it were fire," Jam. v. 3.

10. One star doth incomparably exceed in beauty and worth a golden earth; and if thou be truly God's, and have thy foot already upon the moon, Rev. xii. 1, as thou oughtest, thou shalt hereafter tread everlastingly upon thousands of them. Disdain then, in the mean time, to let thy heavenly spirit dote upon those baser hoards of shining earth, which are making themselves wings to fly away, as an eagle toward heaven; for riches are like transitory streams, which, posting by the side of a city, no man can stay. Were it not a senseless and foolish endeavour and expectation for a town to hope and assay to keep with them the hasty current of a mighty river, which none of a hundred towns before could hold? And dost thou expect any constancy of abode with thee of that thick clay which hath passed through so many hands before? Neither is it so much thine as the world's. A dog follows two

men; it is not known to whom he belongs until they be parted. Upon the arrest of death, thy wealth leaves thee everlastingly, and cleaves unto the world, and therefore it was worldly wealth.

11. Moderation and conscionableness in getting may, by the mercy of God, draw from his bountiful hand a more special extraordinary gracious providence and blessing upon posterity; whereas contrary carriage may bring a heavy curse. The prophet, who was husband to her who came crying to Elisha for comfort, did fear God, saith the text, 2 Kings iv. 1. Whereby he was happily restrained from all wicked ways of gaining and growing into wealth. Durst he have enlarged his conscience proportionably to the corruptions of those times, and shifted his sails according to the setting of every wind, as preachers of smooth things are wont, I see no reason but he might have been advanced to Jezebel's table as well as the four hundred flattering, false, temporizing prophets; and by serving the time also, have risen and enriched both himself and his. But this honest man would rather die in debt, leave his wife and children in extreme poverty, and expose his two sons as bondmen to the creditor, than put his hand to any manner of iniquity in getting, or to raise an outward rotten estate upon the ruin and desolation of men's precious souls. And what follows? Rather than the wife and children of such a man shall want, God will have the prophet do a miracle for their supply and comfort, as appears in the history. But now, on the other side, Gehazi, in the very following chapter, 2 Kings v., hopes, by bribing, to make himself and his children for ever. And what is the issue? He pulls thereby a horrible curse both upon himself and his posterity:

"The leprosy therefore of Naaman shall cleave unto thee, and unto thy seed for ever," ver. 27. Thou hadst better then leave a wallet to thy child to go from door to door, than a cursed hoard of ill-gotten goods.

12. But, above all, to curb thine heart from covetousness, meditate much upon such places as these, Matt. vi. 25—34; Phil. iv. 6; 1 Tim. vi. 9, 10; Jam. v. 1—3; Prov. xxiii. 5

OUR SPIRITUAL STATE.

Lastly, concerning a right and comfortable managing of our spiritual state, a point of deepest consideration and highest consequences, take notice of two extremes, two dangerous rocks upon which the soul may run, and split itself spiritually.

1. The one is a proud overprizing of our own graces, with a conceited, overweening self-admiration.

2. The other a dejected, distrustful undervaluing of God's mercies, the promises of life, and those graces which we possess in truth and holy desire, though not in that degree we desire.

Before I can seasonably and preparedly fall upon the first, to instruct punctually, and arm the christian against it, with whom I principally deal in this whole discourse, give me leave to discover a mystery of spiritual self-deceit, by which Satan sits presumptuously in the darkened minds and deluded imaginations of those whom with his cunning and malice he hoodwinks, and hardens to their endless confusion.

Many thousands, even under the means, and in

this glorious mid-day of the gospel, are groundlessly conceited that they are right, whereas, in truth and trial, they are rotten at the heart-root; that they are sure of heaven, when they are as yet most certainly of the family of hell. Neither is this any strange thing: so deluded were the foolish virgins, Matt. xxv. 11, 12; and so are all such outside christians. Those also in Luke xiii. 26, 27; and so are all who stand only on the work wrought, and bare task of religious duties, without the power of inward holiness. Likewise the young man in the gospel, Matt. xix. 20, with that generation mentioned in Prov. xxx. 12; and so are all such as justify themselves. So the proud pharisee, Luke xviii. 11, 12, who was so confident, that he gave God thanks for his blessed condition, when he was but yet a cursed unjustified rebel; and so are all of his formal strain. Those also in John viii. 39, who held themselves to be Abraham's children, whereas Christ tells them the devil was their father, ver. 44; and so are all those who build only upon the outward privileges of christianity, without personal purity. Likewise Paul, in the state of pharisaism; and so are all those, who, wandering out of the path which is called holy, swell with a proud opinionativeness and furious zeal above the banks of God's blessed book and bounds of all holy discretion, and will needs soar aloft on waxen wings of self-conceitedness and superficialness, to strange and uncouth heights of excellent fancies, without having ever laid a sound foundation in true humiliation for sin, and in self-denial. So deluded was the church of Laodicea, Rev. iii. 14, and all such lukewarm professors. Hence we have a taste what a world of people are wofully blindfolded by the prince of this world; and, through the insinuating imposture and unexamined delusion of spiritual self-deceit, are put into a fool's paradise of being already safe and secure for heaven; whereas as yet they are mere strangers to the mysteries of Christ and the new creation, and shall be certainly damned if they so continue; "for that which is highly esteemed among men is abomination in the sight of God," saith Christ to the self-justifying pharisees, Luke xvi. 15.

And yet some sorts of unregenerate men are here to be excepted from this general deluge of self-delusion, who lie not so grossly enwrapped in the juggling mists of the devil's angelical glory. Not that they are better than those deluded ones, or have any good assurance upon sound undeceiving grounds of their spiritual well-being, (for such an humble true persuasion is confined only to true converts,) but it happens by accident, that, by reason either of the extreme villany of their lives, or desperate positions of their antichristian doctrine, they see clear reasons that stand, like an armed man, in their convinced consciences, that if they continue in their forlorn courses they cannot possibly be saved; or else they feign reasons and coin distinctions upon purpose to exclude all from any infallible certainty of salvation. They are such as these:

1. Gross hypocrites, who deceive others, but not their own hearts, as Judas.

2. Those notorious ones, who in their cold blood will not stick to confess that they are yet quite wrong, and utterly wide from the way that is called holy, and will sometimes set a time when they purpose to cast off for ever, and cashier their sensual courses and swaggering company, and begin at length to look towards heaven, and learn the art of

saving their souls; and in the mean time they make a covenant with death, and are at an agreement with hell, Isa. xxviii. 15.

3. Other sons of Belial, whose hearts by their obstinate wallowing in the work of darkness, hardening their foreheads by their impudent villanies against the face of heaven, and with their own soul-murdering hands and horrible cruelty pressing a hot iron upon their consciences, are grown at length into such a prodigious rock, that though they know themselves to be posting towards the pit of hell, yet they are senseless and fearless of that fiery dungeon.

4. Those who, being convinced of the truth and goodness of the gospel, and approving in their judgment and conscience the power and practice of it, as the only way to everlasting bliss; but then turning their carnal eyes upon the furious enticings of their darling sins, and by the touchstone of sense comparing the pleasures of these which they presently grasp, with the spiritual strictness and promised joys of the other, stand infinitely unresolved and desperately obstinate, by no means and upon no terms to leave the present sensual joys of their earthly paradise; but rather choose, even in their cold blood, to turn their backs upon God, who is blessed for ever, his holy truth, service, servants, and all the glory in the world to come. And then, by good consequence, having thus subscribed and sealed by an irrevocable resolution, and sworn vassalage to be Satan's for ever, and for ever to stand on his side, receive into their hearts an inward certificate that they are utterly forsaken of God, and shall be certainly damned. Whereupon they boil inwardly with much malicious blasphemous rage against

God, whom they have renounced, persecute with implacable spite the blessed gospel and glorious ways of Christ, which they have so desperately rejected; and gnash the teeth, like so many already hellish fiends, against all those happy ones whom they see walk with constancy and comfort in that holy way to innumerable joys, which they, with certain knowledge of their heart, and against the clear light of their conscience, have wretchedly abandoned for ever, and so sin against the Holy Ghost.

5. The papists also, as upon the unblessed grounds of their antichristian doctrine, cannot possibly build any true persuasion of being in God's favour; so they are bound out by the tenour of their heretical tenet from thinking it lawful to entertain any unwavering certainty that way.

6. Nay further, some out of a pharisaical pretence of humility and modesty, but, in truth, from the secret suggestion of a guilty conscience, which ministers unto them more than matter enough of true and just doubting, are notable wranglers for papistical doubting.

Thus you see some there are also who do not assure themselves of future happiness either upon true or false grounds. Yet I am persuaded, the greatest part of those who live within the sound of the gospel are ordinarily confident without cause, and secure of their salvation, whereas in truth and trial they have no surer interest or better claim to the kingdom of heaven, than the foolish virgins, and the rest of that deluded rank, which I mentioned before. Let a minister of some great congregation wherein there are very few professors, which is no hard thing to find, but where there is no real profession, (especially the gospel being peaceably preached, there can ordinarily be no power of christianity; show there may be, indeed, without substance, but not the power of godliness,)—I say, let him interrogate and ask the rest of his people, one after another, be they hundreds or thousands, what views they hold of themselves for the world to come; what they think will become of them after this life; what their present judgment is of their spiritual state; and he shall scarce meet with any who will not, in some kind or other, discover some groundless confidence of his well-being that way. Their answers, ordinarily, would be to this purpose: "We thank God we have a good faith to Godwards: we have believed in Christ ever since we can remember: we hope God will be merciful, though we be not Scripture-men, nor so forward as others, or such followers of sermons, yet we look to be saved as well as the best of them all: upon the whole matter, we doubt not but that we shall go to heaven." And if the minister should reply, "But, I pray you will tell me, you that are so confident, do you believe, and repent, and make conscience of all our ways?" "Yea," would they say, "with all our hearts, else it were a pity we should live." Whereas, God knows, it is neither so nor so; their poor, frozen, flinty hearts never yet melted before the ministry of the word; were never truly touched with remorse for their innumerable sins; never warmed with any saving work of the Holy Ghost, but ever thus far, are mere strangers to the mystery of Christ. (Those that are true of heart are not wont to contest for the integrity, but ever to complain of the naughtiness and untowardness of their hearts.) And therefore if they become not renewed men, in the mean time, the veil of their self-delusion and vain confidence will most certainly at last be frighted and fired from their blinded minds, with that terrible and dreadful doom, "Depart from me, I know you not." Chrysostom, in one of his homilies to the people of Antioch, teaching them not to trust in multitude, speaks thus unto them; "How many do you think are there in our city which be in the state of salvation? It will vex, what I am about to speak, yet I will speak it; there cannot, amongst so many thousands, an hundred be found who are in that state; nay, and I doubt whether all those." Now, had this good father, at the same time, demanded of those many thousands besides, what they conceived of themselves for salvation; do you not think he would have found them all well conceited of themselves? Would not they, with much bitterness and heat, have declared his censure as too peremptory and unmerciful, and been ready to retort, "Howsoever you dote upon the disciples you draw after you, and only approve and applaud the Joanites, (for so they were called, because his name was John,) yet we hope to do as well as they, and come to heaven as soon as the precisest of those you have in such high esteem."

Here then let me a little enlighten, and open in a word, as I promised, the mystery of this spiritual self-deceit.

For which purpose know, that Satan first discovers in our corrupt nature and crooked dispositions, a very suitable ground whereupon to practise this notable imposture; I mean the original poison of natural presumption, whereby we are all apt to be fearless and senseless of our present spiritual misery, and readily to catch at any vain shadow of counterfeit confidence for our future welfare. Secondly, he observes in the party he intends to delude the most plausible matter and self-pleasing apprehensions, which may make the fittest medium to misinfer a false conclusion for his spiritual safety. Lastly, by some flashes of his personated angelical light, he sets upon it the glimmering flourish of a presumptuous impression, and so seals up the deceived soul with the spirit of slumber and groundless security.

Now, the insufficient matter, rotten grounds, false mediums, which Satan, by his sophistry, doth cunningly and cruelly use, to cast many thousands into a pleasing golden dream of imaginary spiritual safety and self-deceit, and into a fool's paradise of a soul cheating conclusion, are such as these:—

1. Measuring a man's self by himself; himself perhaps formerly grossly ignorant and notoriously lewd, by himself now grown moral and somewhat illuminated with Divine knowledge, but yet neither holy, nor ever truly humbled.

2. Comparing himself with others who are Satan's outrageous revellers, in respect of his moral moderation, and something more civil carriage.

3. Arguing God's special love and saving favour from his outward prosperous state and blessings in temporal things. So the fatting ox might think with himself, I shall surely live, because I feed in this green rich pasture.

4. Concluding from crosses that he is a son, and not a bastard; that he hath his punishment here, as they say; whereas they are but the just effects of God's secret curse blowing upon his

counsels, dealings, and undertakings; for his covetousness, unconscionableness, hatred to be reformed; and except he truly turn, in the mean time, will prove the very foretastes and parts, as it were, of hellish torments.

5. Sometimes nothing but self-love serves the devil's turn to lock up a carnal heart in this security and causeless confidence; especially in some extremely ignorant people, who easily believe that which they desire, and have no other ground of their going to heaven, but because they would have it so.

6. Common conceits and corrupt notions, compounded of gross ignorance and popish folly, that a man's good meanings and good doings, as they ignorantly speak; nay, and, as some have said, his day-labour will help him to heaven, and serve his turn for salvation. And if any of these sottish cavillers be questioned, and challenged for the unsoundness of his spiritual state, he will be ready, with absurd rudeness and irksome clamour, to break out into such boasting as this: " Why do you tell me of these high points, or trouble me with this new learning! I was never asked thus much before in all my life, and yet the time is to come that ever our parson threatened to keep me from the communion: I do no man wrong; I pay every man his own ; I am neither thief, nor drunkard, nor adulterer ; I live peaceably amongst my neighbours. I know as much as the preacher can tell me, though he preach out his heart: that I must love God above all, and my neighbour as myself, and that I hope I do." Whereas, poor blinded soul, he is as full of foolish pride, ignorance, profaneness, and impenitency, as the skin will hold, and is smoothly

carried hoodwinked by the devil to hell, without all noise, or any contradiction.

7. The work of God's restraining Spirit, which sometimes, by his power and terror, keeps in and confines a man's inward corruption, that it breaks not out into such open outrages and outward villanies as in some other wicked ones; and that for the sake of his own people, or some other secret ends seen, and seeming good to his heavenly Highness. Now, this restraint, by the delusion of the devil, and deceit of a man's own heart, may be apprehended as a great conquest over corruption, and so a conversion be thence vainly concluded.

8. Education in a religious family. Some, in such a place, being only outwardly warmed with the heat of holy exercises about them, and by custom and for company, grown conformable to religious duties with some contentment; depart thence with a vain-glorious conceit and unsound persuasion that they are also of the right stamp, because they were so long among spiritual tools, and at the fire, which might indeed have truly melted their yet too frozen and flinty hearts. Put a sow into a green meadow, and she will keep herself as fair as the sheep; but let her break out, and she will wallow again in the mire as filthily as before: so it is with too many such.

9. Much knowledge and noble defence of that blessed orthodox truth which we profess, without a kindly saving impression of goodness and grace in the heart. Many great men and great scholars, more is the pity, are empoisoned with this conceit; they are self-conceited, that if they be zealous patrons and protectors of true religion, they are safe enough for salvation, though, alas! they be mere

strangers, nay, too many times opposers, to the power and practice thereof.

10. The benefit of a better nature, and a constitution not so precipitant and prone to some corruptions. For instance, a man hereby may see others lie remorselessly in the most abominable and beastly sin of drunkenness, when his heart riseth against such swinish filth; see others transported with furious and fiery passions, whereas his milder temper knows no such rage; see others hunting after high places, with the hazard of their souls, and certain shipwreck of a good conscience, whereas his solitary disposition affects retiredness and home. Thus, when it is many times the infirmity, impotency, or deformity of nature, or at best but the natural moderation of a better complexion, that disinclines and disables him from the acting of some grosser evils, he fondly conceives that it is the power and sovereignty of grace which makes the difference between himself and other sons of Belial, who, by nature's impetuousness, are more prone and provoked thereunto.

11. The heartless effects of slavish fear, which sometimes will curb some kind of men from committing some notorious sins, and spur them forward to the outward performance of some holy duties; yet they, not marking the motives, manner, or end, nor taking to heart at all the gross exorbitancy of any of them, but only eying the work wrought, may causelessly be too well conceited of themselves, and so deceive their own souls. But, let no true-hearted Nathanael here mistake: I know some of God's dearest children, who make conscience of all sin, and seek to please God in all things, who yet, in the darkness of their melancholy or heat of temptation, may fear all is naught with them because they fear

they do all for slavish fear. But their fears, jealousies, hearty complaints, and holy desires to the contrary, may minister comfort enough if they will be counselled, until they come out of temptation.

12. Even the blessed word of God, misunderstood, and wretchedly abused to the devil's advantage, and damnation of men's souls. For instance: some suck poison out of that heavenly flower, "Whosoever shall call upon the name of the Lord, shall be saved," Rom. x. 13; collecting, and concluding thence, that if they can say, "Lord, Lord," though they be mere strangers to the life of grace, yet they shall live for ever. But such should know, that every one who in that saving sense calleth upon the name of the Lord, must " depart from iniquity," 2 Tim. ii. 19, and must savingly believe, Rom. x. 14. Now, such a fruitful faith ever purifies the heart, Acts xv. 9, and is inseparably attended with a glorious train of heavenly graces, " virtue, knowledge, temperance, patience, godliness, brotherly-kindness, charity," 2 Pet. i. 5—7. I have heard, with mine own ears, that place, Rom. xii. 1, sottishly perverted, to the maintenance of lukewarmness, coldness in religion, and goodfellowship. When purity in heart, holiness of life, universal obedience, and other requisites to salvation have been pressed; it hath been replied in good earnest, "I pray you, why are you so hot? what needs all this? what needs so much ado, when a reasonable thing will serve the turn? Is it not said, Which is your reasonable service?" Now, I often wonder what such men as these mean, who are proctors and pleaders for this Laodicean reserved mediocrity and politic moderation in matters of heaven? what worship and service they would proportion out for the all-powerful God?

Doth any man of sense conceive, that the mighty, dreadful Lord, and Judge of all the world, who offers unto us by the ministry, in the mean time, his own dear Son, with all the rich purchases of his heart's blood; and would give us the full fruition of himself hereafter, with all the glory and endless felicities above, will be satisfied with a heartless, formal outwardness; with a cold, rotten carcass of religion? It cannot be. He is a Spirit, and must be worshipped in spirit and truth. If men will needs harden themselves in bitterness and blasphemies, against the purity and power of godliness; if they will still browbeat and bear down their brethren, for their zeal and fervency in the affairs of God; let them tear those sacred leaves out of God's blessed book, that sparkle out unto us the holy fire of forwardness and heat, and continually press upon us to exercise power, spirit, and quickening in heavenly businesses, and the services of our most bountiful and ever-blessed God. See Matt. v. 29, 30; Luke xiii. 24; Rom. xii. 11; 1 Cor. ix. 24; Eph. v. 15; Phil. i. 10; 1 Thess. v. 22.

13. A bare speculative opposition, and verbal contradiction to the corruptions of the times and controverted ceremonies. For, I doubt there are some, who seeing some of God's dearest children, both godly ministers and other christians, only out of tenderness of conscience, stand unresolved about these latter, are too well persuaded of themselves spiritually, for a mere boisterous masterlike partaking with them in that particular; whereas they have no part at all in their holy graces and humble sanctification.

14. An overheady and furious zeal in will-worship, superstitious forms, and self-conceited services; as

in Paul, yet unconverted, and many ignorant papists; in the pursuit of some religious distempers and spiritual exorbitancies, bred only in some fantastical brain, given over for horrible pride to strong delusion; yet tendered with many holy pretences, and representations of highest perfection; nay, sometimes seconded with strange revelations and raptures, the mere jugglings of the devil's angelical glory in melancholy, or otherwise deluded imaginations: and so Satan can put such even into a trance of imaginary joy.

15. Serious meditation upon that quickening passage of Christ's holy sermon, of the fewness of those who shall be saved, Matt. vii. 14, should properly and naturally sharpen our desires and endeavours to a singular, constant contention after a holy strictness, forwardness, and fruitfulness in every good work, and all the ways of God, that we might be sure to be in the number of those few; yet, by accident, it may confirm some kind of men who are under the means, yet unconverted, in a false persuasion of their good state to Godward, and that thus: some there may be of larger capacity, and more understanding, who out of a contemplation of that great universal deluge of mahommedanism, paganism, judaism, and infidelity, (which at this day doth fearfully overflow the face of the earth, scarcely the fifth part whereof now professeth Christ,) and also out of a nearer consideration of the state of christendom, wherein popery, that foul sink and hydra of all heresies, (besides too many other exorbitant giddy deviations from the sobriety and analogy of true religion, and the path which is truly called holy,) that mightily prevail, and empoison innumerable souls; and which is yet more,

seeing so many amongst those who profess Christ, I mean, in respect of doctrine, notoriously lewd, and profanely naught; so many atheists, drunkards, scorners, swearers, and worldlings :—and then, after this prospect and survey abroad, reflecting a partial eye upon themselves, and their own ways, and finding themselves in the bosom of the church, and moral men, think verily, out of their extreme blindness and spiritual folly, that heaven would be unfurnished, and unfilled, if they should be excluded; and that it were a disparagement to the mercies of God, to rank and arraign them amongst turks and pagans at that last great day. But, if to their moral honesty they add a formal profession, why then, they think, they would be much wronged, if salvation were denied them; then already, in conceit, they knock and bounce, as it were, at the gates of heaven for entrance, with great boldness and confidence, like the foolish virgins, Matt. xxv. 11, and those, Matt. vii. 22, and with the pharisee give God thanks for their good state to himward. Alas, poor souls! let no man deceive you with vain words, neither delude your own souls with idle fancies. To whomsoever the glorious gospel of Christ shines savingly, and breathes spiritual life, they " deny ungodliness and worldly lusts; live soberly, righteously, and godly in this present world," Tit. ii. 11, 12. Mere morality never brought any unto heaven. And every lukewarm professor shall certainly be rejected by Christ.

16. But, amongst all the unsound grounds, insufficient matter, and false mediums, upon which Satan, and the deceitful heart labour to erect their rotten buildings of vain hopes in the credulous

conceits of those who are carried hoodwinked towards hell; all which, in the time of trial, and under the tempest of God's visiting wrath, will prove but " a spider's web: they shall lean upon their house, but it shall not stand; they shall hold it fast, but it shall not endure," Job viii. 14, 15. I say, amongst them all, there is not any that doth set on the counterfeit seal of this false persuasion with more peremptoriness and confidence, than a concurrence of those excellences, perfections, endowments incident to temporaries, and attainable in the state of unregeneration; which may be collected from such places as these, Matt. xxvii. 3, 4; xxv. 1—13; Mark vi. 20; Luke xiii. 26; xviii. 11, 12; Heb. vi. 4, 5; 2 Pet. ii. 20, 22.

Now, these and the like, are the unsound, seeming, and insufficient grounds whereupon the devil works; and doth easily, by the aid of natural presumption, and his own angelical flashes, insinuate and infer his soul-cheating conclusions, and cunningly infuse the poison of spiritual self-deceit, the groundless confidence and false persuasions of a good state towards God.

You may, with some penitent remorse, tremble under the revenging wrath of God for sin, and out of that horror confess and make restitution; and yet so did Judas, Matt. xxvii. You may reverence a godly minister, hear him gladly, and do many things after his doctrine; and yet so did Herod, Mark vi. 20. You may hold conformity in profession with the best; and yet so did the foolish virgins, Matt. xxv. You may be a hearer of the word, and that with quickness, and receive it with joy; and yet so did the stony-ground hearers, Matt. xiii. 20. You may be able to disclaim gross sins, give every man his due, fast, pray, and give alms; and yet so did the pharisee, Matt. vi. 1; Luke xviii. 11, 12. You may be enlightened, taste of the heavenly gift, &c., and yet may afterward fall away irrecoverably, Heb. vi. 4—8.

"But I," may the deluded pharisee and formal professor say, "find and feel all, or most, or many of these in myself;" (for what any unregenerate man hath heretofore attained, it is not impossible but that any now, or hereafter, may attain the same;) therefore doth he conclude falsely, out of Satan's sophistry, "I am safe enough for salvation." And in all this, Satan, lest he should be wanting to his labours, by a lying resemblance, to imitate the work of the Holy Ghost in the hearts of the faithful. For that which the devil, putting on the glory of an angel of light, puts upon his followers in this kind falsely and groundlessly,—that the blessed Spirit performs to those who are really true of heart, and upon good ground.

For it is not the universality, and excellency of all natural, merely moral, politic, and learned endowments, and sufficiencies; but above and besides all these, a supernatural, heavenly, and special work of the Spirit, sanctifying them all for God's glorious service. It is not a bare task of holy duties, religious exercises, presence at the ordinances outwardly performed; but the soul, as it were, of saving grace, animating and informing them with spiritual life, reverent heartiness, and fruitful improvement. It is not the glistering blaze of a visible forward profession of religion; but the power of godliness, and sincere practice of works of justice, mercy, and truth. It is not a general participation of the Spirit, the Spirit only of illumination, or largest speculative comprehensions of sacred knowledge; but a humble, fruitful, experimental skill, and dexterity in the mystery of Christ, and of walking humbly with our God, which doth soundly comfort the heart of a man spiritually wise, about assurance of his happy state to Godward. And, therefore, the true christian, when he would refresh his spirits with the sweet contemplation of his spiritual safety, and being in a comfortable gracious state, causeth his sincere conscience to answer in truth to such like interrogatories, as those which I have proposed for trial, in such a case, in my "Discourse of True Happiness." He ordinarily hath recourse unto, and runs over in his mind, with a humble delightful commemoration, the heavenly footsteps and mighty works of the Holy Ghost in his conversion; special watchfulness over his ways; sincere heartedness, holy strictness, and sanctified singularities in his conversation; which, as they are peculiar to God's people, so they are mysteries and strange things to the best unregenerate man; and that thus, or in the like manner :—

"Blessed be God," saith he within himself, "that ever it was so, yet so it was; the holy ministry of the word, sanctified and guided particularly for that purpose by the finger of God, happily seized upon me, while I did yet abide in the arms of darkness, and the devil's snares, a most polluted, carnal, abominable sinner; and effectually exercised its saving power upon my soul, both by the workings of the law and of the gospel. It was as a hammer to my heart, and broke it in pieces; and by a terrible, cutting, piercing power, it struck a shaking and trembling into the very centre of my soul, by this double effect.

"It first opened the book of my conscience, wherein

I read with a most heavy heart, ready to fall asunder, even like drops of water, for horror of the sight, the execrable abominations of my youth; the innumerable swarms of lewd and lawless thoughts, that all my life long hath stained mine inward parts with strange pollution; the continual wickedness of my tongue; the cursed profanation of God's blessed sabbaths, sacraments, and all the means of salvation I ever meddled with. In a word, all the hells, sinks, and sources of lusts and sin, of vanities and villanies I had remorselessly wallowed in ever since I was born: I say, I looked upon all these engraven by God's angry hand upon the face of my conscience in crimson and burning lines. Whereupon, in the next place, it opened upon me the armoury of God's flaming wrath, and fiery indignations, nay, and the very mouth of hell, ready to empty themselves, and execute their utmost upon mine amazed and guilty soul.

"In these restless and raging perplexities, wherewith my poor soul was extremely scorched and parched with penitent pain; His wrath, who is a 'consuming fire,' wringing my very heart-strings with unspeakable anguish; Jesus Christ, blessed for ever, was lifted up unto me in the gospel, as an antitype to the erecting of the brazen serpent in the wilderness. In whom, dying and bleeding upon the cross, I beheld an infinite treasury of mercy and love; a boundless and bottomless sea of tender-heartedness and pity; a whole heaven of sweetness, peace, and spiritual pleasures. Whereupon, there sprung up and was enkindled in mine heart, an extreme thirst, ardent desires, vehement longings after that sovereign, saving blood, which alone could ease my grieved soul, and turn my foulest sins into the whitest snow. So, that in the case I then was, had I had in full taste and sole command, the pleasures, profits, joys, and glory of many worlds, willingly would I have parted with them all; and had I had a thousand lives, freely would I have laid them all down, to have had the present horror of my confounded spirit comforted from heaven; and my spiritual thirst allayed and a little cooled, but with one drop of Christ's precious blood; the darkness, desolations of my woful heart refreshed and revived, but with the least glimpse of God's favourable countenance. The edge and eagerness of which inflamed affections made me look about with infinite care, how to compass so dear a comfort. Then came into my mind (the Holy Spirit being my merciful remembrancer) those many melting compassionate invitations, more warming and welcome to my heavy heart than many golden worlds, more delicious than delight itself, Isa. lv. 1; lvii. 15, 16; Ezek. xviii. 30—32; xxxiii. 11; Matt. xi. 28; John vii. 37; Rev. xxi. 6. So that at last, oh blessed work of faith! staying myself, and resting my sinking soul upon the Rock of eternity, and the impregnable truth of these sweetest promises, sealed with the blood of the Lord Jesus, and as sure as God himself, I threw myself into the merciful and meritorious arms of my crucified Lord; with this resolution, and reply to all terrors and temptations to the contrary, that if I must needs be cast away, they shall tear and rend me from the tender arms of God's dearest compassions, upon which I have cast myself; if they will have me to hell, they shall pull and haul me from the bleeding wounds of my blessed Redeemer, to which my soul has fled. Whereupon I found, and felt (and I bless God infinitely, and will through all eternity, that ever it was so) conveyed, and derived upon me from my blessed Jesus, the well-spring of immortality and life, a quickening influence of his mighty Spirit, and heavenly vigour of saving grace, whereby I became a new man, quite changed, new created. By this vital moving, and incubation, as it were, of the Spirit of Christ upon the face of my soul, all things became new: mine heart, affections, thoughts, words, actions, delights, desires, sorrows, society, and all things. 'Old things are passed away, behold, all things are become new,' 2 Cor. v. 17.

"And I am sure my change is sound, and saving; for it is not, 1. A mere moral change from notorious sin to morality, and no further. 2. Nor a formal change only, which adds to moral honesty, outward profession, and outside conformity to the ordinances, holy exercises, most duties of religion, and no more. 3. Nor merely mental. I mean it thus: (for I know true repentance is called change of mind, in another sense:) when the understanding only is enlightened with Divine knowledge, gilded over, as it were, with the dazzling splendour of general graces, not without some speculative flashes of fleeting joy, swimming in the brain indeed, but not rooted in the heart. 4. Nor temporary only; such as that, Matt. xii. 43; 2 Pet. ii. 20, 22, when of all gross sins for a time, out of terror, or sudden fright from some son of thunder; or upon trial whether, by his own strength, he be able to endure, a man discontinues the outward practice, perhaps, and digest a divorce from his darling pleasure, and follow the holy ways of those who walk towards heaven, without too much discontentment; for, without too sore a crush to his carnal heart, he could be content to look after a crown of life; or for some other by-end. But because his heart was not honest and good, neither did the word take a humble root in it, nor himself resolve upon a sincere, general, and constant self-denial at first, he falls again upon his former sin, and again wallows in the mire of his sensual pleasures, with more rage and resolution than before. 5. Nor partial, where there may be an outward reformation in the most things; but yet there is still retained a secret and resolved reservation of an impenitent, entire enjoyment of all the delights and full sweetness of the bosom sin, which is utterly incompatible, and cannot possibly consist with a truly religious and regenerate state. I say, my change (I solely and infinitely magnify, admire, and adore the free grace and love of my most holy and ever-blessed God for it) was not only moral, formal, mental, temporary, or partial in the sense I have said, but universal both in respect of the subject and object, as they say, without all reservations, exceptions, sensual distinctions, pharisaical imposture, partialities, hypocrisies, self-delusions.

"For my teachers have told me, by the touchstone of his pure and holy truth, that every true change is of the whole man, from the whole service of Satan to the living God, in sincere obedience to his whole law in the whole course of our lives; that it is discernible, and distinguished from all partial, insufficient, hollow, half conversions. 1. By integrity of change, I mean in all parts and powers of spirit, soul, and body; in the understanding, judgment, memory, conscience; in the will, affections, desires, and thoughts; in the eyes, ears, tongue, hands, feet; for even as they were members of the body before, employed wholly for Satan and sensuality, so now are they also become instruments of righteousness unto God. God has no monster-children, as they say: a child new-born hath all the parts of a man, though not the perfection of his growth. So a new-born babe in Christ is thoroughly and universally changed, though not yet a perfect man in Christ. 2. Sincerity of change, as well in heart and inward parts, as in life and outward carriage. 'O Jerusalem,' saith the prophet, 'wash thine heart from wickedness, that thou mayest be saved. How long shall thy vain thoughts lodge within thee?' Jer. iv. 14. No external privileges of religion, though ever so glorious; no exactness of the work wrought; no pharisaical forms of devotion; no outward behaviour, be it ever so blameless; no cost or contributions in the service of God, will serve the turn, without sincerity of heart. Though a man should come before the Lord with thousands of rams, or ten thousands of rivers of oil; should he give his first-born for his transgression, the fruit of his body for the sin of his soul; should he bestow all his goods to feed the poor, and give his body to be burned; were he able to comprehend the whole book of God, and with the largeness of his understanding devour all the holy sense; yet all this were more than all in vain, and utterly unavailable, without uprightness of the heart and purity in the inward parts. 3. Spiritual growth. Unregenerate men, at the best, grow but in the generalities, flourishes, devout representations, and temporary forwardness of formal christianity; which is like the growth of corn on the house-top, or the seed springing out of the stony ground; but the honest and good heart bringeth forth fruit with patience. Spiritual stuntings there may be, and standings at a stay for a time; but as good corn in a good soil, being refreshed after a binding drought with a ground shower, springs up faster and more freshly; so it is with the sound-hearted christian, after a damp in grace, to which he may sometimes be subject; for being roused and awakened out of such a state by the quickening voice of a piercing ministry, the cutting sting of a heavy cross, or some other special hand of God, he lays hold upon the kingdom of Christ with more holy violence than before, and labours afterward, by the help of God, to repair his former spiritual decay with double diligence in watchfulness, zeal, and heavenly-mindedness. Progress in christianity is resembled to the thriving of a child, which may fall into sickness; but it many times proves a growing ague, 1 Pet. ii. 2, 3. To a man in a race, who may stumble and fall, but after his rising takes surer footing, and runs faster, Phil. iii. 13, 14. To the ascending of the sun towards midday, which may be overcast with a cloud, but after it hath recovered a clear sky, shines more brightly and sweetly. 4. Self-denial; of which, see something before, page 56. He that would soundly comfort his conscience with the true testimony of a true convert, must, at the first giving his name unto Christ, and upon his proclaiming war and entering the lists against Satan, sound, with a sincere heart, the depth of that fundamental principle of christianity and Christ's own holy rule, ' If any man will come after me, let him deny himself, &c.' Matt. xvi. 34. As soon as he resigns up himself to this royal service, under the colours of the Lord Jesus, he must immediately, in our Saviour's sense, make over all his interest in liberty, life, livelihood, all earthly pleasures and treasures, without reservation, or he will certainly faint and fall off in the day of battle. The necessity of this rule and resolution is intimated unto us in two parables, Luke xiv. 28—31. A man that will build, must count the cost beforehand, and make sure means to defray the charge; otherwise, to begin, and not able to make an end, were but to lay a groundwork of his disgrace and scorn in the loss of his cost and pains. A prince who would wisely make war, must first have a true trial of his own, and dexterity to discover his enemy's strength; otherwise to bid him battle, were but to incense him more, and thrust a title into his hands to deprive him of all he hath. He that seriously sets himself to seek God in truth, and to save his soul indeed, must cast up his reckonings beforehand, what will be required at his hands, and consult with his own heart whether willing to forego all such contentments, hopes, pleasures, preferments, worldly comforts, which are incompatible with a good conscience and the path that is called holy; and to endure all those troubles and indignities from the angry world, which ordinarily are wont to crown the heads of all Christ's soldiers, else most certainly he will shrink in the wetting. He must resolve, by the invincible nobleness of his christian courage, to digest the hate and opposition of dearest friends, nearest kindred; the railings and reproaches of men most abject and contemptible, in respect of those whom they revile; he must be content to become the drunkard's song, table-talk to those that sit in the gate, Psa. lxix. 12, and the by-word of basest men, ' viler than the earth, &c.,' Job xxx. 8, 9: in a word, he must prize and prefer his Saviour, his truth, cause, and service infinitely before the whole world.

" Now, besides my blessed change thus qualified,

and this glorious work of the Holy Ghost upon my soul, by the help of God I have stood at the stave's end with the darling pleasure and minion delight of my former days ever since I was new-born. I have ever since made conscience of all sin, and to perform all holy duties. I have had respect to all God's commandments, and all his ordinances. I have dearly loved my blessed Lord, and all things that belong unto him,—his titles, attributes, creatures, works of justice and mercy, his word, sacraments, sabbaths, ministers, services, children, presence, corrections, and coming. I have since delighted in the saints, the only excellent ones upon earth, Psa. xvi. 3, whom I heartily hated before. I have daily, with as great earnestness and fervency as my poor dull heart could possibly, complained and cried unto my God in prayer against my own sins, passionate distempers, rebellious risings, the malice of Satan, the allurements of the world, corruptions of the times, the cruelties of strange injections and horrible temptations, my many and often failings, frailties, and imperfections. Upon due and impartial examination, I have happily ridden mine hands of all that consuming pelf, which any way crept into mine estate, by wicked and wrongful means, in the days of mine iniquity, (for scarce any man in the state of nature but deals falsely in one kind or other.) I have desired and endeavoured to adorn my profession, as well with works of justice, mercy, and truth, as by the outward acts of piety; "Herein do I exercise myself, to have always a conscience void of offence toward God, and toward men," Acts xxiv. 16.

"And in all these passages and particulars, both of my conversion and conversation, had I only reposed upon the outward act, and rested in the work wrought, I had utterly fainted, and been quite undone in the day of adversity. But truth of heart was the touchstone, and sincerity is the sinew of all my assurance and comfort.

"I have been, I confess, (yet full sore against my will and the hearty desire of my soul,) haunted and hindered in passages through my new birth and managing my christian businesses, with the violent intrusion and insinuating mixture of many imperfections, distractions, temptations, wants, weaknesses, infirmities, and failings; inward pride, secret hypocrisy, distrusts, and deadness of mine own wicked heart. I was much wanting, by reason of the natural rebellion of my hard heart, to those workings of the law and gospel mentioned before. I have come far short of that sorrow for sin which I desired, and of that heavenly-mindedness in performing holy duties which was required. But then, I have from time to time grieved and groaned under those too many frailties and defects, as under a heavy burden. I have many a time bitterly bewailed them in secret; they have made me walk more humbly before my God, and towards men; I have continually complained heartily against them at the throne of grace; I have sincerely desired and endeavoured after all those means which might restrain and mortify them, and made conscience to discover and decline their unwelcome insinuations, and so I have gone on still in the holy path with sincerity of heart, and in obedience unto God; still upholding mine heart with consideration of that sweet and merciful disposition of my heavenly Father; who ever, if the heart be upright and truly humble, takes the will for the deed, and accepts us "according to that which we have, and not according to that which we have not," 2 Cor. viii. 12. And therefore I am most sure (neither, by the help of God, shall all the devils in hell drive me from this hold) that they are all buried for ever in the righteous and meritorious blood of my blessed Saviour. And so I still hold up my head against all contradiction of carnal reason, natural distrust, and Satan's cruel suggestions; being well assured, that hearty humiliation and grieving under weakness in well-doing is as true a fruit of sanctification and mark of true conversion, as spiritual ability to do well. It is not so much the quantity, as the truth of grace; not so much the exactness of the outward act in performing holy duties, as sincerity of heart, which qualifies a broken heart for comfort in the promises of life and assurance of God's love. Though I know well there was never any who tasted truly grace but he sincerely thirsted and endeavoured after more. Never did any man well in the worship and services of God, who did not bewail his wants and failings therein, and truly desire and labour to do better. It is the property of pharisees and formal professors to conceive that they are spiritually rich enough already, and have need of nothing; but the better the christian is, the more sensible he is, and heartily complaining of his spiritual poverty, wicked heart, and manifold imperfections."

Here then, may we see in this discourse of the true convert comforting himself in the point of his spiritual state, other kind of sincere matter, sounder grounds, more special workings of the Holy Ghost, than any one of the fore-mentioned deluded ones was ever practically and experimentally acquainted with. Neither is this all: the true christian hath yet more noble, immediate, and demonstrative evidences to strengthen his heart in the assurance of God's everlasting love unto him through Christ, and in the present possession of his favour. For (with submission to better judgments and the sense of the prophets) I conceive that a sanctified man may be assured of his spiritual safety and sound state to Godwards, in divers ways.

1. By the evidence and single act of internal vision. "We have received," saith the apostle, "not the spirit of the world, but the Spirit which is of God; that we might know the things that are freely given to us of God," 1 Cor. ii. 12: that is to say, argue the papists, Christ's incarnation, passion, presence in the sacrament, and the incomprehensible joys of heaven. But it is clear in the text, that the apostle speaks generally of all the gifts that are given us of God; which serveth the argument of comparison, that as a man's spirit teacheth him to know all his thoughts that are in him, so also the Spirit of God teacheth the believers, in some measure, to know all that God hath given them. He doth not say that we know God's gifts, but that we know the gifts that God hath given unto us. See further to this point and purpose, 1 John v. 13; 2 Tim. i. 12. By a secret and sacred irradiation of the Spirit of faith, the sanctified soul is assured of its personal and particular dependence and reliance upon the promises of life and God's mercies through Christ, by which it knows it hath eternal life, John iii. 36.

As certainly as he that hath a corporeal eye knoweth that he sees, so certainly he that is illuminated with the light of faith knows that he believes. The glorious splendour of such an orient and heavenly jewel cannot but show itself, and shine clearly to the heart wherein it dwells. Like a bright lamp set up in the soul, it doth not only manifest other things, but also itself appeareth by its own light. When I see and rely upon a man promising me this or that, I know that I see and rely upon him: shall I, by faith, behold my blessed Redeemer lifted up as an antitype to the brazen serpent for the everlasting cure of my wounded conscience and rest upon him, and yet know no such thing?

Hear how clear learned Augustine is for this internal vision. "Our faith," saith he, "is conspicuous to our own mind. Faith itself is seen in the mind, although that which is believed by faith is invisible. A man holds his faith by most certain knowledge, and plain attestation of conscience. Every man sees his faith in himself." Even Durandus, taking upon him to expound one of those passages in the before-cited place of Augustine, tells us, "That he who hath faith is as certain that he hath it, as he is of any other thing; for he that believes, feels that he believes, and by consequence that he hath faith; and there is nothing more certain than experience." The words of Vegaes, also, in the council of Trent, are to this effect; "As he that is hot, is sure he is so, and should want sense if he doubted; so he that hath grace in him, doth perceive it, and cannot doubt; yet it is by the sense of the mind, not by Divine revelation."

Object. But if these things be so, how comes it to pass, that God's dearest children sometimes complain that they have neither sight nor sense of their faith?

Ans. I speak of that which is ordinary, not permanent. The sun in a clear sky openly discovers and manifests itself; though sometimes it be overcast with clouds, or eclipsed with the moon. This heavenly lamp of faith shines, and shows itself clearly enough to the sanctified heart, in the calmness of a christian course, and serenity of the soul; especially freshly cleared, and purged with showers, as it were, of penitent tears; though in the damp of spiritual desertion, darkness of some stronger temptation, eclipse of earthly-mindedness, it may lie hid and obscured for a time. And yet for all this, if christians would be counselled, and believe the prophets; if they would not undervalue God's infinite mercy, by looking upon him through a slavishly dejected and melancholy humour, which is wont to represent him as terrible, fierce, and inexorable; whereas, in his own nature and sweetest disposition, he is indeed ever most compassionate, tender-hearted, and melting over the bleeding miseries of a truly broken heart; I say, if they would not thus mistake, but conceive aright of that most adored mystery and bottomless depth of his free love, Cant. ii. 4; Jer. xxxi. 3; Ezek. xvi. 8; Hos. xiv. 4; John iii. 16; xvii. 23, they might, even in times of desertions, temptations, spiritual afflictions of soul, sweetly uphold their hearts with assurance of adherence, though for the present they want the assurance of evidence: for such an assurance is intimated, Psa. xxii. 1; xlii. 5, 11; xliii. 5. For instance; many a faithful soul, making conscience of all sin, sincerely following the best things, resolved without reservation to do or suffer any thing for Christ, would give a world to be sensibly assured of God's favour, and fully persuaded that his sins are pardoned. By reason of the want of sense and feeling, whereof he slavishly languishes upon the rack of tormenting fears and terrors, utterly without all cause; and not only so, but thereby also gratifying the devil, dishonouring God's free mercy, disabling himself for a comfortable discharge of his callings, and that which he little thinks on, lying in the sin of not receiving comfort, and of not accepting his own proper legacy which Christ left him, John xiv. 27: for in the mean time his heart doth cleave unto Christ as to the surest rock. He cries, and longs after him, and would not part with him for all the world: he would infinitely rather have his body rent from his soul, than his soul from his Saviour. Ask his affection and resolution this way; and, for all his fears and sorrows, he will tell you that he will still rest and rely upon his Lord and ever-blessed Redeemer, let him do with him as he please; he will trust in him, though he slay him. Now, the internal vision, the consciousness, (the reflexed act, that I may speak in the phrase of the schools,) of this sincere adherence unto Christ, and those exceeding precious promises of life, sealed with his blood, might, and ought to assure him of the everlasting safety and happiness of his soul; and so consequently, to comfort him infinitely more than if he had the crown of the whole world's sovereignty set upon his head. Justifying faith, which gives infallible interest to eternal life, is not (to speak properly and punctually) to be assured of pardon; but to trust wholly upon the mercy of God through Christ for pardon. If there arise a question in thy fearful heart about thy spiritual state, sense and feeling is no substantial ground whereon to build, being a separable accident to the graces of salvation; but the truth and tender-heartedness of Christ in the promises, which can never fail, being as sure as God himself. If some wrangling fellow should lay claim unto thy land, thou wouldest not, in such a case and controversy, consult with an ignorant neighbour; he, perhaps, out of his weakness and want of skill, might raise doubts and dangers where there were none, and put thee into a greater fright; but thou wouldest have recourse to some learned in the law, who, with understanding, searching and surveying thine evidences, and finding no flaw, would put thee out of all fear. When in time of temptation thou art terrified and affrighted with renewed scruples and distractions about thy spiritual well-being, do not in anywise advise with carnal reason, which is stark blind in the mystery of Christ, much less with that evil one, who is a sworn enemy to thy soul, and father of lies. They may tell thee thou hast no sense, no feeling, therefore all is naught: but to the law and to the testimony; let thy trembling heart cleave to the impregnable truth of those sweetest promises, Isa. lv. 1; Matt. xi. 28; John vii. 37; Rev. xxi. 6; and thou art safe for ever. For a more full impression of this comfortable point, I would have you to refresh your memories with a review of those four states of faith, which I have heretofore distinguished, upon purpose for the weakest christian's sake; and know, that the reflex act of the lowest degree and least measure then mentioned, might, upon good ground, if he do not wilfully and wickedly refuse to be comforted, fill his fearful spirit with unspeakably glorious joy as full as the sun is of light, and the sea of waters. These things laid together, and well weighed, may form a precious and sovereign antidote against the slavish terrors, causeless fears, and heavy walking of many who are true of heart, but distressed in conscience about their spiritual state; who, while they labour and long with insatiable greediness (and I blame them not) for a sensible assurance and feeling apprehension of God's favour, do too much neglect and disregard that comfort which their faith might afford them upon good ground, in that, notwithstanding their present distracting amazements and perplexity of spirit, they are able still to commit their souls unto Christ as their faithful Redeemer, and their everlasting strength.

In this point I have let some passages fall, by the way, which may serve to discover and dissolve the vanity and weakness of that dilemma wherein Bellarmine plays the wilfully egregious sophister. It runs thus :—

"The protestants teach," saith he, " that a man is justified by special faith, whereby he persuadeth himself that he is just." He then reasoneth thus: " When I begin to believe that I am just, I am either just or unjust. If just, then I am not justified by faith, by which I believe myself to be just, because this faith is after my justification. If unjust, then this faith is false, and so a man should be justified by a lie."

To this horned argument we answer thus: There are sundry acts of special faith; for my purpose, at this time, we will take notice of two.

A fiducial assent, resting upon the merit of Christ; an affiance, dependence, adherence, reliance, or if there be any other word expressing that act of an humble soul, whereby it casteth and reposeth itself only upon God's promise in Christ, for the obtaining of remission of sins and everlasting life. In this act the poor soul, enlightened and affrighted with sight and sense of its sin and misery, and seeing an infinite impossibility of satisfying God for the one, or freeing itself from the other, by any means or merit in heaven or earth, but only by the propitiatory mediation of Jesus Christ; it throws itself into his arms, grasping fast about him, hides itself in the clefts of this rock, from the storms of God's fiercest and fiery indignation; apprehends in him plentiful redemption and all-sufficiency of salvation, and, therefore, plies him with strong cries and tears for mercy; bespeaks him in all terms of confidence and affiance: My Lord and my God, my hope, my fortress, my rock, my strength, my salvation; save me, or I sink; hold me fast, or I am lost for ever. You may see sometimes a little infant, upon apprehension and approach of some sudden danger, how heartily and hastily it runs into the mother's arms for succour and safety; even so a truly wounded soul, pursued by the terrors of the law, and frighted with the dreadful sight of God's frowning countenance, flies with speed into the arms of its blessed Redeemer, clings inseparably unto his bleeding wounds for everlasting protection, and there rests upon the freeness of his love, merit of his passion, and truth of his promise, as upon an eternal rock, never to be removed; not the concurrent rage of all the devils in hell, or powers of darkness, being ever able to make a divorce. By this act we are accepted for just before the throne of grace, for Christ's sake and sufferings.

An act of certification, which, quickened by the Spirit of grace, when God pleaseth for his own glory and good of his child, reflecteth upon the soul with a comfortable assurance that we are already in the arms of Christ, and his for ever: the least glimpse whereof a true heart would not exchange for all the kingdoms upon earth. The first act makes us just, the second finds us just, and so certifies truly; not by a lie, as lying companions and Satan's sophisters calumniate. It is the saying of an excellent divine, both for depth of learning and height of holiness, " To believe that my sins are now pardoned, and that I am saved, is not the first act of faith, but follows when a man doth see himself to be justified in Christ."

2. By a secret application of the promises of the gospel in form of an experimental syllogism, thus:

Whosoever believes and repents is a child of God: I believe and repent; therefore, I am a child of God.

The major, or first proposition, is clear and evident in the very letter, and by the immediate sense of Scripture. See John iii. 36; Acts x. 45; xiii. 39, &c.

Object. But how do you know the minor, or second proposition to be certainly so?

Ans. By the certainty of internal vision, whereby we as clearly see our faith, as our life, will, thought, and knowledge, as appears in the before-cited place of Augustine. In his opinion, faith is as visible to the internal eye of a sanctified mind, as is a man's life and will: nay, and we are wont to discern with a more eager eye and observation a stranger than an ordinary domestic. Our life and will are inbred; faith is adventitious. Also by the testimony of a renewed conscience, which is as a thousand witnesses. Now, had I a thousand honest witnesses at the bar before an upright judge, to prove my cause and justify my right against the outfacings and perjuries of the worst accuser, I would little doubt but to get the day. It is proportionably so in this present point; I mean, between my regenerate, enlightened conscience, and Satan. Nay, in this case should all the devils in hell swear the contrary; did carnal reason, natural distrust, or any other adverse power cavil and contradict with ever such irksome tediousness, yet, by the mercy of God, I will not withstand that heavenly light that stands in my conscience like an armed man.

Object. But how do you know that you truly believe: we may know, perhaps, that we have some kind of faith, but not that we have the true lively faith, which will serve the turn for salvation?

Ans. St. Paul bids us try and prove ourselves, whether we have that faith by which Christ dwelleth in our hearts, which is the faith of such as are accepted with God, 2 Cor. xiii. 5. Now, it were strange if the blessed Spirit should bid us examine and search for that which could not possibly be found out.

Again; if a man cannot be certain that he believes with all his heart, that is, truly and sincerely, Philip's interrogatory to the eunuch, Acts viii. 37, had been in vain, and the eunuch's reply rash and unadvised.

Augustine was clearly of this mind, that a man may be acquainted with the sincerity of his faith. "There is," saith he, "a kind of glorying in the conscience, when thou knowest thy faith is sincere, thy hope certain, thy love without dissembling."

Object. But many say they believe, and yet are deceived; thinking they have that which they have not: how then can a man be certain?

Ans. So thousands amongst us, by the false spectacles of presumption, making the bridge of God's mercy broader than it is, and larger than his truth, which confines it only to broken hearts, are wofully deluded, and ready every moment to be drowned in the dungeon of fire and brimstone; must, therefore, those few who are sincerely humbled for their sins, truly believe, and upon good ground have part in it, be also deceived? Because madmen rage, and men asleep know not well that they are asleep, must, therefore, men truly waking and wise, not know certainly that they are awake and in their senses? The common people generally conceive of the sun's magnitude that it is not past a foot round; must, therefore, the certainty of knowledge that it is many times larger than the earth be denied to the skilful astronomer? Some men dream that they are rich, and tumble themselves amongst their golden heaps; though it be not so indeed when they awake: doth no man, therefore, certainly know whether he be rich or not?

Conceive proportionably of repentance, an inseparable companion and effect of true faith, which is then saving, when it is serious, sincere, and without hypocrisy, and that may be manifest and clearly discernible to the heart that hath it. Do you think the seriousness of the Ninevites' repentance was not certain unto them? "We have received the Spirit which is of God," saith Paul, "that we might know the things that are freely given to us of God," 1 Cor. ii. 12, which are not only life everlasting, &c., but justification, sanctification, and such like. I say, that savingness of repentance, as also of faith, consists not in the measure and greatness, but in the sincerity and truth, of which the true penitent may be certain, as well as of his sorrow. But whereas the popish doctors, being blind guides, lead their hoodwinked followers into such perplexed mazes of uncertainties, and, indeed, impossibilities, about contrition, in respect of extension, intention, appreciation, and equivalence to sin, no marvel though they plead pertinaciously for the point and purgatory of doubting.

3. By the effects and fruits growing from the root of grace in the heart.

Object. But there may be in the hypocrite an exact outward conformity and obedience.

Ans. True it is, that for the outside and carcass, as it were, the works of unsanctified men may be like to those of the godly; but they are without the soul, life, and spirit, which is in the work of a true believer; to which he is no less privy in his heart, than to the outward work which passeth through his hands. And we hold that works done in uprightness of heart only are they which truly testify in this case.

Let every true-hearted Nathanael then comfortably conclude pardon and peace unto his own soul, from all such fruits so qualified. For instance, in one:—" We know that we have passed from death unto life, because we love the brethren," 1 John iii. 14. I love the brethren, therefore I am translated from death to life.

Object. But is it possible for a man to know that he loves his brethren as he ought, and as the apostle requires?

Ans. St. John makes it a sign of our being so translated, therefore it may be known: for signs manifesting other things must themselves be more manifest. And Augustine tells us that " a man knows more the love with which he loves, than his brother whom he loves."

Thus may the christian infallibly collect that the sanctifying Spirit, justifying faith, saving grace, dwell in his heart, by all the good deeds, holy duties, inward and outward fruits, springing from an upright heart. For, as it follows, and may be infallibly and demonstratively inferred from the effect to the proper cause in other things. For example: It is day; therefore the sun is risen, because day cannot be caused but by the sun's rising: so in this point also, as before explained. If we pursue and ply with true hearts the whole trade of christianity; if we be sincerely exercised in the works of holiness, justice, mercy, and truth, and walk humbly with our God, we may build upon it that we are truly blessed. All such sound fruits of faith are evident signs and demonstrations of our spiritual safety, and standing fast for ever. "If ye do these things," saith Peter, "ye shall never fall," 2 Pet. i. 10.

4. By the testimony of the Spirit, which sometimes,—as in the time of more fervent prayer, holy retiredness of mind, heavenly meditation; or in some quickening exercises of extraordinary humiliation; or after some special important service done to God and his church, with humble sincerity and in true zeal; or upon the soul-searching passage of some well-grounded sermon of comfort and seasonable application of mercy; or in the beginning of spiritual and end of natural life, as most needful times; or in the time of martyrdom, and sincere sufferings for the name of Christ,—I say, at such times, the Spirit may suggest and testify to the sanctified conscience, with a secret, still, heart-ravishing voice, thus, or in the like manner: Thou art the child of God; thou art in the number of those that shall be saved; thou shalt inherit life everlasting; and that as certainly and comfortably as if that angel from heaven should say to thee, as he did to Daniel, "Greatly beloved." And why should any popish

caviller contradict this, since even Bellarmine himself speaks proportionably in another case? Upon a passage in Augustine, acknowledging the inward efficacy of God's Spirit, giving testimony to our hearts concerning the truth of that which is contained in the Scriptures, he saith, " This light of faith is a certain testimony of God, by which it is said to the secret cogitations of our hearts, That is true; thou needest not to doubt thereof." Here is an immediate testimony of the Spirit, granted for the confirmation of the truth of the word; why may not the like be expected for an assurance of the work of the word? Mighty and remarkable was the work of the Spirit this way upon the heart of that noble martyr, Robert Glover, upon the first sight and representation of the stake; so sweetly seasonable is God in all his refreshings. For two or three days before his death he was full heavily oppressed with the spiritual miseries of a dead heart, and spiritual desertion. In which time, no doubt, he cried mightily unto God, and often cast the eye of his renewed conscience upon a truly believing, penitent, humble, holy, and heavenly heart; resolved to sacrifice its warmest blood in the merciless fire for the testimony of Jesus, and yet no comfort would come. But in the very moment of the time of need, the blessed Spirit did suddenly shine into his dark and desolate soul, with the glorious beams of his own immediate comfort, and so sensibly filled it with such overflowing rivers of spiritual joys, that no doubt they mightily abated and quenched the raging fury of those popish flames, wherein he sweetly fell asleep. It was a special and immediate springing of the Holy Ghost in the heart, which made master Peacock, after many days of extreme horror, profess that the joy which he felt in his conscience was incredible. We feel and acknowledge by daily experience that Satan doth immediately inject; and shall not the blessed Spirit, after his holy and heavenly manner, immediately also suggest?

Neither is this to be reputed an extraordinary revelation, or enthusiasm, without or beside the word of God; for that which the Spirit so reveals unto our consciences, we ourselves may collect and conclude out of God's word, upon the evidence of our faith, repentance, other saving endowments, and holy graces shining in our souls, and uprightly exercised in our whole conversation. When we, by these means, have assured our souls that we are the children of God, which is the testimony of our own renewed spirits; the Spirit of God, as another witness, secondeth and confirmeth this assurance by divine inspiration, and by sweet motions and feelings of God's special goodness, and glorious, saving presence; and so, according to the apostle's phrase, " beareth witness with our spirit," Rom. viii. 16. Wherefore, if any man presume upon, or pretend to any immediate suggestion or revelation for his spiritual safety and everlasting well-being, and yet utterly want the testimony of his renewed conscience to the same purpose, the testimony of universal obedience; of not living willingly and delightfully in any one known sin; of crucifying the flesh with the affections and lusts, &c.; I can give him none but this cold comfort,—he is deceived by the devil's counterfeit glory of an angel, casting into his abused imagination such groundless conceits, which in time of trial will vanish into nothing, and fly away as a dream.

By the way, let me tell you, that though this last

manner of assurance be more immediately from the Spirit, yet understand also that the other is not effectual upon the heart, without the excitation, illumination, and assistance of the same blessed Spirit.

For the first, consider the before-cited place, 1 Cor. ii. 2.

For the second: when the conscience, through the ministry of the law, doth testify to a man his state in sin, and under the curse, it is through the spirit of bondage that it doth testify: then, when it doth testify to him his state of grace, and freedom from the curse, it is much rather from the Spirit of adoption. "No man can say that Jesus is the Lord, but by the Holy Ghost," 1 Cor. xii. 3.

For the third: I doubt not but the blessed Spirit, as a comfortable remembrancer, refreshed Hezekiah's memory, when he cried to the Lord, "Remember now, O Lord, I beseech thee, how I have walked before thee in truth and with a perfect heart, and have done that which is good in thy sight," Isa. xxxviii. 3.

Object. But how shall a man discern and distinguish a true persuasion and the testimony of the Spirit, from a groundless, presumptuous conceit, and the devil's delusion?

Ans. If Bellarmine ask me, I will easily stop his mouth:

1. By asking him how his saint Francis and saint Antony knew assuredly that their revelations of the certain remission of their sins were from the Spirit of God? especially, since with him they were revelations quite beside and without the word. For he holds this proposition, that, Francis was truly justified; Antony had his sins forgiven; and so of other particular men, is not to be found in the word either

immediately or by evident consequence; which we upon good ground contradict, if the particular men be true believers.

2. By that saying of Ambrose, urged by Catarinus in the council of Trent: "The Holy Ghost doth never speak unto us, but doth make us know that it is he that speaketh."

But if the doubtful christian, truly troubled about it, would be taught and informed in the point; or, if it be possible that the pharisee, the deluded one, should heartily desire to be enlightened, I advise that they would reflect upon these following marks of difference.

1. A sound persuasion, upon good ground, by the Spirit, is ever exactly agreeable and answerable to the word. The inward testimony of the Spirit, and outward testimony of the word, do always sweetly accord, and one answers to the other, as face to face in water; and, therefore, if thy present state, wherein thou conceivest thyself to be sure and safe enough for salvation, be disabled and condemned by God's word, thy confidence is vain, and Satan deludes thee. The Scripture tells us that, "whosoever is born of God doth not commit sin," 1 John iii. 9; which is not to be understood simply of the act of sinning; for who can say, My heart is clean? But in this sense: he makes not a trade of sinning; he sinneth not with purpose, pleasure, and perseverance; he doth not live, lie, and delight in sin; he suffers it not to reign in him. If then thou allowest any lust in thy heart, or go on in the willing practice of any one known sin, or sensual course, and yet art well conceited of thyself for comfort in the world to come, the devil deceives thee: God will not hear the prayers, but wound the hairy

scalp of every such a one, Psa. lxvi. 18; lxviii. 21. For instance: If thou livest in lying, (for it is one thing to be overtaken that way out of fear, or ere thou be aware, another thing to continue in it habitually and resolutely against an enlightened, but impenitent conscience,) and yet look for heaven, thou art deceived; thou hast made a lie thy refuge, and hid thyself under falsehood. And why? because God's word saith, that " the fearful, and unbelieving, and the abominable, and murderers, and whoremongers, and sorcerers, and idolaters, and all liars, shall have their part in the lake which burneth with fire and brimstone: which is the second death," Rev. xxi. 8. Conceive proportionably of living in any other sin damned in God's book in the sense I have said. If thou abidest in the state of mere moral honesty, and yet thinkest with thyself that thou art thereby furnished sufficiently for future happiness, it is but a false flash. And why? because the word saith, " Without holiness no man shall see the Lord," Heb. xii. 14; which necessarily implies, that no mere civil man can possibly be saved. If thou be a lukewarm Laodicean, and yet conceivest thou art rich enough spiritually, and lookest to be saved, thou art deceived. And why? because the word saith that Christ will cast such a one out of his mouth, Rev. iii. 16. Such are all lukewarm, formal professors to the Lord Jesus Christ. A terrible and flaming sentence uttered from the Judge's own mouth in the mean time; which methinks should horribly affright thousands in our days, who stand for a frozen formality, heartless indifferency, reserved neutrality, and politic moderation in profession and practice of religion. Thus, a true testimony and sound persuasion of a good state to Godward ever holds correspondence to the word, and is infallibly grounded thereupon.

Object. Say you so? In spiritual cases and points of faith, how is it possible that a man should be infallibly certain of that by the word, which is not contained in the word, either immediately or by good consequence? For Bellarmine affirms, that the particular proposition, that " such or such a man is truly justified," is not contained in the word of God either immediately or by good consequence.

Ans. To let pass, at this time, that which some worthy divines press in this point, that such places as these, Psa. ciii 3; Rom. x. 9; Gal. ii. 20, &c., intimate and imply such a particular proposition immediately: I answer, that it is deduced by evident consequence out of the word; for, from such general promises and propositions as these, " He that believeth on the Son, hath everlasting life," John iii. 36; " Whosoever believeth in him shall receive remission of sins," Acts x. 43; " And by him all that believe are justified from all things," Acts xiii. 39, these particulars follow by good consequence, that Paul, Peter, Luther, Calvin, Beza, Bradford, or any other particular man believing in Christ, receives remission of sins, is justified, hath eternal life; even as it followeth directly and infallibly that as every man is a reasonable creature, therefore John, Thomas, &c., are endued with reason.

Though no word saith expressly and immediately, Thou, Thomas, believing, shalt be saved; yet the same word which saith, " He that believeth on the Son hath eternal life," saith also, Thou, Thomas, believing, hast eternal life, or shalt be saved. As, on the contrary, this universal truth, " He that believeth not the Son, shall not see life, but the wrath of God abideth on him," includeth virtually, consequently, infallibly, as though they were written in it these particulars: Judas, or Bonner, not believing, shall not see life, but the wrath of God abideth on him. Otherwise: if the general did not thus sufficiently include and comprehend every particular, and a universal proposition all subordinate singular propositions under it, the law, " Thou shalt not kill: thou shalt not commit adultery: thou shalt not bear false witness against thy neighbour," would not belong to Fawkes' blowing up the parliament; to this or that priest polluting himself in hearing confession; to Bellarmine lying voluminously, because it is nowhere expressly written, Thou, Bellarmine, shalt not bear false witness against thy neighbour; Thou, Fawkes, shalt not tear in pieces the royal limbs of the Lord's anointed.

If John or Thomas, believing, be not bound to be assured of his salvation out of the general promise, except it were said somewhere in Scripture, that Thomas or John by name should be saved; it would follow, that these particular men were not bound to be honest men, or to fear God, because it is nowhere said in the word that Thomas or John ought to be honest men, or are commanded to fear God, but only in the general.

In a word: let the jesuit tell me whether or not, out of the word, he be infallibly certain that his body shall rise again at the last day: he dare not for his heart deny it. And I pray you tell me where it is particularly and expressly said in Scripture, that the body of Robert Bellarmine shall rise again at the last day? All particular infallible assurance in this kind springs out of the general

2 K

proposition and promise that all shall rise, 1 Cor. xv.

2. That heart which doth sweetly enjoy the paradise of a true testimony, and well-grounded persuasion, that it lives the life of grace and immortality, is sincerely affected and inflamed with a reverent love and insatiable longing after the word preached and read, prayer, singing of psalms, meditation, conference, vows, days of humiliation, use of good books, godly company, all God's ordinances, and good means appointed and sanctified for our spiritual good. Because through them, like so many golden conduit pipes, those gracious saving operations of the Holy Ghost are conveyed and continued unto it; which minister sound matter and true grounds of such comfortable assurance, and in the conscionable use and exercise of them also, are wont sometimes to be secretly and sensibly breathed into it such heavenly real refreshings themselves, which the joy of the whole world's enjoyment cannot possibly equal. Now, the affection this way of those who are pharisaically puffed up with a groundless conceit and vain confidence, is faint and formal, partial and reserved; not accompanied with universality and uniformity of reverence and respect to all the blessed ordinances and means of grace. It is ever the manner and cunning of such to qualify their countenance and correspondence to these, with that moderation and temper which may be compatible and plausibly consist with the safety of their temporal happiness, and security of their bosom sin. And no marvel though their affection in this kind be not so hearty, and hold not out, for they draw no special virtue and sweetness from Christ through them; and their conceit of being right is not fed

from the Bible, and with the heavenly manna of a conscionable ministry, but built upon those insufficient grounds and rotten props I before exposed.

3. A sound and undeceiving persuasion that thou art everlastingly locked in the arms of God's mercy and love, grounded upon the word, seconded and set on by the Spirit, is a most rare and rich jewel, which doth infinitely outshine and overweigh in sweetness and worth any rock of diamond, crystal mountain, or this great creation were it all converted into one invaluable pearl; and therefore is infinitely envied, and assaulted mightily on all sides. It is continually hunted, like a partridge on the mountains, by natural distrust, the policy of Satan, and all the powers of darkness. There is not a wicked spirit but is transported with implacable indignation against that heaven upon earth, and therefore, rages and roars about thee still, to rob and bereave thy humble breast of such a heavenly gem: besides the two main ends and general aims of all the malice and machinations of those apostate angels; the dishonour of God, and the discomfort of men's souls. In this point they are peculiarly enraged with extreme hellish anger, to see a mortal man, a child of Adam, crowned by God's merciful hand, even in this life, with right and interest, and as it were an earnest of the inheritance with the saints in light, and of those blessed mansions of glory and rest, of which by their apostasy and pride they have unhappily and everlastingly deprived themselves. Not only so, but they employ also their agents, envious of the grace of God and thine own fearful heart, to charge falsely many times upon thee, hypocrisy and delusion, lest that white stone given thee by the Holy Ghost, the splendour and sweetness

whereof none knoweth but he that hath it, should fairly shine upon thy sad soul with that lightsomeness and comfort as it both may and ought. Whereupon it must needs follow, that if thy persuasion be well grounded, and assurance true, it will be accompanied, and often exercised with fears, jealousies, doubts, distrusts, varieties of temptations, Satan's fiery darts, injected scruples, contradictions of flesh and blood, cavils of carnal reasons, want of comfortable feeling, &c., which will many times necessarily drive thee to cry mightily to God, and complain at the throne of grace against all this hellish ordinance and assaults of thy unbelieving heart; by the wrestling of faith to warm thy soul with meditation upon the promises, to re-examine and revise thy grounds, to confirm thy watch, to resort for counsel, strength, and comfort to the quickening means, experience of former sweet feelings and motions of the Spirit, to truly judicious divines, experienced christians, days of humiliation, and books of best relish to a spiritual taste. But now, on the contrary side, presumptuous confidence and groundless conceit lie in the pharisee's bosom with much quietness and security, without doubting, difficulty, contradiction, or any such ado. The reason is, his carnal heart is well enough content, because it still feeds upon the delights of his darling sin, without disturbance. Satan is too subtle to interpose, tempt, or interrupt, in such a case; for he well knoweth that his foundation is falsehood, his hope of heaven but a golden dream, and therefore in policy he keeps his peace, that he may hold him the faster.

Take notice, by the way, that the very thing which makes many a true-hearted christian doubt of himself, and of the soundness of his spiritual state, should put him out of all doubt; even that of being often exercised with doubts, temptations, multiplied attempts against his faith and assurance of God's love, if prayed against, humbly resisted, and opposed with cleaving unto the tender-heartedness of Christ, and truth of his promises, though for the present he has little or no feeling, no such joy and peace in thus believing. And that very thing upon which the deluded ones build, and many times boast themselves; to wit, that they are untroubled, untempted in point of faith and pretended assurance, may return an infallible remonstrance to their own consciences, that they are certainly deceived. For, doubtless, that faith which is never assaulted with doubting, is but a fancy. Assuredly that assurance which is ever secure, is but a dream. Many a pharisee stands by the bedside of the sincere professor visited with affliction of conscience and many heavy temptations, secretly and sinfully pleasing himself in the unblessed calmness of a groundless confidence, and in his freedom from such terrors and spiritual troubles; when he is like an ox fatting in the green pastures of impunity and outward prosperity for the day of slaughter. But the afflicted party is as precious gold, purifying in the Lord's refining furnace, that he may afterward come out and shine more gloriously.

4. In that heart which the Spirit of God testifies that it is a child of God, Rom. viii. 16, doth the same Spirit create many fervent ejaculations, strong cries, and unutterable groanings, ver. 26. The testimony of the Spirit is ever attended with the spirit of prayer. That glorious glimpse shining into the soul, and assuring it of salvation, is so

sweet, so heavenly, so rapturous, so transcendent, and incomparably above all earthly joy, that it warms the spirit of a man with quickening life and liberty, to pour out itself in the presence of his Lord and his God, before the throne of grace. Sometimes in more hearty triumphant, and, as it were, winged prayers; at other times, in those which are more faint and cold, yet edged with infinite desires, that they were more fervent, and therefore by the way, as it were, mingled and perfumed with the sovereign and satisfactory incense in the golden censer, which the Angel of the covenant holds in his hand, are graciously accepted of Him, who by an excellency and title of highest honour is styled the Hearer of prayers: or at least, with inexpressible groans and inward wrestlings, for preservation, recovery, and enlargement of that same comfortable assurance itself, and of all other holy graces and fruits of the Spirit, purity of heart, conquest over corruption, nearer communion with God, spiritual-mindedness, and such other heavenly guests, amongst whom it is wont to dwell with delight, and represent itself more comfortably. But now, on the other side, every deluded pharisee is a mere stranger to the power of prayer; his presumption and groundless confidence is but a weed which will grow of its own accord, and therefore is not sensible of any necessity, neither feels any want of constant prayer from a broken heart, universal obedience, or the holy preciseness of the saints to support it.

5. An assurance of God's love upon sure ground, doth mightily quicken and spur forward the ingenuous christian to more holiness, hatred of sin, resolution in a good cause, watchfulness over his heart, and walking with God. "Having these promises,"

saith he, "let us cleanse ourselves from all filthiness of the flesh and spirit, perfecting holiness in the fear of God," 2 Cor. vii. 1. Having this hope, I will labour to purify myself, "even as he is pure," 1 John iii. 3. To let the principal motive pass, it is impossible but that the feeling consciousness that God's free love, through Christ, hath freed us from eternity of torments, one hour wherein is infinitely more stinging and terrible than all the tortures that all mankind have, do, or shall endure, from the creation to the end of the world; and hath certainly interested us in an eternity of joys, one hour wherein doth incomparably surpass all the delights of this wide world, were they collected into one lump of pleasure,—I say, it cannot be but that such an assurance should stir up the blessed soul to do or suffer any thing for Christ's sake; to do worthily in Ephrata, and be famous in Bethlehem; rather to die than turn papist. But the other groundless confidence, being in truth but a fancy, must needs be powerless, fruitless, inactive; and makes the deluded rather secure, careless, presumptuous, and only formal.

6. The blessed Spirit is wont to spring in our hearts with heavenly refreshing and his sweetest testimony, especially at such times as when we retire and recollect ourselves to converse with God in a more solemn and solitary manner; opening our consciences, breaking our hearts, and pouring out our souls into his bosom; when we are preparedly and fruitfully exercised in the ordinances; in our innocent patient sufferings, for good causes and conscience' sake; when we feel that we have conquered or well curbed some corruption, by the power of prayer; in the believing contemplation

and examination of our change, and the infallible marks thereof; when we meditate effectually upon the bottomless depth of God's free love unto us, with which he hath loved us from everlasting to everlasting; upon days of humiliation, &c. But that other counterfeit flash keeps a deluded pharisee in a fool's paradise continually; he is ordinarily at all times alike peremptory in the point of assurance. You shall not take him any week in the year, any day in the week, any hour in the day, without a bold persuasion, and protestation, if need be, that he hopes to be saved as well as the precisest. He is as confident this way when he is cavilling against the purity of the saints and power of godliness, as when he is the deepest in his pharisaical devotions.

7. The presumption of the pharisee is ordinarily greatest in the height of outward prosperity, and when God's candle shineth brightest upon his head with worldly blessings. But the persuasion of the christian is for the most part then strongest when the world most frowneth upon him for his forwardness, and in the heat of persecution.

8. Those that are deluded with a groundless confidence, have ordinarily been so conceited of themselves ever since they can remember or had any thoughts of heaven, and that without consciousness of any conversion, change, or supernatural saving work upon their souls at all. For though the devil seals it with more security upon their hearts by his counterfeit angelical glory, yet he finds matter enough in our corrupt nature ministered originally for such a golden dream and imaginary castle in the air. But the testimony of the Spirit and that other true persuasion are supernatural, and never felt before conversion, nor ever to be found but in a re-

generate soul. I doubt not but many christians, to their singular comfort and further assurance, can tell their experience of both: their bold, peremptory, ill-grounded presumption in their unregenerate time; and their now true, kindly, sweet persuasion, accompanying their conversion, which is so much envied and assaulted by Satan.

9. Natural presumption, gilded over with the devil's delusion, ever shrinks in the wetting. Troubles of conscience, fiery trials, heavy crosses, the face of the prince of terror, disastrous and dismal times, dissolve it into nothing. But the other true testimony holds out, like armour of proof, against the thickest hail-shot of all adverse power. Nay, it is wont to shine and show itself with united vigour, and more lightsomeness within; in the greatest damp of outward discomforts and utmost confusions abroad.

10. The christian can give sound reasons for his resolution in the point of assurance; from his conversion, holy conversation, love of the brethren, and universal obedience; those means I mentioned before, which are peculiar to the child of God. But put the pharisee to proof in this case, and perhaps he will not be able to say so much as his formal, deluded brother, Luke viii. 11, 12. Sure I am, all that he can produce for that purpose, being tried by the touchstone of God's truth, will prove too light and inconsequent. Review the false mediums and insufficient grounds discovered before, and you will perceive that none of them can possibly lead to a comfortable conclusion.

11. The Laodicean professor longs far more for gold than growth in grace; thinks himself already rich enough in religion, and that he hath attained

that very temper which every wise man should rest
upon, without any more meddling: that, if he should
stir forward, he would be too precise; if he should
grow any worse, he would be too profane; and therefore concludes, I have need of nothing. But the
enlightened christian, having truly tasted of the assurance of God's love, is infinitely greedy of growing in grace, of conquering corruptions, of nearer
communion with Christ, of doing in the cause of
God all the most glorious and sincere service he
possibly can before he go down into the grave, and
be seen no more. His performances, by the grace
of God, are many; his endeavours more; but his
desires endless, and ever unsatisfied with his degree
of well-doing, his present degree of grace and measure of obedience.

Thus having premised a discovery of spiritual
self-deceit,—whereby many so overvalue themselves
in point of their spiritual state, that they conceive
they are quite right; whereas, in truth and trial, they
are stark rotten at the root: their case herein is like
that man's, who, lying fast asleep upon the edge of
a steep rock, dreams merrily of crowns, kingdoms,
and the very confluence of all earthly contentments,
conceiving that he wallows himself in the overflow-
ings of all worldly felicities, but, upon the sudden
starting for joy, breaks his neck, and tumbles into
the bottom of the sea: they are lulled asleep by
the deluding charms of the devil, upon their beds of
presumptuous security, all their life long, dreaming
of no danger at all, but ever confident their case is
good enough Godward; but their consciences being
awaked upon their beds of death, or at farthest at
God's tribunal, they are suddenly swallowed up of
despair, and drowned in everlasting perdition,—

I come now to forewarn and forearm the true christian, that, with all watchfulness and constancy, he would ever labour to prevent and defeat the secret assaults and insinuations of that " white devil," as a worthy divine calls it, spiritual pride; a gilded poison, which Satan doth first extract out of the very sweetest and fairest flowers in Christ's garden; I mean the most holy virtues and heavenly gifts implanted in the hearts of his people; and then, thereby so envenoms and blasts them, that they lose not only their own native splendour and gracefulness, but also their fruitful communication to others, and comfortable acceptation with God. When he sees a man extraordinarily enriched with spiritual graces, he seeks, might and main, to make him swell with secret pride, and to puff him up with an overweening conceit of his own worth; that so the christian himself may want the comfort of them, his brethren the fruit of them, and God the glory of them. When the strong man can no longer keep goodness out of the soul, but the Holy Ghost, with a merciful violence, breaks in upon him, and dwells there, his next endeavour is to abuse even grace itself, as an unhappy instrument to weaken and wound itself; nay, so subtle is he, and endless in his attempts, that, if he cannot make a man proud of any thing else, he will labour to make him proud that he is not proud, and to glory vainly, because he is not vainglorious. The original and breeding of this canker in the sanctified soul, I have discovered in my " Discourse of True Happiness," and there made known some corrosives and counter-poisons against it; to which, at this time, I add the following.

When thou beginnest, with an overweening conceit,

to admire thyself immoderately, and above that which is meet, cast thine eye,

1. Upon the purity and piercing of God's all-seeing eye, ten thousand times brighter than the sun, and purer than purity itself; which sees sin to be infinitely more sinful and loathsome than thou canst possibly, whereby his holy justice is incensed with infinite indignation and unquenchable severity against it. Witness the turning into devils, the irrecoverable destruction, and everlasting downfal of so many glorious creatures, the top and masterpiece, as it were, of all God's handiwork, shining once so fairly in the highest heaven, and nearest unto his throne. The curse which fell upon Adam and all his posterity for eating the forbidden fruit; the confusions which came upon the first world by the flood; the burning of Sodom with fire and brimstone from heaven; the fearful rejection of his own ancient people; the horrors of a guilty enraged conscience, which is a hell upon earth, and damnation above ground; and the everlasting fire which is prepared for reprobate men and angels. Neither doth God's bright eye only see all thy sins in their native foulness, but also in their truest number. Thou, perhaps, for want of more spiritual eyesalve, beholdest them but as stars in a gloomy evening; but assure thyself he sees them, as motes in the sun, and as stars in the clearest winter's night. Methinks this mortifying meditation should rather make thee grow into further detestation of sin than admiration of thyself.

2. Upon the incomprehensible perfections and absolute pureness of God's most holy nature, the splendour whereof doth dazzle the clearest eyes of the brightest seraphims; doth drown, as it were, all

angelical glory; as the sun's presence doth the light of lesser stars; much more doth it utterly darken the material beauty of all the lights in heaven. Were the sun, which is made all of brightness, and the ever-springing fountain of fresh shining beams, presented before that unapproachable light which besets God's sacred throne, it would vanish away as a darksome mote, and lump of vanity. Where then would a frail sinful man in a house of flesh appear? "Behold," saith Job, "he put no trust in his servants; and his angels he charged with folly: how much less in them that dwell in houses of clay; whose foundation is in the dust; which are crushed before the moth," Job iv. 18, 19. "Behold, he putteth no trust in his saints; yea, the heavens are not clean in his sight. How much more abominable and filthy is man, which drinketh iniquity like water!" Job xv. 15, 16. "Behold, even to the moon, and it shineth not; yea, the stars are not pure in his sight. How much less man, that is a worm! and the son of man, which is a worm!" Job xxv. 5, 6. A glimpse, as it were, of that highest glory, shining everlastingly in that purest uncreated essence, God blessed for ever, did make righteous Job to " abhor himself, and repent in dust and ashes," Job xlii. 6; and holy Isaiah to cry, "Woe is me! for I am undone," Isa. vi. 5. And, if thou also turn thine eye from the vanity of self-admiration toward the infinite Sun of absolute and incomprehensible purity, and then reflect upon thyself, as he that hath gazed too much upon our visible sun, looking down again seeth nothing, thou shalt behold the nothingness of thine overweened worth, and nothing but darkness and deformity; and so shalt find infinite more matter of humiliation and abhorring thyself in dust and ashes, than of self-estimation and conceitedness.

3. Upon the pure crystal glass of God's pure law, which can discover unto thee the least spot that ever stained so much as any one of thy thoughts; which shines with that perfect light, that it would guide aright every step which thou takest in the way that is called holy; and is of that latitude for prohibition of sin, and leading to purity and exact pleasing of God, that, though we may see an end of all perfection, yet it is exceeding broad, Psa. cxix. 96; and, therefore, though such as hate to be reformed, especially if their consciences be waking and working, are drawn to a particular and punctual survey of themselves and all their ways in this pure crystal, even as a bear to the stake, or a foul face to the looking-glass. They are well enough content to hear the commandments read, restraining their understandings only to the gross acts, "Thou shalt not kill," &c., and perhaps justifying themselves pharisaically thereabouts; but come to the holy strictness of Christ's exposition, "Whosoever looketh on a woman to lust after her, hath committed adultery with her already in his heart," and it strikes full cold to their impure hearts, and causeth them to cry out against the men of God, "Why do you torment us before our times?" I say, though it be thus with the unregenerate, by reason of their guilty and galled consciences, yet let it be thy delight, who art blessed with an everlasting impregnable protection, by the blood and merit of Jesus Christ, from the curse and rigour of the law, to examine thyself close by this heavenly looking-glass, for the discovery of thy defects and aberrations; and dive with searching and serious meditation into this

adored depth of perfection and purity, to see how far thou comest short; and then thou shalt find infinitely more cause to press hard towards the mark than to look upon that which is behind, or proudly to prize any thing that is past. Only I advise, when thou settest thyself thus solemnly to rip up thy conscience, and ransack thy heart to the root, to bring it down and into the dust, for increase of humiliation and lowliness in thine own eyes, as thou holdest out in the one hand the clear crystal of God's pure law, to discover the crookedness of thy vile natural disposition, the villanies and scarlet abominations of thine unregenerate time, and the daily spots and stains which light upon thy soul; hold out also, in the other hand, or rather lay hold upon Christ Jesus by the hand of faith, hanging, bleeding, and dying upon the cross, for those very same sins; that thereby thou mayest utterly quench all Satan's fiery darts, prevent drawing towards despair, nay, preserve thy spirit in sweetest peace and unconquerable comfort against, if it be possible, the least distrustful intrusion of any slavish terror.

4. Upon the holiest men that ever breathed the life of grace upon earth, and the most renowned in the church through all generations, for all spiritual sufficiences and excellences, and thou shalt find them ever most humble in their own opinions, vilest in their own eyes, nothing in their own account. Methinks holy Paul's heavy complaint, "O wretched man that I am! who shall deliver me from the body of this death?" Rom. vii. 24:—heavenly David's continual cry, " I am a worm and no man: there is no rest in my bones, because of my sin: my sin is ever before me," Psa. xxii. 6; xxxviii. 3; li. 3:—blessed Bradford's abasing himself, who

was one of the worthiest martyrs, and the heavenliest minded man, that ever breathed out his last in the flames, and ascended to heaven in a fiery chariot; as himself spake at the stake, "I am as dry as a stone," saith he, "as dumb as a nail; as far from praying as he that never knew any taste of it:" he sometime subscribed in this manner to those letters which were full of spiritual life, divinest strains, and demonstration of the Spirit: "The most miserable, hard-hearted, unthankful sinner, John Bradford;" "A very painted hypocrite, J. B.:"—I say, methinks the humble deportment of these, and all truly holy ones, should rather make thee sink yet lower in thine own conceit, than swell with the poison of pharisaical self-conceitedness.

5. Keep in a readiness and in fresh remembrance such humbling considerations as these, when thy heart begins to swell vain-gloriously. 1. That thou hadst thine hand in that fire-work which blew up all mankind; I mean, in Adam's transgression, that brought forth such a sea of sin and sorrow into the world; such a world of miseries and mischiefs upon all the sons and daughters of Adam, all tortures upon earth, and torments in hell through all eternity. 2. That thou camest into this world a sink, a very hell of all filth and impurity; of all corruption and crookedness, even a little devil for darkness and damnation. 3. That thou wofully lost and mispent many years, perhaps the best of thy time, strength of youth, flower of thy age, in Satan's service, and upon thy own abominable lusts. 4. That now upon thy conversion, the mere work of God's free grace, thou, being honoured with part in Christ's passion, with the presence of the blessed Spirit dwelling in thee, with the highest advancement of

being God's favourite, the dearly beloved of his soul, Jer. xii. 7, yet the best sabbath that thou passest over, the holiest duty that thou performest, is stained and distempered with many imperfections, distractions, frailties, and failings. 5. That, while thou yet inhabitest a house of flesh, thou hast inherent in thee secret seeds, and inbred inclinations to all sin, (bless the sanctifying Spirit for thy privilege and preservation,) even to atheism, despairing of God's mercy, &c. 6. That whereas thousands about thee go on in their sins, and perish everlastingly, thyself, it may be, before thy change worse than most of them, yet now being sanctified, thou mayest be assured thy name was wrote in heaven from all eternity, and therefore from everlasting thou layest in the bosom of God's love, and from the same everlasting had the Lord Jesus set apart to shed his blood in the fulness of time for the salvation of thy soul; and have patience but a little, and everlasting refreshing shall come from the presence of the Lord; thou shalt shine as the brightness of the firmament for ever and ever. And in all this who made thee to differ? Thou wast framed of the same mould, made, as it were, of the same cloth, only the sheers going between, with those that perish: it was only God's free grace, the good pleasure of his will. These, and the like considerations, laid together, should infinitely rather move thee with all humble reverence to adore the bottomless depth of God's free love unto thee, than conceitedly to magnify thyself above thy brethren, or proudly insult over those that are without; to praise thy God with a never-satisfied admiration of his inconceivable bounty, than to plague thy soul, and, as it were, empoison thy graces with a humour of pride.

6. Thou must shortly be strictly accountable at the just tribunal of God for the use and employment of all the good things he hath given unto thee; of thy life, and every moment of it; of thy goods, and every farthing of them; of every word thou ever spokest; of every thought that ever sprung out of thy heart; of every sermon thou ever heardst; of every sabbath thou hast solemnized; of every line thou hast written; of every glance of thine eye; of every journey thou hast made; of thy wit, memory, learning; of thy strength, courage, credit; of thine honour, power, and high place; in a word, of every benefit or any good thing in any kind thou ever receivedst from the bountiful and blessed hand of Almighty God. And, the more and more excellent and extraordinary endowments and gracious indulgences have been vouchsafed thee from the ever-springing Fountain of all good, the more exactly must thou be answerable, and in proportion accountable for more Wherefore, since the graces of salvation incomparably excel and outshine all other human abilities; all excellences of nature, art, policy, learning, or what else can be named admirable in the eyes of men; God looks that we should keep those heavenly jewels especially bright and shining, communicate them most frankly and abundantly to our brethren, and with all watchfulness and wisdom, upon all opportunities, employ them to our Master's greatest and most glorious advantage. Now, there is nothing more hinders the fruitful improvement of them than pride; nothing makes them more acceptable and profitable than humility. A proud man, puffed up with an opinion of his good parts, doth ordinarily, out of an itching, ambitious humour, single out such seasons for discovery of

himself, and ostentation of his gifts, when he may win most applause from men, and show himself vain-gloriously, and thereupon is more rare, dainty, and reserved in exercising his talent. But a downright humble christian is in this kind unreservedly and indifferently for all places, times, and persons, where and when he may bring glory unto God, good unto others, comfort to his own soul, in discharging a good conscience. He dares not, either out of humour, or for fear he should make himself too cheap, as they say, or any other vain respect, conceal any thing in his heart or brain, were it the highest strain of his heavenly skill, or any experimental secret in the mystery of Christ, from the meanest christian, could he wisely and seasonably thereby do him any spiritual good. Let us, therefore, infinitely abhor, by filthy vain-glory, to stain the glory and blast the fruitfulness of our graces; but rather, with all humility and watchfulness, observe and apprehend all the ways, occasions, and callings, whereby we may most glorify God with them, and improve them best for our Lord's advantage, that so we may give up our account at the great and universal audit, with more favour, and enter more comfortably into our Master's joy.

7. Let the fear and foresight of the many dreadful effects, and much ill that certainly follows, and is ever found where this white devil, spiritual pride, haunts, hunt it out of thy heart, and keep a continual narrow watch against all its sly insinuations. Besides that it plagues the soul which harbours it with many spiritual miseries, distempers, disacquaintance with God, (for he is ever most familiar with those who are most humble,) pharisaical swellings, inflammations of furious zeal, and the

like; it ever proves also of pestilent consequence and prejudice to the common state of goodness, to the honour and acceptation of christianity.

(1.) A truly proud professor, puffed up with his gifts and supposed sufficiencies, who wickedly aims more at vain-glory than glorifying God, at his own praise than profiting others, is, for the most part, very irksome, tedious, and burdensome to the company of humble, wise, judicious christians. For ordinarily he is swift to speak, and too full of words, far more forward to over-rule and domineer, in opposing, moderating, resolving, than seven men that can render a reason. An itching humour after applause, and of carrying away the credit for ability to discourse and eminency above others, puts him on too often to pour out himself indiscreetly and impertinently in all companies, to press and obtrude upon others with much verbal importunity, and unconquerable stiffness, his master-like conceits, without due respect or seasonable observation of the humble abilities and sufficiencies of bystanders, and that many times when he hath neither calling, fitness, efficacy of matter, nor power of the Holy Ghost. And if a man do not presently, upon the bare and first proposition, accord and accommodate his judgment to every circumstance of whatsoever he holds, and square exactly to his oracles, he begins to shake the head, as though he were a lost man, and is ready to excommunicate him out of his conscience. I speak not thus to stop the current of comfortable talk, edifying discourse, and fruitful conference in any true-hearted Nathanaels. There is infinitely more need to stir them up, and quicken them to more forwardness and communion this way at christian meetings, but only to check the vain-glorious, empty, opinionative talkativeness of such as are possessed with this white devil.

(2.) Such a one also is wont to be too austere, censorious, sour, and imperious in his carriage towards those who are without, whereby he becometh both a stumbling-block to them in their way to christianity, and brings also an unnecessary, scandalous, false aspersion upon the ways of God and yoke of Christ, as though they were harsh, heavy, and unpleasant, whereas they are most sweet, easy, and amiable. I know full well there is not the wisest, holiest, humblest, discreetest christian alive, who can so possibly bear and behave himself, but profaneness will plague him with slanderous imputations of any kind. Jesus Christ our Master was not free this way; which of his servants then can, dare, or will expect and desire exemption? Blessed be God, that our good names are oiled, so that the ink will not stick which is cast upon them. There is scarcely a religious professor, especially of resolution and spirit, to be found, but some men of the world will charge him with surliness and pride. Whereas, many times not only the imputation is ungrounded, mistaken, misimputed, fastened upon him for the most part by reason of his nonconformity to the courses of the world, and corruptions of the times; his shunning the company of profane men; his resolution and undauntedness in good causes; and his innocency and independency, which beget boldness and braveness of mind; but also those fellows themselves who so slander him cannot possibly choose but be passingly proud, because their consciences were never enlightened with the sight, sense, and acknowledgment of the foulness of sin, their own vileness, the exactness of God's law, purity of his most holy nature, and severity and certainty of his judgments. Yet, for all this, I would advise all those who have in earnest given their names to Christ, that they would walk warily, and so demean themselves that they give no just offence in this kind. For, when they have tried both ways, they shall find that mercifulness and meekness to those that are without, humility and humanity, affable, courteous, and loving deportment, and so becoming all things to all men, in Paul's sense, and so far as we may with a good conscience, is the better way, subscribed unto by the manifold experiences of wisest and worthiest christians, to win honour to our profession, to gain more unto God's side, and to preserve ourselves in as much peace amidst a wicked and crooked generation as holiness will possibly permit.

(3.) God, in his just judgment, gives over such a one sometimes to fantastical opinions, odd and absurd tenets, swerving brainlessly and senselessly from the holy harmony of confessions, the truth whereof every honest man, if need required, ought to seal with his blood, which when superficialness, and its ordinary consort, self-conceitedness, have unhappily brought forth, by the midwifery of a kind of spiritual wantonness, be they ever so monstrous and mis-shapen, yet some giddy heads will hearken and hanker after them, so that frequently many weak, ungrounded, unstable young beginners in profession, are wofully entangled, as we too often see in our chief city; whence ensues a vast deal of prejudice, hurt, and hinderance, even to the common state of goodness, to the honour and acceptation of christianity. For thereupon is raised a cry in all conventicles of good fellowship, and consistories of worldly wisdom, that these forward professors will all turn fantastical, arians, or any thing. Which cry awakens the eye of state jealousy, and so, by an unworthy consequence, draws upon those who are true of heart, even God's best servants, and the king's best subjects, discountenance, suspicions, if not molestations, unnecessarily and causelessly. For so might ye root up your rose-trees, because a worm sometimes breeds in the sweetest bud. So might ye extinguish monarchies from the face of the earth, because they sometimes degenerate into tyrannies. So might ye conceive ill of Peter, and the rest of the apostles, because Judas proved an apostate.

Sometimes God suffers him to fall into some gross sin, in the face of the world, and before the watchful eye of scornful enemies; the infamy and scandal whereof, being once on wing, fly abroad as swift as the eagles of the heavens, over a whole country, over a kingdom; the devils and their drunken trumpeters are speedy dromedaries to carry such news, and this concurrent cry resounds from all places with much wicked triumph and insultation, "You see now what these professors are. One so famous for his forwardness is fallen into such a gross sin, and so notoriously; they are even all alike," &c. Which by accident, and in the event, redounds too often to the inexpiable disgrace of our holy profession, the strengthening of the stubborn, the staggering of the strong, the stunting of those which are coming on, the hindering of the weak, the hardening of the wicked, the chaining of the scorner far faster to his chair of pestilence. Woe unto him by whom such offence doth come, except by a remarkable repentance and recovery, after blessed David's example, he re-establish himself in the hearts of

God's people, and stop the mouths of the adversaries, who are equally guilty of impenitency, as of far perhaps grosser impieties. Augustine doth excellently express, and to the life, the wiliness of the wicked and humour of the world upon such unhappy occasions. There was, as it seems, some such scandalous accident befel in his family. Whereupon he writes an epistle to the ministers, seniors, and the whole city of Hippo, and heartily entreats them all, " that themselves would not therefore either faint in that christian course, and holy profession, or fall foul with suspicions and censures upon all, for the faults of a few, for there is no society so happy, which is not stained with some villany. Although," saith he, " discipline be exercised in my family with a watchful eye, yet I am a man, and live amongst men, and therefore cannot presume that mine house should be better than the ark of Noah, than the house of Abraham, than the house of Isaac, than the house of Jacob, than the house of David, &c., in all which some were wicked; nay, than the family of Jesus Christ, in which there was a traitor and a thief. Lastly, than heaven itself, from which the angels fell " But that which I would principally have you take notice of in that epistle, and for which I especially mention it, is Augustine's emphatical, elegant, and effectual expressing the eager, itching, ambitious humour of the wicked, to father and fasten the faults of some upon the whole generation of the just. *Instant*, saith he, *Satagunt, ambiunt;* I cannot express their full significancy in English, but part of his meaning is, they every way infinitely labour, that when some professors of holiness have foully fallen indeed, or be only so slandered, the world would believe that they are all such. Do you not think in Lot's time that the world did thus insult and exclaim, or in the like manner, upon his fall: "Here now you see puritan Lot, who could not endure the good fellowship of the men of Sodom, he is now himself seized upon by incest: they are all such I will warrant you?" In David's time: "What, David! a man so precise that he professeth a liar shall not tarry in his sight, Psa. ci. 7; hath he taken away another man's wife? You see now what they all are." Proportionably in these times, (and it will be the humour of those that hate to be reformed to the world's end so to calumniate,) if any who have given their names unto Christ be detected, nay, or suspected, of any notorious scandalous crime, it is a sufficient warrant for the wicked to raise a general cry, and to proclaim every where that they are all alike. And good fellows, as they call themselves, will think themselves wronged if the world thereupon do not conceive the only difference between them and forward professors to be, that these carry things more cunningly, and have an art in concealing their miscarriages. "We," say they, " are plain-dealing men, and appear as we are; we are flesh and blood, and must have our pleasures, and therefore refresh ourselves at many merry and jovial meetings; we swear sometimes, and drink, and game, and, to tell you the truth, do a great deal worse, but without hypocrisy; whereas these demure holy ones bear themselves more reservedly, wear a vizor in their visible conversation, but assure yourselves sin in secret as well as we." Just as Augustine saith in the forecited place, "The wicked watch and observe, and, if they spy any of the better side to fall, they would presently have the world to think that all the rest are such, only they are not ever discovered." Now, the Lord rebuke thee, Satan, who so infatuatest the judgments, and blindest the understandings of men, otherwise of good parts, and very worldly wise, whom thou wofully hoodwinkest and hardenest to their endless overthrow. 1. That they should wickedly and absurdly condemn all for some, whereby they bar themselves everlastingly from the love of the brotherhood. 2. That they should erect tribunals in other men's consciences, (which is God's royal prerogative,) and so miscensure their hearts, to their own hardening. 3. That they should not be able to discern between being haled and hurried, as it were, into some sin against the general purpose of a man's heart and practice of his life, by the violence of some temptation, passion, or impetuous sudden ensnarement, (which he afterwards heartily bewails with much bitterness of spirit, and exemplary repentance, willing, if God were so pleased, to redeem the scandal of his fall with the shedding of his blood, taking occasion thereupon to walk more warily, and to do more nobly in the service of his God all the days of his life,) and a resolved delightful wallowing in a variety of lusts, pleasures, and gross sins, without any repentance or reformation at all.

I conclude the whole point, and a good part of my meaning, in the words of an excellent writer, not much altered. " I not only hold it lawful to rejoice in those good things wherewith God hath blessed us in any kind whatsoever, especially the saving gifts of the Holy Ghost, but a cause of much unthankfulness, to entertain them with a sullen and unfeeling disposition. Yet all human affections and endowments, wherein due reverence to God is wanting, are no better than obscure clouds, hindering the influence of that blessed light which clarifies the soul of man, and predisposeth it unto the brightness of eternal felicity. So that insolent joy and overweening, which a man, in the pride of his vain imagination, conceiveth of his own worth, doth above all other passions blast our minds, as it were, with lightning, and make us reflect our thoughts upon our own seeming inherent goodness, forgetting the while Him to whom we are indebted for our very being; and besides, it blows upon our gifts with such a malignant humour, that they also become unfruitful and unprofitable to others."

Thus much concerning the first extreme and error in managing our spiritual state; to wit, a proud overprizing of our own graces, with a conceited over-weening self-estimation.

Second. I come now to the second, which is a dejected, distrustful undervaluing of God's mercies, the promises of life, and the graces which we possess.

And here I cannot hold, but must, even with some indignation, expostulate and contend with many of God's hidden ones, about their heavy, pensive, and uncomfortable walking, for that they are so far from entertaining and expressing that unspeakable glorious joy, which upon their new birth is their native portion and patrimony, their just and due inheritance; as certainly theirs by an everlasting propriety and right, (if they would but open their eyes to see it, and enlarge their hearts to grasp it,) being a fruit of that Holy Spirit which dwells in them, and a price of Christ's kingdom established in their souls, as their clothes upon their backs, their hearts in their bodies, and blood that runs in their veins. I say, they are so far from walking in the strength and light of this joy, that they wickedly, I dare say, if not wilfully, abandon and expose their spirits, freed for ever by the Lamb's blood from the hellish fangs of any slavish horror, to the unnecessary rack of much fruitless, unworthy, and slavish sadness, whereby, besides their own needless, sinful, self-created torment, they most unworthily undervalue, abridge, and disparage the infiniteness of God's dearest and tender mercy, who is a thousand times more ready and forward to bind up any broken heart, than it is to bleed before him.

Also, they unnecessarily disable and indispose themselves for the duties and comfortable discharge of both their callings.

Again: they gratify Satan and satisfy his cruel humour; who, if he cannot have a man's company in hell hereafter, (for, if he were sure of that, he would make him live as joyfully and jovially as he could possibly,) he labours, might and main, to hold him upon the rack of slavish, distrustful terrors all the days of his life.

Further: they are thereby many times occasions of discouragement and disheartening to those which are without, that they are more loth to enter into the ways of life, prejudging them to be thorny and rough, dark and deep, full of grass, and drooping of heaviness and horror; whereas, indeed and truth, they are all paved with mercy and love, strewed with violets and roses, full of fresh springs of spiritual comforts, and sweetly enlightened, even in the darkest passages, with the heavenly and healing beams of the Sun of righteousness. For whether it be fit to believe the Spirit of all truth and comfort, or the scornful spirit of impure drunkards and Satan's revellers, judge you. This precise and strict walking, say they, which is pressed upon us with such importunity and confidence, would lead us to mopishness and melancholy; would enchain us to that abridgment of our pleasure, restraint from company; from crowning ourselves with rose-buds, and former courses of good fellowship and mirth, of which our generous and jovial spirits are most impatient and utterly incapable. But what saith the blessed Spirit? " Her ways are ways of pleasantness: and all her paths are peace," Prov. iii. 17. They give them occasion to misconceive that the yoke of Christ is burdensome, and will gall their necks; whereas, in truth and trial, it is easy and light, and would prove a chain of heavenly pearls to adorn their souls. Also that after they have given their names to profession that they shall never have merry days, but must necessarily bid adieu to all delight; whereas their joys should not be taken away, but only changed, as one of the ancients speaks, and that most happily, and with an invaluable advantage. For the filth and froth of their sensual bitter-sweet pleasures, fugitive follies, and furious delights, which pass away in the act, as the taste of pleasant drink dieth in the draught, should be turned into that true unconquerable spiritual joy which the world cannot give, neither man nor devil take away. Their bursts of loud laughter amid their pots and pastimes, which are but as the crackling of thorns under a pot, the devil's wake and music for hell, should be converted into a sweet, constant, habitual contentment of mind: nay more, whereas before in the very height and ruff of their maddest meetings, most roaring outrages and revellings, their hearts, upon the remembrance of death, their secret impenitent guiltiness, that strict account at God's dreadful tribunal, at which they may be arraigned the next hour, were full often touched and stung with many inward bitter gripings, and slavish foretastes of hellish terror; yet upon their change, and change of joys, even in the highest tide and torrent of their penitent tears and sorrow for sin, (and they should be sad for nothing else,) their spirits shall be refreshed and enraptured with a paradise of sweetest peace, and heavenly glimpses of eternal light. In a word, if they would in earnest abandon the devil's service, come out of hell, give their names unto Christ in truth, I dare assure them, on the word of life and truth, they would not exchange the saddest hour of all their life afterward, with the prime and flower of all their former sensual pleasures, might they have ten thousand worlds to boot. Here, then, is no loss in the change. But, in the mean time, much to blame are they, who being truly God's, yet out of weakness, want of wisdom, wilful listening unto the father of lies, will not give way to the counsel of the prophets, that they may prosper in spiritual heart's-ease, and so prevent such occasions.

Let those that hate to be reformed hang down their heads; let swaggering Belshazzar's countenance be changed; let his thoughts trouble him; let the joints of his loins be loosed, and his knees smite one against another; let the hearts of all ambitious Nimrods, courteous worldlings, swinish drunkards, those guilty of licentiousness, cruel usurers, lovers of pleasures, or whosoever live and lie in any beloved sin against an enlightened conscience, tremble as the leaves of the forest that are shaken with the wind. Let a sound of fear be ever in their ears, and sorrow seize upon their hearts, as the pangs of a woman in travail. Let trouble and anguish, and the cup of trembling in the hand of the Lord, make them afraid; and let them every hour look to meet their angry God, "as a bear bereaved of her whelps, to rent the very cawl of their hearts, and to devour them like a lion," Hos. xiii. 8. Let sadness sit upon their foreheads as its proper seat, and furies of conscience still affright their spirits with cries of blood: let no voice of joy or gladness be heard in their habitations, but the most frightful apparitions of horror dwell for ever in the eye of their guilty consciences. For, without repentance, this is their lot, and this is their everlasting portion. And most happy were they if any thing would fright and fire them out of the arms of darkness and snares of the devil; I say, let the aspiring Lucifers look heavily upon foresight of their dreadful downfal; for though they exalt themselves as the eagle, and though they set their nests among the stars, thence will I bring them down, saith the Lord, Obad. 4. Though their excellency mount up to the heavens, and their head reach unto the clouds, yet they shall perish for ever like their own dung, Job xx. 6, 7. Let all covetous worldlings cry out, for so the Holy Ghost commands them, "Go to now, ye rich men, weep and howl for your miseries that shall come upon you. Your riches are corrupted, and your garments moth-eaten. Your gold and silver is cankered; and the rust of them shall be a witness against you, and shall eat your flesh as it were fire. Ye have heaped treasure together for the last days," James v. 1, 2. Let all impure drunkards hold down their heads, and howl for the horrible woe which follows them at their heels: "Woe to the crown of pride, to the drunkards of Ephraim. Behold, the Lord hath a mighty and strong one, which as a tempest of hail and a destroying storm, as a flood of mighty waters overflowing, shall cast down to the earth with the hand. The crown of pride, the drunkards of Ephraim, shall be trodden under feet," Isa. xxviii. 1—3; see also ch. v. 11, 12; and 1 Cor. vi. 10. Let the very heart-strings of all lascivious wantons tremble at the terror of that cutting threatening, " Whoremongers and adulterers God will judge," Heb. xiii. 4. Let that stinging " but," Eccles. xi. 9, strike cold to the hearts of all sensual gallants and sons of pleasure: " Rejoice, O young man, in thy youth; and let thy heart cheer thee in the days of thy youth, and walk in the ways of thine heart, and in the sight of thine eyes: but know thou, that for all these things God will bring thee into judgment." Nay, let the heart of every man, whosoever he be, of what cloth soever his coat be made, that goes on in the willing allowed practice of any one known sin, fall asunder in his breast like drops of water, for the day of horror that is at hand, and the sword of vengeance which hangs over his head. For certainly, at length, the Lord, " shall wound the hairy scalp of such an one as goeth on still in his trespasses," Psa. lxviii. 21. In a word, wailing and wringing of hands, woe and alas, is the merriest song that any wicked man upon earth can sing upon good ground, while he yet abides in his unregenerate state. Who doth not see and acknowledge it, except he wilfully shut his eyes, or be grossly hoodwinked by the devil, or a rank atheist? For there is a cup which is called a cup of God's fury, and a cup of trembling in the hand of the Lord, Isa. li. 17, whose little finger is able to beat the greatest mountain to powder, and to rend the hardest rock in pieces: and the wine is red; which intimates unto us the sharpness and fierceness of God's fiery indignation: it is full of mixture; brimfull of stinging ingredients; and he poureth out of the same, to stir up and quicken, as it were, the bitterness and very bottom; and " all the wicked of the earth shall," whether they will or not, " wring out the dregs thereof and drink them," Psa. lxxv. 8.

But now, on the other side: let all those of the brotherhood, I use the phrase of the Holy Ghost, all those who have given their names to Christ in truth, and are true of heart in his holy service, upon whose heads everlasting light doth rest, lift up their heads. Let the amiable aspect of sweetness and peace ever dwell upon their foreheads; let heavenly beams of spiritual lightsomeness and mirth shine fresh in their faces; let no uncomfortable damp of any slavish sadness or touch of hellish terror vex their blessed hearts; let them never more be afraid of any evil tidings, or of destruction when it cometh. In a word, let them be infinitely and for ever merry, and sweetly glad at the very heart root. And good cause why. It is the charge and command of the Spirit of all truth and comfort; " Be glad in the Lord, and rejoice, ye righteous: and shout for joy, all ye that are upright in heart," Psa. xxxii. 11.

Oh that the Lord would be pleased so to perfume and sweeten the ensuing passages with the refreshing glimpses of his glorious face, and dear infusions of divine joy, that I might be vouchsafed the honour of being his humble instrument to raise up and quicken the drooping spirits of all that are true of heart; of all that bear a sincere and invincible affection to the gospel of Jesus Christ and power of godliness; that they would be everlastingly cheerful; that they would arise and shake themselves from the dust, and put on their beautiful garments; that they would for ever, with a resolution never to be shaken with all the powers of hell, banish and bar out of their happy souls, all their unnecessary scruples, distrusts, dejections, sad thoughts, and heaviness of heart; that they would, out of sensibleness of their present unutterable felicity, and strength of their truly heroical spirits, bear and behave themselves as heirs of heaven indeed, and as the favourites of the King of kings! So should they infinitely more honour the sweetness of God's merciful disposition, the dearness of his love, the tenderness of his compassion, the bottomless mystery of his free grace, the preciousness and truth of his promises, the invaluableness of his Son's blood, the pleasantness of the ways of grace, and the glorious work of the Holy Ghost upon their own blessed souls.

Let them ever keep fresh and strong in their minds for this purpose, such considerations as these:

1. True joy, the most noble, sweet, and amiable affection, that ever warmed the heart of man, is, by warrantable proprietorship and rightful interest, only peculiar and proper to honest, humble, and holy hearts. Such gracious and golden cabinets are only fit for this heavenly jewel. The beauty and deliciousness of it are confined only to the communion of saints, the sealed fountain, the spouse of Christ. The brotherhood alone is blessed with its refreshments and rapturous influence. It never did, and never will shine or sparkle out the least glimpse upon the world, or upon any earthly heart. The most ambitious eager hunters after pleasures, the world's greatest favourites and dearest minions, have only engrossed and grasped a madman's counterfeit of it. "I said of laughter," said Solomon,

"it is mad." For the truth is, no wicked or unregenerate man hath any true cause or good ground at all to rejoice, laugh, or be merry. I will, in a word, make it plain even to the scorner.

Suppose a great man, convicted and condemned for treason, going towards the place of execution a mile off; and let there be a table all along furnished with variety of dainties; let him tread upon violets and roses, cloth of arras, cloth of gold, or what you will, all the way; let him be attended on both sides with most exquisite music and honourable entertainments; do you think all this would make him laugh heartily, carrying this in his heart, that he must lose his head at the mile's end? I trow not. As far less true cause hast thou to laugh, whosoever thou art, that walkest on impenitently in any wicked course, or liest delightfully in any beloved sin, as a temporal death is less than endless torments. For he is but going to lose his head, but thou, as an already condemned man also, art posting towards hell. "He that believeth not," saith Christ, "is condemned already," John iii. 18. If we examine the happiest state of the most glorious worldling and all his ways, we shall find no matter at all for true joy, either to breed in or feed upon. Let us walk into his fool's paradise, and survey all the fading flowers of his imaginary felicities. It may be we shall find wealth, power, pleasures, honours, pomp, and magnificence of state; perhaps an imperial crown, the top of all earthly happiness. And what of all these? Alas! gold and pearl, as one says, are but shining dust: power is but a flash of lightning, and forthwith it is suddenly extinct: pleasure is but a bait, and yet passeth away in the act, as the taste of a pleasant drink dieth in the draught: honour is but a breath, and yet binds a man in gilded fetters, and blasts his spirit with far more care and fear than when he was most mean; even as highest boughs are most shaken by the winds, and the points of steeples beaten most with storms and lightning. All worldly splendour and pomp is but a smoke which vanisheth as it riseth, and draws tears from the eyes. Even a regal diadem, in the opinion of a heathen king, is attended with such a weighty, irksome, and painful charge, that, saith he, "He who foreknew the weight of a sceptre, should he find it lying upon the ground, he would not deign to take it up." And what is himself, the owner and lord of all these? A little walking earth, a coloured piece of clay, a warm piece of dirt; to-day a man, to-morrow none: his breath is in his nostrils; stop but his breath, and he is dead. And what is his abode amongst these painted vanities and things of naught? For sudden passage and change it is like a shepherd's tent, a weaver's shuttle, or a water bubble; like a quick post, or a flying cloud; like a ship under sail, or an eagle on her wings; like a fading flower, or a falling leaf; like foam that is scattered, or dust that is driven with the wind; like a vapour, a thought, a smoke, a wind that passeth, and cometh not again; like a flying shadow, yea, the very dream of a shadow, as one says, and that a morning dream, which is even as soon ended as begun. But let us look within, and examine the state of his soul, and see if we can there find any more peace, comfort, or constancy. No; there you shall behold a lively resemblance of the very restless tumultuations of the raging sea; the never dying worm breeding and growing big in the froth of his filthy lusts, and rottenness of his rebellious heart: in a word, his poor soul bleeding to eternal death.

Let us come unto his death, from the inevitable stroke whereof all the gold and pearl of east and west can no more redeem him than can a handful of dust: and there he shall find despair and horror, like two evening wolves, enraged with hunger, ready to tear his soul in pieces, when there is none to help. And what follows? He must lay down his cold carcass among the stones of the pit, at the roots of the rocks; his name, by reason of his former pride, luxury, oppression, opposition to goodness, shall rot as fast, and stink as bad above ground, as his body in the grave. And lastly, the forethought only whereof should make him tremble all the days of his life; his immortal soul sinks irrecoverably by the weight of sin into the bottom of the burning lake, where there are torments without end, and past imagination; exceeding not only all patience, but all resistance: where there is no strength to sustain, nor ability to bear, that which, whilst God is God, for ever must be borne. And when they have been endured millions of years, yet are no nearer an end than when they began, nor the soul nearer out than when it came in. Tell me then, I pray you, in all this is there any room for rejoicing? Is there any matter for true mirth? No more than taste in the white of an egg, than strength in a broken staff of reed, than sweetness in the apples of Sodom. Why then, it is a shame for the weakest christian that breathes but the spiritual life even of holy desires, not to be infinitely more merry than the most glorious and magnificent worldling upon earth. Shall a graceless wretch, going towards hell, to whom God himself hath proclaimed there is no peace, "no joy," as the Septuagint render it; who is a mere thief, robber, and usurer, in respect of all the joys upon which he intrudes, and which way soever he casts his eyes, if he wear not false spectacles, or be blindfolded by the devil, can see nothing but the ugly face of horror, and true cause of trembling. If he look backward upon the time past, he may see all the abominable lusts of his youth, all the sins of his former life, registered with an iron pen in the book of his conscience, and lurking there like so many sleeping lions, who upon the very first touch of God's visiting hand, will awake, arise, and rend him in pieces. If he look upon his present state, through the clear glass of God's righteous law, he may see Divine vengeance dogging him hard at the heels, ready to strike him down into hell, upon the next riot and rebellion against his patient Lord; that most horrible fiery tempestuous storm, Psa. xi. 6, ready to fall upon his head, even when he is warmest in his wealth, and in the hottest gleam of his worldly prosperity; sudden destruction ready to seize upon him unavoidably, as travail upon a woman with child, when he is singing the securest requiem to his soul of safety and peace, 1 Thess. v. 3. If he look forward to future time, he sees death, the grave, God's strict tribunal, the last judgment, and endless miseries of the other world; the sting, poison, and terrors of which he shall never be able either to avoid or abide. I say, shall such a fellow laugh and boast? and shall not a true-hearted Nathanael rejoice, to whom Jesus Christ hath bequeathed a legacy of peace; whom the Spirit of God bids rejoice evermore; and who, which way soever he looks, if he open his eye of faith, shall see nothing but matter of sweetest contemplation, infinite cause of truest joy and spiritual ravishment. If he look backward upon the time whilst he yet lay under the tyranny of the devil, and dominion of the first death, he shall see the catalogue of all his former sins, should it be as black as hell, as foul as Sodom, as red as scarlet, fairly and for ever washed away in that " fountain opened for sin and for uncleanness," Zech. xiii. 1, even the precious blood of the immaculate Lamb, Jesus Christ, the Holy and the Righteous. If he look upon his present state, he shall find himself preserved as a jewel, most safe in the precious cabinet of God's dearest providence, environed with a glorious guard of mighty angels, " kept by the power of God through faith unto salvation, ready to be revealed in the last time." If he look forward, he shall see death indeed, but the sting taken out of it by the death of Christ; the grave perfumed by his Saviour's blessed burial, wherein he may lie down as in a bed of down, fenced with the omnipotent arm of God, waiting for the glory of the resurrection; the throne of grace in heaven, standing upon pillars of mercy and love, where Jesus Christ sits as Judge, who shed his heart's blood for him, and is his Advocate while he yet abides in this vale of tears; the bosom of Abraham, the arms of God Almighty wide open, and stretched out to receive him, at the end of his pilgrimage, into his Master's joy:—I say, shall such a happy soul not have a heaven in his heart, but be heavy-hearted? Shall a vassal of the devil laugh, and an heir of heaven look heavy? Monstrous absurdity!

2. Every christian, after his new creation, hath always incomparably more matter of joy than mourning; infinitely greater cause to be enraptured with

spiritual joy, than to be dejected by grief. Though this may seem a paradox to the clearest eye, and best apprehension of worldly wisdom, yet, in truth, it is a true principle in the mystery of Christ. I do thus manifest it, and make it good to the saddest mourner in Sion, if he do not give more ear to the lying and malicious dictates of the devil, and distrusts of his own heart, than to the well-grounded counsel of the prophets, and impregnable truth of God's blessed word. In the right estimate and valuation, all the afflictions and sufferings of this life, whether of soul, body, outward state, or any way, are but dust in the balance, in respect of that " exceeding and eternal weight of glory," purchased and prepared for him by the blood of his dearest Lord. In the original it is, as a worthy divine well says, a superlative, transcendent phrase of speech, which far surpasseth the height of all human oratory, and all the rhetoric of the most eloquent heathens, because they never treated upon such a theme, they were not inspired with such a spirit. Whereupon the apostle in another place saith, " I reckon that the sufferings of this present time are not worthy to be compared with the glory which shall be revealed in us," Rom. viii. 18. Whence it followeth, that a very fore-imagination of that most inconceivable happiness to be had hereafter, to wit, the shining splendour and sun-like glory of our bodies, the unspeakable perfections and excellences of our souls, the admirable beauty of the place, the glorious comfort of our heavenly company, the beatifical fruition of the most blessed Trinity, and that which crowns our bliss with impossibility of further addition, endlessness of all these;—I say, a serious preconception hereof, enlightened and strengthened by faith, is able to hold up the christian's heart with infinite strength, and to refresh it with a secret unutterable gladness, even amidst variety and extremity of all worldly troubles; and doth minister far more matter of rejoicing, than of mourning, as that an "exceeding and eternal weight of glory," is to be preferred before a little momentary light affliction, 2 Cor. iv. 17. Hence it was that the holy martyrs of Jesus were so joyful and sweetly contented in the midst of all their outward miseries, pressures, persecutions, and even martyrdom itself. "I was in prison," saith Lawrence Sanders, "till I got into prison." "I feel no more pain,' saith Bainam, "in the fire, than if I were in a bed of down; it is as sweet to me as a bed of roses." "I believe," saith Adolphus Clarebacchius, "there is not a merrier heart in the world at this instant than mine is." To one objecting to Faninus, Christ's agony and sadness, to his cheerfulness, "Yea," saith he, "Christ was sad that I might be merry. He had my sins, and I have his merit and righteousness." But, especially, let us look upon Paul, a blessed and precious pattern for us to imitate in this point. He was troubled on every side; without were fightings, within were fears. He was in stripes above measure: in prisons more frequent: in deaths oft: of the jews five times received he forty stripes save one: thrice was he beaten with rods: once was he stoned: thrice he suffered shipwreck: a night and a day was he in the deep: in journeying often, in perils of water, in perils of robbers, in perils by his own countrymen, in perils by the heathen, in perils in the city, in perils in the wilderness, in perils in the sea, in perils amongst false brethren: in weariness and painfulness, in watchings often: in hunger and thirst, in fastings often: in cold and nakedness, 2 Cor. xi. 23—27. He was called "a pestilent fellow," Acts xxiv. 5. He was accounted as the filth of the world, and offscouring of all things, 1 Cor. iv. 13. And yet for all this, he professeth of himself, that he "took pleasure in infirmities, in reproaches, in necessities, in persecutions, in distresses for Christ's sake," 2 Cor. xii. 10. Nay, which is more, and more to my purpose, he saith in another place, that he was filled with comfort, and exceeding joyful in all his tribulation, 2 Cor. vii. 4. Now, every sincere-hearted professor is bound to over-abound exceedingly in this joy, as well as Paul. Not so, saith the weak christian, for Paul had a stronger faith than I, and more grace. It is true; but yet thy faith is as true as his. And it is not so much the greatness, as the truth of faith, which gives right and interest to a crown of life, comfort in all afflictions, and everlasting happiness. Therefore, well said Francisco Varlute, "Paul and Peter were more honourable members of Christ than I, but I am a member: they had more store of grace than I; but I have my measure, and therefore sure of glory." It is strange then, that any true-hearted Nathanael, having such good ground of rejoicing, and joy being so sweet and welcome a guest to the heart of man, should wear out a few and wretched days in unnecessary heaviness and sinful sadness, whereby he highly dishonours God's free love, hinders others from the ways of life, hurts full sore his own soul, and only gratifies Satan.

3. It is a constant mark of every regenerate man, to make conscience of all God's commandments, Psa. cxix. 6; now, the Holy Ghost doth not only in many several places give us charge to rejoice, but

is very earnest upon us in this point; nay, doth so often double and treble, with extraordinary emphasis and elegant gradation, his entreaty and importunity in the same place. "Let the saints," saith he, "be joyful in glory," Psa. cxlix. 5. "Let all those that seek thee, rejoice and be glad in thee," Psa. xl. 16. "Rejoice in the Lord, O ye righteous," Psa. xxxiii. 1. "Rejoice evermore," 1 Thess. v. 16. "Rejoice in the Lord alway: and again I say, Rejoice," Phil. iv. 4. "Let all those that put their trust in thee rejoice: let them ever shout for joy," Psa. v. 11. "Let the righteous be glad: let them rejoice before God; yea, let them exceedingly rejoice," Psa. lxviii. 3. "Be glad in the Lord, and rejoice, ye righteous: and shout for joy, all ye that are upright in heart," Psa. xxxii. 11. It is not an arbitrary or indifferent thing, as some may suppose, to rejoice, or to be sad. But a comfortable commandment is sweetly enforced upon us by the Fountain of all comfort, to rejoice; and we break a commandment if we rejoice not. And therefore we are bound in conscience to shake ourselves from the dust, to pluck up our spirits, to expostulate and be angry with our hearts, if they grow heavy, as David did: "Why art thou cast down, O my soul? and why art thou disquieted within me?" For we must answer as well for not rejoicing, as for not praying; for breaking this commandment, "Rejoice evermore," as that other, "Thou shalt not kill:"— I know full well there are difference and degrees in sin.

But here a weak professor, being pressed to the entertainment and excellency of this joy, may be troubled and tempted upon the survey of the definition and nature of it. For this spiritual, christian joy is a delicious motion of the mind, stirred up by the Holy Ghost, from the presence and possession of Christ Jesus, our sovereign God, dwelling in the soul by faith, whereby the heart is extraordinarily refreshed with a sweet, holy, unspeakable delight. Now, saith he, if it be so, I must tell you, I find and feel no such sensible grasping of Jesus Christ in the arms of my faith, or assured possession of him, that I dare admit of this joy, or meddle with it.

But know, that now thou art in the time of thy spiritual infancy, and liable to temptations, desertions, and other damps and dejections of soul; yet let thy feeling or acknowledgment be what it will, thou dost most certainly enjoy the Lord Jesus, even by a sincere hunger and thirst after him and his righteousness, Matt. v. 6, and by thine upright heart's adhering and cleaving unto him as thy only and chief joy; and, by consequence, art upon good ground, and by true right interested in all that joy which the blessed Spirit doth so importunately press upon thee in so many places. Here refresh thy memory with a review of my former distinction of assurance of evidence and adherence.

4. What canst thou think upon, or what can possibly befal thee, out of which thou, being turned unto God, and true of heart, mayest not collect matter of comfort, and by the mighty help of faith extract some joyful meditation?

(1.) If thou survey thy graces, with which the free mercy of God hath glorified thy soul, thou shalt see in them a sacred heavenly sunshine, which is able to enlighten the darkest midnight of all thine outward miseries, to disperse and dissolve the blackest and most tempestuous clouds of temporal troubles. Thou shalt feel in them such an inexplicable and excessive sweetness, which were the world around thee a sea of bitterness and gall, might turn it all into sugar. Thou shalt find in them such an impregnable mortal vigour, that will most certainly uphold thy spirit unconquerably at thy dying hour, and before that last dreadful bar, when all impenitent sinners shall roar like wild bulls in a net, full of the terrors of God, and cry upon the hills and rocks to hide them from his unquenchable wrath, which they shall never be able either to avoid or abide. Hence springs that abundant and unexhausted matter of joy, that the joy of harvest, of dividing great spoils, and that which is of such joyful temper that we think we are but in a dream, is but a toy and trifle, a type and shadow to it, and which ever predominates and incomparably transcends all matter of mourning.

(2.) If thou look out upon thine outward state; upon thy wife, children, friends, health, goods, good name, orchards, gardens, possessions, honours, or whatsoever thou hast attained, or dost enjoy with good conscience and sanctifiedly, thou art bound to rejoice in them as temporal tokens of God's eternal love; notable encouragements to do more nobly in his glorious service, and comfortable additions to thine hope of heaven; but in such order, that as thy clothes first receive heat from thy body before they can comfortably warm it, so some inward joy of reconcilement to the Creator, must first warm thine heart before thou canst take any kindly comfort from the creatures.

(3.) Concerning crosses, afflictions, troubles, persecutions, which are wont to present themselves to the apprehension of carnal men with much horror, even in the very bitterness and extremity of them, if thou cast the enlightened eye of thy soul upon such places and promises as these, 1 Cor. x. 13; 2 Cor. iv. 17; Rom. viii. 28; Heb. xii. 6; xiii. 5; Isa. lxiii. 9, and xliii. 2; and then reflect upon thy afflicted self, thou mayest, by the marvellous work of faith, draw a great deal of joy from them. A patient submission unto, and fruitful exercise under God's visiting hand, is an infallible demonstration that thou art a son, and not a bastard. Is there then not more sweetness in those afflictions, which are evident marks that thou art in the right way to heaven, than in worldly pleasures, which clearly demonstrate to thy conscience that thou art posting towards hell? Hence it was that the apostles rejoiced, being beaten, that they were counted worthy to suffer shame for the name of Jesus; that Paul and Silas sung in prison at midnight; that Ignatius cried, " Let fire, racks, pullies, yea, all the torments of hell come on me, so that I may win Christ."

(4.) Nay, even contumelies and contempt, reproaches and scorn from the world for thy profession, which naturally much nettles a noble spirit, do crown thy head, and should fill thy heart with abundance of glory, blessedness, and joy. " If ye be reproached for the name of Christ, happy are ye," saith Peter, " for the Spirit of glory and of God resteth upon you," 1 Pet. iv. 14. " Blessed are ye," saith Christ himself, " when men shall revile you, and persecute you, and shall say all manner of evil against you falsely for my sake. Rejoice, and be exceeding glad," Matt. v. 11, 12. Scurrilities and scoffs, spiteful speeches, odious nick-names, lying imputations cast upon thee in this kind, by tongues which cut like a sharp razor, are in their due estimate, and true account, as so many honourable badges of thy christian magnanimity and resolute standing on the Lord's side; and at the throne of Christ will be certainly reputed as characters of special honour, and remembrancers of thy worthy service, whereby thou shalt appear more acceptable and amiable in the eyes of almighty God, and all that glorious triumphant church above. Let no cowardly christian then decline them with wounding of his conscience.

(5.) If thou rightly temper and well weigh even thy sorest sorrow, and the very bleeding of thy heart for sin, it should be so far from damping the delight of thy spirit, that it ought to open unto thee a wellspring of purest joy. For the penitent melting of our affections, and kindly mourning over Him whom we have pierced with our sins, infallibly argues, and sweetly assures the presence and sanctifying power of the Holy Spirit. And what greater comfort or sweeter delight than that which ariseth from a well-grounded evidence that the Fountain of all comfort dwells in our souls? Such tears as burst out of a heart oppressed with grief for sin, are like an April shower, which though it wet a little, yet it begets a great deal of sweetness in the herbs, flowers, and fruits of the earth. As even in laughter the heart of the wicked is sorrowful, so contrarily, even in such mourning the heart of the true penitent is lightsome and comfortable. For habitual joy may not only consist with actual sorrow, and contrarily; but also even actual joy with actual sorrow. This is no strange thing in other cases: when we see a good man persecuted for a good cause, and stand to it nobly, we grieve for his troubles, but rejoice in his resolution and undauntedness. As we ought then to grieve bitterly for our sins, so let us rejoice immeasurably for such ingenuous grieving. Let us lament heartily over Him whom we have wounded with our abominable lusts, but let us also be infinitely glad at the very heart root, that they are all pardoned by the pouring out of his blood. Not the most exquisite quintessence and extraction of all manner of music, vocal or instrumental, can possibly convey so delicious a touch and relish to the outward ear of a man, as a certificate brought from the throne of mercy, by the blessed Spirit, sealed with Christ's blood, to the bruised heart and grieved soul of an humble sinner, in the very depth of his sorrow.

(6.) If thou be troubled with temptations, and exercised even with variety of them, hear the Holy Ghost: " Count it all joy when ye fall into divers temptations," James i. 2. To let other particulars pass: from the very foulest and most grisly suggestions of Satan, thou mayest collect this common glorious comfort, that thou art none of his. For as he is wont to keep unconverted men in as merry a mood, and fair a calm of outward contentment and inward security as he can possibly; retiring and reserving his most fiery darts and hideous temptations, until he have them at some unavoidable strait: so all that are broke out of his hellish prison, by the help of the Holy Ghost, he ordinarily pursues with deadly rage and all the powers of darkness. He hunts them in his fittest seasons, like a partridge on the mountains, with troubles without, and terrors within. The less peace thou hast, therefore, from him, the more pleasure mayest thou take in thine escape out of his hands. The more restlessly he follows thee with the fury and variety of his temptations, the more sweetly and securely, if thou wilt give way to the counsel of the prophets, and the work of faith, mayest thou repose thy wearied soul upon the comfortable assurance of being certainly God's.

5. Every one that hath part in Christ's death, is bound in conscience, and bidden by the blessed Spirit, to lead a most happy life, even to keep a feast, a spiritual holiday, as it were, from all servile terrors, slavish sadness, uncomfortable dejections of spirit; "for even Christ our passover is sacrificed for us; therefore let us keep the feast," 1 Cor. v. 7, 8.

The sweetness and excellency of this feast is notably set out and amplified by, (1.) The beautiful garments we put on and wear when we are admitted unto it; (2.) The matter and magnificent provision; (3.) The music; (4.) The frank and bountiful entertainment and plenty; (5.) The extraordinary pomp and princeliness of it.

(1.) For the first, meditate joyfully upon that rich attire, and those royal attributes, glorifying and crowning Christ's blessed spouse, with most admirable and enrapturing beauty: "Who is she that looketh forth as the morning, fair as the moon, clear as the sun, and terrible as an army with banners?" Cant. vi. 10. And know that all the essential glory and fairness which is to be found in the whole church, the "woman clothed with the sun," Rev. xii. 1, as that of justification and sanctification, belongs to every member thereof, to every faithful christian.

"As the morning." 1. The morning springs out of the greatest darkness. The night is most dark, as they say, a little before day: the illuminated soul arises out of the most darksome grave of ignorance and sin. 2. The beauty of the morning is principally seen in her ruddiness: the soul that is newly delivered out of the horror of Egyptian darkness, and hands of the hellish Pharaoh, is all ruddy with passing through the red sea of Christ's blood; that is the ground upon which all its beauty and blessedness are built. 3. The glory of the morning, after its first peeping in the east, spreads fairer and fairer in all beauty and brightness, until the mid-day and full illustration of the world: grace in the soul, after the first plantation, grows stronger and stronger, shines fairer and fairer, until it set in the bottomless ocean of endless glory. See Prov. iv. 18.

" Fair as the moon." 1. The moon receives all her light and lustre from the sun: all the graces, holiness, inherent righteousness, shining in a sanctified soul, are the image and impressions of the Sun of righteousness. 2. The moon hath some spots in her face, but yet is very beautiful by her borrowed light: the christian is somewhat black with the remnants of original corruption, and by reason of his unavoidable frailties and imperfections, but yet comely as the curtains of Solomon, by the glory of his new creation, and gracious beams that shine upon his soul from the face of Christ. 3. The further the moon is removed from the sun, the fairer she is, and fuller of light: the more an humble soul, upon sight of the holy majesty and purest eye of Deity, ten thousand times brighter than the sun, which cannot look on iniquity, doth retire with lowliest thoughts into himself, to abhor himself in dust and ashes, as most vile, and far worthier to be thrown into the lowest dungeon of the kingdom of darkness, than to be honoured with the love and light of his countenance, is more beautiful and amiable in the eyes of God.

"Clear as the sun." The moon shadows out inherent fairness; the sun resembles and represents our imputed purity; so that this royal robe, the Sun of righteousness, the unspotted justice of Jesus Christ, doth glorify the soul. 1. With an entire, unstained beauty; our inherent holiness hath some spots and stains of imperfection, like the moon, but that imputed for our justification is much more spotless and bright than the sun. 2. Universally: we are washed, as it were, all over in the blood of Christ, and covered wholly with his perfect righteousness. 3. Constantly: the exercise of spiritual graces, and sense of inward comfort, may sometimes ebb and wane for a time, but the robe of Christ's royal justice, once put on by the hand of faith, is sure and the same for ever.

"Terrible as an army with banners." Besides this rich and royal attire, all this abundance of spiritual fairness and beauty, we are to put on also, lest hellish harpies, if I may so speak, snatch away our delicious and divine dainties, that glistering armour, thick set with heavenly pearls, described Eph. vi. 13—17, the glorious splendour whereof is able to dazzle the devil's eyes, to daunt his courage, and drive him out of the field. For he well knows it to be tried, and of proof, worn by our Captain, Christ Jesus, who foiled him by the "sword of the Spirit," in that great combat in the wilderness, Matt. iv.; and it is that by which the weakest christians shall shortly, by the blessing of the God of peace, bruise Satan under their feet, Rom. xvi. 20.

The sum is: the heavenly attire of a sanctified soul is far fairer and more amiable than the exquisite concurrence of all earthly beauties and visible glory. Were the light of all the stars above collected into suns, and added unto that great bright body, the prince of all the lamps in heaven, nay, if besides, there were an accession of all the splendour of all the pearls and jewels of all the crystal and glistering things in this lower world, and all compacted into one beautiful body, it would be but as a lump of darkness, to the glory and fairness of a sanctified soul. For the beauty and amiableness of a holy soul inflames the heart and affections of the Son of God with an extraordinary pang of spiritual fervent love, Cant. iv. 10; whereas, not all the glory of the world, though represented to his eye with the fairest lustre, and in the most refined form, could move him ever a whit, Matt. iv. 10. Plato was wont to say, If moral virtues could be seen with the outward eye, they would stir up in the heart extraordinary flames of admiration and love: what unspeakable raptures then would christian graces enkindle, were they visible to the eyes? They would be able to make persecutors, professors; to turn even drunkards into puritans, as they call them; the most sensual epicure into a mortified saint.

(2.) For the second, let thy spiritual appetite feed cheerfully upon that sweetest place, " And in this mountain shall the Lord of hosts make unto all people a feast of fat things, a feast of wine on the lees, of fat things full of marrow, of wines on the lees well refined," Isa. xxv. 6. Here is provided, as we may see, a magnificent and glorious feast, composed all of marrow and fatness, of most refined and purified wines, which shadow unto us spiritual delicacies, those golden dainties dug out of the rich mine of the mystery of Christ, by the hand of faith, in the word, sacraments, prayer, communion of saints, solemn humiliations, sweet soliloquies, solitary conferences with our God, feeling forethought of infinite joys through eternity, &c. Every circumstance breathes out nothing but sweetness.

"In this mountain." It is dressed in mount Zion, "the perfection of beauty, the joy of the whole earth, the glory of all lands;" which represents unto us, by way of shadow and type, the overflowing glory of the christian church, the very heaven of all human societies, our only sun in this inferior world, which though so much maligned, yet were it removed, there would be a little hell upon earth, and nothing left but a dark midnight of villany and horror, for incarnate devils to domineer in.

"A feast of fat things, a feast of wines on the lees, of fat things full of marrow, of wines on the lees well refined." Hereby is intimated the matter of the feast, and royal provision, amplified with extraordinary emphasis of words, elegancy of phrase, and iteration of the same sense, with variety of expression; which also argues its excellency. It is not enough to have said, "of fat things," but there is added, "of fat things full of marrow;" and so proportionably of the wines; to intimate the most exquisite refined flower of all delicacies and dainties. The marrow of the fatness; as if a man should say, The spirit of the quintessence, the diamond of the ring, the sparkle of the diamond; and yet all this comes infinitely short of what the Holy Ghost would shadow and show unto us by the most sumptuous materials of earthly feasts. But, above all, that which makes the feast most matchless is, the feast-maker; Jehovah is the founder and furnisher of it;

the Maker of heaven and earth makes it. The
poets describing men of most ambitious appetites
after choicest dainties, say, that they rob all the
elements to please their palates. The master of
this feast, the ever blessed Jehovah, tells us of his
store and treasuries this way: " Every beast of the
forest is mine, and the cattle upon a thousand hills.
I know all the fowls of the mountains: and the wild
beasts of the field are mine," Psa. l. 10, 11. But
all these being but only matter of corporeal food,
are yet nothing to the spiritual sweetness of this
heavenly banquet. The secret and sacred delight
of those divine dainties intended here by the Holy
Ghost, being unspeakable and glorious, doth infinitely transcend the possibility of all creatures to
contribute, and the capacity of the largest natural
understanding to conceive. So must be construed,
as a worthy divine truly says, that text, 1 Cor. ii.
9, 10, not of the joys of heaven, which here the
spiritual man himself cannot tell what they shall
be; but of the gospel joy, of the wine and fatlings
ready prepared, and now revealed to the believer by
the Spirit.

(3.) For the third, hear the voice of sweetness
and peace: " Sing unto her: a vineyard of red
wine," Isa. xxvii. 2. " Sing," sounds nothing but
joy, lightsomeness, and mirth. " Unto her;" the
sex of more amiableness, tenderness, and love.
" A vineyard;" vineyards, orchards, gardens, and
such inclosed plots, are, as it were, the flowers,
stars, and paradises of the earth. " Of wine;" as
though the vine-trees of this inclosure brought not
forth the grosser and uncrushed grapes, but more
immediately the refined and pure blood of the grape
" Red;" the most generous, sparkling, delicious

wine. A vineyard is, as it were, the diamond of the ring; wine, the sparkle; red, the splendour of the sparkle; all excellences, sweetnesses, transcendences, where God opens and expresses his heart and love to his church, or any of his chosen.

(4.) For the fourth, let thy faith peruse, with enlarged meditations, those precious passages of gracious invitation and bountiful entertainment, Matt. xxii. 3, 4; Isa. lv. 1, 2; Prov. ix. 2, 3; Cant. ii. 3, 4. Thou shalt suck, and be satisfied even with the breasts of consolations. Thy dearest and most glorious mother, who is clothed with the sun, treads upon the moon, and wears on her head a crown of twelve stars, shall sweetly and tenderly bear thee upon her sides, and dandle thee upon her knees, Isa. lxvi. 11, 12.

(5.) For the fifth, it is compared to a wedding-feast, and that of a king's son, which is wont to be honoured and crowned with height and variety of all magnificence and majesty, joy and triumph, mirth and music. When a humbled soul is first made sure to the Son of God, the joyful harmony of all good hearts that hear of it, and the triumphant hallelujahs of the blessed angels in heaven, concur in concert, as it were, of congratulation for so happy a match, in gladness and joy for so holy a change. This feast begins at thy first betrothing, when thou receivest a ring, as it were, beset with five precious stones: 1. righteousness, 2. judgment, 3. loving kindness, 4. mercies, 5. faithfulness, Hos. ii. 19, 20. It is afterward continued with many gracious passages of love and sweetest entertainments on both sides, even in this life, as appears in Solomon's spiritual love-song. It shall at last be crowned with an everlasting jubilee, and pleasures more than

the stars of the firmament in number; when the
Lamb receives his wife into his nearest and dearest
embracements, even into full possession of the most
blessed, never-ending kingdom of heaven, bought
for her full dearly with his own heart's blood. Then
our feast of grace ends in the endless fruition of
glory. How merry then ought we to be in the
mean time, who are admitted and have a right to
this gracious and glorious feast? Of expressing
which to the life, the finest fare and most exquisite
delicacies of all earthly feasts come as far short, as
the dull earth comes short of the glistering heaven,
a gross mortal body of the preciousness of an ever-
living soul, an inch of time of the length of eternity.
Spiritual food fills an immortal soul with heavenly
manna, out of the mystery of Christ, attended with
purest joy and sincerest pleasures through all eternity.

6. As thou dost honour God's justice in trembling
at his threats, and throwing thyself into the dust
as extremely vile, and deserving hell under his
mighty hand; and the piercing majesty of his pure
word, representing clearly unto thy conscience, and
pressing terribly upon it, the heinousness of all thy
lusts, iniquities, abominable provocations before the
eyes of his glory, and divine indignation flaming
against them; so when thou findest and feelest thy
heart truly wounded by the sword of the Spirit, with
remorse and sorrow for thy sins, weary with the heavy
weight and burden of them, possessed with sincere
hatred and loathing of every evil way, thou oughtest,
and are bound in conscience, and by the commandment of the Holy Ghost, to glorify God's truth in
his promises of mercy, by throwing thyself into the
blessed arms and bleeding embracements of the
Lord Jesus dying upon the cross, in whom they are

all yea and amen, with much assurance and peace, with unspeakable and glorious joy. And the rather, because the special season and only opportunity of thy magnifying and honouring the sweet influence of God's dearest mercies, tender-heartedness, and truth upon humble souls, through the precious promises of life, is in this life. In the world to come they shall all be accomplished upon thee to the utmost, and crowned with a clear vision and full fruition of that ever blessed and most glorious Majesty. Then faith for ever expires, and we see face to face.

These things being so, and most certain, let every true-hearted Nathanael be heartily entreated, nay, justly charged in the name of Jesus Christ, by the blessed Spirit, the fountain of all comfort, as he will answer it at the glorious throne of mercy, erected in heaven upon purpose to make him everlastingly happy, that he henceforth most resolutely and for ever cast out of his conscience, sprinkled with the blood of the Lamb, and out of the kingdom of Christ, overflowing with peace and joy, now comfortably established in his soul, those intruding usurpers and tyrants, (only natural lords over natural men,) I mean, horrors of guiltiness, false fears, slavish terrors, damps and droopings, all uncomfortable pensiveness, dejections and fear. And leaving such harpies as these, and heart-eaters, only to the grumbling and guilty consciences of all those that hate to be reformed, and Satan's slaves, as their proper furies, let him with a holy violence against the devil's cruel assaults, and contradictions of his own distrustful heart, and with a cheerful spirit, lay hold upon his just inheritance and everlasting portion, purchased for him by the bitter and painful sufferings of the Son of God; even floods and fresh successions of sweetest joys, shed and showered down continually from the throne of grace upon his upright heart in great abundance, if he will but only vouchsafe to open the door by the hand of faith, that the blessed beams of such lightsomeness and comfort, shining from the face of Christ, may come in. Let his soul, full fairly arrayed with its heavenly robes, to which the beauty of the morning, brightness of the moon, and glory of the sun, are but a shadow; and, listening sweetly to that melodious song, composed all of peace and joy, pleasures and pardon of sin, which the mercy of God makes in the ear of its faith, fall to and fill itself at the wedding-feast of the king's son, with those ever-springing rivers of spiritual refreshing, out of the bottomless depth of God's free love revealed in the mystery of Christ, by the ministry of the word and sacramental grace, as with marrow and fatness; let it suck abundantly, and be satisfied with the breasts of everlasting consolations. And since he is incorporated into Jesus Christ, and at all times hath the wings of faith in readiness to outsoar the height of all human miseries; let him for ever stand, like mount Zion, impregnable and unshaken with the most furious incursions of the floods and tempests of all worldly troubles, pressures, and persecutions. Let all those monstrous and most abhorred injections, filthy temptations, and fiery darts, pointed with the very malice of hell, ordinarily offered to the imagination of the best, be resolutely repelled by the shield of faith, and hurled back upon the tempter's face. Let all ungodly oppositions from man or devil, or fearful distrust, be but as so many proud and swelling waves dashing against a mighty rock, which the more boisterously they beat upon it, the more are they broken and turned into a vain foam and froth.

But to descend with thee to some particulars; tell me truly, thou who hast given thy name to Christ in truth, what is it that troubles thee? What is it that still detains thine heavy heart in the chains and fetters of horror and sadness, and locks it up so long from the entrance and entertainment of spiritual joy? And if I be not able to confront and confound it by some well-grounded counter-comfort and antidote out of the oracle of truth; if I be not able to discover it to be a self-created cross, and to dissolve it into an imaginary and groundless fancy, by the light of the word, then walk heavily still. Only believe the prophets, and thou shalt prosper. Thou must then be contented to be counselled by the faithful physicians of thy soul, who can show unto man his uprightness, and are instructed unto the kingdom of heaven, especially fetching all their prescriptions, receipts, and counterpoisons out of the rich treasury of the book of life.

Thou must learn,

1. To put a difference between nullity of grace, and imperfection of grace. Many good souls desire sincerely that their hearts were broken in pieces, and bled at the root, for their many and heinous sins, grieving much that they can grieve no more; they hunger and thirst for Christ's righteousness, more than for the wealth of the whole world; they groan mightily in spirit for God's favour, pardon of sin, power over their corruptions, ability to pray better, &c. But yet because they feel not that measure of sensible smart and anguish of heart in lamenting their former life as they desire, because

they have not their wished-for joy and peace in believing, because they cannot now pray as fervently and feelingly as they perhaps were formerly wont, nor with that freedom and heartiness as they would; in a word, because they are yet but smoking flax and bruised reeds, not full shining lamps, and strong pillars in the house of God, they will needs have all to be nought. Whereby they (I will not say belie the Spirit) but most unworthily deny, and in their conceits nullify his already wonderfully glorious work upon their souls, to their, I know not how great, spiritual hurt and hinderance. For such intolerable unthankfulness may be justly punished, and paid home with longer detainment upon the rack of distrustful slavish fear, and under the bondage of legal terrors. It is a special point, then, of spiritual wisdom, and of singular importance for the soul's quiet and welfare, to discern weakness of grace from want of grace. Christ Jesus declaring in his heavenly sermon who are blessed, doth not instance in the perfections, excellences, and heights of christianity, though all that are true of heart sincerely pray for and press after them, but in the least and lowest degrees, lest the smoking flax should be quenched, and bruised reeds be broken. He doth not say, Blessed are the strong in faith, the full assured; blessed are those that take on for their sins, as for their only son, and for their first-born; but, " Blessed are they which do hunger and thirst after righteousness: blessed are the poor in spirit," &c.

2. Not always to make sense and feeling the touchstone for the truth of thy spiritual state. A man in a swoon or asleep feels not his life, and yet is a living man. It is one thing to have grace,

another to feel grace. One thing the life of faith, another the life of sense.

3. Not to disgrace thy own graces, by casting thine eye too dejectedly upon other christians' perfections and precedencies. Let it not fare with thee in this case, as it doth with one gazing too much upon the sun, who looking downwards again can see just nothing, whereas before he clearly discerned all colours about him. Look upon them for imitation and quickening, not for slavish dejection and self-blinding.

4. To acknowledge and expect that heavenly graces, as faith, &c., while they inhabit these earthly houses, ebb and flow, wax and wane, faint and flourish, by reason of the combat between the flesh and the Spirit. So that if a man should tell me, that he hath always prayed alike without temptation or damps, without any sense at any time of deadness or spiritual distempers; that he hath ever believed alike, without those doubts and scruples, that faintness and fear, of which most christians so much complain, I durst confidently reply, that then he never either prayed acceptably, or believed savingly. The fathers fitly compare the state of the church to the variable condition of the moon, which sometimes shines more gloriously, sometimes not so; it is so also with every true member thereof, in respect of the exercise of grace, comfort in holy duties, sense of God's favour, and spiritual feeling.

5. To believe the Spirit of truth, the word of God, and voice of Christ, before the father of lies, dictates of natural distrust, and suggestions of flesh and blood. To which, methinks, thou shouldest be easily persuaded, and then all the mists of thy spiritual miseries would be quickly dispersed. It is a

mighty work, if not a great miracle, to get any soft-ness at all, or true sorrow for sin, into the heart of a man; it is naturally so stony and impatient of grief, and the devil such a stirrer against it, so that the most are mere strangers unto it; yet for all that, when this penitent sorrow is once sincerely on foot in an afflicted soul, so endlessly and on every side are we pressed with the policies of hell, it is often too forward to feed upon tears still, and still too wilful in refusing to be comforted. Satan then will be ready to say, Thou seest now, thy conscience being enlightened, thy sins are so horrible and heinous that they are too heavy a burden for thee to bear, there is no way with thee but to sink into horror and despair. But what saith Christ? Nay, now is the season: "Come unto me all ye that labour, and are heavy laden," with thy sin, " and I will give you rest," Matt. xi. 28. Here now, if thou wilt believe the sweet voice of Christ Jesus, rather than the muttering sophistry of Satan; if in good manners thou wilt come when thou art called, and not retire in a sinful and cruel modesty, thou shalt be presently lightened. Yea, but saith the tempter, thy heart hath been so strangely hardened and soaked in sin heretofore, now such a hellish cloud of darkness hath seized upon it, that there is no hope nor possibility. But what saith the word? "Seek him that maketh the seven stars and Orion, and turneth the shadow of death into the morning," Amos v. 8. It is he alone that can most easily change the dismal midnight of thy present spiritual misery into the glorious mid-day of sweetest peace, and lightsomeness of heart. Yea, but saith he further, thou hast lain long upon the rock of guilty horror, had much counsel, and been under the hands of many spiritual physicians, and yet no comfort comes. And what then? Hear what the Spirit of truth tells us: "Since the beginning of the world, men have not heard, nor perceived by the ear, neither hath the eye seen, O God, beside thee, what he hath prepared for him that waiteth for him," Isa. lxiv. 4. Waiting patiently for the Lord's coming to comfort us, either in temporal or spiritual distresses, is a right pleasing and acceptable duty and service unto God, which he is wont to crown with multiplied and overflowing refreshings, when he comes. See Isa. xl. 31. Nay, and shouldest thou die in this state of waiting, if thy heart in the mean time sincerely hate all sin, heartily thirst for the mercy of God in Christ, and resolve truly upon new universal obedience for the time to come, thou shalt be certainly saved, because the Holy Ghost saith, "Blessed are all they that wait for him," Isa. xxx. 18.

6. That defects, distractions, failings in our spiritual exercises, and undertakings groaned under, grieved for, and striven against, by an upright heart, are so far from nullifying grace, that they should not bereave us of peace of conscience, or interrupt our sweet communion and comfortable walking with our God.

7. Not to confine, undervalue, and extenuate the mercies of God, promises of life, the Holy Spirit's saving work upon thy soul, and the present graces thou possessest in truth.

These cautions premised, let us come to the examining and answering of some complaints and counter-pleas against entertainment of comfort, which are wont to arise in troubled consciences, out of ignorance and misconception of the merciful ways of God, and the mystery of his free love through Christ; and do thou believe that proportionable sovereign antidotes and counter-comforts may be collected also in abundance out of God's blessed book, against the rest, or any reply whatsoever.

And to begin with the first cries of a christian in the pangs of his new birth.

1. A poor soul having wallowed long in vanity of vanities and villanies, of lusts and licentiousness, is now, by Divine grace, at this or the other sermon, struck through by the sword of the Spirit, with penitent grief, and his heart broken into pieces by the hammer of the law. In this depth of heaviest distress, and bleeding case, he casts his eyes upon Jesus Christ lifted up in the ministry, as an antitype to the brazen serpent, for his comfortable binding up, and everlasting cure. Those messengers of God, who are able to declare " unto man his uprightness," Job xxxiii. 23, assure him in the word of life and truth, and charge him in His name who was anointed by the Lord for that purpose, and appointed by the Father of mercies to comfort all mourners in Sion, Isa. lxi. 1, 2, that now being truly cast down under God's mighty hand, thirsting for the blood of Christ, and sincerely resolving upon a new course for the time to come, he would turn his legal terrors into evangelical, weeping joy; put on beauty for ashes, the garment of praise for the spirit of heaviness, " that they might be called trees of righteousness, the planting of the Lord, that he might be glorified," Isa. lxi. 3. Oh no, says he, out of the deep sense of his bottomless vileness, the news is too good to be true, to wit, that now the blessed Son of God, and all the precious

rich purchases of his invaluable passion should belong unto me, the most sinful wretch that the earth bears, who have desperately spent my days and strength so long in the furious service of Satan, and my own sensual lusts: whereupon he refuses comfort, and chooses rather to sink again and languish under the horrors of guiltiness and fear. Whereas he should incomparably more honour and please the God of all comfort, by trusting his mercy, sealing to his truth, than by unseasonably suspecting his justice and power.

Here then he wofully fails and forgets himself, in a distrustful underprising God's incomprehensible greatness, almighty mercy, unlimited liberality, and freeness of his love. He is, in this case, not so much to consider what is fit for him to receive, as convenient for the ability and bounty of so great and good a God as the mighty Lord of heaven and earth to give, who doth all things like himself. If he build, he makes a world. If he be angry with the world, he sends a flood over the face of the whole earth. If he goes out with the armies of the saints, he makes the sun stand still, the stars to fight, the seas to swallow up the most dreadful armadas. If he love, the precious heart's blood of his own Son is not too dear. If he deliver any man, he pulls him out of the hand of the prince of darkness, and frees him from everlasting flames. If any become his favourite through Christ's mediation, he will make him a king, give him a paradise, and set a crown of eternity upon his head. Earthly princes at their pleasure ennoble those they love, with dukedoms, marquisates, earldoms, what then do you think shall be done unto the man whom the King of heaven desires and delights to honour? Let us then, I say, in such cases, consider not so much what is fit for us silly worms to receive, as for so great a God to bestow. If we can once bring hearts, bruised and broken with the burden of our sins, bleeding and weeping, unto his mercy-seat, he will think all the meritorious sufferings of his Son, all the promises in his book, all the comforts of his Spirit, all the pleasures in his kingdom, little enough for us. If we look upon ourselves, sinful wretches, we might justly fear the extremest torments, fiercest flames, and lowest dungeon in hell, infinitely rather than expect a kingdom. But he loves us freely, Hos. xiv. 4. It is his pleasure to give us a kingdom: "Fear not, little flock," saith Christ, "for it is your Father's good pleasure to give you the kingdom," Luke xii. 32. If it be the good pleasure of the King of kings to bestow a kingdom upon a truly humbled soul, which he makes in the mean time his royal throne here upon earth, Isa. lvii. 15, what can man, or devil, or any distrustful heart, say against it? And why shouldest thou, being such a one, be so unmannerly and unthankful, nay, so unnecessarily cruel to thy own heavy heart, as not to open the everlasting door of thy soul by the key of faith, to let the King of glory, knocking with his hand of mercy, come in, and crown it with grace and glory, with comfort and everlasting peace?

2. But alas, says he, my sins are more than any man's. Now, when I am searching into the sink of them, I can find neither bank nor bottom. Unnumbered swarms of gross impieties and iniquities through my whole life; of abominable impurities and pollutions, which have continually defiled my mind, heart, and affections, armed with several stings of terror, do so restlessly press upon my wounded

conscience and oppress it, that I cannot, I dare not think upon, or look towards any comfort.

Let them be what they are, and add thereunto all the sins which have, are, and shall be committed by all the sons and daughters of Adam, from the creation to the end of the world, excepting sin against the Holy Ghost, and yet in a heart truly humbled under them, heartily hating them all, coming with a sincere spiritual hunger at Christ's call to be disburdened of them; they can make no more resistance against the mercies of God, than a little spark of fire against the mighty sea thrown into the midst of it; nay, infinitely less. For all these sins would still be finite both in nature and number, but God's mercies are every way infinite. Now, between that which is finite, and that which is infinite, there is no proportion, and so no possibility of resistance. Whence it is that the prophet inviting his people to repentance, Isa. lv. 7, by assuring them of God's sweet, merciful, and gracious disposition, lest any too fearful and dejected spirit, undervaluing God's mercy, should think thus within itself: Be it so; yet alas, my sins are so many, and such a son of Belial have I been, and so endlessly provoked the glory of the pure eye of God, that I can expect no mercy; the pollutions of my youth have been so prodigious and infectious, that I have no face to press unto his throne of grace. God himself doth there purposely prevent the objection, and speaking to our capacity, which cannot comprehend infinity, replies to this sense: Oh say not so! stay all such despairing thoughts; do not cast the incomprehensibleness of my mercy in the narrow mould of thy finite shallow conception; do not so unworthily abridge and confine the unlimited and boundless compassion of the mighty Lord of heaven and earth; "for my thoughts are not your thoughts, neither are your ways my ways, saith the Lord. For as the heavens are higher than the earth, so are my ways higher than your ways, and my thoughts than your thoughts," Isa. lv. 8, 9. Many a bruised reed would not exchange the comfort which the weakest faith may extract out of this sweetest place, for all the kingdoms of the earth. For he saith not, that his ways and thoughts of knowledge and wisdom, but his ways and thoughts of mercy, are as far above ours, as the heavens are above the earth; indeed, as he himself is above man, which is infinitely. But take notice, by the way, that the mercies of God do exercise this infinite and irresistible power only in truly humbled, believing souls, heartily hating, and sincerely set against all sin. I say so, lest any impenitent should pervert this precious point, or trample upon this pearl. For as in such a soul no sins, either for number or notoriousness, can possibly withstand, or stand before God's infinite mercies; so not one drop of all those infinite mercies belongs unto any that goes on willingly and delightfully, hating to be reformed in any one known sin, or that he might know, and wilfully forbears to be informed. As the invaluable blood of Christ turns the very scarlet sins of the truly broken believing heart into whitest snow, so it will never wash away the least sinful stain from the proud heart of any unhumbled pharisee. Let no one, therefore, that goes on still in his trespasses, take up any vain confidence, or misgrounded conclusion of false comfort from hence, by misconceiving thus: Is it so, that the infiniteness of God's mercy cannot be resisted by the greatness or multitude of sins, being ever finite both in their number and nature? How is it possible then that I should miss of those infinite mercies? Why may not I comfortably hope that my sins also shall be swallowed up in that bottomless sea? I will tell thee why. As the power of God, though it be infinite, yet is limited by his will, so the mercies of God, though they be infinite, are regulated by his truth. His mercies transcend with immeasurable distance, the height of heaven, and depth of hell, and are, indeed, as himself, infinite: but his truth hath told us, that none shall have part in them but those alone who repent and believe. God's truth revealed in his word, must ever confine the current of his compassions, and is the touchstone to try and qualify those to whom his mercies belong. See then what kind of people are partakers of God's infinite mercies, by the testimony of that word of truth by which we must be judged at the last day, Isa. lv. 7; lxi. 1—3; Psa. xv; xxxiv. 18; cxlvii. 3;' Ezek. xviii. 21; Luke iv. 18. Solomon saith, "Whoso confesseth and forsaketh his sins, shall have mercy," Prov. xxviii. 13. How then can he expect any mercy who takes them not to heart, but lies in them still?

3. Of the pardonableness of my other sins, saith another, I could be reasonably well persuaded, but alas, there is one above all the rest, which now upon discovery and remorse I find to be full of rank and hellish poison, of such a deep and damnable dye, to have struck so desperately in the days of my sinfulness at the very face of God himself, and far more deeply into the heart of Jesus Christ than the spear that pierced him bleeding upon the cross, and thereupon, at this present, stares in the eye of my newly awakened and wounded conscience with such

horror and frightfulness, that I fear Divine justice will think it fitter to have this most loathsome, inexpiable stain, rather at length fired out of my soul with everlasting flames, (if it were possible that eternal fire could expiate the sinful stains of any impenitent damned soul,) than to be fairly washed away in the mean time with his blood, whom I so cruelly and cursedly pierced with it. Oh! this is it that lies now upon my heart like a mountain of lead, far heavier than heaven and earth, and enchains it with inexplicable terror to the dust and place of dragons. This alone stings desperately, keeps me from Christ, and cuts me off from all hope of heaven. I am afraid my wilful wallowing in it heretofore hath so reprobated my mind, seared my conscience, and hardened my heart, that I shall never be able to repent with any hope of pardon.

And why so? Is this sin of thine greater than Manasseh's familiarity with wicked spirits? Than Paul's drinking up the blood of saints? Than any of those mentioned in that black account, 1 Cor. vi. 9, 10, who notwithstanding were afterwards, upon repentance, washed, sanctified, and justified, in the name of the Lord Jesus, and by the Spirit of our God? Than Eve's transgression, who opened the flood-gate to all the sins which have been or shall be committed from the creation to the end of the world, and to all those torments which shall flame in hell through all eternity? Than that horrible sin of killing Christ Jesus? And yet the murderers of that Just and Holy One, upon their true compunction of heart, were saved by that precious blood, which they had cruelly spilt as water upon the ground But be it what it will, a scarlet sin, a crimson sin, a crying sin, and add unto it Satan's malicious aggravations, and all that horror which the dejectedness of thy present afflicted spirit, and darkness of thy melancholic imagination can put upon it, yet Paul's precious antidote, Rom. v. 20, holds triumphantly sovereign as well against the heinousness of any one sin, as the confluence of many: "Where sin abounded, grace did much more abound." It is indeed a very heavy case, and to be deplored even with tears of blood, that thou shouldest ever have so highly dishonoured thy gracious God with such a horrible sin in the days of thy vanity, and thou oughtest rather choose to be torn in pieces with wild horses, than commit it again; yet if thy heart, now truly wounded with horror and hate of it, will but cleave to the truth and tender-heartedness of Jesus Christ in his promises, and fall into his blessed and bleeding arms, stretched out most lovingly to ease and refresh thee, as the heinousness of it hath abounded heretofore, his grace will now abound to the same proportion, and much more. Nay, I will show thee a pearl. In this case, by accident, God's mercies shall be extraordinarily honoured in pardoning such a prodigious provocation, because they are thereby, as it were, put into it, and their dearness, sweetness, and infiniteness improved to the greater height and excellency, and the blood of Christ made, as it were, more bright and illustrious, and the honour and preciousness of it advanced, by washing away such a heinous and hellish spot. If we bring broken, believing hearts towards his mercy-seat, it is the Lord's name to forgive all sorts of offences, "iniquity, transgression, and sin," Exod. xxxiv. 7. It is his covenant to sprinkle clean water upon us, that we may be clean, and to cleanse us from all our filthiness, and from all our idols, Ezek. xxxvi. 25, even from idolatry, the highest villany against the majesty of heaven; so that a papist, upon repentance, may be saved. It is his promise not only to pardon ordinary sins, but those also which be as scarlet, and red like crimson, Isa. i. 18. It is his free compassion to cast all our sins into the depths of the sea, Mic. vii. 19. Now, the sea, by reason of its vastness, can drown as well mountains as molehills; the boundless ocean of God's mercies can swallow up our mightiest sins much more. It is his merciful power, that blots out our sins as a cloud, Isa. xliv. 22. Now, the strength of the summer's sun is able to scatter the thickest fog, as well as the thinnest mist; nay, to drive away the darkest midnight: so the irresistible heat of God's free love, shining through the Sun of righteousness upon a penitent soul, can far more easily dissolve to nothing the most desperate work of darkness, and the most horrible sin. But this mystery of mercy, and miracle of God's free love, is a jewel only for truly humbled souls. Let no stranger to the life of godliness meddle with it. Let no swine trample it under his feet.

THE END.

London: Printed by W. Clowes and Sons, Stamford-street